Codifying Cyberspace

Can the Internet regulate itself? Faced with a range of 'harms' and conflicts associated with the new media – from gambling to pornography – many governments have resisted the temptation to regulate, opting instead to encourage media providers to develop codes of conduct and technical measures to regulate themselves. The European Commission has consistently encouraged a broader scope for self-regulation of digital media during the first years of the Internet, and continues to do so through the 2007 Audiovisual Media Services Directive. As this book shows, despite the attractions of this strategy, significant questions remain about its effectiveness.

Codifying Cyberspace looks at media self-regulation in practice, in a variety of countries. It also examines the problems of balancing private censorship against fundamental rights to freedom of expression and privacy for media users. Self-regulation is not a new strategy and has already been used in established media formats such as print, broadcast and film, but the new media, such as the Internet, mobile telephony and online gaming, present new and unexpected challenges and dilemmas. This book is the first full-scale study of self-regulation and codes of conduct in these fast-moving new media sectors and is the result of a three-year Oxford University study funded by the European Commission.

Damian Tambini is Senior Lecturer at the London School of Economics. He was previously Head of the Programme in Comparative Media Law and Policy, Oxford University. He is also Associate Fellow at the Institute for Public Policy Research (IPPR), the Oxford Internet Institute and at Oxford University's Said Business School. Tambini's previous publications include *Privacy and the Media* (2003), *Collective Identities in Action: Theories of Ethnic Conflict* (2002), *New News: Impartial Broadcasting in the Digital Age* (2002), *Nationalism in Italian Politics* (2001), *Citizenship, Markets, and the State* (2000) and *Cyberdemocracy* (1998).

Danilo Leonardi is Head of PCMLP (Programme in Comparative Media Law and Policy) at the University of Oxford's Centre for Socio-Legal Studies. He also coordinates the IMLA (International Media Lawyers Association), an international network of lawyers working in the areas of media law, media freedom and media policy. He is a founding member of the Legal Human Academy, a group dedicated to innovation in methods for teaching law.

Chris Marsden LL.B., LL.M. is Lecturer at the University of Essex. Marsden has conducted research into better Internet regulation as a consultant for the UK communications regulators, for the European Commission and for the Council of Europe. His previous publications include *Convergence in European Digital TV Regulation* (1999) and *Regulating the Global Information Society* (2000).

Codifying Cyberspace

Communications self-regulation in the age of Internet convergence

Damian Tambini, Danilo Leonardi and Chris Marsden

Routledge
Taylor & Francis Group

LONDON AND NEW YORK

First published 2008
by Routledge
2 Park Square, Milton Park, Abingdon, Oxon OX14 4RN

Simultaneously published in the USA and Canada
by Routledge
270 Madison Ave, New York, NY 10016

Routledge is an imprint of the Taylor & Francis Group, an informa business

© 2008 Damian Tambini, Danilo Leonardi and Chris Marsden

Typeset in Baskerville by
Book Now Ltd, London
Printed and bound in Great Britain by
The Cromwell Press, Trowbridge, Wiltshire

British Library Cataloguing in Publication Data
A catalogue record for this book is available from the British Library

Library of Congress Cataloging in Publication Data
A catalog record for this book has been requested

ISBN10: 1–84472–145–0 (hbk)
ISBN10: 1–84472–144–2 (pbk)
ISBN10: 0–203–94706–1 (ebk)

ISBN13: 978–1–84472–145–0 (hbk)
ISBN13: 978–1–84472–144–3 (pbk)
ISBN13: 978–0–203–94706–7 (ebk)

Contents

Illustrations

Figures

Tables

Preface

This book began as a two-and-a-half-year research project carried out in 2001–4 by the Programme in Comparative Media Law and Policy at the Centre for Socio-Legal Studies, Oxford University. The research was funded by the European Commission under the Internet Action Plan. The project investigated self-regulatory codes of conduct across National, EU and International boundaries covering a wide range of media from the Internet, film, video games and digital television to mobile communications. We are grateful to the European Commission for permission to reproduce material that appeared first in the 2004 report of the IAPCODE project.

The overarching concern of the authors has been to place the study of self- and co-regulation bodies and their codes of conduct in the context of the protection of freedom of expression, and the challenges posed by new technological developments. Our focus in this research was, of course, on the then-15 Member States of the European Union but we also cast a brief glance over the eastern border of the European Union. We believe that the ideas, processes and institutions discussed in this study are not exclusive to the European Union. We hope, therefore, that some of the ideas and the models discussed in this study could be of interest beyond the EU borders.

The authors wish to thank Germaine DeHaan, David Canter, Marcus Alexander, Christian Ahlert, Benoit Frydman, Susan Crawford, Beth Noveck and Isabelle Rorive for empirical and theoretical research they conducted into the various sectors, as well as the initial reports regarding aspects of self-regulation which they prepared.

We thank the European Commission, and in particular Richard Swetenham at the EC, for the grant that supported two-and-a-half-years of research of the IAPCODE project. We are indebted to Professor Monroe Price and Stefaan Verhulst (formerly co-directors of PCMLP) for the design and preparation of the successful grant proposal, and for developing the initial methodology of research that was the point of departure for this study.

Thanks are due to scholars, practitioners, researchers and staff of self-regulatory bodies and of other organisations whom we interviewed in the course of the research or with whom we discussed many of the issues addressed in this book when they participated in seminars and other activities of the IAPCODE project, as well as those of a parallel project simultaneously being conducted at PCMLP dealing with self-regulatory initiatives in Russia (the Russia Media Law Networking Project supported by the UK Department for International Development). We wish to thank: Ian Mayes (The Guardian Newspaper); Mark Stephens; Eve Salomon, Tim Toulmin, Will Gore and Robert Pinker (UK PCC); George Kidd (ICSTIS); Claude-Jean Bertrand (University of Paris); Angela Campbell and Patrice Chazerand (IFSE);

Cormac Callanan (INHOPE); Stephane Marcovitch (ISPA France); Roger Darlington (Internet Watch Foundation); Nick Lansman (EuroISPA); Andree Wright (Australian Communications and Media Authority); Stephen Whittle (BBC, OfCom); Andrea Millwood-Hargrave (Broadcasting Standards Commission and ATVOD); Andrei Richter (MMLPI); David Goldberg (PCMLP), and the many others that answered our queries on self-regulation over the years.

Parts of this book have been presented in various forms over the years, and we would like to acknowledge the input of participants in discussions, at seminars and conferences at the Centre for Socio-Legal Studies, the Westminster Media Forum, the European Audiovisual Observatory, the Oxford Media Convention and the Institute for Public Policy Research, as well as those organised by DG Information Society at the European Commission.

We recognise the interns and research support staff of the programme for their assistance at different stages of the research and preparation of this work: Chester Yung, Anna Pisarkiewicz, Oli Bird, Meera Javeeri, Simone Gruenhoff, Emily Hensby and Daniel Stenner. We thank Louise Scott, the Administrator of PCMLP, for her efficient support in the different phases of the IAPCODE project, and then the preparation of the book. We also thank Paul Honey and Nadine Antun for their assistance in preparing the manuscript.

We must recognise the support of the editors at Cavendish/UCL Press: Beverly Brown, whom we contacted initially with the idea of the book and which she immediately supported, and Briar Towers for helping us steer the manuscript through the required stages. We are also grateful to the artist, William Holton, for kind permission to use his work on the cover.

The views expressed in this book are of course those of the authors, who take responsibility for any remaining errors or inaccuracies.

Damian Tambini, Danilo Leonardi and Chris Marsden
London, Oxford, Essex, September 2007

1 The 'classic' model of self-regulation on the Internet

> You claim there are problems among us that you need to solve. You use this claim as an excuse to invade our precincts. Many of these problems don't exist. Where there are real conflicts, where there are wrongs, we will identify them and address them by our means. We are forming our own Social Contract. This governance will arise according to the conditions of our world, not yours. [. . .]
>
> We are creating a world where anyone, anywhere may express his or her beliefs, no matter how singular, without fear of being coerced into silence or conformity.
>
> Our identities have no bodies, so, unlike you, we cannot obtain order by physical coercion. We believe that from ethics, enlightened self-interest, and the commonweal, our governance will emerge.
>
> John Perry Barlow, *A Declaration of the Independence of Cyberspace*, 1996[1]

In this chapter, we outline the basis for Internet self-regulation, explaining the origins and development of US Internet content regulation, the industry structures and content liabilities that have been enshrined in law, and the manner in which private enforcement of liability has developed in the governmental vacuum that developed in the late 1990s. We then analyse the European Union's response to the prevailing Internet content self-regulatory paradigm of the United States, and the development of what became known as co-regulation: self-regulation with a legislative backstop or 'lurking threat'.

Internet design and libertarian non-regulation

It is claimed by some pioneers such as John Perry Barlow that the Internet is a global phenomenon beyond nation-state control, in which unregulated any-to-any communication is possible. Ten years on, comparing 'cyberspace' to outer-space when the majority of EU citizens have accessed the Internet, and when the boundaries between 'virtual' and real life are blurring, negates the democratic importance of preventing harm occurring on the Internet. The preface to the 'Internet Commons Treaty' of 2004 recognises this, even while continuing to proclaim the non-governmental libertarian ideal:[2] 'The Internet seems to have lost the special status that led most governments [sic] to "hands off" policies during the 90s.'

The Internet was largely a US government creation, ARPANET, with architecture originally intended to survive thermonuclear strike. Developed by university science departments, and later in European universities, it became a cultural artefact and is now a key driver of economic integration across national boundaries. The British inventor of the World Wide Web (WWW), Tim Berners-Lee, has explained that the openness of the WWW describes:

> a vision encompassing the decentralized, organic growth of ideas, technology, and society. The vision I have for the Web is about anything being potentially connected with anything. It is a vision that provides us with new freedom, and allows us to grow faster than we ever could when we were fettered by the hierarchical classification systems into which we bound ourselves.[3]

Lawrence Lessig explains what that architectural principle[4] means in practice:

> This end-to-end design frees innovation from the past. It's an architecture that makes it hard for a legacy business to control how the market will evolve. You could call it distributed creativity, but that would make it sound as if the network was producing the creativity. It's the other way around. End-to-end makes it possible to tap into the creativity that is already distributed everywhere.[5]

The 'end-to-end' principle is hard-wired into the Internet's architecture by the technical standards and protocols that govern the engineering of the Internet. In this narrow engineering sense, much of the Internet is self-regulated, for instance by:

- W3C (World Wide Web Consortium), a US–EU consortium of private and public universities and researchers, including corporate researchers;
- the similarly constituted IETF (Internet Engineering Task Force);
- ICANN (Internet Corporation for Assigned Names and Numbers).

Gould demonstrates that the consensual model of standard setting which sufficed in the development of the Internet, a legacy model which is still effective in the more technical policy arena, is increasingly placed under strain by the advanced consumer adoption of the Internet.[6] The legacy of such technical self-regulation is that minimal direct government interference has been seen.[7] The self-regulatory bodies are international in character and were begun as non-commercial self-regulatory organisations.[8] The end-to-end principle dictates that any content control be embedded in code by the content creator, and filtered by browser software installed and controlled by the end-user.

Running throughout this book are some fundamental questions: does technical architecture prevent the realization of public policy goals in content regulation? Can 'public' control be re-exerted over media content, not just on the Internet but also in media as diverse as video games, feature films, mobile phone content, print and traditional broadcasting? In the following section we consider the events that led the US Internet community to its technologically led libertarian position.

Internet content, codes of conduct and technical self-regulation

Concerns regarding inappropriate and potentially harmful content on the Internet are as old as the public Internet itself.[9] Once the general citizen was first allowed to use the Internet, in 1992, rapid consumer adoption led to a need for rule-making. This began to surface in public policy debate around 1994, when Vint Cerf[10] classified three types of Internet regulation: technical constraints, legal constraints and moral constraints. He stated that, 'In reality, all of these tools are commonly applied to channel behavioural choices.' He explains that it was public service Internet service providers' – university and research institute – conditions of use, including codes of conduct (CoCs), that regulated online behaviour from the Internet's invention. After the opening of the Internet, CoCs, inherited from the public service past, continued to be the default approach. Cerf emphasised the need to set up incentive structures for self-regulation: 'guidelines for conduct have to be constructed and motivated in part on the basis of self-interest'.

In these early years, a pattern of negotiation between self-regulatory bodies for the Internet and government began to emerge. Price and Verhulst assert the limits of both government and private action in this sphere, and assert the interdependence of both – there is little purity in self-regulation as there is usually a lurking government threat to intervene where market actors prove unable to agree.[11]

An early threat to libertarianism emerged in 1994, with proposed US child protection legislation against illegal and harmful material on the Internet, the *Communications Decency Act*.[12] In 1996, this particular content law was struck down under the strict standards of the US Constitution's First Amendment in the landmark *American Civil Liberties Association v. Reno* case. In a 1995 response the World Wide Web Consortium began to develop the Platform for Internet Content Selection (PICS),[13] the basis of filtering that was immediately incorporated into browser software and used to classify web pages by the major Internet service provider (ISP) portals in the United States – and by default worldwide. The idea was simple: to engineer websites and user software to enable control of content at the device – the end of the network – rather than by ISP or another intermediary.

In addition to the administrative sanctions, generally informal, triggered by the original CoCs of Internet users described by Vint Cerf, the Internet also developed its own form of lynch-mob to enforce norms of behaviour. Sanctions included the spread of viruses which incapacitate recipients' PCs via e-mail, hacking into government or corporate sites, or reputation damage (consider the eBay auction site's user ratings as a benign example). Clearly these lack legitimacy. Formal democratic decision-making for the global issues which Internet governance raises is extremely immature, as Froomkin demonstrates in his assessment of ICANN processes.[14] Citizen demands for protection and security create a classic global public goods issue, which governments are now addressing.[15] Environmental, labour and financial market analysts will find these reflections unsurprising examples of both the limitations of global governance and the rapid maturing and increasing complexity of 'civil society'.

Public policy towards Internet content liability

'Visionaries' such as Barlow were not the only advocates of a self-regulatory structure for new media during the first years of the rapid consumer adoption of the WWW. The Clinton Presidency launched two major self-regulatory initiatives for the digital media sector: a US Presidential Advisory Committee on digital television, and another on privacy in electronic commerce.[16] The Council of Europe and the European Commission issued a series of reports and recommendations promoting Internet self-regulation during the same period.[17] The intervening years have seen the emergence of a fertile ecology of rule-making, regulatory competition, alternative dispute resolution and a complex interaction between state, co- and self-regulatory practices in the media sectors. And this complex and changing regulatory ecology has been further challenged by two major trends: convergence between previously distinct technologies such as telecommunications, broadcasting, games, the Internet and press; and convergence between different national and regional regimes of self- and co-regulation.

To view all rule-making on the Internet in terms of a Manichean divide between state and 'freedom' may provide an edge to Barlow's social critique, but it is unhelpful for our purpose here, which is to analyse and monitor the emerging structures of self- and co-regulation that apply to the Internet and other convergent media sectors. As the Internet is critically important for communication (and, in turn, for culture and commerce) then broader issues of trust and externalities will lead to legitimate demands for regulation. It will be clear that imagery of state 'invasion' of a self-governing Internet is misleading. Internet development does entail some public policy issues that engage the institutions of democratic governance, and it is only within the legal framework for Internet liability that Internet users and service providers can enjoy the relative freedoms to self-regulate that Barlow invokes. Our emerging structures of media regulation develop through competition in response to a demand for regulation which is in a constant negotiation between private and public institutions.

The first decade of WWW content rule-making has been the subject of little systematic European legal analysis. This study therefore examines the background to self-regulation in terms of the earliest rules for Internet conduct, and then explicates some of the key aspects of the demand for regulation in terms both of the economics of information and communication services and of apparent consumer harms associated with the Internet in particular, and communications in general. We provide the first detailed European analysis of Internet CoCs, comparing different countries' use of codes of conduct, and also comparing Internet self-regulatory codes and procedures with those that are used in other converging media sectors.

Throughout the 1990s self-regulation was heavily advocated by the European Commission, most notably under the Safer Internet Action Plan, but this approach seems to have fallen out of favour with recent measures promoting a more 'co-regulatory' approach. Whereas 'self'-regulation implies a degree of independence from direct state regulation, 'co'-regulation implies that the state is involved in jointly developing rules and regulations. This might be thought more desirable to the extent that research on self-regulation has shown that many self-regulatory models in the Internet industry lack proper procedures for oversight and enforcement, and amount to little more than declarations of good will.

Self-regulation is the laboratory of law and regulation for the Internet. Only by understanding the broader issues that are at stake – such as the nature of trust, harm and freedom of expression in the various media sectors – can a broader policy approach to co- and self-regulation be adopted. With greater understanding of the structures and processes of self-regulation comes a strategic shift. There is some evidence that the broad policy consensus in favour of media self-regulation in the late 1990s is breaking down. Frustrated at what they see as a lack of effectiveness of self-regulatory techniques and the observation that rules are sometimes flaunted, there have been numerous instances, some examined in this book, where public authorities seek a larger co-regulatory role regarding Internet content.

This is seen most clearly in the debates on the proposal for a new Audio Visual Media Services Directive which will regulate video content on the WWW. The language of self-regulation remains, however. European Commissioner Viviane Reding in September 2005 stated (emphasis in original):[18]

I have heard and read here and there, that Brussels intends to regulate the Internet, to introduce new red tape. Frankly, this is nonsense! Never ever has the Commission had such a foolish idea! But let me ask you some questions: who in this room is in favour of child-pornography on the new media? Who stands for the freedom to spread incitement to racial hatred on the new media? . . . It is the duty of the Commission to propose a framework under which these shared European values are protected. But I have no intention to 'regulate the Internet'!

For those who use the Internet, and for those who are professionally involved in providing information, developing strategy, or building a business on the Internet, the emerging rules are fundamentally important. The combination of self-regulatory codes and law, and the subtle relationship between them, can define the difference between a situation in which a company has legal liability for content, and one in which the liability for content remains with others in the value chain. There may be cases in which the adoption of a self-regulatory code of conduct could lead to an increase in the due diligence burden, and others in which it is sensible business practice to adopt a code of conduct in order to reduce risk.

Of course the Internet has always been regulated. As Reidenberg[19] and later Lessig[20] stated, the environment of the Internet is itself a determinant of its physical and virtual boundaries. The software that makes the Internet work is a pre-existing 'law' of the Internet, just as gravity and other laws of motion regulate the humans and their artefacts who interact via the Internet. But the use of legislative and jurist's tools to regulate the Internet has largely been by means of applying existing offline laws to the online environment: for jurisdiction, for criminal obscenity, for libel and, more prevalent, for copyright infringement.[21] 2006 saw the announcement of several publications and policies that reflect this broadband Internet crisis: first, academically, the announcement of new books from a cyber-realist perspective on the extent to which national legislation and implementation can affect the Internet, reflecting the six years of the Yahoo! cases, China's censorship model and eight years of Microsoft's case with the European Commission;[22] second, both Google's decision to reject US government data requests yet launch a google.cn Chinese search engine which blocks access to anti-government sites, and the reflection on the fracturing of Internet standards because of those censorship and security issues raised by Yahoo!, Google, Microsoft and others.[23]

In the field of Internet regulation, there is a much more relevant and broad field of legal declarations and recommendations than useful case law (with the exceptions of intellectual property rights and criminal law cases, not covered in this book).[24] The non-binding policy instrument is, as will be seen, a staple of self-regulation backed by the threat – but not implementation – of specific legal authority to impose direct state regulation.[25] 'Soft law' has specific meaning in European law as a non-binding legal instrument that is followed as a matter of informal practice by Member States, such as a Recommendation. The usage here is less specific, referring to any non-binding regulatory direction issued by an inter-governmental organisation (IGO), government agency or ministry.[26]

Current dilemmas can only be understood against the background of the previous regime: in particular the current market actors' legal liability for Internet content, which we consider in the following section.

How Internet liability operates: the role of ISPs

Noam has shown that consolidation in the Internet industry increased in the United States from about 1996, though most sectors remain competitive.[27] He examines eight sub-sectors:

- Internet backbones, which connect the global Internet;
- Internet service providers (ISPs);
- broadband access providers, providing high-speed access in the local loop;
- portals which aggregate content and functions as a 'home page' for users;
- browser software such as Microsoft Explorer or Netscape Navigator;
- search engines, such as Google or Altavista;
- media-player software, such as RealPlayer or Windows Media;
- Internet Protocol (IP) telephony.

He explains that 'common elements are high economies of scale (scalability) based on the high fixed costs and low marginal costs, and the way they are often complemented on the demand side by network effects (which economists call "positive externalities")'. Representing the value chain diagrammatically:

- network encompasses *broadband providers* and *backbone providers*, such as UUNet;
- ICP (Internet Content Producer) encompasses *portal* (though often integrated into ISP functions) and *search engine*;
- *IP telephony*, Instant Messaging and the two most common *browsers*, Netscape and Internet Explorer, are owned by two large ICPs, AOL and MSN respectively;[28]
- the two largest *media player* companies are integrated into ICP conglomerates (Windows Media, Real Networks).

ISPs provide the actual connectivity to the end-user. Throughout the history of the Internet, ISPs have integrated with content services and access suppliers. Most large ISPs provide a default home page 'portal', with news, features and search facility. The largest ISPs are subsidiaries of either access providers (local cable or telephone companies) or software companies such as Microsoft and AOL-Netscape-Compuserve (though note the new strategy of the latter in the broadband environment). The italics in Figure 1.1 illustrate Microsoft products and services, the underlined items belong to AOL Time Warner, and those offered by both conglomerates are italicised and underlined.

Often, ISPs are joint venture partners with content or access providers, such as BT Yahoo! (UK), Yahoo! Softbank (Japan) or AOL Deutschland (formerly a Bertelsmann joint venture). Both Microsoft and AOL are also content providers, own

Access	Content	ISP	Peer to Peer	Browser Software
Common carrier • Broadband local network • Backbone peering	MSNBC AOL Time Warner Music Movies Television News	Microsoft Network AOL Netscape Compuserve	Instant Messenger Services IP Telephony Search Engines	Microsoft Explorer Netscape Navigator

Figure 1.1 Internet value chain.

search engines, and have Instant Messenger services. All European access providers and US cable companies provide proprietary Internet services for their customers, making AOL and Microsoft unusual ISPs in that their content-software focus has prevented their leveraging their ISP dominance into access. In broadband markets, those ISPs who also control access include T-Online, Orange in France, Telefonica and BT Yahoo! Though other ISPs can access the local loop at wholesale prices, competitors fear that the regulated access price leaves them disadvantaged.

Public access, through work, government institution, cybercafe or school, and the device itself, are not included in Noam's list; but the filtering software that end-users and these intermediaries rely on is integrated into such software as search engines, media players, portals and especially browser software. Filtering software is now compulsory in libraries in the United States[29] and schools in France,[30] amongst other places – where the state can control public access to illegal and harmful content, it does so.

Liability for harmful and potentially illegal content on the Internet

Internet operation requires the passive reproduction and distribution of material. ISPs automatically reproduce and distribute material to subscriber requests. Content creators upload to web pages by instructing the ISP's computer to store a copy of the uploaded material. The ISP's computer also makes copies of the material every time a computer asks to view the subscriber's web page and sends those copies through the Internet. That file does not travel directly to the user. Instead, it generally goes through other computers hooked up to the Internet. Each of these computers makes at least a partial copy of the relevant file. As Yen has described, 'a practically unlimited scope of liability soon follows'.[31] In order that these nodes on the network between content provider and end-user are not all held strictly liable[32] for the billions of web files they continually copy in the act of transmission, legislators in the United States and European Union have held that only a limited liability holds for these intermediaries, typically ISPs.[33] In the United States, liability regimes have differed according to speech-based and copyright-based liabilities. The *Communications Decency Act* 1996 provides that 'No provider or user of an interactive computer service shall be treated as the publisher or speaker of any information provided by another information content provider.'[34] Yen states: '[T]he general philosophy motivating these decisions – namely, that the liability against ISPs for subscriber libel would result in undesirable censorship on the Internet – remains vitally important in assessing the desirability of ISP liability.' Holznagel has indicated that US courts have applied these 'safe harbour' provisions to protect the ISP, even (a) where it was aware of unlawful hosted content; (b) if it had been notified of this by a third party; (c) if it had paid for the data.[35] Frydman and Rorive observe that courts 'in line with the legislative intent . . . applied the immunity provision in an extensive manner'.[36]

In Europe, 'safe harbour' protection of ISPs from liability was implemented on 17 January 2002, when the E-Commerce Directive of 2000 came into force. Article 12 protects the ISP where it provides 'mere conduit' with no knowledge of, nor editorial control over, content or receiver ('does not initiate [or] select the receiver'). Benoit and Frydman establish that it was based on the 1997 German *Teleservices Act*, though with 'slightly more burden on the ISPs in comparison with the former German statute'.[37] Where ISPs provide hosting services, under Article 14 they are protected from liability, in two instances:

[a] if the provider does not have actual knowledge of illegal activity or information and, as regards claims for damages, is not aware of facts or circumstances from which the illegal activity is apparent; or

[b] if the provider, upon obtaining such knowledge or awareness, acts expeditiously to remove or to disrupt access of the information.

Like the proverbial three blind monkeys, ISPs, IAPs and web hosting services should 'hear no evil, see no evil, speak no evil'. As mere ciphers for content, they are protected; should they engage in any filtering of content they become liable. Thus, 'masterly inactivity' except when prompted by law enforcement is their only rational choice as it is the economically most advantageous course of action open to them. Frydman and Rorive state 'undoubtedly the Directive seeks to stimulate co-regulation'. It does this by formally permitting national courts to over-ride the safe harbour in the case of actual or suspected breach of national law, including copyright law and certain types of illegal content, such as hate speech or paedophilia.

Whereas in the United States the absolute speech protection of the First Amendment and procedural concerns mean that Notice and Take Down is counterbalanced by 'put back' procedures, in Europe no such protection of free speech exists, and speech freedom is qualified by state rights. In both jurisdictions, Notice and Take Down regimes cause Frydman and Rorive to state that 'this may lead to politically correct or even economically correct unofficial standards that may constitute an informal but quite efficient mechanism for content-based private censorship'.[38] It is clear that the economically rational course of action for ISPs is simply to remove any content notified, and otherwise do nothing to monitor content and let end-users, the police and courts, and ultimately the content providers, decide what is stored and sent over their access networks. Frydman and Rorive state that:

> Business operators should never be entrusted with . . . guidelines defining the limits of the right to free speech and offering procedural guarantees against censorship . . . which belong to the very core of the human rights of a democratic people.[39]

That is nevertheless the situation which ISP CoCs find themselves.

Should ISPs be responsible for a class of their content, where it serves their commercial benefit? Vicarious liability tests the ability to benefit and control, (i) the right and ability to supervise and (ii) a financial direct interest. This tends to make ISPs choose not to monitor even for law enforcement. The financial direct benefit is interesting in view of the 'killer application' for broadband: does this include peer-to-peer if the access charges received by the ISP are based on traffic, i.e. adverts on portal or bandwidth usage? ISPs arguably benefit from the existence of copyright infringement on the Internet. Thousands of users desire Internet service precisely because it offers free access to copyrighted materials. As Yen argues,[40] an ISP could make copyright compliance part of its system rules and then monitor for violations. How about mobile networks and unsolicited electronic mail (spam) removal – do ISPs there exercise the right and ability to monitor content? Can they control information on their network? Vicarious liability could therefore follow.

The debate regarding the intervention of ISPs in the traffic of their users has become entangled in the broader debate about privacy, security and Internet quality of service. 'Masterly inactivity' is exactly the charge that dominant ISPs are least vilified for by academic scholars. We briefly explain the Net Neutrality debate – which is exactly about whether ISPs should be allowed to inspect and discriminate between packets on their networks.

Lemley and Lessig in 1999 argued against permitting cable companies to discriminate between Internet traffic.[41] Their claim was that innovation at the edge of the network is opposed by traditional media and network businesses, as it makes business cases based on controlling distribution bottlenecks redundant: where there is peer sharing, there is less opportunity for traditional bottlenecks and therefore control of revenues. However, the inverse applies also: without some means to secure revenues for the increased bandwidth necessary for applications to flourish, do network operators have an incentive to upgrade? As Ed Whitacre of AT&T stated: 'The Internet can't be free in that sense, because we and the cable companies have made an investment and for a Google or Yahoo! or Vonage or anybody to expect to use these pipes [for] free is nuts!'[42]

Content charging relies on a type of quality of service for the Internet, enabling network providers to discriminate (in Lessig's terms, to regulate) between packets. The standards body for 3G mobile telephony, 3GPP, has been working since 2000 on a set of standards called IMS, for IP Multimedia Subsystem.[43] This is an operator-friendly environment intended to generate new revenue via deep packet inspection. Fixed line carriers and equipment vendors have created the 'IPsphere', a new set of standards for network intercession in IP application flows.[44] Both sets of standards support the ability to filter and censor by file type on the Internet. This enables the carrier to discriminate, to decide which content to delay and which to permit to travel at normal speeds to the end-user. As Cisco standards expert John Waclawsky puts it: 'This is the emerging, consensus view: That IMS will let broadband industry vendors and operators put a control layer and a cash register over the Internet and creatively charge for it.'[45]

The interoperability debate is broader than simply an Internet access debate, as it affects innovation in software – indeed, the origin of the argument lies with software industry disputes over interoperability, an argument captured by Lessig in his contribution to the Microsoft litigation.[46] The debate has centred on the legislation in the US Senate[47] and Congress permitting US network operators to discriminate between Internet traffic they carry. In Europe, the debate has developed more slowly, and the new proposed Electronic Communications package does not propose so-called 'net neutrality' provisions, instead continuing to permit national regulators to make policy.[48]

Those wishing to see ISPs regulate their content should be careful what they wish for – they may find that the economic incentives to police that content outweigh the child protection and free speech arguments. In this case, it is wise to recall Frydman and Rorive's comments that private actors should never be entrusted with censorship. However, as the Internet is a network of mainly private networks, binary distinctions should be analysed with great care. Price and Verhulst rightly stated that public and private interact in messy hybrid regulatory processes.

The following section contains a more technical analysis of the grounds for regulation of the Internet, taken in large part from US academic and practitioner analyses of how to regulate using technical, economic and social tools, as well as legal instruments. Its lessons are central to any self-regulatory examination and, though the language is specialised, the basic messages can be comprehended by non-specialists.

Public goods and private ISPs

Public communications markets, by which we mean those intended for use by the general population and regulated as such by government, are the essential means of delivering what is referred to by economists as a 'public good' in information. A public good is non-rival, which means that the provision of a public good may simultaneously benefit more than one person. A public good is also non-exclusive, which means that, once a public good is produced, it is nearly impossible to prevent others from simultaneously benefiting from its production. The end-to-end design of the Internet means that its content is a public good, with control only exerted by its final user. Free-to-air broadcasting shares the same features, but control over its production and transmission by governments is possible.

Free-riders: Since a public good is non-exclusive, there is little incentive for anyone to pay for its production, thus leading to the free-rider problem, in which the optimal strategy for an individual consumer is to let someone else pay for production and, since there is non-exclusivity, free-ride on what is produced. If everyone decides to free-ride, then no one will pay, and no public goods will be produced. Similarly, responsible Internet content providers might find that many irresponsible, harmful or even illegal providers are free-riding their attempts to self-regulate.

The probability of free-riding is proportional to the community's size and commonality of interest, i.e. the smaller the community, the more impact a person's action or lack thereof will have on the community's other members. Furthermore, knowledge of members' identities is important; once a community's members can identify the free-riders, the community can exert social pressure upon them to contribute back to the community. In the case of Internet content providers, such a community does not exist on a global level, but sub-groups, for instance ISPs at a national level, arguably constitute sufficient community interest to self-regulate.

Government provision of public goods: Free markets would not adequately address societal and communal needs for public goods. Given the propensity for free-riders to exploit public goods, government should regulate to ensure that public goods are being adequately supplied for the benefit of all. Businesses generally recognise individuals primarily as consumers, and their fiduciary duty to their investors fails to recognise fully non-economic issues including the right to privacy, access to harmful material, and free speech. If companies collude in the free market, they could achieve higher profits at the consumers' expense. Other businesses might engage in predatory behaviour.[49] Even self-regulatory groups of well-resourced companies might choose high-cost technical or legal solutions to raise those compliance costs to rivals.

Government action to encourage private provision of public goods includes the favourable sales tax and postal charge treatment given to printed papers (the press), the distribution of broadcasting, telecoms, and therefore the Internet. The problem of collective action which the Internet's globalisation presents is intensified by the capabilities and potential of the technology, and the characteristics of information markets. Where public goods are non-excludable and non-rival, the privatisation of information flows offers possibilities for private monopoly and sub-optimal exclusion of social groups and individuals. This is a justification for the strong European tradition of public service broadcasting. The high fixed and low marginal costs of information goods have been exacerbated by the Internet, and the potential benefits of positive externalities from the wider flow of information are threatened by the closure of this formerly open network.

Where initial European public reaction to the Internet resembled that associated with environmental pollution, and negative externalities are highlighted for public concern,[50] McGowan and Samuelson[51] indicate that the challenge lies in the potential removal of the end-to-end positive externalities of the free flow of information and innovation. The excludability of information from users by strong filtering and cryptography, secure payment systems and the like may be essential in order to advance a safer, more trusted Internet, but changes the nature of the medium from a public to an increasingly private sphere. The regulation of this new global space is essential to address this contradiction to maintain global public goods of free information, privacy, interconnectedness and development.

Code as law and technological determinism: *lex informatica*[52]

The architecture of the Internet influences behaviour. This architecture is built on software code and hardware engineering. The Internet has of course gone through many maturing phases since its anarcho-libertarian and vehemently public sphere (or 'Commons') origins up until the early 1990s. A new type of radical free-market libertarianism grew up from then, consistent in its espousal of free speech but more concerned with corporate and commercial freedom, avoiding government economic and access, as opposed to social, regulation. This raises a dilemma, however; as it becomes institutionalised through standardisation processes and the deployment of technologies such as filtering and digital rights management, the software itself begins to regulate speech. Lessig therefore views software as the 'code of cyberspace', not in a narrow engineering sense, but more widely, in the civil law sense as the constitution of cyberspace.[53] He sees regulation developing from law, economics, normative values and architecture (Figure 1.2). The last of these is – for Internet regulation – the software code that designs the Internet.

Norms are here defined as a rule supported by a pattern of informal sanctions, following Ellickson,[54] who observes three faults in individual actor analysis: neglect of socialisation, of socially enforced norms, and of the human quest for status. Lessig aims to model explicitly the three Ellickson constraints, in addition to market constraints. He terms socialisation 'architecture', viewing society in these terms. His version of regulation is broader than intentional policy action,[55] including 'architectural'

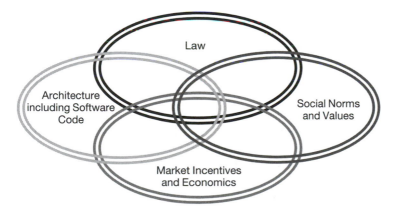

Figure 1.2 The intersecting elements in Lessig's model of regulation.

constraints, for instance geographical distance.[56] Lessig aims not to diminish law in relation to the three exogenous constraints, but to examine its effects on those restraints. That law is a clumsy blunt instrument is itself relatively well founded, and an attempt to reassert the role of law by Lessig is a statement of the interdependence between the four constraints described (Table 1.1). Legal effects can thus be both direct and indirect, in that they can regulate the regulatee (e.g. ISP), or regulate the other three constraints – while those constraints act upon each other and the ISP.[57] He admits that the theoretical application shares the universalist dilemma: 'The regulation of this school is totalizing. It is the effort to make culture serve power.'[58]

The prior design of the Internet regulates behaviours between users without needing any intervention by the conventional apparatuses of social control – the market, social forces, or political and legal activity. This engineering solution, which applies to much of the basic protocols of the Internet, raises challenges for the policy makers' presumption that legitimacy stems from the social and political. If engineering can either protect users in a space, or otherwise prevent normal social controls from applying, is the presumption of social control reversed, replaced by a technologically determined environment in which policy makers must establish harm before intervening? The potency of this argument has lost much of its force in the 'democratising' period of mass Internet adoption, for at least three reasons:

- harm is seen to have occurred as online behaviour prompted offline crime;
- technologically determinist legitimacy claims for such a pervasive medium of communication are increasingly difficult to maintain in the face of public scepticism concerning the role of experts in nanotechnology, biotechnology, environmental science, and now the Internet;
- governments have increasingly intervened in the Internet's architecture to secure surveillance and other tools to invade users' anonymity, puncturing the myth of the 'unregulable' Internet, particularly in surveillance post-9/11.

Social and economic regulation: commerce and code

The new means of distribution and transaction via electronic commerce now penetrating the previously open public space of the Internet represent the 'commerce'

Table 1.1 Adapting Lessig's 'realms of social order'

	Architecture – 'code'	Economics	Social norms	Law
Enforcement agent	Designers	Market	Peer group	Police courts
Prior or post facto constraint	Prior – design	During – process	Prior/Post – reputational	Post – sanction
Constraint type	Physical	Economic	Opprobrium	Sanction
Basis of interaction	Structural design	Production and exchange	Social/group	Power
Basis of participation	User	Buyer/seller	Group member	Citizen/subject
Primary institutions	Protocols Engineering institutes	Corporation Enterprise Market	Family Community Church/faith	State public information

which, in the views of those sympathetic to free expression but sceptical of monopolistic corporate control of the underlying architecture of the Internet, were taking over the 'code'[59] in the late 1990s. The architectures of cyberspace are causing such re-examination of regulation and legitimacy.

Government no longer attempts to control access to widespread provision of public goods, as it did in analogue television broadcasting, as it is recognised that this may stifle innovation. Internet and telephony access, and control of content, are central to societal development, and controlled by private (often foreign) corporations. The Freeserve, Hotmail or Amazon model for e-commerce success is to attract and retain customers – often by incurring enormous losses in providing free services until critical mass is accomplished – thus creating a 'bottleneck' where other service providers' need to access customers can be excluded, or exploited commercially: the rents involved in a successful model create incentives for anti-competitive conduct.[60]

There is thus a three-way conflict of values, between cyber-libertarians epitomised by John Perry Barlow, corporate free-marketers, and those espousing social responsibility on the part of Internet social and commercial entrepreneurs. The question is how to maintain the Internet's dynamism, freedom and vitality, but control its wilder anarchic excesses. Often the debate is highlighted by sensational excesses, such as webcasts of celebrity births, or crimes inspired by the Internet, such as convicted murderers in Germany and England, whose fantasies for cannibalism and necrophilia were expressed on the Internet with tragic offline results.[61]

Opening markets through 'races to the bottom'

Briefly summarised, public choice analysis[62] of central government in the United States 'diagnosed regulatory capture and unchecked central government growth as principal ailments . . . [critics] looked in part to the devolution of regulatory authority to junior levels of government for a cure'.[63] The information asymmetries between government and market actors can lead to regulatory distortions in favour of the market actors.[64] Public choice has a weakness beyond an over-simplistic reliance on economic resources: it reveals taxpayer preferences where mobility is assumed (and hence competition between geographically fixed regulatory jurisdictions) rather than the total electorate, and therefore the interests of business (e.g. Internet content providers) rather than those of the vulnerable (e.g. children):

> Competition causes the content of regulation and the level of public goods and taxation to be dictated by the private preferences of a narrow, arbitrarily identified class of itinerant at-the-margin consumers or investors . . . competition can force the pursuit of policies . . . removed from the public interest.[65]

Internet policy may be biased in favour of multinational ISPs, therefore, rather than consumers. However, the mobility of companies, and the weak bargaining position of government, can be exaggerated. North explains that[66] 'It is no accident that economic models of the polity developed in the public choice literature make the state into something like the mafia.' He then explains why the parameters of investigation must be broadened:[67] 'Informal constraints matter. We need to know much more about culturally derived norms of behaviour and how they interact with formal rules to get better answers to such issues.' Where market failure leads to regulatory intervention on an institutional basis, it acknowledges that regulatory processes may be captured by incumbent interests. Thus, regulation may begin as a response to market failure, or to broader social intervention in markets, but becomes a feature of regulatory capture, as regulation is identified with regulated actors.[68]

ISPs, evolving into much more complex content, service and access providers, are the key link in control of the end-user's Internet experience, and the focus of this study.

Broadband service providers: liability increasing?

Since the WWW was introduced in 1993, more than a billion people have used the Internet. Over 250 million households now have broadband access to the Internet, of some form, with many accessing broadband at school, college or work. These two progressions of the Internet, from a research and business tool to a consumer activity, and from narrowband to broadband,[69] have transformed the community on the Internet. By March 2004, European BSPs (broadband ISPs) such as Tiscali were challenging incumbents by selling voice-over Internet protocol. The marketing costs and potential revenue gains of entering a combined data–voice-content market immediately permanently and significantly raised the costs of providing a full ISP service. AOL, formerly the world's largest ISP, announced its withdrawal from the US broadband market. From a universe of thousands of European ISPs in 2000, no more than twenty-five large BSPs can be expected to dominate the European consumer market by end-2008. The regulatory implications are profound.

Governments' belief that their regulatory goals could be met by ISP activities in self-regulation were exposed in a series of court cases in the period from 2001. As ISP incomes from narrowband Internet access, which used the national public telecoms network as 'free-riders', were replaced by less favourable broadband access charges, ISPs increasingly found their financial resources for self-regulation eroded. The 'triple whammy' of local-loop-unbundling access delays, advertising-revenue falls and the absence of profitable content services on either narrow- or broadband meant that the period 2001–3 was one of enormous economic failure for ISPs.

The large or dominant, well-resourced and carrier-backed BSPs indicated in Figure 1.3 are in a position to provide the effective self-regulation that failing narrowband ISPs are increasingly unable effectively to resource.[70] BSPs face major legal challenges. The copyright bottleneck caused by record/movie companies and their contractors'[71] failure to release material online was overcome first by illegal file-sharing between users on peer-to-peer networks. While governments, conscious of exposing the convenient fiction of ISP liability online, have not prosecuted breaches, copyright owners are pursuing BSP customer records vigorously, the Recording Industry Association of America (RIAA) leading.[72] The broad issue of ISP response to copyright infringement is considered in Chapter 6.

International and European jurisdictional response to the Internet

The Internet creates multiple competing regulatory jurisdictions, both in European law[73] and in broader international comparisons, not least in broadcasting[74] and e-commerce regulation.[75] This search for a more holistic explanation is approached from law by Weiler, in his study of the European Union constitution[76] 'with particular regard to its living political matrix: the interaction between norms and norm-making, constitution and institutions, principles and practice'. The decision whether, when, how, why and whom to regulate is political, however bounded by technological

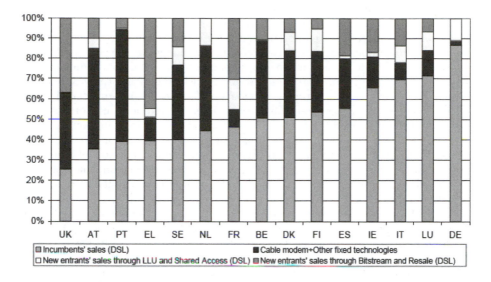

Figure 1.3　Incumbent share of EU15 broadband market (start of 2004). (From http://europa. eu.int/information_society/policy/ecomm/doc/implementation_enforcement/ annualreports/10threport/sec20041535vol1en.pdf at p. 57.)

factors.[77] Ayres and Braithwaite state:[78] 'Practical people who are concerned with outcomes seek to understand the intricacies of interplays between state regulation and private orderings . . . '

As indicated by the positions adopted by US policy makers, the choices of regulatory venue adopted have been chosen in public–private partnership between the economic super-powers, the United States and European Union, and their high-technology private partners. The choices made have been largely private, from the ICANN domain names procedures to the self-regulatory standards setting procedures which have overtaken the traditional United Nations agency, the ITU.[79] The UK E-Commerce Green Paper of 1999 states: 'E-commerce is essentially a global, rather than a national, issue.'[80] It further states that initiatives have been taken by the OECD (Organisation for Economic Cooperation and Development) in a cryptography conference of October 1998,[81] by the United Nations Commission on International Trade Law (UNCITRAL) in a Model Law on Electronic Commerce,[82] and in other EU initiatives.[83] The US government took the view that the challenges of global e-commerce over the Internet should be met through private, and avowedly economically rational, mechanisms of self-regulation. The sustainability of this model in view of its lack of consumer/citizen representation is a central dilemma in the future development of the Internet, e-commerce and the Information Society.[84] Functionalist and technologist concerns regarding security, encryption and domain name allocation become increasingly difficult to separate from individual rights concerns regarding privacy, freedom of expression and public governance of the commons. The tension between new dynamic processes of self-regulation and existing institutions of more formalised and accountable government-mediated regulation is central to an understanding of twenty-first century communications regulation.

As in most European responses to technologically led change in the socio-economic landscape since 1945, the policy and market lead in technological convergence has been taken by US corporations, academics and government. There is a *defi american*[85] in European response to convergence. Language also separates the European and US debates on the macro questions of industrial policy: the future of both European delivery networks, and the content which they will carry. Where the United States says 'video', Europe says '*l'audiovisuel*', reflecting the traditional policy distinction between the socio-cultural aspirations of European communications policy and the caricatured US profit maximisation market-led philosophy. (Such distinctions are more distinct in theory than in fact.) The markets for cinema exhibition of film, pay-TV subscription of thematic channels, and the model of regulation chosen for Internet and video-on-demand, are links in a value chain which must be examined in the round, rather than separately. This reflects a different regulatory legacy. European telecommunications markets were liberalised on 1 January 1998, belatedly following the 1984 example set by the United Kingdom[86] and United States. The importance of the Internet as the primary information network for the creation of the Information Society has been recognised by the European Union, from the Bangemann Report of 1994 to the eEurope+ Progress Report of 2004.[87] The European Commission has declared in its Communication of 25 February 2004[88] that the pillars of Information Society development are the regulatory framework, government investment in attractive content and support for research and innovation. In its eEurope Action Plan Review of 18 February 2004, the Commission[89] further identified eliminating legal barriers to e-commerce, the copyright bottleneck for broadband content, and the increasing nuisance of spam as priorities.[90] Regulation is declared to be a key element in the development of an inclusive and safe Information Society in which users make full use of the potential of the Internet.

The Bangemann Report of 1994[91] shared some free-market characteristics with the US 'Information Superhighway' which Al Gore had claimed prior to the 1992 Presidential campaign, but Europeanised the Gore/Clinton 'Information Superhighway'[92] of early 1993 to the 'Information Society' analogy. DG Information Society[93] was established to consider regulation and promotion of the Information Society. Bangemann[94] acknowledged the need for continued sectoral regulation: 'a single European regulatory authority for communications may one day prove necessary'. He appeared less convinced of the need for command-and-control regulation of content: 'a new approach is required as content becomes network-independent and as control of content (and responsibility for its use) shifts from government to the individual'. The goals of content regulation in the digital economy are however easier espoused than implemented.

European Internet users are increasingly using the Internet for electronic commerce, information and entertainment, education, forming friendships and virtual communities. However, trust in the medium is affected negatively by software viruses, spam, inappropriate or harmful contact and content, threat of prosecution for copyright and even criminal activity online. Invasion of privacy is a constant source of concern to Internet users. The European Commission expresses some of the pitfalls of web surfing compared with television or radio:

> Whereas in traditional broadcasting (analogue or digital) the individual broadcaster is easily identifiable, it is difficult and sometimes impossible to identify the source of content on the Internet. Access to harmful and illegal content is easy

and can even occur without intent. In addition, the volume of information in the Internet is massive in comparison to broadcasting.[95]

It has long been maintained that Internet service is not analogous to broadcasting, but print publishing. In this view, the lack of control of the network by any one company, relatively low entry and distribution costs to publishers and authors, and pluralism of supply means that there is competition for users. In this case, the only 'control' is on the distribution of the material to the final user, as in a newsagent's kiosk, and the editorial choice of the end-user. In the tangible case of print, newsagents might refuse to sell pornography to minors, but in the case of the Internet, that choice is more difficult due to the technology. End-user tools such as filtering, imposing rules on children's use of the Internet, and reporting inappropriate or illegal content to hotlines established by Internet companies have had only limited success.

In European debate,[96] the regulatory response was considered in a 'convergence' report commissioned by DG InfoSoc, published in September 1996.[97] This report formed the backdrop for the debates[98] which led to the 1999 Commission proposals for a new framework for communications regulation,[99] coming into force in August 2003. The July 1997 Declaration at the Bonn Ministerial Conference made plain the Council of Ministers' desire to see end-user filtering rather than intermediary liability:[100]

Responsibility of the actors

41. Ministers underline the importance of clearly defining the relevant legal rules on responsibility for content of the various actors in the chain between creation and use. They recognise the need to make a clear distinction between the responsibility of those who produce and place content in circulation and that of intermediaries.
42. Ministers stress that the rules on responsibility for content should be based on a set of common principles so as to ensure a level playing field. Therefore, intermediaries like network operators and access providers should, in general, not be responsible for content. This principle should be applied in such a way that intermediaries like network operators and access providers are not subject to unreasonable, disproportionate or discriminatory rules. In any case, third-party content hosting services should not be expected to exercise prior control on content which they have no reason to believe is illegal. Due account should be taken of whether such intermediaries had reasonable grounds to know and reasonable possibility to control content.
43. Ministers consider that rules on responsibility should give effect to the principle of freedom of speech, respect public and private interests and not impose disproportionate burdens on actors.

Facilitating users' choice

53. Ministers urge the software industry to provide the necessary tools to enable users to select categories of content which they do or do not wish to receive so as to deal with information overload and undesired or harmful content.
54. Ministers therefore welcome the development of powerful services and software tools which enable information search and retrieval, and delivery directly to the user of specifically requested information.

55. Ministers stress the importance of the availability of filtering mechanisms and rating systems which allow users to decide on categories of content which they wish themselves, or minors for whom they are responsible, to access.

A further allusion to the international challenge of Internet regulation, even in the case of criminal law, is made:

65. Ministers recognise the specific challenges posed by the misuse of Global Information Networks. They consider, therefore, that international co-operation is essential in this area. Ministers will actively encourage the reinforcement of police and judicial co-operation, particularly in the area of technology training and mutual assistance, to prevent and combat illegal content and high technology crime. They support the establishment of international networks of hot-lines.
66. Ministers welcome the recent initiative of the OECD aiming at a comparative study of national legislations and an exchange of experiences on the issue of illegal content on the Internet. Supporting a multilateral as well as a European approach, they consider that the international dimension is crucial in the building of trust and confidence in the Global Information Networks.

State regulatory discussion during the 1997 renegotiation[101] of the 'Television Without Frontiers' Directive[102] led to a co-regulatory Recommendation in 1998 that continues to serve as the Commission's policy towards content regulation.[103] Further Commission legal instruments including the E-Commerce Directive of 2000 have maintained the co-regulatory approach to Internet regulation laid out in the 1998 Recommendation.[104]

Is an international consensus emerging on Internet content liability?

The US government adoption of a free-market libertarian approach was encapsulated in the Magaziner Report of 1997.[105] Michael Froomkin has described this Report as a paradoxical mix of heavy government intervention to secure property rights for corporations, combined with a libertarian language designed to minimise regulation in areas other than property rights. As for its claim to be providing a 'global framework', he claims that it 'fails to grasp the consequences of the means proposed to achieve its short-term ends for long-term global governance'.[106] The global growth of the Internet – despite its phenomenal US national growth – was therefore hampered by rival visions of the role of the state.[107] During the early consumer development of the WWW, when most information was unencrypted and e-commerce was relatively crude, competing visions co-existed. Tensions over privacy, domain name allocation, freedom of speech and other issues continue to exist between the United States and Europe, reflecting deep-seated unresolved differences in the approach to market, state and society.

The broadband Internet is a more powerful and more pervasive medium than its narrowband predecessor. It offers new 'regulability' in the form of the BSPs, more profitable and well-resourced actors than their failing narrowband forebears. It also requires well-funded BSPs, given the range of access and content control costs, notably increased by peer-to-peer file sharing. In Chapter 2, we consider the range of self-regulatory types and techniques available, before going on in later chapters to assess their successes and failings. In concluding chapters, we must return to the development of the Internet, in order to draw some conclusions for self-regulation from its further development. First, we explore how media policy has developed at national and European level.

Notes

1 John Perry Barlow and the Electronic Freedom Foundation (1996) *A Declaration of the Independence of Cyberspace*, www.eff.org/~barlow/Declaration-Final.html, accessed 28 February 2005.
2 See Treaty on Principles Governing the Activities of States in the Exploration, Development and Use of The Internet Commons at http://www.internationalunity.org/, accessed 28 February 2005. This is the 2004 version of John Perry Barlow and the Electronic Freedom Foundation's 1996 *Declaration of the Independence of Cyberspace*.
3 Berners-Lee, T with Fischetti, M (1999) *Weaving the Web: The Original Design and Ultimate Destiny of the World Wide Web by Its Inventor*, HarperCollins, at: www.harpercollins.com/catalog/redir.aspl?0062515861
   Tim Berners-Lee invented the WWW in his spare time at CERN, the particle accelerator laboratory which was an inter-governmental funded research initiative in Switzerland.
4 Saltzer, J W, Reed P D and Clark, D D (1984) 'End-to-End Arguments in System Design', *ACM Transactions in Computer Systems* 2(4), 277–88.
5 Lessig, L (14 November 1999) 'Architecting Innovation', at: www.thestandard.com/article/display/0,1151,7430,00.html
6 Gould, M (2000) 'Locating Internet Governance: Lessons from the Standards Process', Chapter 10 in Marsden, C (ed.) *Regulating the Global Information Society*, London: Routledge. Lessig has characterised this as the 'newbie' issue of pervasive adoption of the Internet, creating a cultural problem where there is less common knowledge of 'netiquette'. The resultant mission creep 'has been described by Jean Camp of the Kennedy School at Harvard University as a three-stage process: adhocracy-technocracy-bureaucracy' (interviewed by Chris Marsden: April 2000, Toronto).
7 See Gillett, S, Eisner, S and Kapor, M (1996) 'The Self-Governing Internet: Coordination by Design', in Kahin, B and Keller, J H (eds) *Coordinating the Internet*, Cambridge, MA: MIT Press.
8 See Lemley, M (1999) 'Standardizing Government Standard Setting Policy for Electronic Commerce', *Berkeley Technology Law Journal* 14(2), 745–58, and Lessig, L (1999) 'The Limits in Open Code: Regulatory Standards and the Future of the Net', *Berkeley Technology Law Journal* 14(2), 759–70.
9 Lessig, L (1996) 'Reading the Constitution in Cyberspace', *Emory Law Journal* 45, 869. ARPANET, the original scientist-controlled network, was handed over to commercial control in 1992, when the World Wide Web, based on HTML for URLs, was also popularised. The first browser to integrate text and images, Mosaic, was launched in 1993. Netscape Navigator and Microsoft Internet Explorer were released in the following two years. Yahoo was formed in 1994, AOL in 1985, but jumped from 500,000 to 4.5 million subscribers in two years from the start of 1994.
10 Cerf, V (14 August 1994) Guidelines for Conduct on and Use of Internet, Draft v0.1 at: www.isoc.org/Internet/conduct/cerf-Aug-draft.shtml. Though an incomplete draft it is fascinating as an example of very early public policy making on Internet content.
11 Price, M and Verhulst, S (2000) 'In Search of the Self: Charting the Course of Self-Regulation on the Internet in a Global Environment', Chapter 3 in Marsden, C (ed.) op. cit. One must acknowledge the strength of the democratic principle enunciated: see Mayer-Schonberger, V and Foster, E T (1997) 'A Regulatory Web: Free Speech and the

Global Information Infrastructure', in Kahin, B and Nesson, C R (eds) *Borders in Cyberspace: Information Policy and the Global Information Infrastructure*, Cambridge, MA: MIT Press; Volkmer, I (1997) 'Universalism and Particularism: The Problem of Cultural Sovereignty and Global Information Flow', in Kahin, B and Nesson, C R (eds) op. cit.; Price, M (1995) *Television, the Public Sphere and National Identity*, Oxford: Oxford University Press.

12 Title 47 USCA, 223(a) and (d), The Communications Decency Act 1996 was introduced on 30 January 1995, passed by Congress in December 1995 and signed into law by President Clinton in January 1996, before being substantially but not wholly declared unconstitutional by the Supreme Court in *ACLU v. Reno*, Supreme Court Case No. 96–511, 1997.

13 Resnick, P and Miller, J (1996) 'PICS: Internet Access Controls Without Censorship', *Association for Computing Machinery* 39(10), 87–93, at: www.w3.org.PICS.iacwcv2.htm

14 Unsurprisingly, ICANN falls far short of the inclusive participatory standard required. Froomkin, Michael A (2000) 'Semi-Private International Rule-Making: Lessons Learned from the WIPO Domain Name Process', Chapter 11 in Marsden, C (ed.) op. cit.

15 See Kaul, I, Grunberg, I and Stern, M (eds) (1999) *Global Public Goods: International Cooperation in the 21st Century*, New York: Oxford University Press.

16 Discussed further in Campbell, Angela J (1999) 'Self-Regulation and the Media', *Federal Communications Law Journal* 51, 711.

17 A non-exhaustive list of EU reports and recommendations in the 'early' period of Internet policy discussion would include:

  - White Paper on Growth, Competitiveness, and Employment – The Challenges and Ways Forward into the 21st Century, COM(93)700, Brussels, 5 December 1993;
  - Europe and the Global Information Society, Recommendations of the Bangemann Group to the European Council, 26 May 1994;
  - Green Paper on Strategy Options to Strengthen the European Programme Industries in the context of the Audiovisual Policy of the European Union, COM(94)96, 6 April 1994;
  - Europe's Way to the Information Society: An Action Plan, COM(94)347, 19 July 1994;
  - Communication of the Commission to the Council, the European Parliament, the Economic and Social Committee and the Committee of the Regions on the Information Society: From Corfu to Dublin – The New Emerging Priorities, COM(96)395, 24 July 1996;
  - Commission Communication on The Implications of the Information Society for European Union Policies: Preparing the Next Steps, COM(96)395, 24 July 1996;
  - Commission Communication on Europe at the Forefront of the Global Information Society: Rolling Action Plan, COM(96)607 final, 27 Nov. 1996;
  - Council Resolution on New Political Priorities Regarding the Information Society, 21 Nov. 1996, OJ C386, 12 Dec. 1996, p. 1;
  - Commission Communication, A European Initiative in Electronic Commerce, COM(97)157, April 1997;
  - Building the European Information Society for Us All, Final Report of the High Level Experts Group, April 1997.

18 Reding, V (2005) Better Regulation for Europe's Media Industry: The Commission's Approach, Speech 05/532.

19 See further Reidenberg, J (2005) 'Technology and Internet Jurisdiction', *Univ. of Penn. L. Rev.* 153, 1951: http://ssrn.com/abstract=691501

20 Lessig, L (1996) 'Reading the Constitution in Cyberspace', *Emory Law Journal* 45, 869.

21 See Reidenberg, J (2004) 'States and Internet Enforcement', *Univ. Ottawa L. & Tech. J.* 1, 1; Goldsmith, J (1998) 'Against Cyberanarchy', *U. Chi. L. Rev.* 65, 1199; Bick, J D (1998) 'Why Should the Internet be any Different?', 19 *Pace L. Rev.* 41, 63; Goldsmith, Jack (1998) 'What Internet Gambling Legislation Teaches About Internet Regulation', *Intl Law.* 32, 1115.

22 See Geist, M (2006) 'New Yahoo Decision Raises Old Questions', at: http://news.bbc. co.uk/2/hi/technology/4641244.stm and www.michaelgeist.ca/index.php?option=com _content&task=view&id=1083; Goldsmith J and Wu T (2006) 'Digital Borders: National Boundaries Have Survived in the Virtual World – and Allowed National Laws to Exert Control over the Internet', at: www.legalaffairs.org/issues/January-February-2006/ feature_goldsmith_janfeb06.msp; Murray, A (2006) *Regulating Cyberspace: Control in the Online Environment*, London: Routledge-Cavendish; Zittrain, J (2006) 'The Generative Internet', *Harvard Law Journal* 119(1), 1–67; Zittrain, J (2006) 'Without a Net', at: www.legalaffairs. org/issues/January-February-2006/feature_zittrain_janfeb06.msp

23 See Wakefield, Jane (2006) 'Google Faces China Challenges', BBC News, 25 January, at: http://news.bbc.co.uk/1/hi/technology/4647468.stm and Rhoads, Christopher (2006) 'Should the World Make Room for Another Wide Web?', *Wall Street Journal* 22 January, p. 1, at: www.courant.com/business/hc-wsjinternet.artjan22,0,4344057.story?coll=hc-headlines-business

24 For a practitioner viewpoint see National Consumer Council (2001) 'Soft Law in the European Union', at: www.ncc.org.uk/europe/softlaw.pdf

The NCC references several European legal instruments that give rise to self-regulatory soft law obligations:

Directive 97/7 on distance selling, especially article 11.4
Directive 95/46/EC on data protection
Recommendation 98/257/CE on out-of-court settlements
Directive 92/59/EEC on general product safety.

25 For a treatment attempting to exhaustively deal with European and German case law, see Scheuer, Sections 5–6, in Held, T and Scheuer, A (2006) Draft Report: Study on Co-Regulation Measures in the Media Sector. Study for the European Commission, Directorate Information Society and Media Unit A1 Audiovisual and Media Policies, Hans Bredow Institute.

26 For the increasing use of soft law as a regulatory instrument, see Morth, U, ed. (2004) *Soft Law in Governance and Regulation: An Interdisciplinary Analysis*, Edward Elgar.

See further the Commission's 'soft law' website: http://europa.eu.int/comm/development/body/legislation/softlaw_en.htm

27 Noam, E (2003) 'The Internet: Still Wide Open and Competitive?', *Oxford Internet Institute Issue Brief* No. 1, August. He defines the Internet sector as: 'the core industries that provide instrumentalities and infrastructure components underlying the Internet's basic functioning' (p. 2).

28 The terms Internet Access Provider (IAP) and Internet Service Provider (ISP) are often used interchangeably, though some people consider IAPs to be a subset of ISPs. Whereas IAPs offer only Internet access, ISPs may provide additional services, such as leased lines and Web development. In contrast to both IAPs and ISPs, Internet Content Providers provide their own proprietary content, often in addition to Internet access. See Yen, A (2000) 'Internet Service Provider Liability for Subscriber Copyright Infringement, Enterprise Liability and the First Amendment', *Georgetown L. J.* 88, at: http://papers.ssrn. com/sol3/Delivery.cfm/SSRN_ID236478_code000726304.pdf?abstractid=236478

29 Child's Internet Protection Act 2003, building on the Communications Decency Act 1996.

30 Reuters (18 March 2004) 'Central Filter Against Web Hate for French Schools', at: www. reuters.com/newsArticle.jhtml;?storyID=4599516

31 President Clinton's 1995 Copyright Taskforce supported such liability: Working Group on Intellectual Property Rights, Information Infrastructure Task Force (1995) *Intellectual Property and the National Information Infrastructure* 1–6, 114–24.

32 Some legal commentators forcefully argued that strict liability should apply. See Hardy, T (1994) 'The Proper Legal Regime for Cyberspace', *U. Pitt. L. Rev.* 55, 993, 1042–46 (advocating strict ISP liability); Tickle, K (1995) 'Comment: The Vicarious Liability of Electronic Bulletin Board Operators for the Copyright Infringement Occurring on Their Bulletin Boards', *Iowa L. Rev.* 80, 391, 416 (favouring limited ISP liability).

33   See, for example, Elkin-Koren, N (1995) 'Copyright Law and Social Dialogue on the Information Superhighway: The Case Against Copyright Liability of Bulletin Board Operators', *Cardozo Arts & Ent. L. J.* 13, 345, 399–410, who argues opposing liability.

34   Section 30, 47 USC § 230(c)(1) (Supp. II 1996). This language might shield ISPs from liability for subscriber copyright infringement as well. However, Section 230(e)(2) specifically states: 'Nothing in this section shall be construed to limit or expand any law pertaining to intellectual property.'

35   Holznagel, B (2000) 'Responsibility for Harmful and Illegal Content as Well as Free Speech on the Internet in the United States of America and Germany', in Engel, C and Keller, H (eds) *Governance of Global Networks in Light of Differing Local Values*, Baden Baden: Nomos.

36   Frydman, B and Rorive, I (2002) 'Regulating Internet Content Through Intermediaries in Europe and the USA', *Zeitschrift für Rechtssoziologie* Bd.23/H1, July, 41–59.

37   Ibid., p. 54.

38   Ibid., p. 56.

39   Ibid., p. 59.

40   Ibid., p. 19.

41   This testimony to the FCC was later published as Lemley, M A and Lessig, L (2001) 'The End of End-to-End: Preserving the Architecture of the Internet in the Broadband Era', *UCLA L. Rev.* 48, 925.

Other notable contributions to the debate include: Wu, Tim (2003) 'Network Neutrality and Broadband Discrimination', *J. Telecom. & High Tech L.* 2, 141; Yu, Christopher (2004) 'Would Mandating Network Broadband Neutrality Help or Hurt Competition? A Comment on the End-to-End Debate', *J. Telecom. & High Tech L.* 3(2), 23–57; Farrell, Joseph and Wesier, Philip J (2003) 'Modularity, Vertical Integration, and Open Access Policies: Toward a Convergence of Antitrust and Regulation in the Internet Age', *Department of Economics UCB Paper* E02–325; Woroch, Glen A (2002) 'Open Access Rules and the Broadband Race', *L. Rev. M.S.U.–D.C.L.* 3, 719–42.

42   Business Week International Online Extra (2005) 'At SBC It's All About Scale and Scope', 7 November, at: www.businessweek.com/

43   See Wadawsky, John (2005) 'IMS 101: What You Need to Know Now', at: www.bcr.com/carriers/public_networks/ims_101_what_need_know_now_2005061514.htm

44   See IPsphere (2006, May) 'Creating a Commercially Sustainable Framework for IP Services Realizing Next Generation Revenues', IPsphere Forum Work Program Committee Version 1b.0 at: www.ipsphereforum.org/home/IPsphere_CommercialPrim erExec050806.pdf

45   See note 32.

46   Lessig, L (1999) Brief as *Amicus Curiae US* v. *Microsoft*, 65 F.Supp.2d 1 (D.D.C. 1999) (No. Civ. 98–1232 (TPJ), Civ. 98–1233 (TPJ)), at: http://cyber.law.harvard.edu/works/lessig/AB/abd9.doc.html

47   See Communications, Consumer's Choice, and Broadband Deployment Act of 2006, at http://thomas.loc.gov/cgi-bin/bdquery/z?d109:SN02686:

48   See EC Staff Working Document 28 June 2006 at Section 6.4 Net Neutrality: 'In Europe the regulatory framework allows operators to offer different services to different customer groups, but does not allow those who are in a dominant position to discriminate between customers in similar circumstances. However, there is a risk that, in some situations, the quality of service could degrade to unacceptably low levels. It is therefore proposed to give NRAs the power to set minimum quality levels for network transmission services in an NGN environment based on technical standards identified at EU level. The existing provisions for NRAs to impose obligations on operators with significant market power, and the powers for NRAs to address access and interconnection issues could be used to prevent any blocking of information society services, or degradation in the quality of transmission of electronic communication services for third parties, and to impose appropriate interoperability requirements.'

49 Goldring, J (1997) 'Netting the Cybershark: Consumer Protection, Cyberspace, the Nation-State, and Democracy', in Kahin, B and Nesson, CR (eds), op. cit., p. 322.

50 See Whitehead, P (1997) *Draft Report on the Commission Green Paper on the Protection of Minors and Human Dignity in Audiovisual and Information Services* (COM[96]0483 – C4–0621/96), PE 221.804, 24 April.

51 See Gifford, D J and McGowan, D (1999) 'A Microsoft Dialog', *Antitrust Bulletin* 44, 619; Samuelson, P and Opsahl, K (1999) 'Licensing Information in the Global Information Market: Freedom of Contract Meets Public Policy', *EIPR* 21, 386.

52 Several legal authors have discussed the technical engineering of the Internet and its effect on law and policy, notably Reidenberg, J (1993) 'Rules of the Road for Global Electronic Highways: Merging the Trade and Technical Paradigms', *Harvard Journal of Law and Technology* 6, 287. Reidenberg is also notable for her international perspective, when much of the US scholarship is insular.

53 Lessig, L (1999) *Code and Other Laws of Cyberspace*, New York: Basic Books, Chapter 7.

54 Ellickson, R C (1998) 'Law and Economics Discovers Social Norms', *Journal of Legal Studies* Part II: XXVII, 537–52, at 549, fn 58.

55 See Ogus, A I (1994) *Regulation: Legal Form and Economic Theory*, Oxford: Clarendon Press, pp. 1–3.

56 Bentham, J (1995) *The Panopticon Writings*, edited and introduced by Miran Bozovic, London: Verso; Foucault, M (1991) *Discipline and Punish: The Birth of the Prison*, Harmondsworth: Penguin Books; Lessig (1999), op. cit., at 665, 691.

57 Lessig (1999), op. cit., at 667.

58 Lessig (1999), op. cit., at 691.

59 Lessig (1999), op. cit., at 691.

60 A comprehensive and complete analysis is offered by Larouche, P (1998) 'EC Competition Law and the Convergence of the Telecommunications and Broadcasting Sectors', *Telecommunications Policy* 22(3), 219–42. See also Harcourt, A (1998) 'Regulation of European Media Markets: Approaches of the European Court of Justice and the Commission's Merger Task Force', *Utilities Law Review* 9(6), 276–91, at 277. A *communitaire* legal justification for national application of EC competition law under the Treaty of Rome is provided in Temple-Lang, J (1998) 'The Duty of National Authorities under Community Constitutional Law', *European Law Review* 23, 109, at 119.

61 See Wearden, Graham (2004) 'UK Police Chief: Shut Down Abhorrent Websites', at: http://news.zdnet.co.uk/Internet/0,39020369,39147312,00.htm

62 Moe T M (1997) 'The Positive Theory of Public Bureaucracy', in Mueller, Dennis C (ed.) *Perspectives on Public Choice: A Handbook*, Cambridge University Press.

63 McCahery, J, Bratton, W W, Picciotto, S and Scott, C, eds (1996) *International Regulatory Competition and Coordination*, Oxford University Press, p. 12.

64 Tiebout, C (1956) 'A pure theory of public expenditures', *Journal of Political Economy* 64, 416–24.

65 McCahery *et al.*, ibid., p. 15.

66 North, D C (1990) *Institutions, Institutional Change and Economic Performance*, Cambridge University Press, p. 140.

67 Ibid.

68 It is then entirely explicable that governments, responsive to dynamic technological change, would adapt regulation, with imperfect use of competition policy, in order to strategically influence international markets. Such a view of market failure on a local basis in both political and economic terms may appear cynical. However, information plays an important role in comprehending markets. Further, technology has also played an under-emphasised role. Stiglitz, J E (1985) 'Information and Economic Analysis: A Perspective', *Economic Journal* 95(suppl), 21–41. The growth of firms and other market institutions is explained by the first, and intellectual property rights and other non-disclosure the second. When one combines the two in information technologies, which are both disproportionately strategic and equally tend to market failure on a global scale, one has the ingredients

for a compelling market failure scenario. Where information and communication technology has become the primary driver of growth, and is ubiquitous in internationally competitive industries, one may anticipate the intervention of governments in markets to increasingly bear the hallmark of these institutionally based strategic analyses. Hodgson, G M (1988) *Economics and Institutions: A Manifesto for a Modern Institutional Economics*, Cambridge: Polity Press; North, D C (1990), op. cit.; Levy, B and Spiller, P (1994) 'The Institutional Foundations of Regulatory Commitment: A Comparative Analysis of Telecommunications Regulation', *J. Law, Economics and Organization* 10(2), 201–46.

69   From 150 Kb/s in some Western European entry levels to 20 Mb/s where VDSL has been deployed.

70   Independent cable operators, retail broadband ISPs as well as third-party broadband providers erode market share: KPN in the Netherlands has strong retail competition on its own network, some local loop unbundling competition and strong cable network competition. German competition is limited.

71   Typically collecting societies for publishers/authors, musicians/actors.

72   In January and February 2004, the RIAA brought actions against over 1000 file-sharers known only by their IP addresses, in 'John Doe' litigation. See www.riaa.com/news/newsletter/021304.asp, accessed 28 February, for the broad alliance International Intellectual Property Alliance. See www.riaa.com/news/newsletter/pdf/sampleJohnDoeLawsuit.pdf for an example of the RIAA proceedings.

73   For a theoretical discussion of policy convergence, accompanied by communications case studies, see Levy, D A L (1997) 'Regulating Digital Broadcasting in Europe: The Limits of Policy Convergence', *West European Politics* 20(4), 24–42; Holznagel, B (1998) 'European Audiovisual Conference – Results from Working Group III', *International Journal of Communications Law and Policy* 1(1), at: www.digital-law.net/IJCLP/final/current/ijclp_webdoc_9_1_1998.html.

The more general role of the European Court of Justice is examined by Weiler, J (1991) 'The Transformation of Europe', *Yale Law Journal* 100, 2405; (1993) 'Journey to an Unknown Destination: A Retrospective and Prospective of the European Court of Justice in the Arena of Political Integration', *Journal of Common Market Studies* 31, 417; and (1994) 'A Quiet Revolution: The ECJ and Its Interlocutors', *Comparative Political Studies* 17, 510.

74   Beltrame, F (1996) 'Harmonising Media Ownership Rules: Problems and Prospects', *Util L. R.* 7, 172; Hitchens, L P (1994) 'Media Ownership and Control: A European Approach', *Modern Law Review* 57(4), 585–601.

75   Spar, D L (1996) 'Ruling Commerce in the Networld', *J. Computer-Mediated Communication* 2, 1.

76   Weiler, J H H (1999) *The Constitution of Europe*, Cambridge University Press, p. 15. His Chapter 2, from which this methodological note is taken, is updated from his classic 1991 essay 'The Transformation of Europe', *Yale Law Journal* 100, 2403.

77   Florini, A M (2000) *Who Does What? Collective Action and the Changing Nature of Authority*, in Higgott *et al.* (2000), Chapter 1, pp. 15–31, especially at 20–27.

78   Ayres, I and Braithwaite, J (1992) *Responsive Regulation: Transcending the Deregulation Debate*, Oxford University Press, p. 3.

79   Formal legitimacy is offered by ITU, or WIPO in the case of ICANN, but there is no doubt that private actors such as Motorola, IBM, Nokia, Ericsson and others play a critical role as non-state actors. Drake describes the formation of the ITU as a classic government-sponsored functionalist problem-solving activity, and its latter history as hijacked by the US government and its clients, whether carriers or manufacturers, leaving no doubt of the fact that non-state actors are intimately involved in the formerly state-controlled process of rule and standard-setting for the Internet and telephony. Drake, William J (2000) 'The Rise and Decline of the International Telecommunications Regime', Chapter 4 in Marsden, C (ed.) op. cit.

80   Department of Trade and Industry (5 March 1999) *Building Confidence in Electronic Commerce: A Consultation Document*, p. 6, 'International Context'.

81   See Ypsilanti, D (1999) 'A Borderless World: The OECD Ottawa Ministerial Conference

and Initiatives in Electronic Commerce', *Info* 1(1), 23–34. For a critical perspective, see Love, J (1999) 'Democracy, Privatization and the Governance of Cyberspace: An Alternative View of the OECD Meeting on Electronic Commerce', *Info* 1(1), 15–22.

82 See United Nations General Assembly Resolution 51/162 of 16 December 1996, at: www.un.or.at/uncitral/en-index.htm

83 Additionally, work in this field is conducted through various self-regulatory bodies. See Bangemann, M (1999), 'Which Rules for the Online World? The European Union Contribution', in *Info* 1(1), 11–15.

84 See below for details.

85 Servan-Schreiber, Jean (1967) *Le Defi American* (translated (1968) *The American Challenge*, Penguin).

86 c.12, Telecommunications Act 1984, as amended by c.41 of the Competition Act 1998.

87 eEurope Progress Report (February 2004) 'Analysing Accession Countries Progress to eEurope Targets', at: www.emcis2004.hu/dokk/binary/30/17/3/eEurope–Final_Progress_Report.pdf

88 IP/04/261 (2004) 'Towards a Global Partnership in the Information Society: Way Forward for the EU', at: http://europa.eu.int/rapid/start/cgi/guesten.ksh?p_action.gettxt=gt&doc=IP/04/261|0|RAPID&lg=EN&display =

89 COM (2004) 108 final 'eEurope 2005 Mid-term Review', at: http://europa.eu.int/information_society/eeurope/2005/doc/all_about/acte_en_version_finale.pdf of 18 February 2004.

90 COM (2004) 28 'Unsolicited Commercial Communications or "spam"'. More at: http://europa.eu.int/information_society/topics/ecomm/highlights/current_spotlights/spam/index_en.htm

91 Bangemann, M *et al.* (1994) 'Europe and the Global Information Society, The Report of the High Level Group', www.ispo.cec.be/infosoc/backg/bangeman.html; see further Bangemann, M (1997) 'A New World Order for Global Telecommunications – The Need for an International Charter', *Telecom Inter*, 'The Policy Response to Globalization and Convergence', speech presented in Venice, 18 September, available at: www.ispo.cec.be/infosoc/promo/speech/venice.html; Bangemann, M (1999) 'Which Rules for the Online World? The European Union Contribution', *Info* 1(1), 11–15.

92 www.ntia.doc.gov/

93 www.ispo.cec.be/infosoc/

94 www.ispo.cec.be/infosoc/promo/speech/venice.html

95 See *Second Evaluation Report from the Commission to the Council and the European Parliament on the Application of Council Recommendation of 24 September 1998 Concerning the Protection of Minors and Human Dignity* COM(2003) 776 final of 12 December at: http://europa.eu.int/comm/avpolicy/legis/reports/com2003_776final_en.pdf at p. 6.

96 European Commission (1996) *Green Paper on the Protection of Minors and Human Dignity in Audiovisual and Information Services* of 16 October 1996; *Council Resolution on Illegal and Harmful Content on the Internet* of 17 February 1997 OJ C 70, 6. 3. 1997; Economic and Social Committee Opinion OJ C 214, 10. 7. 1998; European Parliament Opinion OJ C 339, 10. 11. 1997; Economic and Social Committee Opinion OJ C 287, 22. 9. 1997; Committee of the Regions Opinion OJ C 215, 16. 7. 1997.

97 KPMG (1996) *Public Policy Issues Arising from Telecommunications and Audiovisual Convergence, A Report for the European Commission*, at: www.ispo.cec.be/infosoc/promo/pubs/exesum.html

98 Commission of the European Communities, 1997, *Green Paper on the Regulatory Implications of Convergence Between the Telecommunications, Media and Information Technology Sectors: Towards an Information Society Approach. The Convergence Green Paper.* COM (1997) 623, Brussels, December, at: http://europa.eu.int/ISPO/convergencegp/97623en.doc (accessed 16.03.03).

99 See variously: Commission of the European Communities (1999) Communication of the Commission to the European Parliament, the Council, the Economic and Social Committee and the Committee of the Regions, *Review of the Telecommunications Regulatory Framework – A New Framework for Electronic Communications Infrastructures and Associated Services.*

The 1999 Communications Review. COM (1999) 539, Brussels, December, at: http://europa.eu.int/ISPO/infosoc/telecompolicy/review99/review99en.pdf (accessed 16.03.03).

Commission of the European Communities (2002a) *Eighth Report on the Implementation of the Telecommunications Regulatory Package,* COM (2002) 695 final, Brussels, December, at: http://europa.eu.int/information_society/topics/telecoms/implementation/annual_report/8threport/finalreport/annex2.pdf

Commission of the European Communities (2002b) Directive 2002/21/EC of the European Parliament and of the Council on a common regulatory framework for electronic communications networks and services ('*Framework Directive*'), OJ L 108, at: http://europa.eu.int/information_society/topics/telecoms/regulatory/maindocs/index_en.htm

Commission of the European Communities (2002c) Directive 2002/20/EC of the European Parliament and of the Council on the authorisation of electronic communications networks and services ('*Authorisation Directive*'), OJ L 108, at: http://europa.eu.int/information_society/topics/telecoms/regulatory/maindocs/index_en.htm

Commission of the European Communities (2002d) Directive 2002/19/EC of the European Parliament and of the Council on access to, and interconnection of, electronic communications networks and associated facilities ('*Access Directive*'), OJ L 108, at: http://europa.eu.int/information_society/topics/telecoms/regulatory/maindocs/index_en.htm

Commission of the European Communities (2002e) Directive 2002/22/EC of the European Parliament and of the Council on universal service and users' rights relating to electronic communications networks and services ('*Universal Service Directive*'), OJ L 108, at: http://europa.eu.int/information_society/topics/telecoms/regulatory/maindocs/index_en.htm

Commission of the European Communities (2002f) Directive 2002/58/EC of the European Parliament and of the Council of 12 July 2002 concerning the processing of personal data and the protection of privacy in the electronic communications sector ('*Directive on Privacy and Electronic Communications*'), OJ L 108, at: http://europa.eu.int/information_society/topics/telecoms/regulatory/maindocs/index_en.htm

Commission of the European Communities (2002g) Decision No. 676/2002/EC of the European Parliament and of the Council of 7 March 2002 on a regulatory framework for radio spectrum policy in the European Community ('*Radio Spectrum Decision*'), OJ L 108, http://europa.eu.int/information_society/topics/telecoms/regulatory/maindocs/index_en.htm

100 Bonn Ministerial Declaration 8 July 1997 at http://europa.eu.int/ISPO/bonn/Min_declaration/i_finalen.html

101 See Whitehead, P (1997) *Draft Report on the Commission Green Paper on the Protection of Minors and Human Dignity in Audiovisual and Information Services* (COM [96] 0483 – C4–0621/96), PE 221.804 of 24 April 1997, which formed the basis of European Parliament debate.

102 Directive 97/36/EC of the European Parliament and of the Council of 30 June 1997 amending Council Directive 89/552/EEC on the coordination of certain provisions laid down by law, regulation or administrative action in Member States concerning the pursuit of television broadcasting activities, OJ L 202, 30.7.1997.

103 *Green Paper on the Protection of Minors and Human Dignity in Audiovisual and Information Services,* COM (96) 483, 16.10.97; Communication on Illegal and Harmful Content on the Internet, COM (97) 487, 16.10.97; Council Recommendation 98/560/EC on the development of the competitiveness of the European audiovisual and information services industry by promoting national frameworks aimed at achieving a comparable and effective level of protection of minors and human dignity, OJ L 270, 7.10.1998.

104 See further Directive 2002/58/EC of the European Parliament and of the Council of 12 July 2002 concerning the processing of personal data and the protection of privacy in the electronic communications, OJ L 201, 31.7.2002; Directive 2000/31/EC of the European Parliament and of the Council of 8 June 2000 on certain legal aspects of information society services, in particular electronic commerce, in the Internal Market, OJ

L 178, 17.7.2000; Decision No. 276/1999/EC of the European Parliament and of the Council of 25 January 1999 adopting a Multiannual Community Action Plan on promoting safer use of the Internet and new online technologies by combating illegal and harmful content primarily in the area of the protection of children and minors, OJ L 33, 6.2.1999, p. 1 as amended by Decision No. 1151/2003/EC of the European Parliament and of the Council of 16 June 2003, OJ L 162, 1.7.2003.

105 Clinton, W J and Gore, A Jr (1997) *A Framework for Global Electronic Commerce* at: www. ecommerce.gov/framewrk.htm (henceforth the Magaziner Report after the head of the President's Taskforce and Senior Adviser to the President for Policy Development).

106 Froomkin, M A (1999) 'Of Governments and Governance', *Berkeley Technology Law Journal* 14(2), 617–33, at p. 620.

107 Reidenberg, Joel (1996) 'Governing Networks and Rule-Making in Cyberspace', *Emory Law Review* 45, 911–30.

2 Self-regulation of media content in Europe

From state control to regulation to self-regulation to co-regulation

During the 1990s, key decisions on Internet regulation were taken that marked out the paths upon which the Internet's development would depend. It was a time of intense debate, which is examined in this chapter. We see that those developing the institutions of Internet regulation, knowingly or otherwise, drew upon existing models in other media sectors, and were influenced by the Anglo-American-inspired vogue for deregulation and liberalisation combined with a concern not to 'break' the technically and economically 'miraculous' new technology. At the birth of the World Wide Web, it was theoretically possible that Internet technology and content could have been regulated by economic competition, by social norms, by detailed legislation, by independent regulatory agencies, or by 'purely' self-regulatory agencies. It is to the debate about the relative merits of these forms of regulation, and the problematic distinctions between them, that we now turn.

This chapter begins by defining regulation in the first section, then explores in the second whether regulatory convergence is occurring, and in the third examines previous attempts to regulate via expert independent agencies, in telecoms and broadcasting. It then investigates the increasing trend towards 'co-regulation' in the fourth section, and in the fifth the ability of large ISPs and other multilateral actors to 'game' the weak enforcement by self-regulation. Finally we consider the pan-European and pan-sectoral possibilities of consolidation of self-regulatory mechanisms in an attempt to simplify the European media co-regulatory maze.

Soft law and the ecology of regulation and self-regulation

Regulation may be defined as 'the act of controlling, directing, or governing according to a rule, principle or system'.[1] This is taken to exclude punitive general legal norms (criminal law). Baldwin *et al.* explain that: 'At its simplest, regulation refers to the promulgation of an authoritative set of rules, accompanied by some mechanism, typically a public agency, for monitoring and promoting compliance with these rules.'[2]

They argue that recent regulatory design has generally separated rule-making from enforcement/monitoring activities, the former remaining in parliamentary competence, the latter delegated to independent regulatory agencies (IRAs) whose decisions could be judicially reviewed in some cases. From the perspective of judicial review there is need 'to develop a conception of "public"'[3] to identify areas amenable to judicial supervision. For the economist, regulation 'in its widest conception is state intervention in the economic decisions of companies'.[4] A broader sociological definition 'considers all mechanisms of social control' to be forms of regulation, which encompasses self-regulatory models, the role of firms and social norms. This enables the consideration of non-legal factors, and the interaction of private companies, civil society and state.

This wider definition is useful because self-regulatory rules and procedures develop in an interdependent relationship with legal codes. Where one fails the other is under more pressure to succeed, and where one develops the other may wither. It is therefore useful to speak of an ecology of regulation. The rules and agencies described by Baldwin *et al.* are, in the case of the Internet, private actors' CoCs, with very little or no sanction for non-compliance. Positivists can rightly point to the absence of sanction as demonstrating no legal structure to Internet regulation at all, and the impact of these codes on behaviour is indeed extremely difficult to estimate. This makes all the more urgent the examination of the 'hybrid processes'[5] of non-state regulation. Harden and Lewis state that 'as constitutional lawyers, this causes us considerable concern in terms of the mechanisms available for rendering state business generally accountable'.[6] In brief, the continuing deregulation and foreign control of content causes concern in policy towards the fundamental public good of mass communication. However, the 'soft law' of a CoC may be seen as demonstrating implied state sanction tempered by its forbearance where market actors are seen to impose self-enforced rules, or at least norms, of behaviour.

The debate on self-regulation in the 1990s was fundamentally influenced by enthusiasm for soft law, and the approach of New Public Management. The concept of 'soft law' has developed from two sources with broad application to Internet regulation. These are:

- *lex mercatoria*, the system of international law generally held to have developed amongst the Renaissance merchants of the Hanseatic League, an example of customary international law;
- the role of 'soft' law in European and then international law, more particularly non-sanctions-based instruments of the European Union, including Declarations, Recommendations and other policy instruments which create no legal duty or sanction, but upon which market actors rely in planning their activities in a chosen sector.[7]

Hood describes the rise of the regulatory state as 'New Public Management', characterised by: the rolling back of the frontiers of the state, privatisation and quasi-privatisation, increased use of information technology, and internationalism.[8] Harlow explains that New Public Management 'has swept like a tidal wave up our estuaries and into our rivers, shattering the post-war interventionist consensus'.[9] Ayres and Braithwaite state:[10]

> by working more creatively with the interplay between private and public regulation, government and citizens can design better policy solutions . . . administrative and regulatory practice is in a state of flux in which responsive regulatory innovations are politically feasible.

Responsive regulation – or reflexive regulation – reflects a more complex dynamic interaction of state and market, a break with more stable previous arrangements. It is the interplay between private and public actors which provides richness and complexity.

The growth of the regulatory state has been examined in theoretical terms by Beck,[11] in his study of 'risk society' and the usurpation of democratic functions by unaccountable experts. Luhmann,[12] in his systemic theory of specialisation, concludes that such apolitical fragmentation of the legislative communion with democratic institutions is both inevitable and irreversible. Teubner has been very influential in European conceptions of law as 'moving away from the idea of direct societal guidance through a politically instrumentalised law . . . Instead, reflexive law tends to rely on procedural norms that regulate processes, organisation, and the distribution of rights and competencies.'[13] Teubner uses the concept of reflexive law to explain a legitimation crisis in contemporary governance in Western Europe.

The attraction of this systemic critique of regulation for the Internet sector is clear: the fast-changing globalising nature of the Internet will require a systematically adaptive regulatory structure. It was vigorously argued that conventional regulation, involving legislative lag and inexpert courts, would be entirely inappropriate and would risk breaking the architectural principles of this new technology. This position has been applied in the case of other globalising phenomena than the Internet, for instance financial and environmental law.

The early development of the Internet as a mass-market phenomenon therefore coincided with a deep and far-reaching problematisation of conventional legislative approaches to regulation in Europe. Not only was there a presumption in favour of non-state regulation drawing on the tradition of the 'free press', but there was a broad shift towards independence of regulators across all sectors and, as we shall now see, resulting constitutional instability: independent regulatory agencies were charged with oversight of Internet content in some cases, but concerns about over-regulation and speech freedoms favoured self-regulation over regulation by public authority.

Technical convergence and self-regulation[14]

One of the central means by which communications policy makers have traditionally dealt with the dilemma of communications regulation is by developing forms of self- and co-regulation. Particularly in the press sector, but increasingly in games, advertising, broadcasting and other media sectors, self-regulation has been seen as an acceptable response where political interference with media has been viewed with justifiable suspicion yet there remains a need for some form of regulation. In some cases, as with many press councils, the line between government and self-regulation is clearly drawn in the constitution and procedures of the councils. In others, for example broadcasting, we more often find an arm's-length relationship: self-regulatory codes are applied independently by an independent council, but there is a clear statutory relationship between the broadcast licensee, the regulator and the broadcast code.

To say there is a clear line of separation between self- and co-regulation would be an illusion, however: public and governmental debate about communications issues continues perpetually, and governments always carry the threat of external regulation of communications providers, including the press, should self-regulation fail. Debate about audiovisual industry and policy within Europe has been overshadowed by the concept of convergence since the mid 1990s. There has been a prevailing sense that previously distinct industry lines between computing, telecommunications and broadcasting are blurring or disappearing, and that destabilising changes are occurring at an unpredictable rate. Digitisation is claimed to be at the heart of developments that are not merely technological, but also economic and social. Hence the assumption that convergence is the crux of the information society.

All policy analysts agree that technology is changing fast, that markets are changing more rapidly than previously, and that regulation is too subject to procedural constraints to maintain the pace of either technology or markets. It should be added that in telecoms regulation, national appeals mechanisms through the court system, whether administrative or standard, are even slower than regulation or even legislation in achieving change. The differential is illustrated in Figure 2.1.

The 'step change' is that from regulation by government IRA, always subject to national and European legislation and national and European due process through the court systems, to self-regulation. In the economic arena, much can be achieved through alternative dispute resolution and use of industry-led standards bodies. In the licensing and content regulation context, there is a more radical challenge. This has been described by Towers Perrin as moving from 'silo-based regulation' to converged regulation, so that broadcasters and Internet actors are not treated differently according to medium, but according to function in the vertical value chain.[15] Thus content providers of Internet, print and television are regulated by the same regulator; access providers, whether of satellite or terrestrial television, broadband or narrowband, fixed or wireless Internet are treated the same. In this section, we examine Internet content from this converged perspective.

The debate on how to regulate convergence and whether regulation within this context is a barrier rather than a facilitator, has roughly been divided between two main camps, the *maximalists* and the *minimalists*.

- For *maximalists*, most current regulation originated in an era when distinctions between sectors were clear, but which no longer applies: convergence will increasingly blur all the distinctions between services; all networks will be able to

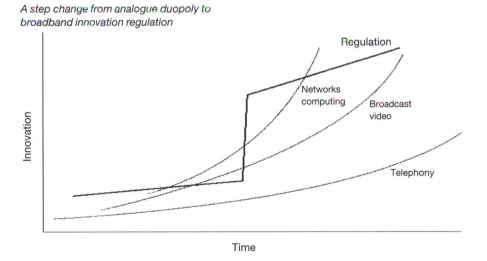

A step change from analogue duopoly to broadband innovation regulation

Figure 2.1 Can regulation keep pace with digital convergence?

(From Marsden, C (2001) 'Reinventing Broadband Regulation, Re: Think!', White Paper, at p. 6: www.croxford.org/ivan/rethink/pdfs/rethink_regulation.pdf.)

deliver any service to any platform. Much of today's regulation has a national focus, increasingly inappropriate, according to this viewpoint, as the services market becomes international, or global on the Internet model.

- The *minimalist* point of view holds that convergence will have a more limited impact, that it will not alter the specific nature of different types of service. Its proponents argue that media policy should actively promote social, cultural and ethical values, whatever technology is used for delivering services. They favour two sets of rules, one for economic aspects and another for service content, in order to guarantee efficiency and quality, as in broadcasting in the discussions in late 2005.

The developments currently underway in the broad communications field represent a fundamental paradigm shift away from conventional policy modes. Whilst in many countries in Europe converged communications regulators are being set up for tele-communications and broadcasting, cooperation between the fragmented, voluntary self-regulation bodies is likely to be sporadic and uncoordinated. The aim of this section is to highlight the fundamental shift in attitudes and assumptions concerning the definition of the public interest in communications, largely driven by the globalisation of technology, and the economic and social benefits fostered by convergence.

The complexity and scope of convergence requires a basic analytical framework for considering its meaning and implications. A common understanding of the concept, its importance for regulators, and the perspective with which to assess its impact are required, before it is possible to consider specific regulatory responses.[16]

Technical convergence

Digital convergence is mainly used as an umbrella term for some of the technological changes within the media, from technical and consumer market perspectives. At the heart of technical convergence lies digitisation, whereby all forms of data (alphanumeric text, graphics, still and moving pictures and sounds) are translated into binary form ('noughts and ones').[17] Digitisation leads to other key technological advances such as compression, optical fibre and extended switching, which in turn contribute to convergence. A legal definition of the networks and markets that are converging is offered by the competition analysis of UK and European regulators: here are markets for regional and/or national television, radio, newspapers, telecoms, satellite and cable pay-TV, all recognised in case law.[18]

The integration of different kinds of content breaks down the strict demarcation between different media[19] (what Negroponte calls 'mediumlessness'[20]) and makes possible new forms often defined as 'multimedia'. All levels of the value chain are affected by technical convergence.[21] Different services that had previously been carried by different physical media might be carried by a single medium (e.g. the Internet), and a service that had previously been carried by a single medium may be distributed through several different physical media (e.g. the electronic newspaper). Furthermore, as a result of this digitisation of content, almost every message can be transported from point A to any point B in numerous physical ways. The movement from a single-purpose network or transmission mode towards multipurpose networks is thus the result.[22] No longer do the separate media involve physical carriers with widely differing characteristics; all new communications services can be delivered in off-line or on-line mode.[23] The use of data compression and increases in cost-effective bandwidth such as Digital Subscriber Lines (DSL) allow more and more data delivery.[24] Capacity will therefore be abundant. The obstacle of spectrum scarcity, which has shaped the network architecture and history of the information industry to date, can be largely overcome and the number of channels available for conventional broadcasting, for example, will exponentially expand. All this clearly has implications for traditional regulatory systems – as will be discussed below – which are based around spectrum shortage and a relatively small and discrete group of incumbent media actors.

Content types and convergence

Convergence enables many networks to carry the same form of content, or for several content types to be combined, creating multimedia and new media content.[25] Wildman sees multimedia as an 'umbrella term', generated from three phenomena: first the integration of separate media; secondly, 'de-specialisation of transmission technologies', caused by digitisation; thirdly, the convergence phenomenon of the delivery of broadcast, telephony and Internet via the same transmission network.[26] As the first and second are technical mechanisms, it is the third – a market development controlled by regulation – which concerns us.

Consumer market convergence

Converged digital media require a display terminal and a decoder, in order for the consumer to access information. There are essentially three user devices for accessing new communications services: the mobile handset, the personal computer and the television. Besides a battle for 'eyeballs' between these platforms, there is a much more significant battle for the software or conditional access system.[27] This is not only a large market in its own right, it also gives bottleneck control over content design and billing systems. In addition, potential users are going to require some way of finding what they want among the plethora of rival offerings. Advanced computer software such as search engines or electronic programme guides (EPGs) may provide a way to sift, sort and manage all these data, a further example of how key bottlenecks within the system may pose new and important regulatory problems.

We now discuss the convergence of broadcasting (the audiovisual) onto Internet delivery platforms, which raised many difficult issues in the mid-1990s prior to 1997 review of the Television Without Frontiers (TVWF) Directive, and has been discussed in detail in the period since 2003 as the Commission attempts to account for convergence between regulated (TVWF) broadcasting content and unregulated (E-Commerce Directive) Internet content.

Regulatory convergence

The changes in technical, service/application, business strategy and policy responses to audiovisual and multimedia convergence have been far-reaching since the 1997 revision of the TVWF Directive and the Convergence Green Paper provided the 'blueprint' for the development of the European communications environment. They were followed by the 2002 regulatory package, the MEDIA programme's evolution, and the 2005–7 revision of TVWF. The questions in telecoms and broadcasting are relatively well known by the Commission, involving various longer-term bottlenecks as well as those addressed in full in the 2002 package (though implementation is thus far at best sporadic in the Member States, as evidenced in the Tenth Implementation

Report). Progress has been rapid, but turbulent and multi-paced, towards a ubiquitous Information Society, and the goals are now expressed as 'i2010'.[28]

The European Commission proposed in its Issues paper[29] for the UK Council Presidency's Liverpool Conference of September 2005 that it follow a comprehensive approach to revision of the Directive, with two tiers of rules, with audiovisual services to be defined as linear and non-linear. This raises two evidential issues:

1. What to regulate and what the implications of the definition of audiovisual content services indicate. It is necessary therefore first to scope and then to assess the implications of regulation on these non-traditional audiovisual services, which include:
    *   webcasting (linear)
    *   streaming (linear)
    *   near video on demand (linear)
    *   video on demand (non-linear)
    *   web-based news services (non-linear).
2. Having undertaken the scoping of markets, we can examine the regulatory implications – how to regulate each of the basic and linear tiers, according to:
    *   type of actor anticipated to require regulation – e.g. commercial mobile websites, commercial web hosts, or streaming media companies;
    *   numbers of such actors in terms of magnitude and regulatory burden created thereby;
    *   processes therefore required to implement such a schematic, including cost–benefit and the risk of regulatory flight and arbitrage by non-EU host nations.

The Issues papers refer to the forms of self- and co-regulation extant in media policy, and it is anticipated that various of these models will prove applicable to the various regulatory tasks proposed.

Audiovisual linear 'broadcast' markets

Broadcasting and datacasting over mobile networks has been taking place, and peer-to-peer exchanges have supplied the pent-up demand for multimedia content since the phenomenon of Napster.[30] Audiovisual markets in the European Union have changed very rapidly in 1994–2004, and can be expected to change even more rapidly in the next decade (Figure 2.2). This prior change was driven by exponential change in channel capacity, especially via digital cable and satellite, increased market penetration of multichannel homes (using sports and feature-film premium content), and an increasing number of platforms.[31] Further, the introduction of digital terrestrial television, largely driven by public service broadcasters, has been delayed but is now successful in Sweden, UK and Germany, amongst others.[32]

Non-linear sectors: multimedia content and services

We now consider the non-television delivered market. Stylistically we describe this as non-linear, because at least currently it is largely unscheduled and non-streamed audiovisual content which is delivered using this medium. (Note that digital radio is already prevalent for even narrowband Internet users.) Non-linear is a far less developed and much less defined market to describe, and extremely heroic presump-

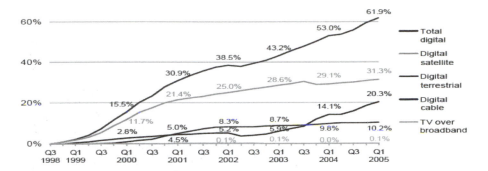

Figure 2.2   UK digital television penetration by household.

Source: Ofcom Digital Television Update.

tions are needed to predict its future development. The multimedia environment has been changing rapidly, driven by user demands for greater interactivity and 'pull' of content, notably in the use of SMS voting and competition participation in reality television shows, which can also be viewed via computer and mobile handset.[33] The pan-European development of 'Big Brother' by Netherlands-based independent producer Endemol (a division of Telefonica) with its multimedia supports has been a forerunner for interactive cross-format programming. The unpredictable nature of 'hit' multi-platform interactive formats is demonstrated by this case study. Experimental broadcasting over mobile networks and DVB-H frequencies supports deployment on a commercial basis.

The decreasing cost of high-density storage for mobile devices (and advances in video compression, battery power, and bandwidth cost reductions) means that the MP3 downloader to a personal computer of 2000 becomes the MPEG4 downloader to a mobile device of 2006. TiVo-type home media servers and personal video recorders, not yet fully interoperable in most cases, portend an environment in which wireless multimedia networking throughout the household becomes commonplace. Using personal area networks for wireless connectivity and multimedia sharing is now common in Europe, using Bluetooth devices, and soon ultra wide band (UWB). Blogging, video-blogging and mobile blogging generate content that is increasingly competing for user attention with conventional linear and online media.

By around 2015 in the larger EU countries, digital television will be available to all, urban cable and telephone networks will be upgraded to carry digital video channels, and mobile networks will carry multimedia content. It is, however, unclear what effect this will have on citizens' use of communications media. There are several plausible scenarios. It is extremely difficult to predict with any degree of accuracy which user group – or another yet undefined usage pattern – will be most accurate in which time period for which European Member State. The EC 10th Implementation Report demonstrates the variable adoption of broadband connections which enable audiovisual content to be delivered via the Internet (Figure 2.3).[34]

The extreme nature of the predictive challenge is due to the unusual volatility of content markets and citizen tastes in media consumption, which rely on network effects to a great extent (especially in non-linear demand patterns) as well as having extreme economies of scale because of the perfect reproducibility of digital content. This latter factor can have both market-enhancing and market-delaying effects: the

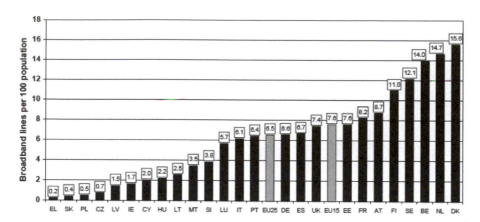

Figure 2.3 EU25 fixed broadband penetration rate, 1 July 2004. (EC 10th Implementation
    Report, Figure 74, at p. 72.)

Source: Commission services based on COCOM data.

growth of music downloading has been driven by the peer-to-peer sharing of MP3
files. By contrast the growth of video sharing (in peer-to-peer networks) has been
slowed by producer actions designed to prevent reproduction without secure digital
rights management. The technical standard for MP3 encouraged distribution; the
lack of a common standard and the preoccupation with security of the video industry
means that the path to consumer mass markets is indeterminate.

It is clear that different media have converged on the broadband Internet. In
particular, video gaming, music distribution, streamed radio stations and online
newspaper readership appear to be highly substitutable between their traditional
analogue and new digital media of consumption. Internet users claim to use the
Internet more than any other medium except television – which includes use of radio
and print media via the Internet. Television use appears far lower amongst Internet
users, according to the World Internet Project (Figure 2.4).[35]

However, overall television viewership amongst non-broadband users is not significantly different to viewership in the population as a whole. Further, Internet penetration has stabilised at about 65 per cent by household, with mobile phone
penetration at about 85 per cent.[36] There is a significant minority of the population
that does not intend to use digital media platforms, and there is evidence that this
group is both the most vulnerable in society and least likely to change (typically
comprising the most elderly, non-formally educationally qualified and poorest quar-
tiles). Against this background, any attempt to measure accurately the development
of the non-linear audiovisual market over time will be fraught with difficulty.

This convergence of technology has several consequences. The development of
convergence gives the customer a certain level of control over the information being
delivered,[37] for example over timing or destination (e.g. video on demand). The
services offered will be more and more customised to an individual's specific needs
(client profiling or personalisation). As a consequence of the interactivity of the
new communications services, the ability to control communications in a traditional

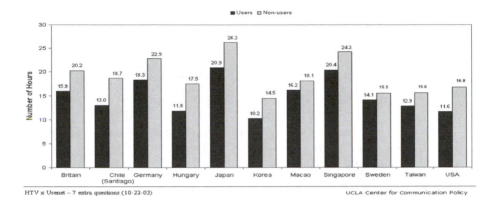

Figure 2.4 Television viewing between broadband users and others in 11 countries, 2003.

hierarchical manner could be undermined, or at least it is claimed that a new approach is needed.

There are dangers in over-emphasising convergence. It would be naive to suggest at this stage that a single super-industry will arise with a huge influence upon the rest of economy and society. More realistically, three elements have to be taken into account when analysing those trends:

- market development is expected to be evolutionary. Television services will merge with online services as and when telecoms networks are sufficiently advanced, although this may not occur in the near future;
- two distinct service categories compete within the communications industries which dominate the present debate in Europe: TV-type services versus online-type services (the Internet). In the long run they could converge or at least be linked via gateways; at present, however, the online and TV markets still have different cultures and their actors still operate differently;
- the word 'convergence' is misleading since it suggests 'narrowing'. What really happens in the market is diversification and the creation of new industries and sectors. Blackman calls the phenomenon 'coalescence' rather than convergence,[38] to reflect the nuanced adoption of technology in the market and society.

The most extreme example of network convergence is the Internet – as a simple digital network of networks, it can carry all digitally encoded information: radio, television, music, newspapers, film, voice telephony, chat. The Internet did not emerge from the ether without precedent, however. In Europe, models for television, print media and telecom regulation all existed. Without acknowledging this prior art, it is not possible to contextualise current debates. We therefore turn our attention to IRAs for broadcasting and telecoms.

Media regulation by independent agency

The business of regulating communications markets requires firstly an understanding of general processes of regulation, and secondly an appreciation of the unique qualities of communications. In this section we briefly consider telecoms and broadcast markets as examples of 'utility regulation' – essential public services delivered by corporations. This is the model of regulatory arrangement adopted in Europe in the 1980s and 1990s.

While central government economic management[39] was existent in the early six-teenth century, the root of recognisable national regulation of networked industries dates to the maturing of those networks, notably railways and telegraphs, in the nine-teenth century. As economies of scale in maturing technologies contributed to market failure and dominance in the first half of the twentieth century, government response to increased cartelisation was to take ownership of the networks into public hands.

In the case of communications systems, strategic considerations of the public interest in ensuring reliability and surveillance of the networks ensured that first postal distribution, then telegraphy, then radio and television, were all developed under public ownership in Europe. Non-network communications systems such as publishing remained in private hands, even where their content offended govern-ment sensibilities, as with national newspapers. There was thus the co-existence of both economic and political controls on communications networks, with blurred lines of public and private governance. The second half of the century saw an increased emphasis on competition within markets, and the eventual reintroduction of those publicly owned network industries into private ownership. Accompanying this trend has been the reversion from overt government involvement in economic planning more generally, and outright ownership of many industries under direct ideological influence of first socialist, and then corporatist, planning. Thus a nationalisation policy was most vigorously introduced in the immediate post-1945 years, to be followed by a gradual retreat in the face of technological innovation facilitating competition, and the ideological preference for private ownership under competitive conditions which is closely associated with the Thatcher–Reagan governments.

A reaction to the growing interdependence of states and markets, and the evidence of 'capture' of the former by the latter, was to develop a more robust regulator: the independent regulatory agency (IRA). Baldwin and McCrudden state:

> [Agencies] undertake important government functions but are constitutionally awkward because they combine powers that have traditionally been kept sepa-rate. Their perceived effectiveness, moreover, derives from the same property which makes them constitutionally awkward: their ability to engage in disparate and apparently conflicting activities.[40]

Government ownership and control of strategic markets gave way to privatisation in the period since 1980. This is as true of communications markets as other sectors, despite their strategic and constitutional role in information dissemination. Baldwin identifies four reasons for the development of specialist regulators in the post-war period, of which the British commercial television regulator, ITA, founded in 1954, was a prototype:

1 *Market failure:* areas such as broadcasting required constant supervision, in order to ensure public interest overcame market failure, which in such an industry was endemic.
2 *Expertise:* sectoral regulation required a relatively large and specialist staff.
3 *Specialism:* the range of powers required to carry out such a brief would require a range of specialisations (enforcement, industrial promotion, monitoring and political lobbying are the examples given).

4   *Social complexity:* the growth of complexity in society required these specialisations, both for social welfare and technological manipulation.

Broadcasting fulfilled all four functions.

Baldwin and McCrudden write that the original UK television regulator 'was
provided with a new and, for Britain, unique combination of powers'.[41] Baldwin has
identified it as the first attempt to import US-style board regulation into European
public law regulation.[42] The novelty was the separation of regulation from both the
activity to be regulated and central government. Some commentators consider
constitutional structures as regulating 'private initiative with public control',[43] in the
public interest, or at least 'connivance',[44] despite a 'very wide . . . unstructured discretion'.[45] Despite these critiques from both democratic accountability and expertise
claims, the growth of the IRA has attended the growth of privatised and liberalised
communications markets, notably in broadcasting and telecoms.

Birkinshaw *et al.* explain that 'public-private interactions have become a permanent and vital part of the British constitutional landscape, but that such interactions
are rarely given legal form and that their subjection to requirements of accountability
is unduly haphazard and meagre'.[46] Critics have suggested three flaws in the IRA-
based regulatory system:

1   *Independence:* it is difficult if not impossible to ensure independence from political
control.
2   *Capture by regulatees:* regulators in dynamic markets are accountable to their corporate licensees for the sector's viability, and hence prone to capture under agency
theory.
3   *Lack of democratic accountability:* once appointed, regulators are accountable only to
the courts with no effective democratic control.

Hogwood doubts the conceptual utility of independence claims for agencies:[47]

in many cases . . . independence of government is limited, that some depend on
the industry being regulated for resources, and that all depend on the industry
being regulated for information . . . The full range of regulatory control often
depends on the joint involvement of a number of regulatory bodies.

He believes that regulatory effectiveness is therefore a measure of 'interdependence'
rather than 'independence'.

Baldwin states the contextualisation of legitimacy relies on 'a wider sense of political accountability'.[48] Baldwin's views are therefore based on 'a common recognition
that certain values are relevant[49] . . . it is their cumulative force that justifies'.[50]
Baldwin identifies eclectic liberalism as a subjective ground for recognition of legitimacy,[51] in similar terms to the jurisprudence of Dworkin.[52] Libertarians including
many Internet policy advocates espouse a view alien to this liberalism. Craig argues
that deregulation is based on a rejection of communitarianism: 'Any suggestion that
[regulation] should be legitimated by a concept of participatory rights which flow
from a communitarian thesis would simply be rejected by those who do not espouse
any such thesis.'[53] He further cautions that:

Regulation is often informal, characterised by negotiation, persuasion and
cajoling . . . The potential economic advantage of informal regulation in

achieving a cost-effective level of regulation must be weighed against the danger of regulation becoming *ad hoc* and circumventing procedural safeguards in legislation.[54]

The trade-off between flexible self-regulation and more formal law is examined further below.

Telecoms regulatory agencies

In communications reform, the decline of the direct control of corporate actors by the state in favour of regulation has occurred since the passing of the UK Telecommunications Act 1984 and the US AT&T divestiture effective the same year, used to persuade OECD members to pursue similar liberalisation.[55] This reasoning is also applied to suggest that benefits may accrue to the television production sector through such liberalisation. Network access or 'interconnection' is essential in proprietorial infrastructure ownership of national telecoms markets.[56] Three alternative approaches to telecom regulation have been suggested:[57]

- specific structural control in the public interest;
- bottleneck control through specific regulation;
- generic competition law.

Cave and Cowie caution that 'a policy of minimum regulation would appear appropriate',[58] as specific regulation may lack flexibility, and lead to technological by-pass and regulatory obsolescence in a dynamic market.

Broadcast regulation as a precursor to European Internet regulation

The end of the basic service European telecoms monopoly in 1998 accompanied a gradual liberalisation of broadcasting in the 1980s. The feature which distinguishes terrestrial broadcasting from the Internet is the absolute state control over the producer and content of production (though note the exception of Luxembourgeois RTL). Licensing allows for strong control over the broadcast sector, even when undermined by transnational communications such as direct broadcast satellite television. In broadcasting, shortage of effective spectrum, combined with the pervasiveness and potential of the medium, led to government licensing as a barrier to entry. Consequently, specific prior structural regulation was instituted to prevent abuse of monopoly power, integrated in Europe with positive content regulation in the public interest.[59]

The development of commercial and international provision of satellite television services to the home, begun in 1983, and the growth of US cable television systems in the UK, Germany, Netherlands, Belgium, Poland and other states, are phenomena of a commercial rather than regulatory origin which necessarily influence the regulatory environment (Table 2.1). Satellite television has been the political scientist's regional communications case study par excellence.[60] While the issue of consumer reception of non-terrestrial signals is something of a *cause célèbre* in international politics,[61] terrestrial spectrum remains in the gift of the national government.[62]

We can therefore conclude that claims of technological by-pass or extra-territorial by-pass of jurisdiction predate the Internet. Cyberspace is an extension in this regard of the Astra satellite's occupation of outer space. However, as RTL, News

Corporation and others exploited extra-territorial loopholes in domestic broadcast regulation, so it is that foreign innovators such as AOL, UUNet, Yahoo! and Microsoft have pioneered the international development of the Internet.

Media models for Internet regulation

The early development of the Internet governance drew on previous models from other media sectors. The controls used for analogue free-to-air and digital pay-TV, the printed press and basic voice telecommunications are shown in Table 2.2.

Table 2.1 Regulatory concerns and television distribution technologies

	Narrowband analogue		Broadband digital 'multi-channel'	
	Carriage scarcity	Regulation	Carriage scarcity	Regulation
Cable	Strong	Local	Removed	Local
Satellite	Weak	International	Weakened	International
Terrestrial	Very strong	National	Strong	National

Table 2.2 Vertical layer control of the media industries

Control stage	Analogue 'free-to-air' TV	Printed press	Digital pay-TV
Content creation and production	Monopoly of terrestrial broadcasters – self-regulation supervised by state agency	No – low entry barriers	Yes – premium sports rights and movies
Bundling content into 'portals' or channels	Command and control – licensed by state agency	No – low entry barriers	Yes – economies of scale and long-term exclusivity result in dominance
Packaging multiple software into multimedia	Command and control – broadcasters only allocated single channel by agency	No – low entry barriers	Yes – control over interactive services by platform owner
Transmission and delivery	Command and control – transmission controlled by state agency	No – multiple distributors, Post Office subject to common carriage	Yes – access regulated but only light touch regime
Navigational control of user	No – TV remote control only	No – newsagent supplies thousands of media	Yes – 500 channels and electronic programme guide
Limits on access to specific content	No – tax on TV households; content imposed by evening 'watershed'	No	Yes – PIN for premium and adult content

Adapted from Cowie, C and Marsden, C (1999) 'Convergence: Navigating Through Digital Pay-TV Bottlenecks', 1 *Info* 1, at p. 55. Flynn offers 16 separate bottlenecks in the transmission chain: Flynn, B (1999) 'Opening the Box: Issues in Digital Gatekeeping', in *Montreux Symposium '99*, 10–15 June, Symposium Records, pp. 698–706, at p. 699.

Table 2.3 Vertical layer control potential of the press, telecom and Internet industries

Control stage	Printed press	Telecoms	Internet
Content creation and production	No – low entry barriers	Peer-to-peer except premium content self-regulated by IARN	No – 100 billion web pages. Note importance of peer-to-peer file sharing of music and video
Bundling content into 'portals' or channels	No – low entry barriers	Not applicable	Yes – economies of scale and long-term exclusivity result in dominance
Packaging multiple software into multimedia	No – low entry barriers	Not applicable	Control over interactive services, e.g. media players, voice-over Internet Protocol
Transmission and delivery	No – multiple distributors, Post Office subject to common carriage	Common carriage	Access regulated at wholesale level
Navigational control of user	No – newsagent supplies thousands of media; subscription available	Not applicable – open interface	Yes – virus scanning, spyware denial and search engines
Controls on viewing: decoder box or software browser	No	Not applicable – open interface	Possible – PIN for premium and adult content; PICS filtering; by NetNanny, SurfPatrol

In addition to these regulatory models, there are other purer self-regulatory models in broadcast advertising, film and video classification, and computer games rating, that rely on rating the content and using information regulation to inform the end-user that content may be unsuitable for minors. These will be examined in detail in further chapters, but Table 2.3 outlines some fundamental differences between content control during various stages of content production and distribution.

'Co-regulation' develops as a hybrid between self-regulation and regulation

The international and multimedia impact of the Internet creates serious coordination problems, which the European Commission addressed in 2004:[63] 'The Recommendation (see Chapter 1) on the protection of minors has a *cross-media approach* and emphasises the *cross-border exchange of best practices* and the development of *co-regulatory and self-regulatory mechanisms*' (emphasis in original).

It explains how best to achieve the regulatory goals:

A co-regulatory approach may be more flexible, adaptable and effective than straight forward regulation and legislation. With regard to the protection of minors, where many sensibilities have to be taken into account, co-regulation can often better achieve the given aims. Co-regulation implies however, from the Commission's point of view, an appropriate level of involvement by the public authorities. It should consist of cooperation between the public authorities, industry and the other interested parties, such as consumers. This is the approach laid out in the Recommendation. In order to promote national frameworks aimed at achieving a comparable and effective level of protection of minors and human dignity, the Recommendation enumerates different objectives to be fulfilled by (i) the Member States, (ii) the industries and parties concerned and (iii) the Commission.

Co-regulation expresses a dialogue process between stakeholders, which results in a form of regulation which is not state command-and-control regulation in its bureau-cratic central or IRA specialised functions, but is also not 'pure' self-regulation as we observed in industry-led standard setting in Internet infrastructure. The state, and stakeholder groups including consumers, are stated to explicitly form part of the insti-tutional setting for regulation. Co-regulation constitutes multiple stakeholders, and this inclusiveness results in greater legitimacy claims. However, direct government involvement including sanctioning powers may result in the gains of reflexive regula-tion – speed of response, dynamism, international cooperation between ISPs and others – being lost. It is clearly a finely balanced concept, a middle way between state regulation and 'pure' industry self-regulation.

Regulated self-regulation and European concepts of co-regulation

Schulz and Held have investigated co-regulation in the German context, specifically in the case of protection of minors.[64] In their view, self-regulation in Anglo-American debate is concerned with 'reconciliation of private interests', whereas their formula-tion – regulated self-regulation[65] – is indirect state regulation based on constitutional principles. It is the combination of 'intentional self-regulation' – the actions of market actors, whether in social or economic settings – with the state sanction in reserve which results in self-regulation which is 'regulated' by the possibility of state interven-tion. At the Birmingham 'Assizes Audiovisuel' in 1998, the formulation used was: 'Self-regulation that fits in with a legal framework or has a basis laid down in law.'[66]

The French term 'co-regulation' also gives a sense of the joint responsibilities of market actors and state, short of outright command-and-control, in the activity under investigation. It has been used by the UK's telecom regulator to suggest a state role in setting objectives which market actors must then organise to achieve – with the threat of statutory powers invoked in the absence of market self-regulation.[67] However, co-regulation is used in such a wide variety of circumstances that its specific meaning must be seen in the national, sectoral and temporal context in which it is used.[68] The German concept of regulated self-regulation gives the state a role when basic constitutional rights need to be upheld: 'The extent of possible delegation [to self-regulation] depends . . . on the relevance . . . in terms of basic rights.'[69]

Schulz and Held suggest that 'regulated self-regulation' can be any of these cate-gories:

- co-regulation
- intentional self-regulation
- 'audited self-regulation'.

Independent audit of self-regulation is a US concept of using an independent standard or professional body to audit a self-regulatory organisation or individual company according to pre-set standards.[70]

In the case of ISPs, audited self-regulation might involve at least a standard being set that an audit firm could certify organisations against (or at least that organisations could self-certify with reporting requirements), but could involve the setting of an international standard, as increasingly occurs in accountancy, for instance. At a minimum, dedicated budgetary and personnel resources, with activity reports, would be required to demonstrate regulatory commitment. We expand on this concept in the concluding chapter.

A typology of co-regulation

Self-regulation in the European context must also be proportionate to the aims of the legal instrument, as well as conforming to the competition law of the European Union (Figure 2.5). Enforcement is the ultimate responsibility ('the safety net') of the state.

In Schulz and Held's case study, Australia, practical self-regulation is illustrated in the application of the 1997 Telecoms Act and 1992 Broadcasting Services Act, where four types of regulatory scheme can be identified (see Table 2.4).

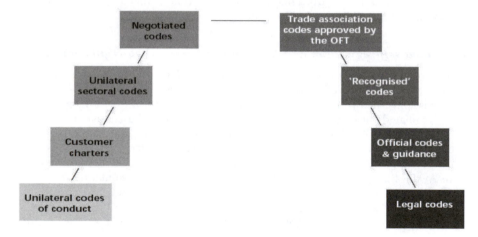

Figure 2.5 The spectrum of self-regulation. (From 'An Overview of Models in Business and the Professions', National Consumer Council 2001.)

Table 2.4 Regulatory types and state roles

Regulatory type	State role
1. Intentional or 'pure' self-regulation	No state IRA involvement
2. Industry codes	Registered with the state IRA
3. Industry standards	Mandatory codes set in the absence of pan-industry code agreement
4. Command-and-control	Set by state IRA pre-empting attempts at self-regulatory action

However, there are clearly nuanced approaches that industry can take, in choosing the menu of 'regulated self-regulation' to adopt. Multinational actors can choose to engage in game-playing with the regulator and other actors in order to secure their preferred environment for regulation, and it is here that national 'regulated self-regulation' is arbitraged by multinational actors. That is not to suggest the extreme and celebrated case in which Yahoo! attempted to substitute US First Amendment speech standards over French government controls on illegal Nazi memorabilia auctions (clearly a Type 4 regulatory discussion),[71] but to suggest that Types 1–3 above afford substantial latitude for rational multinational actors to seek to arbitrage regulators in favour of their 'home state' standards for speech and commercial freedom (which in the US coalesce more frequently than in Europe, which does not protect commercial speech to the same extent).

ISP actors: self-regulatory resources and Internet policy

Economies of scale in Internet industries do not apply only to provision of services: they also apply to self-regulation. A company with operations in six sectors is able to use lawyers and policy makers across the different sectors because the basic skills needed to identify copyright and privacy policies, interconnection and competition law issues and child protection and content filtering are closely related. Further, a company with international subsidiaries can deploy across international markets not only its browser software but also its privacy policy. Policies and regulatory strategies are information goods just like browser software: once created (at high fixed cost) they can be redeployed according to national market characteristics (at low variable cost). Companies such as AOL, Microsoft, WorldCom and Yahoo! have a decade of experience in Internet regulatory policy, which they have redeployed in several dozen territories internationally. It is not unreasonable in the absence of strong government rejection of US self-regulatory policy towards the Internet (considered in more detail below) to expect the policies espoused by these 'first movers' in Internet regulation to achieve a regulatory convergence between the various markets in which they operate: a convergence of Internet policy to accompany market convergence.

Regulatory compliance can form part of a marketing strategy, in content as in carriage. Quality of service is defined in ISP service largely by reliable speed of connection, but companies such as AOL, Yahoo! and Microsoft Network also market their superior spam filtering and parental control filters. Where an industry self-regulates, it can set standards at levels that make compliance relatively low or high cost – depending on the participants' views of best commercial outcome. In a rapidly growing market with little or no government social regulatory intervention, low costs might guarantee expansion, but in a mature market with active social regulation, higher costs might protect actors from new competition. Regulatory initiatives such as Rightswatch, the copyright regulatory body, are expensive and voluntary participation by smaller ISPs was prohibitively expensive. In a more consolidated market with higher compliance and other regulatory costs, ISPs can free more regulatory resource because they are guaranteed that other ISPs also take their regulatory responsibilities seriously.

Self-regulation: the European co-regulatory maze

The promise of self-regulation on the Internet, to sum up, was to provide flexible responses to enhance public welfare in information goods. The goal was to control externalities associated with information provision online, both negative and positive, and do so in a way that was in keeping with our existing approach to free speech and the public interest. Yet the 'Internet sector' was developing at a time of ever-expanding awareness of convergence. Codes, rules and standards conceived for the Internet alone sometimes overlap or conflict with those developed for older media, and self-regulation may follow the convergent path that statutory regulation has recently followed.[72]

The following seven chapters map out the self-regulatory instruments adopted in the major media sectors converging on the Internet. We can graphically illustrate these in Figure 2.6, demonstrating the potential for pan-sectoral and pan-European convergence of regulators, codes and other instruments that may be possible as these sectors converge on the Internet. Each acronym represents a separate self-regulating body.

An optimistic perspective holds that the emerging ecology of self-regulation is a healthy means to the end of securing the public interest with regard to Internet content. It develops organically, through trial and error, building on win–win situations

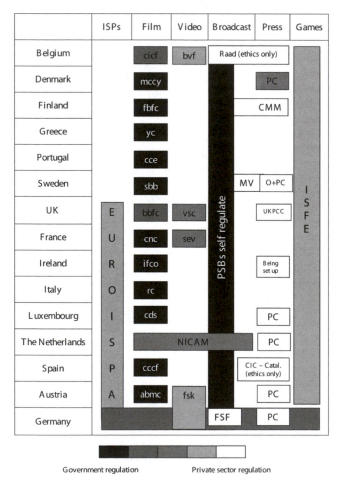

Government regulation   Private sector regulation

Figure 2.6 The European media self-regulatory maze.

whereby companies benefit from increased trust as codes drive up standards of service. Critics argue that what in fact happened was that symbolic debate led to symbolic self-regulation. Codes of conduct and self-regulatory schemes were developed in abundance, but many of these were 'fig-leaf' codes with scanty compliance mechanisms: their primary objective was cosmetic, and the extent to which industry codes impacted in the public interest was limited.

Only by examining in more detail the codes that emerged from this process, and comparing the Internet sector with other media sectors, can we begin to comment more definitively on the progress of self-regulation in convergent media sectors. It will be clear that neither the optimists nor the critics offer a complete picture. Analysis of the codes themselves in context offers insights that are valuable to those who are subjects, objects or beneficiaries of Internet self-regulation.

Notes

1   Prosser, T (1997) *Law and the Regulators*, Oxford: Clarendon Press, p. 4. He problematises the definitional aspect of regulation in the industries he examines as threefold: regulating monopoly; regulating for economic parameters; regulating for social purposes. He rebuts the critique that social policy lacks the legitimacy of other forms of regulation.

2   Baldwin, R, Scott, C and Hood, C (1998) *A Reader on Regulation*, Oxford University Press, p. 3.

3   Black, Julia (1996) 'Constitutionalising Self-Regulation', *MLR* 24, p. 25.

4   Foster, C D (1992) *Privatization, Public Ownership and the Regulation of Natural Monopoly*, Oxford: Blackwell, p. 186; Prosser (1997) op. cit., p. 5.

5   Ibid., p. 1, and see Teubner, G (1993) *Law as an Autopoietic System*, translated by Anne Bankowska and Ruth Adler; edited by Zenon Bankowski, Oxford: Blackwell.

6   Ibid., p. 1.

7   See Majone, G in Baldwin *et al.*, op. cit.

8   Hood, C and Jackson, M (1991) *Administrative Argument*, Aldershot: Dartmouth.

9   Harlow, C (1997) 'Back to Basics: Reinventing Administrative Law', *Public Law* 42, 245. Adopting Lord Denning's memorable phraseology regarding the fourth characteristic, internationalism, in his description of European law: *Blackburn* v. *Attorney-General* [1971],1 *Weekly LR* 1037 (CA).

10   Ayres, I and Braithwaite, J (1992) *Responsive Regulation: Transcending the Regulation Debate*, Oxford University Press, p. 4.

11   Beck, U (1992) *Risk Society: Towards a New Modernity*, translated by Mark Ritter, London: Sage.

12   Luhmann, N (1985) *A Sociological Theory of Law*, translated by Elizabeth King and Martin Albrow; edited by Martin Albrow, London: Routledge & Kegan Paul.

13   Teubner, G (1986) 'The Transformation of Law in the Welfare State', in Teubner, G (ed.) *Dilemmas of Law in the Welfare State*, Berlin: W de Gruyter, p. 8.

14   Higgott, R (1999) 'Economics, Politics and (International) Political Economy: The Need for a Balanced Diet in an Era of Globalisation', *New Political Economy* 4(1), 23–36, and Strange, S (1970) 'International Relations and International Economics: A Case of Mutual Neglect', *International Affairs* 46(2), 304.

15   Towers Perrin (2001) *Report to Regulators' Steering Group: Ofcom Scoping Project*, Towers Perrin, London.

16   See also Goldberg, D, Prosser, T and Verhulst, S (1998) *Regulating the Changing Media*, Oxford: Clarendon Press.

17   Negroponte, N (1995) *Being Digital*, London: Hodder and Stoughton, p. 12.

18   See Harcourt, A (1998) 'Regulation of European Media Markets: Approaches of the European Court of Justice and the Commission's Merger Task Force', *Utilities Law Review*

9(6), 276–91; Larouche, P (1998) 'EC Competition Law and the Convergence of the Telecommunications and Broadcasting Sectors', *Telecommunications Policy* 22(3), 219–42.

19 Cable, V and Distler, C (1995) *Global Superhighways. The Future of International Telecommunications Policy.* London: The Royal Institute of International Affairs, p. 2.

20 See note 17, above.

21 Wallis, R and Cross, T, 'The Common Digital Environment and Industrial Convergence', at: www.city.ac.uk/multimedia

22 Ducey, R V (1995) *A New Digital Marketplace in Information and Entertainment Services: Organizing Around Connectivity and Interoperability*, Washington DC: NAB.

23 Van Bolhuis, H E and Colom, I (1995) *Cyberspace Reflections.* European Commission, DG XII, Social Research Unit, p. x.

24 See Marsden, C (2003) 'Video over IP: The Challenges of Standardization – Towards the Next Generation Internet', Chapter 8 in Eli M Noam, Jo Groebel and Darcy Gerbarg (eds) *Internet Television*, New York: Lawrence Erlbaum; Marsden, C (2001) 'The Start of End-to-End? Internet Protocol Television', *Intermedia* 29, 4–8.

25 The definition of multimedia varies according to context. See Wallis, R, 'Lack of Clarity in Multimedia Definitions Can Hinder Developments of Useful Applications', at: www.city. ac.uk/multimedia

26 Wildman, S (1998) 'Media and Multimedia: The Challenge for Policy and Economic Analysis', *Information Economics and Policy* 10, 1–7.

27 Marsden, C with Campbell Cowie (1999) 'Convergence: Navigating Bottlenecks in Digital Pay-TV', *Info* 1(1), 53–67.

28 Commissioner Reding unveiled the new programme 'i2010', which aims to make Europe a borderless information space, stimulating innovation through investment in research; achieving an inclusive and accessible society.

29 http://europa.eu.int/comm/avpolicy/revision-tvwf2005/ispa_cultdiv_en.pdf

30 See Noam, Groebel and Gerbarg (2003), op. cit., and infra Marsden (2003), op. cit.

31 See generally Brown, A and Picard, R (eds) (2004) *Digital Television in Europe*, New York: Lawrence Erlbaum, and particularly Marsden and Arino (2004), infra.

32 Switching off the analogue signal in the next 6–10 years will permit universal reception of digital terrestrial services.

33 There are many other important examples: selecting video music clips to play on the plethora of digital and satellite TV music channels, contributing to charities (i.e. 'bidding' for Live 8 tickets), competing for Sudoku prizes (e.g. the *Times* competition), Eurovision Song Contest voting, BBC Podcasting, etc.

34 http://europa.eu.int/information_society/policy/ecomm/doc/implementation_ enforcement/annualreports/10threport/com20040759en.pdf

35 www.worldinternetproject.net/home.html; source for October 2003.

36 See Oxford Internet Survey (OXIS), February 2005, at: www.oii.ox.ac.uk

37 Interactivity or switchability.

38 Blackman, C (1998) publicity material accompanying the launch of *Info: The Journal of Policy, Regulation and Strategy for Telecommunications, Information and Media*, Cambridge: Camford Publishing.

39 'Monopoly' described as the government gift of sole trading rights in allocated markets to favoured firms.

40 Baldwin, R and McCrudden, C (1987) *Regulation and Public Law*, London: Weidenfeld and Nicolson, p. 3.

41 Baldwin, R and McCrudden, C (1987), op. cit., p. 19.

42 Baldwin, R (ed.) (1995) *Regulation in Question: The Growing Agenda*, London: LSE, p. 5.

43 IBA, *Guide to Independent Television* (1973), p. 9.

44 Harlow (1997), op. cit., pp. 245–61.

45 Lewis, N D (1975) 'IBA Programme Contract Awards', *Public Law* 20, 319.

46 Birkinshaw, P, Harden, I and Lewis, N (1990) *Government by Moonlight: The Hybrid Parts of the State*, London: Unwin Hyman, p. xi.

47 Hogwood, B W (1990) 'Developments in Regulatory Agencies in Britain', *International Review of Administrative Sciences* 56(4), 595–612, at p. 611.

48 Baldwin, R (1995), op. cit., p. 39.

49 Ibid., p. 50.

50 Ibid., p. 42.

51 Ibid., pp. 50–54.

52 For example, in Baldwin, R (1995), op. cit., Baldwin's reference at his n.113 to Dworkin, R (1977) *Taking Rights Seriously*, London: Duckworth.

53 Craig, P in Baldwin and McCrudden (1987), op. cit., p. 213.

54 Craig, P in Baldwin and McCrudden (1987), op. cit., p. 197.

55 *OECD Working Papers* Vol. III, No. 7 (1995). For OECD competition policy convergence, see *OECD Working Papers* Vol. II, No. 79 (1994).

56 See OFTEL: *Response to Trade and Industry Committee Report on Optical Fibre Networks* (November 1994) and *Beyond the Telephone, the Television and the PC* (August 1995). London: OFTEL.

57 Cave, M and Cowie, C (1998) 'Not Only Conditional Access. Towards a Better Regulatory Approach to Digital TV', *Communications and Strategies*, No. 30 (2nd Quarter), pp. 77–101.

58 Ibid. at conclusion, pp. 100–1.

59 See for instance, Hoffmann-Riem, W (1996) *Regulating Media: The Licensing and Supervision of Broadcasting in Six Countries,* Guilford Communication Series, New York: The Guilford Press. A US business economics perspective is provided in Noam, Eli M (ed.) (1985) *Video Media Competition: Regulation, Economy, and Technology Change*, Columbia University Press.

60 See Nobre-Correia, Jean-Marie (1995) 'Luxembourg: Local, Regional, National or Transnational?', in Miguel de Moragas Spa and Carmelo Garitaonandia (eds) *Decentralization in the Global Era: Television in the Regions, Nationalities and Small Countries of the European Union*, Chapter 9. London: John Libbey.

61 See UNESCO (1981) *One World, Many Voices* (The MacBride Report), Paris: UNESCO.

62 Despite the encroachment of radio signals, from Radio Luxembourg in the 1930s, documented by Coase, R (1950) *British Broadcasting: A Study in Monopoly*, London: Longman, Chapter 2, in his seminal study of radio broadcasting, terrestrial television has remained under domestic control.

63 European Commission (2004) *Second Evaluation Report on the Safer Internet Action Plan*, COM (2003) 776.

64 Schulz, W and Held, T (2001) *Regulated Self-Regulation as a Form of Modern Government,* Hamburg: Verlag Hans Bredow Institut.

65 See Hoffman Reim, Wolfgang (1996) *Regulating Media: The Licensing and Supervision of Broadcasting in Six Countries,* New York: The Guilford Press.

66 See typologies and quotation at p. 7 in Schulz and Held (2001), op. cit.

67 See further Ofcom consultation on self-regulatory body 'certification' and the development of the telecoms ombudsmen in the UK, under Oftel 'patronage' and reinforced by the Universal Service Directive (2002) Article 34.

68 Schulz and Held (2001) op. cit. detail different meanings used in the UK, Australia and France, at pp. 7, 14.

69 Schulz and Held (2001) op. cit., p. 8.

70 Report of the Joint Committee on the Draft Communications Bill, House of Lords, 25 July 2002 ('Puttnam Report').

71 See Reidenberg, J (2004) 'States and Law Enforcement', *Uni. Ottawa Law & Technology Journal* 1, 213, summarising Reidenberg, J (2002) 'Yahoo and Democracy on the Internet', *Jurimetrics* 42, 261.

72 Countries as diverse as Switzerland, Italy, the UK and Australia have recently merged telecommunications and broadcasting regulation into a single institution.

3 Methodology and media self-regulatory codes of conduct

Introduction

This chapter focuses on the methodology used in our analysis of self-regulatory codes of conduct (CoCs) either at the level of the media industry association, or of the individual media company.

This tool of analysis is an elaboration of a framework developed at Oxford University in research carried out by Monroe E. Price and Stefaan G. Verhulst.[1] Elements of this tool were used in a 1999 Oxford study of Parental Control in Television Broadcasting for the European Commission,[2] later updated and published as 'Shifting Paradigms: Reconsidering Regulation of Digital Content'. The '4C approach' (analysing a CoC in terms of coverage, content, communication and compliance) set by Price and Verhulst[3] for the examination of self-regulation was elaborated upon in their 2005 work *Self Regulation and the Internet*.[4]

We have called our development the '5C plus (5C+) Approach'. We supplement the 4Cs with in-depth interviews of the individuals responsible for drafting, revising and enforcing CoCs. These provide information about whether and how particular issues are coded for, although we do not consider why the organisation does or does not include particular issues in their code. This methodology can serve a fast-changing field in a number of ways: as a tool of analysis, as a tool for the creation of codes (or model codes) and as an aid in the necessarily constant update of existing codes.

On one level we want to chart the basic parameters of CoC development in European countries: of interest both to policy makers and researchers monitoring the development of industry rule making. On another, we ask what evidence can be brought to bear on questions of quality of self-regulation. Does it conform to expected levels of accountability, transparency and public involvement? Are there patterns of development that would impact on the ability of self-regulatory organisations to collaborate and cost-save across countries or across sectors? This will lead us to questions such as what explains country differences (law or political culture), which we expect could inform recommendations as to the 'exportability' of self-regulation from Western European countries where it is well established.

Codes analysis: methodology and limitations

Much of this research has focused on the analysis of codes themselves. This has strengths but also limitations, and must be set in context. We can see what rules code subjects want to publicly commit to and be held accountable with (assuming that the drafters of codes are also the subjects of codes and that the self-regulatory mechanism permits effective accountability). But this study of codes should be accompanied by contextualising research on the drafting, adopting and revision of codes, and the process of their application. That is why we also draw upon background research, expert interviews, historical archives, the websites of the self-regulatory bodies themselves and secondary analysis conducted by other researchers.

Code analysis cannot ascertain the effectiveness of the code, though it can identify cases in which a code does not contain provisions for its enforcement or is not in fact justiciable and therefore likely to be less effective. Even these inferences are of limited reliability, as trust, mutual observation, participation in a network of colleagues and/ or a sense of obligation can be key mechanisms in the process of self-regulation. Nor can code analysis offer information about the sustainability of self-regulatory mechanisms. This, as we argue elsewhere in this book, is a product of a combination of industry configuration, cost of the regulatory structure and the standards of transparency and due process that are maintained. With these disclaimers, analysis of codes does offer one of the most reliable objective indicators of patterns in self-regulation development.

The various media sectors required modifications to the framework in certain areas to take account of different focus points, technologies and cultural diversities. We examined emerging issues, including enforcement, procedures, content issues, preventing government legislation, avoidance of liability, and child/consumer protection.

Codes are adopted for one or more of the following reasons,[5] which are not mutually exclusive (in fact, several are mutually reinforcing):

• as an alternative to or to prevent command-and-control regulation;
• to build trust among users, readers, audiences, etc.;
• to avoid liability (legal and/or user-perceived);
• to protect users (minors, etc.);
• to impose professional standards (and as an indicator of professional status);
• to reinforce a network;
• to raise the public image of an industry.

Code drafting and revising can include outside participation and consultation, with interest organisations such as consumer associations, trade unions and non-governmental organisations. Under evolving processes, issues we address include:

• the convergence of national, regulatory and corporate cultures;
• the changing nature of the relationship between government and industry;
• the evolving technological architecture that underwrites self-regulation;
• the further development of standards, codes and rules;
• the growth and change of cultural norms and of public understanding surrounding self-regulation;
• revision through third-party consultation or audit;
• the bringing of standards and principles from 'traditional' media sectors into the newer ones.

Comparative analysis framework – the 5C+ approach

The variables identified and used to compare/classify the selected codes are covered in the following five broad analytical areas, which may have different subsections and questions, depending on the media branch:[6]

- Constitution
- Coverage
- Content
- Communication
- Compliance.

Those 5Cs represent our interpretation of the following core questions that have surfaced in coming to grips with how to analyse self-regulatory codes of conduct:

- How should a code be drafted? (Coming to an understanding of the internal procedural processes involved in making a code.)
- Who is subject to a code? (Whose actions are governed by the code and also whose *should?*)
- What is the objective of the code? (Regulating content, privacy, protecting minors, or illegal content, etc.)
- How should the code be enforced? (What is the enforcement mechanism, sanctions, frequency of application, results?)

Data collection methods

We assembled codes from ISPs, broadcasters, press councils, games and film regulators and providers of mobile communications.[7] These were initially reviewed under the 5C approach, as follows.

Project methodology: the 5Cs

1. Constitution

Constitution refers to the organisational structure and governance of the code-drafting and -enforcing body, its composition, and the roles and responsibilities of its various members in drafting, revising and enforcing the code. It also includes issues of whether the code includes provisions for review and amendment. This first 'C' was not contemplated by the original '4C' methodology.

Analysis of the code alone does not address all of the required issues: the in-depth interviews are needed, particularly for information on code drafting and revisions. Constitution also refers to the regulator entrusted with the application of the code(s).

For print media, 'constitution' therefore refers to the organisation and character of a press council as a mechanism of code implementation, focusing on its governance and its relationships with the government, the industry and society. In the creation of press councils in Europe, a recurrent theme is crisis of some sort (discontent with intrusions by the press, dissatisfaction with low standards of journalism, etc.); there is a threat of legislation; and as a reaction the industry offers to improve its performance by raising standards. For print media, this means standards of journalism ethics.

For broadcast media, the research tool had to be adapted: we searched for available self-regulation in an area which has traditionally been highly regulated.

2. Coverage

By coverage, we understand the scope of application of the code (e.g. to ISPs vs. Internet content providers) including its geographical scope. Geographical scope is usually the question of whether the organisations are country-specific or pan-

European. The questions we address are, for example, whether there is industry membership in the self-regulatory body, and provisions for amending the code. Questions included:

- in the ISP review, whether the code applies to only ISPs or also ICPs;
- in the games review, producers of the games vs. suppliers;
- in the print media review, the scope of the journalistic standards of ethics set out in the code;
- whether the code is also applicable to online content.

These questions were supplemented in interview by *why* the above decisions to include or exclude groups from coverage of the code were made.

3. Content

Content identifies the panoply of areas for concern. The principal of these is 'illegal and harmful content'. But we have cast a relatively wide net, and there are various others. For example, the ISP analysis content issues covers questions concerning whether the code regulates:

- illegal content
- access to material that is harmful to minors
- racist and xenophobic speech
- information regarding best practices in business
- bulk e-mail
- data protection and privacy.

In the games review, because content issues are so intimately tied to a rating, the types of content instead of falling under the umbrella of 'harmful to minors' are much more delineated and deal individually with the levels of:

- violence
- sex and nudity
- offensive language
- racist/xenophobic speech
- controlled substances.

In the print media review, content refers specifically to the ethical standards of the journalistic profession and the accountability of the media in relation to readers/ audiences. Provisions include:

- accuracy
- appearance and reality of objectivity
- prohibition of members of the press from receiving gifts
- privacy
- duty to distinguish between fact and opinion
- racist/xenophobic speech
- protection for vulnerable people (e.g. minors)
- payments to criminals and witnesses, etc.

Again, as in previous examples, this information was supplemented with interviews to understand why certain areas were or were not coded for.

4. Compliance

Compliance is defined as those significant aspects of the code that determine how violations of the code are resolved, including whether there are sanctions, and if so, the modes for enforcing them. Cooperation with law enforcement and third parties is also addressed.

In both the ISP review and games study, compliance is addressed by inquiry into:

- presence of a complaint mechanism;
- sanctions for violation of the code;
- cooperation with third parties such as the Internet Watch Foundation (IWF) and law enforcement.

Interview questions concern the frequency of enforcement actions, common violations and common sanctions, as well as the reasons behind the choice of sanctions.

In the case of the print media study, compliance refers to actual application of the code and consequences for breaches of its rules. The area of study focuses on mechanisms for appeals, resolution of disputes, and sanctions at the council's disposal (e.g. duty to publish the rulings of the press council).

5. Communication

The final C in the 5C approach is communication. By this, we hope to identify the areas of coding that concern the relationship between industry and users. These include:

- consumer and user group interaction at the level of code formulation;
- privacy concerns;
- consumer and consumer group consultation in code amendment and enforcement.

Note some exceptions:

- In the ISP review and games study communication is dealt with in part with questions dealing with the presence of privacy provisions or guidelines within the code.
- In the games study in particular, issues of how the ratings are communicated to the end-user are addressed by questions concerning packaging and display.
- In the print media study, communication refers to mechanisms by which the standards contained in the code are communicated to readers and/or audience.

Finally, another area of inquiry within the ISP review is questions concerning rating and filtering and whether these options are presented to end-users. Interview questions cover why the provisions mentioned were or were not coded for as well as detailed inquiry into the role of consultation with end-users and consumer groups in the formulation, enforcement and amendment of the code.

Matrices developed from the 5C+ approach

This basic outline is meant to be illustrative, not exhaustive, of the types of questions we asked. The 5C+ approach identifies the core issues at a significant level of abstraction and then permits inquiry by carefully selected questions, which vary among media.

Complementing the initial research with questions aimed at the 'why', the 'plus' aspect of the approach offers a deeper understanding into the complex nature of codes at the level of those who are drafting, revising and enforcing self-regulatory CoCs in the media environment.

The three matrices in Appendix 2 illustrate the approaches used for different ISPs/ICPs, games and print.

APPENDIX 1

Council Recommendation of 24 September 1998 on the development of the competitiveness of the European audiovisual and information services industry by promoting national frameworks aimed at achieving a comparable and effective level of protection of minors and human dignity (98/560/EC).

Annex: Indicative Guidelines for the Implementation, at National Level, of a Self-regulation Framework for the Protection of Minors and Human Dignity in On-line Audiovisual and Information Services.

Objective

The purpose of these guidelines is to foster a climate of confidence in the on-line audiovisual and information services industry by ensuring broad consistency, at Community level, in the development, by the businesses and other parties concerned, of national self-regulation frameworks for the protection of minors and human dignity. The services covered by these guidelines are those provided at a distance, by electronic means. They do not include broadcasting services covered by Council Directive 89/552/EEC or radio broadcasting. The contents concerned are those which are made available to the public, rather than private correspondence. This consistency will enhance the effectiveness of the self-regulation process and provide a basis for the necessary transnational cooperation between the parties concerned.

While taking into account the voluntary nature of the self-regulation process (the primary purpose of which is to supplement existing legislation) and respecting the differences in approach and varying sensitivities in the Member States of the Community, these guidelines relate to four key components of a national self-regulation framework:

- consultation and representativeness of the parties concerned,
- code(s) of conduct,
- national bodies facilitating cooperation at Community level,
- national evaluation of self-regulation frameworks.

1. Consultation and Representativeness of the Parties Concerned

The objective is to ensure that the definition, implementation and evaluation of a national self-regulation framework benefits from the full participation of the parties concerned, such as the public authorities, the users, consumers and the businesses which are directly or indirectly involved in the audiovisual and on-line information services industries. The respective responsibilities and functions of the parties concerned, both public and private, should be set out clearly.

The voluntary nature of self-regulation means that the acceptance and effectiveness of a national self-regulation framework depends on the extent to which the parties concerned actively cooperate in its definition, application and evaluation.

All the parties concerned should also help with longer-term tasks such as the development of common tools or concepts (for example, on labelling of content) or the planning of ancillary measures (for example, on information, awareness and education).

2. Code(s) of Conduct

2.1. General

The objective is the production, within the national self-regulation framework, of basic rules which are strictly proportionate to the aims pursued; these rules should be incorporated into a code (or codes) of conduct covering at least the categories set out at 2.2, to be adopted and implemented voluntarily by the operators (i.e. primarily the businesses) concerned.

In drawing up these rules, the following should be taken into account:

* the diversity of services and functions performed by the various categories of operator (providers of network, access, service, content, etc.) and their respective responsibilities,
* the diversity of environments and applications in on-line services (open and closed networks, applications of varying levels of interactivity).

In view of the above, operators may need one or more codes of conduct. Given such diversity, the proportionality of the rules drawn up should be assessed in the light of:

* the principles of freedom of expression, protection of privacy and free movement of services,
* the principle of technical and economic feasibility, given that the overall objective is to develop the information society in Europe.

2.2. The content of the code(s) of conduct

The code (or codes) of conduct should cover the following:

2.2.1. Protection of minors

Objective: to enable minors to make responsible use of on-line services and to avoid them gaining access, without the consent of their parents or teachers, to legal content which may impair their physical, mental or moral development. Besides coordinated measures to educate minors and to improve their awareness, this should cover the establishment of certain standards in the following fields:

(A) INFORMATION TO USERS

Objective: within the framework of encouraging responsible use of networks, on-line service providers should inform users, where possible, of any risks from the content of certain on-line services and of such appropriate means of protection as are available. The codes of conduct should address, for example, the issue of basic rules on the nature of the information to be made available to users, its timing and the form in which it is communicated. The most appropriate occasions should be chosen to communicate the information (sale of technical equipment, conclusion of contracts with user, web sites, etc.).

(B) PRESENTATION OF LEGAL CONTENTS WHICH MAY HARM MINORS

Objective: where possible, legal content which may harm minors or affect their physical, mental or moral development should be presented in such a way as to provide users with basic information on its potentially harmful effect on minors.

The codes of conduct should therefore address, for example, the issue of basic rules for the businesses providing on-line services concerned and for users and suppliers of content; the rules should set out the conditions under which the supply and distribution of content likely to harm minors should be subject, where possible, to protection measures such as:

- a warning page, visual signal or sound signal,
- descriptive labelling and/or classification of contents,
- systems to check the age of users.

Priority should be given, in this regard, to protection systems applied at the presentation stage to legal content which is clearly likely to be harmful to minors, such as pornography or violence.

(C) SUPPORT FOR PARENTAL CONTROL

Objective: where possible, parents, teachers and others exercising control in this area should be assisted by easy-to-use and flexible tools in order to enable, without the former's educational choices being compromised, minors under their charge to have access to services, even when unsupervised. The codes of conduct should address, for example, the issue of basic rules on the conditions under which, wherever possible, additional tools or services are supplied to users to facilitate parental control, including:

- filter software installed and activated by the user,
- filter options activated, at the end-user's request, by service operators at a higher level (for example, limiting access to predefined sites or offering general access to services).

(D) HANDLING OF COMPLAINTS ('HOTLINES')

Objective: to promote the effective management of complaints about content which does not comply with the rules on the protection of minors and/or violates the code of conduct.

The codes of conduct should address, for example, the issue of basic rules on the management of complaints and encourage operators to provide the management tools and structures needed so that complaints can be sent and received without difficulties (telephone, e-mail, fax) and to introduce procedures for dealing with complaints (informing content providers, exchanging information between operators, responding to complaints, etc.).

2.2.2. Protection of human dignity

Objective: to support effective measures in the fight against illegal content offensive to human dignity.

(A) INFORMATION FOR USERS

Objective: where possible, users should be clearly informed of the risks inherent in the use of on-line services as content providers so as to encourage legal and responsible use of networks. Codes of conduct should address, for example, the issue of basic rules on the nature of information to be made available, its timing and the form in which it is to be communicated.

(B) HANDLING OF COMPLAINTS ('HOTLINES')

Objective: to promote the effective handling of complaints about illegal content offensive to human dignity circulating in audiovisual and on-line services, in accordance with the respective responsibilities and functions of the parties concerned, so as to reduce illegal content and misuse of the networks.

The codes of conduct should address, for example, the issue of basic rules on the management of complaints and encourage operators to provide the management tools and structures needed so that complaints can be sent and received without difficulties (telephone, e-mail, fax) and to introduce procedures for dealing with complaints (informing content providers, exchanging information between operators, responding to complaints, etc.).

(C) COOPERATION OF OPERATORS WITH JUDICIAL AND POLICE AUTHORITIES

Objective: to ensure, in accordance with the responsibilities and functions of the parties concerned effective cooperation between operators and the judicial and police authorities within Member States in combating the production and circulation of illegal content offensive to human dignity in audiovisual and on-line information services.

The codes of conduct should address, for example, the issue of basic rules on cooperation procedures between operators and the competent public authorities, while respecting the principles of proportionality and freedom of expression as well as relevant national legal provisions.

2.2.3. Violations of the codes of conduct

Objective: to strengthen the credibility of the code (or codes) of conduct, taking account of its voluntary nature, by providing for dissuasive measures which are proportionate to the nature of the violations. In this connection, provision should be made, where appropriate, for appeal and mediation procedures. Appropriate rules to govern this area should be included in the code of conduct.

APPENDIX 2

The 5C matrix: ISPs/ICPs

1. Constitution	1.1 Do you/your company have a code of conduct/guidelines? (yes/no)
	1.2 When was your code of conduct adopted?
	1.3 Why did you adopt your code of conduct? (ordinary industry practice, fear of external regulation, consumer complaints, legal advice)
	1.4 How was your code of conduct drafted? (in-house, external consultation, consumer groups, based on third party code – please specify original code)
	1.5 Who was/were responsible for drafting/updating your code?
	1.6 How many times has your code been revised?
	1.7 Why was your code changed/revised? (changes in law, changes in business model, external complaints, customer conduct)
	1.8 Number of clients in specific member state
	1.9 Does the code have any formal provisions for review and amendment?
2. Coverage	2.1 Type of organisation (content provider, trade organisation, regulator, interest group)
	2.2 Media industry (ISP/ICP)
	2.3 Primary country of operation
	2.4 Do you have offices/affiliates in other EU member states? (yes – please specify/no)
	2.5 Is the code designed to apply to both ISPs and ICPs?
3. Content	3.1 Who pre-screens your content? (in-house, third party, consumer groups, focus group)
	3.2 Do you pre-screen your content before it is made public? (yes/no)
	3.3 Do you use any quality labels or other icons to identify different types of content? (yes – please specify/no)
	3.4 Does the code contain content that regulates information regarding business?
	3.5 Does the code contain provisions limiting access to material harmful to minors?
	3.6 Does the code contain provisions regarding hate speech?
	3.7 Does the code contain provisions regarding bulk e-mail?
	3.8 Does the code contain data protection and privacy provisions?
4. Communication	4.1 Packaging: how does the code govern display of ratings?
	4.2 Marketing: does the code contain marketing guidelines for television/print/Internet?
	4.3 Information: how are consumers educated about what the ratings mean?
	4.4 Data protection and privacy: does the code contain provisions on protection of consumer's privacy and the producer's copyright?
5. Compliance	5.1 Is your code of conduct: required by national legislation; partially based on national/EU legislation (please list relevant sections); self-regulatory?

5.2 Has there been any litigation/arbitration/mediation relating to your code of conduct? (yes – please specify/no)
5.3 What are the enforcement/dispute resolution procedures, if they are not clearly outlined in your code?
5.4 What are the consequences when the code is broken? (legal sanction, penalty, warning, ban, other)
5.5 Estimate annually the number of code-related enforcement actions (number). Please list the top five most frequently violated aspects of the code.
5.6 Estimate annually for the past five years the number of user accounts that have been cancelled due to code of conduct violations (number). Please list the top five most frequently violated aspects of the code.
5.7 As an industry specialist, do you know of any other exceptional cases relating to codes of conduct in your field?
5.8 Does the code contain a complaint mechanism?
5.9 Does the code contain provisions that regulate cooperation with law?
5.10 Does the code contain sanction mechanisms?

The 5C matrix: games industry

1. Constitution
1.1 What is the structure/governance of the rating body?
1.2 What is the rating body's relationship to:
    1.2.1 the government,
    1.2.2 the industry,
    1.2.3 the consumers,
    1.2.4 other rating bodies?

2. Coverage
2.1 What is the legal grounding for the code?
2.2 Does the code apply only to publishers/producers? Or does it also apply to suppliers, distributors, and advertisers?
2.3 Does the code apply to the Internet, and/or other media of interest to the electronic game industry?
2.4 Are there provisions for consolation and amendments to the code?

3. Content
3.1 Who does the screening?
3.2 What are the age categories?
3.3 What are the major content concerns, and standards regarding:
    3.3.1 violence,
    3.3.2 sex and nudity,
    3.3.3 language,
    3.3.4 controlled substances,
    3.3.5 other concerns?

4. Communication
4.1 Packaging: how does the code govern display of ratings on the packaging?
4.2 Marketing: does the code contain marketing guidelines for television/print/Internet?
4.3 Information: how are consumers educated about what the ratings mean?
4.4 Data protection and privacy: does the code contain provisions on protection of consumer's privacy and the producer's copyright?

5. Compliance
5.1 Does the code contain a complaint mechanism?

5.2 Does the code contain provisions that regulate cooperation with law enforcement and third parties?
5.3 Does the code contain sanction mechanisms?

The 5C matrix: press codes

1. Constitution

1.1 Media industry (print media, online services of print media, other related industry)
1.2 Full name of regulator
1.3 What is the structure/governance of the regulator body?
1.4 Does the regulatory body apply one or several codes? (e.g. journalistic ethics code, advertising code, or more than one code of ethics, etc.)
1.5 Was there involvement of the public in the preparation of the code? (if yes, please specify/no)
1.6 What is the regulatory body's relationship to
   a. the government
   b. the industry
   c. the readers
   d. others? (if applicable, please specify)

2. Coverage

2.1 Geographic area of coverage
   a. Does the code apply to newspapers distributed locally, regionally, nationally?
   b. Does the code apply to newspapers distributed outside the country?
   c. Are complaints taken from overseas? (e.g. newspapers distributed outside the country or online version of the newspaper)
2.2 To what does/do the code(s) apply?
   a. printed versions of newspapers
   b. advertisements
   c. online versions of newspapers
   d. online versions of advertisements
2.3 What is the legal grounding for the code(s)?
2.4 Are there provisions for amendments to the code(s)? (yes/no)
2.5 Are your code(s)
   a. required by national legislation (yes/no)
   b. partially based on national/EU legislation (yes/no)
   c. entirely self-regulatory? (yes/no)
2.6 Is there a 'pre-screening' assessment in place? (e.g. a telephone helpline) (if yes, please specify/no)

3. Content

3.1 In what year was (were) the code(s) adopted?
3.2 How was (were) the code(s) drafted?
   a. in-house
   b. external consultation
   c. consumer groups
   d. based on third party code – please specify original code
3.3 Who was (were) responsible for drafting/updating the code(s)?
   a. government (yes/no)
   b. industry (yes/no)
   c. consumers (yes/no)
   d. interest groups (yes/no)
   e. in-house (yes/no)

3.4 How many times has (have) the code(s) been revised?

3.5 Why was (were) your code(s) changed/revised? (changes in law, changes in business model, external complaints, customer conduct)

3.6 Do media outlets you regulate pre-screen content before it is made public? (yes/no)

3.7 If yes to the above question, how is content pre-screened? (in-house by the media outlet, third party, consumer groups, focus group)

3.8 What does the code contain?

    a. accuracy (yes/no)

    b. objectivity (yes/no)

    c. prohibition to members of the press from receiving gifts (yes/no)

    d. privacy (yes/no)

    e. duty to distinguish between facts and opinion (yes/no)

    f. hate speech provisions (yes/no)

    g. rules on protection for vulnerable people, e.g. minors (yes/no)

    h. rules on payments to criminals and witnesses (yes/no)

    i. rules on depiction of violence (yes/no)

    j. rules on manner in which information is gathered (yes/no)

    k. duty not to divulge confidential sources (yes/no)

    l. duty not to prejudge the guilt of an accused (yes/no)

    m. other area not covered above (please specify)

4. Communication

4.1 Marketing: does (do) the code(s) contain guidelines for the communication to readers, etc. of the code contents?

4.2 Information: how are readers educated about what the code(s) cover(s)?

5. Compliance

5.1 Do any of the codes contain a complaint mechanism?

5.2 Do any of the codes contain provisions that regulate cooperation with law enforcement and third parties?

5.3 Do any of the codes contain sanction mechanisms?

5.4 What are the enforcement/dispute resolution procedures, if they are not outlined in your code(s)?

5.5 What are the consequences when the code(s) is (are) broken? (legal sanction, penalty, warning, ban, other)

5.6 Annual estimate of the number of code-related enforcement actions (number)

5.7 Which are the most frequently violated aspects of the code?

5.8 Has there been any litigation (judicial review/arbitration/mediation) in relation to the code?

5.9 Is the code required by national legislation, partly based on national/supranational legislation?

Notes

1 See: Price, M and Verhulst, S (2000) 'In Search of the Self: Charting the Course of Self-Regulation on the Internet in a Global Environment', in Marsden, C (ed.) *Regulating the Global Information Society*, London: Routledge, and Price, M, Verhulst, S and Blinderman, E (2000) *Internet Codes of Conduct. An Analytical Report* (PCMLP/Bertelsmann Foundation Working Paper).

2 The original report from 1999 is COM/99/371 Final, the results of which were adopted by the European Commission on 19 July 1999 and presented in its consequent Communication on the Study on Parental Control of Television Broadcasting to the Council, European

Parliament and Economic and Social Committee. The research results were published as Price, M and Verhulst, S (2001) *Parental Control of Television Broadcasting*, New York: Lawrence Erlbaum Associates.

3 See: Monroe, P and Verhulst, S (2000) 'The Concept of Self-Regulation and the Internet', in Waltermann, J and Machill, M (eds) *Protecting Our Children on the Internet: Towards a New Culture of Responsibility*, Gutersloh, Germany: Bertelsmann Foundation Publishers.

4 Price, M and Verhulst, S (2005) *Self Regulation and the Internet*, New York: Kluwer Law International.

5 See: Baldwin, R and Cave, M (1999) *Understanding Regulation: Theory, Strategy and Practice*, Oxford University Press, pp. 125–37.

6 Details about this methodology are available at: www.selfregulation.info/iapcoda/iapcode-meth-grid-020530.htm

7 It is relevant to consider at this stage the Annex to the Council Recommendation which forms the basis for ISP Codes of Conduct, as a preliminary framework (see Appendix 1).

4 Press councils

Codes and analysis of codes in the
European Union

Introduction

The print media are subject to various codes of conduct setting out standards of journalistic ethics. Historically, the control of content of the print media has been carried out via journalist ethics codes. Some codes are internal to a media outlet, or specific to a publication, others adopted by professional associations of journalists or applied by a press council. Some publications, for example, rely on an in-house ombudsman applying a code (e.g. newspapers such as *The Guardian*, *The Observer* and *The Independent on Sunday* in the United Kingdom; *El País* and *La Vanguardia* in Spain; *Politiken* in Denmark; and a number of newspapers in the United States[1]). There is therefore a plethora of codes available for a study of EU print media[2] but this chapter is confined to eight European countries in which there is a press council as the enforcement mechanism for accountability of the print media regarding newspapers within their authority. There is considerable international interest in the self-regulation of print media, as evidenced by the activity of organisations such as ONO (the Organisation of News Ombudsmen)[3] and IPC (Independent Press Councils),[4] and the adoption of mechanisms of media accountability in developing and transitional countries.

For present purposes press councils are defined as independent bodies which deal with complaints from the public about the content of the print media. Although there is no single model for a press council, the press councils in this study all administer a code of journalistic ethics, and in all cases proprietors of media outlets fund – or help to fund – the running of the press council. Representatives of proprietors, journalists and in some cases members of the public sit as members of the council.[5]

The list of countries in this study comprises: Denmark, Finland, Germany, Luxembourg, The Netherlands, Spain (but only Catalonia has a press council), Sweden and the United Kingdom (codes for Catalonia, Germany, Denmark and the United Kingdom are reproduced in Appendix 2). Other countries are mentioned as illustrations.

France is conspicuous by its absence from the list. In France, there never was a press council. The media scholar Claude-Jean Bertrand explains that the late establishment of press freedom – and the (at least formal) stricture of the 1881 Press Law – may have fuelled distrust of a journalist-managed 'law court'. There is also the scattering of the profession among many unions, and the lack of dialogue with publishers. Perhaps another reason is the old (although now fading) fierce Left–Right dichotomy in French politics: any criticism of a Right-wing or Left-wing newspaper would have been considered a partisan attack.[6] In Ireland, there is a committee negotiating the establishment of a press council, following the model of the Swedish press council, in which publishers have expressed commitment to funding but the council is recognised by law.[7] In Ireland all national newspapers have had readers' representatives since 1989 to receive complaints.[8]

This analysis of press councils needs to be placed against two background concerns. The first concern is the wider analysis of media self-regulation in the other industries performed in the research on which this book is based, and therefore, to enable comparisons across industries, the general methodology of analysis discussed previously (with a few necessary adjustments[9]) is applied here. We should mention that by print media we refer to newspapers. Books are excluded from consideration. The second background concern refers to the revolutionary changes brought about to the print media by technological progress, which now allow the individual to participate in 'one-to-many' type of communications, such as the phenomenon of the 'citizen journalist'. Blogging,[10] wikis[11] and citizen journalism bypass the editorial controls of traditional print media, and hence circumvent the mechanisms of accountability provided by self-regulatory bodies such as press councils, in-house ombudsmen and other systems aimed at the enforcement of rules of journalistic ethics. These issue will be addressed in the section 'Dilemmas and challenges: the impact of convergence and other challenges to self-regulation of the print media' also in this chapter.

Self-regulation and the experience of press councils

Key indicators: what empirical evidence is there of usage of the self-regulatory code?

Statistics on the usage of press council mechanisms show the following:

United Kingdom: The Press Complaints Commission (UK PCC) deals with the highest volume of complaints in the group of councils surveyed. It received 2,630 complaints in 2002, significantly more than the average of the previous three years; 56 per cent of complaints concerned accuracy, while approximately 25 per cent dealt with privacy.[12] The level increased to near 3,500 in 2004. Almost all UK print media outlets are part of the system and contribute to it (only some fringe publications do not, such as some UK-based foreign language newspapers, although the PCC can hear complaints about those newspapers as well).

Germany: The German *Presserat* receives an average of 600 complaints a year. Approximately two-thirds of all complaints can be dealt with at an early stage without requiring a formal decision.[13] A newspaper or magazine that has been censured by the press council must print the reprimand in its next issue: about 90 per cent of the German publishing companies have signed a voluntary agreement committing themselves to do so.

Sweden: There is an Ombudsman and a Press Council, which can apply fines of up to approximately €2500, and deals with 350–400 complaints per year. About 30 per cent of the complaints have been reviewed by the Press Council either on the Ombudsman's request or, if the Ombudsman has struck the case off the list, on appeal by the complainant; 10–15 per cent of all complaints have resulted in formal criticism of the newspaper in question by the Press Council.

Netherlands: The Dutch Press Council hears a much lower number of complaints: 71 judgements were delivered in 2000, 53 judgements were delivered in 2001, 66 judgements were delivered in 2002 and 70 judgements were delivered in 2003.[14]

Other Councils: Denmark: The Danish Press Council heard 163 complaints in 2003. Switzerland: The Swiss Press Council heard 100 complaints in 2004. Cyprus: The Press Council of Cyprus hears approximately 20 complaints per year. Belgium: The Flemish Council established in 2002 heard 45 complaints in 2003.

Best practice examples

Constitution

Many European press councils were created in response to a crisis of some sort – e.g. discontent with intrusions by the press, dissatisfaction with low standards of journalism, etc. – that prompts either calls for legislation from the public, or a threat of legislation from the authorities, and as a reaction the industry offers to improve its performance by raising standards. The answer in the countries in this study was the creation of an enforcement mechanism for a code of journalistic ethics. Some writers consider self-regulation as a public relations exercise: Robertson and Nicol view it that way in the United Kingdom, for example, as an exercise funded by the media industry to avert legislative action.[15] O'Malley and Soley concur:

> A critical evaluation of the evidence therefore provides powerful support for the view that self-regulation in the UK was not a positive institution designed to promote high standards, deal effectively with complaints and protect press freedom. It was there to defend the proprietors, who funded it, from the encroachments of the politicians, journalists and members of the public who wanted the press to be more responsible than the owners were prepared to allow.[16]

Let us look closer at this relationship between legislative threat and the offer to introduce industry self-regulation, in the stories behind the councils in this study.

United Kingdom: A Press Council was originally established in 1953, and a revised Press Complaints Commission (PCC) was established in 1991. The original Press Council's apparent inability to deal with privacy issues led to its demise:

> The main reason for the abolition of the Council was the increasing intrusion by the press, especially the tabloids, into private lives of people and the inability of the Council to curb it. The main difference between the original Press Council and the PCC[17] is while the Council was also responsible for preservation of the freedom of the press, the latter only ensures a decent standard of conduct by newspapers.[18]

Another important difference was that submission of a case to the original Press Council involved a waiver to pursue other means of redress.

Germany: Similarly an industry initiative, the German Press Council, was founded in 1956 in the context of discussions on a project for a federal press law. In 1952 the Federal Ministry of the Interior submitted a draft, which provided for the establishment of a self-monitoring body under public law. The project met with tremendous opposition from journalist and publisher associations and, following the example of the British Press Council of 1953, those two associations formed the German Press Council on 20 November 1956.[19] We can see clearly the corporatist traditions of Germany in the composition of the council. There is no lay membership.[20]

Sweden: Similar dynamics between the industry and the threat of legislation led to the creation, reforms and relaunches of what is the oldest press council in Europe. The Swedish Press Council was established in 1916.[21] It was the result of an initiative of three press organisations, The Publisher's Club, The Swedish Union of Journalists and The Swedish Newspaper Publisher's Association. It had a slow start and World War II interrupted its work. In the 1960s a deep reform was carried out when the Swedish Parliament contemplated legislation to curb sensationalism in the press. The industry responded by setting up in 1969 the first Press Ombudsman, which is part of the system of the Press Council, and the code of ethics was strengthened. The Swedish system of self-regulation is therefore entirely organised by the industry, and it consists of three pillars: the code of ethics, the Office of the Press Ombudsman and the Press Council.[22]

Catalonia: In Spain the press council is not national, but there does exist a regional body for the press in Catalonia. An important method of self-regulation in Spain is the ombudsmen based at newspapers,[23] a practice initiated by the newspaper *El País* in 1986 which others followed. The initiative that led to the creation of the Catalonian Council of Information (CIC) was grass roots, initiated by the Union of Journalists of Catalonia. Later the initiative was widened to include members of civil society in all stages of the creation of the council, and of course, currently in its functioning. The launching of the project involved signing a document that stressed the voluntary and consensual character of the council and code. The voluntary nature of the code and council was highlighted by the formal signature of the document of creation, and the fact that the council was established for a limited period of time, which is renewable. The protocol[24] in question was signed in 1996 during the Third Congress of Catalan Journalists. Signatories to the protocol were the representatives of the Union of Journalists, the Association of Journalists, and the Faculties of Journalism of universities in the region, as well as individual journalists and a total of 48 media companies (press, radio and television). The protocol in question is an agreement that involves the provision of support, cooperation and financial support to the Council, and a promise to accept its moral authority and its decisions. Its experience can be regarded as successful.[25]

The Netherlands: The press council in The Netherlands was also the result of a struggle between the authorities and the profession about plans to legislate on journalistic standards. The body eventually created in 1960 originally involved the presence of the judiciary in its board. The origins of the press council in The Netherlands, however, date back to 1948. When the press was rebuilt after World War II, journalist organisations became concerned about the standing of the profession. They founded a tribunal in 1948 which functioned until 1960.

Belgium: The Belgian Press Council is a regional council for the Flemish community. It draws on the precedent of the ethics tribunal of the union of journalists. In December 2002 the council of ethics of the Association of Journalists was replaced by a press council in the Dutch-speaking part of Belgium.[26] As is the case of its Finnish and Catalan counterparts, this council can hear complaints on alleged breaches of rules of ethics by journalists in the print and the broadcast media.[27]

Luxembourg: In contrast with the countries surveyed up to this point, the press council in Luxembourg is a statutory creation.[28] In Luxembourg the composition of the press council was determined by the 1979 Law on 'The Recognition and the Protection of the Professional Degree of Journalist'. Council members are renewed every two years.[29] The Luxembourg Council was relaunched in 2004 by a new Press Law.

Denmark: The Danish Press Council was founded in 1964, also by statute. Its basis is Article 41 of the Danish Media Liability Act.[30] In Denmark the partnership between the industry and the authorities is evidenced in the membership of its eight-strong board: the chairman and vice-chairman are appointed by the President of the Danish Supreme Court of Justice and should be lawyers, two members are appointed by the Union of Journalists, two members represent the print media or broadcast management, and two members come from the public at large. The partnership between the authorities and the industry is also clear in the sources of funding for the council: the union of publishers and the Ministry of Justice.

Content

This section considers the ethical standards set out in the codes of conduct applied by the councils.[31] Let us first place those rules in the general regulatory scheme applied to the media in the countries under study. Although regulatory convergence is taking place in this sector (which we will address in more detail below when discussing online newspapers) the influence of history is still relevant. If we consider the content of codes from the traditional point of view of regulation (based on the mode of delivery) we see that on one side we have print media regulation based on ordinary law (e.g. issues such as defamation, privacy, contempt of court and court reporting) and on the other, the heavily regulated broadcast media. These traditional regulatory models are justified by the 'scarcity of frequencies' reasoning of the pre-digital world.[32]

For print media, journalistic ethics apply in an area where ordinary law is not directly engaged. The press councils' task is to ensure that the press adheres to its professed ethics, and they therefore focus on violations with no direct statutory control.[33] Ordinary law might be engaged either at a later stage if the solution offered is challenged, or in place of the press council, if a complaint is routed directly towards the court system. Despite the detailed legal restraints set out in ordinary law, the media could still damage reputations, invade privacy or conduct partisan campaigns.

If we were to put this in graphic terms, we see that the codes of ethics provide the underpinning principles for a variety of self-regulatory mechanisms. If we imagine a triangle (Public Contentedness with the Print Media), and at its base we see complaints and disputes coming into being, disputes may be settled before they involve ordinary law. Of course, in certain circumstances ordinary law is engaged, for example, judicial review. This area of standards of conduct contained in the codes falls into what could also be termed media accountability.[34] The rules dealt with in codes of conduct applied by press councils and other mechanisms for the implementation of ethical standards (e.g. ombudsmen) apply to an area where there tends to be no statutory control. It has been argued that a press council could solve the difficulty of making a free press (protected by ordinary law) also a fair press (a press which follows standards of ethics, for example).[35] (See Figure 4.1.)[36]

The boundaries between standards and ordinary law are drawn differently in different countries. In some countries, the journalistic profession or the industry may resist codes for fear of increasing their due diligence duties, as in the case of the National Press Council of the United States which was reportedly 'killed through neglect'.[37] In contrast, we see that in Scandinavian countries the political culture supports the idea of state presence in the press councils, as well as an element of state funding.

We see that even though there are differences in the detail of their content, the codes under study are based on widely accepted standards of professional conduct

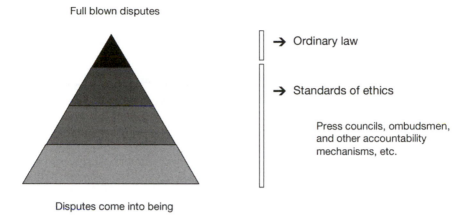

Figure 4.1 Public contentedness with the print media.

such as honesty, objectivity, protection of human rights and accuracy. They express these expected standards with different levels of clarity.

All codes under study had provisions regarding accuracy and discrimination/hate speech. Most contained provisions concerning the duty to distinguish between fact and opinion; a majority had clauses to protect privacy. We can observe this in the issue penetration matrix (Table 4.1) which shows the variation between countries' codes and the range of rules deployed.

Communication of the content of the code

For a code and a complaints mechanism to be effective, knowledge about both is crucial. All the press councils under review have websites (see Appendix 1). Some are quite elaborate and contain easy-to-follow guidance on how to complain (the UK PCC and the German Press Council are good in this regard). Other information which should be easily available relates to previously decided controversies. (Again, the PCC makes available a quite comprehensive database of these.)[38] This increases transparency – the work of the council can be more easily scrutinised – and also aids prospective complainants. As well as on council websites, it is also desirable for a decision against a media outlet to be published in a prominent place in the same offending publication.

Trends

The main similarities across the different countries are: that Press councils are set up with safeguards aimed at making them independent from the industry and the authorities; and emerge from struggle between industry and authorities. The struggle resurfaces from time to time, leading to new settlements and revisions (for example, the incorporation of lay membership in the Swedish Council in the 1960s, the current plans to do so in Germany, or the metamorphosis of the UK Press Council into the UK Press Complaints Commission in the early 1990s). There is a strong corporatist aspect in the composition of councils (owners, editors, journalists) with participation

Table 4.1 Issue penetration matrix

Y/N	D	F	G	L	N No code	Sp	Sw	UK	
Issue 1	Y	Y	Y	Y	–	Y	Y	Y	Provisions regarding accuracy
Issue 2	Y	Y		Y	–		Y	Y	Provisions regarding appearance as well as reality of objectivity
Issue 3		Y	Y		–	Y			Prohibition of members of the press from receiving gifts
Issue 4	Y	Y	Y		–	Y	Y	Y	Provisions concerning privacy
Issue 5	Y	Y	Y	Y	–	Y	Y	Y	Duty to distinguish between fact and opinion
Issue 6	Y	Y	Y	Y	–	Y	Y	Y	Provisions regarding hate speech/ discrimination
Issue 7		Y			–	Y	Y	Y	Rules on protection for vulnerable people (e.g. minors)
Issue 8					–		Y		Rules on payments to criminals and witnesses
Issue 9			Y		–				Rules on depiction of violence
Issue 10		Y	Y	Y	–			Y	Rules on manner in which information is gathered
Issue 11		Y	Y	Y	–				Rules on protection of confidential sources
Issue 12	Y	Y	Y		–	Y	Y		Rule not to prejudge the guilt of an accused
Issue 13		Y			–				Other content area not covered above
Issue 14					–				Complaint mechanism?
Issue 15		Y	Y		–				Provisions that regulate cooperation with law enforcement, and third parties or information embargoes
Issue 16					–		Y		Sanctions, duty to publish rulings of press council

Note
D: Denmark; F: Finland; G: Germany; L: Luxembourg; N: The Netherlands (no code, the press council offers mediation services); Sp: Spain (Catalonia); Sw: Sweden; UK: United Kingdom.

in most cases of lay members too. Critics point out the closeness between industry and councils, particularly as the industry funds all or part of the running of the council. Sometimes the state co-funds. Councils have an internal procedure for evaluating their standards and changing their code. All councils offer a formal complaint and appeal procedure for settling disputes, usually laid out in documents outside the code. The codes address editorial and news content of print media (advertising is addressed by separate mechanisms and codes not studied here). Finally, there is similarity in the standards of ethics laid out in the codes, although this may be deceptive, due to codes being written at a high level of generality.

The main differences are:

- The formal relationship to government: some councils are entirely funded by industry and arguably put a high priority on protecting industry interests, others (Council for Mass Media, CMM, in Finland) receive a grant from the government with 'no strings attached'.
- Some councils (Denmark) have statutory origin, others do not (United Kingdom, Germany).

- Corporatism is more present in some (Germany, and the previously existing Austrian council) as there is no openness to lay membership.
- Codes may be statutory (Denmark) or industry-written (United Kingdom, Germany), even absent (the Dutch Press Council exists as a mechanism for dispute resolution with no code of its own, although in its decisions it may formulate standards that can be found in codes of ethics or quote a particular code).
- Some councils go beyond print media, addressing ethical standards of broadcast journalism (Catalonia, Sweden, Finland), notwithstanding existing statutory regulators for broadcasting (although the complaint would be made before the broadcast regulator and not the press council).
- The degree of information disclosure varies from high (the UK PCC, which has a searchable database of adjudications and annual reports available online), to somewhat high (the German Press Council), to very low (the Luxembourg Press Council).

Dilemmas and challenges: the impact of convergence and other challenges to self-regulation of the print media

Convergence

An important use of the Internet is for access to news. Most newspapers are now distributed electronically as well as in hard copy. The self-regulatory mechanisms for print media are adapting to this. Online newspapers can be carried by a range of platforms; Internet users can join the readership via any device. We see therefore an area of regulatory convergence as online content is now in some cases subject to codes originally developed for the most traditional of the media.

The new medium introduced changes to the process of publication. For example, it is now significantly easier to update the edition of a daily several times in the course of a 24-hour period. The effect of these changes on the future readership of a newspaper is unclear, but the growth of online news introduces the question of whether large national papers will survive.[39] It is not only newspapers providing online news content. Broadcasters and news aggregators are as well, amongst others.

Can the print media codes simply be applied to the Internet? The press councils, asked to respond to complaints made about online news, responded by placing limits on what they could hear, to avoid a potentially exponential increase in workload. The German Press Council in 1996 extended its jurisdiction and its code to complaints originating in online publications, but these must 'relate to published material containing journalistic or editorial contributions which is circulated by newspaper or magazine publishers or by press services solely in digital form or also in digital form'.[40] The Swedish Code (used by both the Ombudsman and the Council) applies to an Internet publication if the company who publishes it is a member of The Swedish Newspaper Publishers' Association or The Swedish Magazine Publishers Association.[41] Similarly, the UK PCC extended its code to cover certain online publications.[42] The Catalan Code, in its Annex 3, also extends the code to online publications of its members. We see regulatory convergence in that some elements of the press tradition are coming into the Internet via the press councils.

What about influence in the other direction? The NTD (notice and take down) procedure which has emerged in the last few years as the key tool in Internet content regulation, does not resolve the liability issue for electronic newspapers. NTD places an obligation on ISPs to remove illegal content only when the ISP 'obtains actual knowledge': it is not suitable for a newspaper that is not a mere conduit for content posted by third parties.[43] The print media face other dilemmas. If they make archives available online, should these reflect accurately what was published on the original date or should tags/notices be put next to material successfully challenged via a self-regulatory mechanism or the courts?[44] Members of the public may want to clean up their record on the web. Search engines have improved considerably in recent years and it is now very easy to have access to newspaper articles, even published regionally or some time ago; actions against newspapers based on archived material are more likely. On the other hand, there is the possibility of a newspaper taking down material from their website too quickly after what in the end turns out to be an unsuccessful complaint. Lack of time or resources may mean that non-defamatory material may not ever be put back online.

The Internet also poses an issue of jurisdiction.[45] As no newspaper can be expected to have lawyers knowledgeable of all the legal systems of the world, technological solutions may be implemented, such as blocking website access to certain countries (for example, if the laws of the country are problematic).[46] Technology can also aid the defence of a newspaper; for example, it matters to a court if the site is a subscriber or a non-subscriber site. It is possible to determine how many visitors a website had (important for determining cause of action, and also, to establish if the numbers of hits are negligible),[47] and for how long the website was accessed (if the allegedly offending article is long and would reasonably require a certain time to read, one might infer that the offending piece had not been read, for example). Hyperlinks present additional challenges, as does the unauthorised reproduction of an article.[48]

Citizen participation

Changes in the media landscape are driven by changes in technology. Particularly in developed societies, access to the Internet (via a computer, a handheld device such as an advanced mobile phone or an organiser, etc.) means that individuals can post content accessible to many. This ability is no longer the preserve of the 'mass' media. It has been said therefore that 'the Internet is enabling conversations among human beings that were simply not possible in the era of mass media'.[49] The citizen journalist turns the news from a lecture into a conversation.[50] The effect of these changes on the future readership of traditional newspapers is unclear, but the phenomenon of the citizen journalist may pose a deeper challenge to the current business model of the print media than the growth of online news. The lack of editorial control may certainly have a detrimental impact on quality, and the readership may continue relying on more traditional forms of media for credibility and accuracy. At the moment there is juxtaposition[51] of traditional media, distributed electronically by a range of platforms as well as in hard copy, and the blogs, wikis, etc. accessible by Internet users via any device. The citizen journalist can distribute widely news items which have not been filtered through the editorial control in place in established media. The content put on the Internet by the citizen journalist is not covered by the framework of rules set out in codes of journalistic ethics and their enforcement mechanisms. The blogosphere is not subject to the mechanisms of accountability discussed in this chapter, in contrast with the online versions of newspapers, to which traditional accountability systems are being extended. As J D Lassica puts it: '[t]he underlying ethical considerations of journalism transcend the medium. In other words, journalism demands high standards, no matter the medium.'[52]

Visibility, transparency and disclosure

A challenge for self-regulatory bodies in the print media as well as in other industries is to increase the visibility of the complaints mechanism and dispute resolution system, to encourage the public to refer complaints to them. Since the press council is entrusted with the task of taking decisions it is desirable to make past adjudications available. This accumulation of 'case law' provides valuable guidance as regards the stringency of the codes as they are in fact interpreted and applied. While on the one hand annual reports, a searchable adjudications database and other materials are easily available on the UK PCC's website, other press councils offer very little information via their websites. Disclosure and transparency are important tools to ensure legitimacy and many of the councils in this survey seem to be ignoring that point.

Composition: lay and stakeholder participation

Press councils are not simply for industry self-monitoring; a way of opening up their mechanisms is by including members of the public in their boards. Although one of the advantages claimed for self-regulation is industry expertise, non-industry membership makes the bodies less 'corporative' and distinguishes press councils from the tribunals created at professional organisations. The UK PCC has a majority of lay members and a minority of senior editors from across the industry. The approaches of the press councils differs as to the background of members. Legal knowledge is deemed of importance at some councils (for example, the chair is filled by lawyers in The Netherlands or Sweden, and outside the European Union, in Australia). The chairman of the PCC is appointed by the industry, but not engaged or connected with it.[53]

In the literature, closeness between industry and its regulator is presented as a challenge for the independence of self-regulation.[54] Non-industry membership helps bring independence. But there is another side to the coin. Richard Shannon in his history of the first decade of the UK PCC mentions that closeness with industry is a 'networking' factor that helps the self-regulatory body to function: 'A free press must persuade itself to be responsible. This is what the PCC does for it. It cannot be other than an intimately internal debate. The more intimate, it might well be argued, the better.'[55]

The proportions of lay membership vary in different councils, from 25 per cent in the Danish council to a little over half in the Catalan CIC. There is 30 per cent lay membership in the Finnish CMM. It has a president and nine board members: six represent areas of expertise in the media, and three represent the public at large. The president and representatives of the public are elected by the council itself, and may not be employees or board members of any media organisation. The media representatives are appointed by a separate selection committee of representatives of media organisations affiliated to the Finnish CMM.[56] The Netherlands Press Council has 40 per cent lay membership. The Dutch Press Council consists of three vice-chairmen, 10 journalist members and 10 non-journalist members, who serve part time on the council. The chairman and his substitute are members of the judiciary. The secretary must be a lawyer. The appointments are for four years and can be extended for another four years.[57] The proportion of non-industry membership is higher in the Catalan council, however, where of 15 members on its board of directors, all respected people in the region, eight are drawn from civil society and seven connected with the media industry.

Stakeholder participation seems to be a component of successful self-regulation in the Catalan experience.[58] Stakeholder participation is understood narrowly in other cases, to mean industry only. The German Press Council is a specialist body that currently excludes lay membership. The same approach was followed by the Austrian Press Council, which no longer exists. Arguably these councils reflect the corporatist traditions of Germany (and Austria): publishers and journalists participate in the council but there is no civil society representation.[59]

Financial journalism

Financial reporting has to meet the disclosure rules of the EU Market Abuse Directive 2003.[60] Accountability under a self-regulatory system[61] allows journalists to meet the requirements of the Directive. The alternative could be control by the securities regulatory authority. In some EU countries such as France,[62] where there is no press council or tradition of self-regulation of the press, implementation of the Directive presents more challenges and it may encourage the development of self-regulatory initiatives to meet the requirements.

Challenges / reviewability in court

The submission of a complaint to a self-regulatory body usually does not preclude other means of redress (for example, lodging a complaint with the UK PCC does not involve a waiver of the right to sue). Reviewability by courts may indirectly reinforce the authority of a self-regulatory body, which otherwise may appear as less relevant as an institution whose decisions are not worthy of attention by the courts.[63] As we indicated, self-regulation could take other shapes. In the United Kingdom, for example, the in-house ombudsman mechanism of a newspaper has been recognised by the courts as able to offer an impartial and prompt apology and hence as grounds (under the offer of amends procedure) to set a reduced award for damages against the newspaper in defamation cases.[64]

Conclusions

In all the press councils in this study we see an experience of giving a legalistic treatment (together with the provision of a mechanism for dispute resolution) to rules that belong in the realm of ethical, moral and/or professional conduct and not in that of ordinary law. The legalistic nature of these systems is confirmed by the presence of lawyers or judges in the membership of the boards and decision-making commissions. At times the councils are open to the criticism that they are not legalistic enough to offer remedies equivalent to those afforded by the legal process and ordinary law.

The institution of the press council was created for an 'old medium', newspapers. As the industry faces new technological challenges, there has been a move to apply this self-regulatory mechanism to new domains of online news and even to content produced by broadcasters. This presents challenges of scope: increased volume of complaints, and a future uncertainty as to where the inclusion of new delivery platforms will end.

In general terms of the relation between ordinary law and self-regulation, we have seen that for the most part the ethical standards being applied here operate in a region where there is no statutory regulation. There are, of course, important areas of overlap. We can expect further developments in the area of privacy, in view of the rules of the European Convention on Human Rights and national legislation incorporating it. The press councils offer a means of alternative dispute resolution, with the possibility of achieving redress via a complaints mechanism which is faster and less onerous than courts, but perhaps with less protection for rights than the protection offered by the law. Speedy redress is no doubt advantageous. Provided that there is adequate protection for rights of complainants, and transparency, self-regulation may have the effect of making the print media more accountable to their audience. This in turn may lead to a virtuous circle in which the enlightened self-interest of the industry ensures funding for code implementation, and obedience of council decisions. It is important to balance the self-interest of the industry with public considerations, such as fostering confidence and involving civil society. If the argument in favour of print media self-regulation of content (via some form of supervision of professional ethical standards) is enlightened self-interest, then sources of legitimacy such as transparency in decision making, good communication to the public and full disclosure are of great relevance. Legitimacy earned over a period of time could encourage compliance, in view of the weak enforcement powers of press councils.

For the Press Council as a mechanism for dispute resolution the key to achieving independence lies in the membership of the board and the sources of financial support. Political culture is an important backdrop. In the Scandinavian examples there seems to be more partnership between state and press council than in the case of the United Kingdom or Germany, for example, where the industry seems more fearful of any interference, even in areas such as privacy where self-regulation may need statutory reinforcement.

The experiences reviewed in this chapter suggest that the efficacy and sustainability of self-regulatory bodies dealing with print media content depend on legitimacy and transparency, as well as political culture, and how the line between statutory control and self-regulation is drawn and kept under review.

APPENDIX 1

European press councils studied and links to codes

Country	Organisation	Code	Link
Belgium (regional: Flemish-speaking community)	Raad voor de Journalistiek	Reglement	(Home) www.rvdj.be (Code) www.rvdj.be/reglement.php
Denmark	Danish Press Council	Vejledende regler for god presseskik	(Home) www.pressenaevnet.dk/english/index.htm (Code) www.pressenaevnet.dk/lovgivning/index_presseskik.html
Finland	Council for Mass Media in Finland	Guidelines for good journalistic practice	(Home) www.jsn.fi/english/index.html (Code) www.jsn.fi/english/guidel.html
Germany	Press Council (Deutscher Presserat)	Code	(Home) www.presserat.de/index.shtml (Code) www.presserat.de/site/pressekod/kodex/index.shtml

continued

European press councils studied and links to codes (contd)

Country	Organisation	Code	Link
Luxembourg	Conseil de Presse Luxembourg	Code de deontologie de la presse	(Home) www.rvdj.nl (Code) www.press.lu/datas/info_code.html
The Netherlands	Press Council (Raad voor de Journalistiek)	No code	
Spain (regional: Catalonia)	Consell de la informacio de Catalunya (News Council of Catalonia)	Codi deontologic	(Home) http://periodistes.org/cic/home.htm (regional council only) (Code) http://periodistes.org/cic/cat/Codi.htm
Sweden	Pressens Opinionsnämnd (Swedish Press Council)	Code of Ethics for Press, Radio and Television in Sweden	(Home) www.po.se/english.jsp?avd=english (Code) www.po.se/Article.jsp?article=1905& avd=english
United Kingdom	The UK PCC	Code of Practice	(Home) www.pcc.org.uk (Code) www.pcc.org.uk/cop/cop.asp

APPENDIX 2

Declaration of Principles of the Journalistic Profession in Catalonia

The deontological Code is an initiative of the *Collegi de Periodistes de Catalunya* [CPC; Union of Journalists of Catalonia] aimed at reasserting the ethical principles of the journalistic profession. The present declaration has been prepared over the last three years. An ad hoc committee – created on the initiative of the CPC's Board of Government and consisting of the committees of Professional Defence and Culture – took charge of the analysis and drafting of the text, which since has been subject to revision and debate by the Advisory Council of the CPC, as well as a consultation process involving all collegiate members. The final text was approved by the CPC Government Board on 22 October 1992.

Barcelona, October 1992

Foreword

The CPC and its Advisory Council, representing the different mass media in Catalonia, have felt the need to foster this collective initiative by journalists, which will reaffirm the rights to freedom of speech and information and defend the existence of a free and responsible press in a plural and democratic society.

This initiative is in harmony with the acknowledged democratic and independent tradition of the Catalonia press, and inspired by similar recent moves in other democratic countries with a strong journalist tradition. This proposal is part of a permanent debate in society about the function of the mass media. We want to promote a collective critical reflection in order to improve the relationship between the press and the society it addresses and serves.

With this aim, we invite and encourage bodies and professionals in the field of communication to reaffirm the deontological principles that support journalistic activity.

Introduction

Freedom of speech and the right to information are two essential pillars of a democratic society. Both are rights protected by the constitution. The existence of plural and independent public opinion depends on the strength, respect and full validity of these rights, and they are essential for good development of public life and the full democracy.

The guarantee of these citizens' rights requires the defence of a free, plural and critical press, open to the society whom it serves. The importance of the journalist's social function is such that these principles must be guarded from any attempted restriction or compulsion, including through inobservance by the media themselves and by those who work in the media.

In this capacity, the media must carry out their function with double obligations, derived from their important task and from their own conscience, according to the constitutional order and to journalistic ethics.

To maintain these principles, the journalist must defend and strictly apply the following rules.

Criteria

Always to observe a clear distinction between facts and opinion/interpretation, avoiding any confusion or intentional distortion, and the diffusion of conjectures and rumours.

To spread only properly founded information, avoiding imprecise statements, or information that could damage people's dignity or bring unjustified disrepute to institutions, public and private bodies; to avoid the use of offensive expressions or epithets.

To rectify quickly and with appropriate treatment any false information – and opinions derived from this – which might damage the rights and interests of the people and/or bodies involved. Not to avoid apology, if it is necessary, independently of law.

To use worthy methods to obtain information or pictures, not illicit ones.

To respect requests for information to be 'off the record', according to the usual practice of this rule in a free society.

To respect the individual and/or legal person's right not give information or answer questions, without dismissing the duty of the journalists to satisfy the right of citizens to information. With regard to affairs concerning the authorities, the fundamental right to information must always prevail over any restriction that violates without justification the principle of information transparency.

Never to accept retributions or rewards from third parties in return for influencing or publishing pieces of news or opinion. The practice of journalism must not be combined with other professional activities incompatible with its ethics, like advertising, public relations and consultancy, whether in public or in private bodies.

Never to use for one's own good privileged information obtained confidentially as a journalist.

To respect the right of people to their own privacy and public image, especially in cases or events provoking situations of affliction or harm, avoiding gratuitous inter-fering and unnecessary speculations over their feelings and circumstances, particu-larly when people request privacy.

To observe scrupulously the principle of presumption of innocence in news and opinion concerning cases or penal proceedings under way.

To treat with particular care information concerning minors, avoiding the identifi-cation of minors who are victims (except in the case of homicide), witnesses or accused in criminal cases, especially in affairs of special social sensitivity, as it is in cases of sexual crimes. The families of those accused or convicted in penal proceedings – or those close to the accused/convicted – should not be identified against their will.

To act with special responsibility and precision in the case of information or opin-ions that could cause discrimination based on sex, race, beliefs or social or cultural identity, and that could cause the use of violence, and to avoid language hurtful to the personal condition of the individuals and their physical and moral integrity.

Final Declaration

Journalists must have the indispensable means and instruments in order to carry out their activity with full independence, freedom, initiative and sense of responsibility.

In this sense – and for a full guarantee of their individual rights and obligations on behalf of citizens – journalists will have to be protected by the clause of conscience and professional confidentiality, as stated in the Constitution.

We also consider necessary the establishment of Editorial Charters, as a more appropriate instrument for defining rights and duties within the media enterprises and for achieving greater transparency in the practice of the profession *vis-à-vis* the citizenry.

The representative professional bodies and organisations must ensure the good image of the journalistic profession; strive to avoid corruptive practices that infringe journalistic ethics; and protect the rights of citizens to freedom of speech and infor-mation, against acts or opinions aimed to restrict or injure the free activity of the media.

In order to fulfil this task, we propose the creation of a dedicated arbitral body, which is representative, plural and independent of government and which, without ignoring the constitutional rights enjoyed by individuals and enterprises, is able to make decisions independent of the judiciary.

German Press Code

Guidelines for journalistic work as recommended by the German Press Council

Drawn up by the German Press Council in collaboration with the Press associations and presented to Federal President Gustav W. Heinemann on 12 December 1973 in Bonn.
(Updated version of 3 March 2005)

The freedom of the Press guaranteed by the Basic Law (Constitution) of the Federal Republic of Germany embraces independence and freedom of information, expres-sion and criticism. Publishers, editors and journalists must in their work remain aware of their responsibility towards the public and their duty to uphold the prestige of the

Press. They must perform their journalistic duties to the best of their ability and belief and must not allow their work to be influenced by personal interests or extraneous motives.

The Press Code embodies the professional ethics of the Press. These include the duty within the framework of the Constitution and constitutional laws to maintain the standing of the Press and speak up for the freedom of the Press.

The regulations pertaining to editorial data protection apply to the Press in gathering, processing or using information about persons for journalistic-editorial purposes. From research to editing, publishing, documenting and storing these data, the Press must respect people's privacy and right to self-determination on information about them.

The professional ethics grant everyone affected the right to complain about the Press. Complaints are justified if professional ethics are infringed.

1. Respect for the truth, observance of human rights and accurate informing of the public are the overriding principles of the Press.
2. The publication of specific news and information in text and photographs must be carefully checked for accuracy in the light of existing circumstances. Its sense must not be distorted or falsified by editing, headlines or picture captions. Documents must be accurately reproduced. Unconfirmed reports, rumours or assumptions must be quoted as such. It must be clear, or made so, that symbolic photographs are such.
3. Published news or assertions, particularly those related to persons, which turn out to be incorrect must be rectified promptly in an appropriate manner by the publication concerned.
4. Dishonest methods must not be used to acquire person-related news, information or photographs.
5. Agreed confidentiality is to be observed as a fundamental principle.
6. All those employed by the Press shall preserve the standing and credibility of the media, observe professional secrecy, use the right to refuse to give evidence, and not disclose the identity of informants without their express consent.
7. The responsibility of the Press towards the public requires that editorial publication is not influenced by the private or business interests of third parties or by the personal commercial interests of journalists. Publishers and editors must reject any attempts of this nature and make a clear distinction between editorial and commercial content.
8. The Press shall respect people's private lives. If, however, the private behaviour of a person touches upon public interests, then it may be reported upon. Care must be taken to ensure that the personal rights of non-involved persons are not violated. The Press shall respect people's right to self-determination on information about them and guarantee editorial data protection.
9. It is contrary to journalistic decorum to publish unfounded claims and accusations, particularly those that harm personal honour.
10. Publication in words and photographs which could seriously offend the moral or religious feelings of a group of persons, in form or content, are irreconcilable with the responsibility of the Press.
11. The Press will refrain from inappropriately sensational portrayal of violence and brutality. The protection of young persons is to be considered in reporting.
12. No-one may be discriminated against due to a handicap or their membership of a racial, ethnic, religious, social or national group.

13. Reports on investigations, criminal court proceedings and other formal proce-
    dures must be free from prejudice. For this reason, before and during legal
    proceedings, all comment, both in reports and headlines, must avoid being one-
    sided or prejudicial. An accused person must not be described as guilty before
    final judgement has been passed. Court decisions should not be reported before
    they are announced unless there are serious reasons to justify such action.
14. Reports on medical subjects should not be of an unnecessarily sensationalist
    nature that could raise unfounded fears or hopes among readers. Research find-
    ings that are still at an early stage should not be portrayed as conclusive or almost
    conclusive.
15. The acceptance or granting of privileges of any kind which could influence the
    freedom of decision on the part of publishers and editors are irreconcilable with
    the prestige, independence and mission of the Press. Anyone accepting bribes for
    the dissemination of news acts in a dishonourable and unprofessional manner.
16. It is considered fair reporting when a public reprimand issued by the German
    Press Council is published, especially by the publications concerned.

The Danish Code

The Press Ethical Rules

THE NATIONAL CODE OF CONDUCT

*A legal code adopted by the Danish Parliament with the acceptance of the national union of journalists
in 1992.*

FUNDAMENTAL POINTS OF VIEW

The safeguarding of the freedom of speech in Denmark is closely connected with the
free access of the press to collect information and news and to publish them as
correctly as possible. The free comment is part of the exercise of the freedom of
speech. In attending to these tasks the press recognises that the individual citizen is
entitled to respect for his personal integrity and the sanctity of his private life and the
need for protection against unjustified violations.

Breach of good press practice comprises the withholding of rightful publication of
information of essential importance to the public and compliance towards outsiders if
this compliance can lead to doubts as to the freedom and independence of the mass
media. It is also considered to be breach of good press practice if tasks that are in
conflict with these rules are placed upon a journalist.

A journalist ought not to be placed on tasks that are contrary to his conscience or
convictions.

The rules comprise all editorial materials (text and picture) published in the
written periodical press, in radio, television and remaining mass media.

The rules also comprise advertisements and publicity in the written periodical
press, in radio, in television and remaining mass media. The rules also comprise
advertisements and publicity in the written periodical press and the rest of the mass
media to the extent, where no special rules have been established.

The rules comprise persons mentioned and depicted, including deceased persons,
and also corporations and similar associations.

THE CONTENT OF THE CODE

A. CORRECT INFORMATION

1. It is the duty of the press to bring correct and prompt information. As far as possible it should be controlled whether the information is correct.
2. The sources of news should be treated critically, in particular when such statements may be coloured by personal interest or tortuous intention.
3. Information which may be prejudicial or insulting to somebody or detract from other persons' opinion of the person concerned shall be very closely checked.
4. Attacks and replies should, in cases in which doing so is reasonable, be published consecutively and in the same way.
5. It shall be made clear what is factual information and what are comments.
6. Headlines and intermediate headlines shall as regards form and substance be substantiated by the article or publication in question. The same rule shall apply to the so-called contents bills.
7. Incorrect information shall be corrected on the editor's own initiative if and as soon as knowledge of errors of importance in the published information is received. The correction shall be given such as a form that the readers are given an easy possibility of noticing the correction.

B. CONDUCT CONTRARY TO GOOD PRESS PRACTICE

1. Information which may violate the sanctity of private life shall be avoided unless an obvious interest requires press coverage. The individual man is entitled to protection of his personal reputation.
2. Suicides or attempted suicides should not be mentioned unless an obvious public interest requires or justifies press coverage, and in such a case the mention should be as considerate as possible.
3. Victims of crimes or accidents should be paid the greatest possible regard. The same rule applies to witnesses and the relatives of the persons concerned. Collection and reproduction of pictorial material shall be made in a considerate and tactful way.
4. There should be kept a clear dividing line between advertising and editorial text. Text and pictures occasioned by direct or indirect mercantile interests should be brought only if a clear journalistic criterion calls for publication.
5. Other people's confidence must not be abused. Special regard should be paid to persons who cannot be expected to realise the effects of their statements. Other people's feelings, ignorance, or failing self-control should not be abused.

C. COURT REPORTING

1. The general ethical rules for journalists mentioned under A and B should also apply to court reporting.
2. The rules for court reporting shall also apply to the preparatory steps of a lawsuit or a trial, including the preparation of criminal bases by the police and the prosecution.
3. Court reporting should be objective. At any stage of the preparation of lawsuits and trials and during the hearing by the court, the journalists should aim at a qualitatively equal representation of the points of view of the parties – in criminal cases the points of view of the counsel for the prosecution and the counsel for the

defence, respectively. A mention of a criminal case should be followed up by an account of the end of the case, whether this takes place in the form of a withdrawal of the charge, acquittal, or conviction.

4. The mention of persons' family history, occupation, race, nationality, creed, or membership of organisations should be avoided unless this has something directly to do with the case.

5. As long as a criminal case has not been finally decided or the charge has not been withdrawn, no information must be published which may obstruct the clearing up of the case, nor must pronouncements to the effect that a suspect or an accused is guilty be published. When a criminal case is mentioned, it shall clearly appear from the report whether the suspect/accused has declared himself guilty or not guilty.

6. To the widest possible extent a clear objective line shall be followed in deciding which cases shall be mentioned and in which cases the names of the persons involved shall be mentioned. A suspect's or an accused's names or other identification should be omitted if no public interest calls for the publication of the name.

7. Caution should be exercised in publishing statements to the effect that the police have been informed about a crime committed by a person mentioned by name. Such information should as a rule not be published, until the information to the police has resulted in the intervention of the police or the prosecution. This rule shall not apply, however, if the conduct which the police have been informed about is beforehand known in wide circles or is of considerable public interest, or if on the existing basis it must be assumed that the information to the police is solidly substantiated.

8. A suspect, accused, or convicted person shall be spared from having attention called to an earlier conviction if it is without importance in relation to the facts which he is suspected of, charged with, or convicted of. In connection with other news, the earlier criminal cases against a named person should, as a rule, not be mentioned.

United Kingdom: UK PCC

THE CODE

All members of the press have a duty to maintain the highest professional standards. This Code sets the benchmark for those ethical standards, protecting both the rights of the individual and the public's right to know. It is the cornerstone of the system of self-regulation to which the industry has made a binding commitment.

It is essential that an agreed code be honoured not only to the letter but in the full spirit. It should not be interpreted so narrowly as to compromise its commitment to respect the rights of the individual, nor so broadly that it constitutes an unnecessary interference with freedom of expression or prevents publication in the public interest.

It is the responsibility of editors and publishers to apply the Code to editorial material in both printed and online versions of publications. They should take care to ensure it is observed rigorously by all editorial staff and external contributors, including non-journalists, in printed and online versions of publications.

Editors should co-operate swiftly with the PCC in the resolution of complaints. Any publication judged to have breached the Code must print the adjudication in full and with due prominence, including headline reference to the PCC.

1   Accuracy
- i) The Press must take care not to publish inaccurate, misleading or distorted information, including pictures.
- ii) A significant inaccuracy, mis-leading statement or distortion once recognised must be corrected, promptly and with due prominence, and – where appropriate – an apology published.
- iii) The Press, whilst free to be partisan, must distinguish clearly between comment, conjecture and fact.
- iv) A publication must report fairly and accurately the outcome of an action for defamation to which it has been a party, unless an agreed settlement states otherwise, or an agreed statement is published.

2   Opportunity to reply
A fair opportunity for reply to inaccuracies must be given when reasonably called for.

3*   Privacy
- i) Everyone is entitled to respect for his or her private and family life, home, health and correspondence, including digital communications. Editors will be expected to justify intrusions into any individual's private life without consent.
- ii) It is unacceptable to photograph individuals in private places without their consent.

Note – Private places are public or private property where there is a reasonable expectation of privacy.

4*   Harassment
- i) Journalists must not engage in intimidation, harassment or persistent pursuit.
- ii) They must not persist in questioning, telephoning, pursuing or photographing individuals once asked to desist; nor remain on their property when asked to leave and must not follow them.
- iii) Editors must ensure these principles are observed by those working for them and take care not to use non-compliant material from other sources.

5   Intrusion into grief or shock
- i) In cases involving personal grief or shock, enquiries and approaches must be made with sympathy and discretion and publication handled sensitively. This should not restrict the right to report legal proceedings, such as inquests.
- ii) When reporting suicide, care should be taken to avoid excessive detail about the method used.

6*   Children
- i) Young people should be free to complete their time at school without unnecessary intrusion.
- ii) A child under 16 must not be interviewed or photographed on issues involving their own or another child's welfare unless a custodial parent or similarly responsible adult consents.
- iii) Pupils must not be approached or photographed at school without the permission of the school authorities.
- iv) Minors must not be paid for material involving children's welfare, nor parents or guardians for material about their children or wards, unless it is clearly in the child's interest.

v) Editors must not use the fame, notoriety or position of a parent or guardian as sole justification for publishing details of a child's private life.

7* Children in sex cases
1. The press must not, even if legally free to do so, identify children under 16 who are victims or witnesses in cases involving sex offences.
2. In any press report of a case involving a sexual offence against a child –
   i) The child must not be identified.
   ii) The adult may be identified.
   iii) The word 'incest' must not be used where a child victim might be identified.
   iv) Care must be taken that nothing in the report implies the relationship between the accused and the child.

8* Hospitals
i) Journalists must identify themselves and obtain permission from a responsible executive before entering non-public areas of hospitals or similar institutions to pursue enquiries.
ii) The restrictions on intruding into privacy are particularly relevant to enquiries about individuals in hospitals or similar institutions.

9* Reporting of crime
i) Relatives or friends of persons convicted or accused of crime should not generally be identified without their consent, unless they are genuinely relevant to the story.
ii) Particular regard should be paid to the potentially vulnerable position of children who witness, or are victims of, crime. This should not restrict the right to report legal proceedings.

10* Clandestine devices and subterfuge
i) The press must not seek to obtain or publish material acquired by using hidden cameras or clandestine listening devices; or by intercepting private or mobile telephone calls, messages or emails; or by the unauthorised removal of documents or photographs; or by accessing digitally-held private information without consent.
ii) Engaging in misrepresentation or subterfuge, including by agents or intermediaries, can generally be justified only in the public interest and then only when the material cannot be obtained by other means.

11 Victims of sexual assault
The press must not identify victims of sexual assault or publish material likely to contribute to such identification unless there is adequate justification and they are legally free to do so.

12 Discrimination
i) The press must avoid prejudicial or pejorative reference to an individual's race, colour, religion, sex, sexual orientation or to any physical or mental illness or disability.
ii) Details of an individual's race, colour, religion, sexual orientation, physical or mental illness or disability must be avoided unless genuinely relevant to the story.

13   Financial journalism
  i) Even where the law does not prohibit it, journalists must not use for their own profit financial information they receive in advance of its general publication, nor should they pass such information to others.
  ii) They must not write about shares or securities in whose performance they know that they or their close families have a significant financial interest without disclosing the interest to the editor or financial editor.
  iii) They must not buy or sell, either directly or through nominees or agents, shares or securities about which they have written recently or about which they intend to write in the near future.

14   Confidential sources
Journalists have a moral obligation to protect confidential sources of information.

15   Witness payments in criminal trials
  i)   No payment or offer of payment to a witness – or any person who may reasonably be expected to be called as a witness – should be made in any case once proceedings are active as defined by the Contempt of Court Act 1981.
       This prohibition lasts until the suspect has been freed unconditionally by police without charge or bail or the proceedings are otherwise discontinued; or has entered a guilty plea to the court; or, in the event of a not guilty plea, the court has announced its verdict.
  *ii) Where proceedings are not yet active but are likely and foreseeable, editors must not make or offer payment to any person who may reasonably be expected to be called as a witness, unless the information concerned ought demonstrably to be published in the public interest and there is an overriding need to make or promise payment for this to be done; and all reasonable steps have been taken to ensure no financial dealings influence the evidence those witnesses give. In no circumstances should such payment be conditional on the outcome of a trial.
  *iii) Any payment or offer of payment made to a person later cited to give evidence in proceedings must be disclosed to the prosecution and defence. The witness must be advised of this requirement.

16* Payment to criminals
  i) Payment or offers of payment for stories, pictures or information, which seek to exploit a particular crime or to glorify or glamorise crime in general, must not be made directly or via agents to convicted or confessed criminals or to their associates – who may include family, friends and colleagues.
  ii) Editors invoking the public interest to justify payment or offers would need to demonstrate that there was good reason to believe the public interest would be served. If, despite payment, no public interest emerged, then the material should not be published.

The public interest

There may be exceptions to the clauses marked * where they can be demonstrated to be in the public interest.

1. The public interest includes, but is not confined to:
    i)   Detecting or exposing crime or serious impropriety.
    ii) Protecting public health and safety.
    iii) Preventing the public from being misled by an action or statement of an individual or organisation.
2. There is a public interest in freedom of expression itself.
3. Whenever the public interest is invoked, the PCC will require editors to demonstrate fully how the public interest was served.
4. The PCC will consider the extent to which material is already in the public domain, or will become so.
5. In cases involving children under 16, editors must demonstrate an exceptional public interest to over-ride the normally paramount interest of the child.

Notes

1 See Nemeth, N (2003) *News Ombudsmen in America: Assessing an Experiment in Social Responsibility*, Westport, CT: Praeger, pp. 127–37, for a description of ombudsmen placed in broadcasters and Internet in North America.
2 Among the many compilations available see Aznar, H (1999) *Etica y Periodismo: Códigos, estatutos y otros documentos de autorregulación*, Barcelona: Paidós, and the following websites: Codes of ethics of various media organisations collected by the American Society of Newspaper Editors: www.asne.org/ideas/codes/codes.htm; and more codes: http://jcomm.uoregon.edu/about/ethics/index.html
3 www.newsombudsmen.org/index.htm
4 www.media-accountability.org
5 For a general definition applicable worldwide, see: www.presscouncils.org/html/frameset.php?page=index
6 Bertrand, Claude-Jean (2002) *Arsenal of Democracy: Media Accountability Systems*, chapter 'M*A*S in France', Creskill, NJ: Hampton Press.
7 Frank Cullen, Co-ordinating Director, National Newspapers of Ireland (NNI), in his address to the Conference to Consider the Report of the Legal Advisory Group on Defamation, 1 December 2003: www.nni.ie/presrel18.htm. The National Newspapers of Ireland is the representative body for Ireland's national newspapers, and Irish editions of UK national newspapers. The Office of the Press Ombudsman and the Press Council of Ireland have a website (www.presscouncil.ie). Appointments are currently being made (website last visited June 2007).
8 McGonagle, M (2003) *Media Law*, Dublin: Thomson Round Hall, 2nd edn, at p. 170.
9 It should be acknowledged that particularly the section on on-line newspapers benefited from informal conversations with members of press councils and newspaper ombudsmen from many countries, newspaper in-house lawyers and lawyers whom one of the authors met at the 6th Annual Meeting of AIPCE (Association of Independent Press Councils of Europe) in Nicosia, 7–8 October 2004, and at the ONO – Organisation of News Ombudsmen – Annual Conference in London, 22–25 May 2005.
10 A blog is 'a frequently updated web site consisting of personal observations, excerpts from other sources, etc., typically run by a single person, and usually with hyperlinks to other sites; an online journal or diary' (from Oxford English Dictionary, OED.com).
11 'A wiki is a type of website that allows users to add, remove, or otherwise edit and change most content very quickly and easily, sometimes without the need for registration. This ease of interaction and operation makes a wiki an effective tool for collaborative writing. The term wiki can also refer to the collaborative software itself (wiki engine) that facilitates the operation of such a website, or to certain specific wiki sites, including the computer science site (and original wiki), WikiWikiWeb, and the online encyclopedias such as Wikipedia' (from http://en.wikipedia.org/wiki/Wiki).

12 UK PCC website: www.pcc.org.uk/2002/statistics_review.html

13 Wassink, E (2004) 'Statistiken zum Jahr 2003', p. 303, in: *Deutscher Presserat 2004 Jahrbuch*, Constance: UVK, at p. 306: the council received 682 complaints in 2003.

14 Scherphuis, A G, 'Jaarverslag Raad voor de Journalistiek 2002', www.rvdj.nl/jaarv.html

15 Robertson, G and Nicol, A (2002) *Media Law*, Sweet & Maxwell, p. 681.

16 O'Malley, T and Soley, C (2000) *Regulating the Press*, London: Pluto, p. 141. For a report on the main arguments of the organisation's perspective on the matter see, for example, Byrne, Ciar (2002) 'Press self-regulation works, says PCC chief', *The Guardian*, 19 June, http://media.guardian.co.uk/Print/0,3858,4436867,00.html

17 The UK PCC's website: www.pcc.org.uk

18 Shivakumar, S, *Press Council of India*, background paper for the workshop on Press, Ethics and Law jointly organised by the Indian Society of Interdisciplinary Studies and Press Club, 23 and 24 March 1998, in Thiruvananthapuram, Kerala, India.

19 Website of the German Press Council: www.presserat.de/site/service/lang_english/ aufgabe/enghist.html. See also: Lutz Tillmanns, 'Media accountability in Germany: the German press council', in 'Organising Media Accountability', www.ejc.nl/hp/mas/tillmanns.html

20 Humphreys, P (1996) *Mass Media and Media Policy in Western Europe*, Manchester: Manchester University Press, p. 61. The German Press Council is currently considering the incorporation of non-industry membership.

21 See the website of the Department of Journalism and Ethics at Stockholm University: www.jmk.su.se/global03/project/ethics/sweden/swe2a.htm

22 Jigenius, P-A, 'Media Accountability in Sweden: The Swedish Press Ombudsman and Press Council', in *Organising Media Accountability*: www.ejc.nl/hp/mas/jigenius.html

23 Jimenez, R, 'Media Accountability in Spain: The Spanish Press Ombudsman', in *Organising Media Accountability*: www.ejc.nl/hp/mas/jimenez.html

24 http://periodistes.org/cic/cat/Protocol.htm (in Catalan) and www.periodistes.org/cic/ esp/Protocol.htm (in Spanish).

25 Aznar, H (1999) *Comunicación Responsable: Deontología y autorregulación de los medios*, Barcelona: Editorial Ariel, p. 215.

26 Belgian Press Council, description in English: www.rvdj.be/engels.php and www.iit.edu/ departments/csep/PublicWWW/codes/coe/jour-belgium.html (the Code in English translation is available at: www.rvdj.be/ethiek_code.php).

27 Voorhoof, D (2003) 'First Decision of Council for Journalism – No Infringement of Journalistic Ethics by Commercial Television', *IRIS* 6:7/11.

28 There were recommendations in other countries for the creation of statutory bodies. The Calcutt report, for example, recommended a statutory tribunal for the UK if self-regulation were to fail. The Press Complaints Tribunal envisaged would be able to award compensation (within statutory limitations unless complainant can show financial loss), and in privacy cases it would be able to restrain publication by injunction. The Chairman would be a judge or senior lawyer appointed by the Lord Chancellor. See: Review of Press Self-Regulation (Chairman Sir D Calcutt QC), Department of National Heritage, London: HMSO, Cm 2135, 1990. A summary of the report is available in the *Entertainment Law Review* (*Ent. L. R.* 1990, 1(5), E 84–86), full text on Westlaw.

29 Rules of the Luxembourg Press Council: www.press.lu/datas/info_ordre.html

30 Danish Press Council: www.pressenaevnet.dk/english/indhold.html

31 See, for example, The American Society of Newspaper Editors: 'Ethics Codes and Beyond (or Create a Good Code if You Don't Have One?): Here's a cookbook of the ingredients of codes currently used by 33 papers', www.asne.org/kiosk/editor/99.feb/steele1.htm; also, Frost, C (2002) *Media Ethics and Self-Regulation*, Harlow: Longman – see Chapter 6 'Codes of Conduct and Self-Regulation'.

32 Barendt, E and Hitchens, L (2000) *Media Law: Cases and Materials*, Harlow: Longman, at p. 404.

33 Thorgeirsdottir, Herdis (2003) *Journalism Worthy of the Name: A Human Rights Perspective on Freedom Within the Press*, Lund University, p. 463.

34   For a discussion of this point see Bertrand, Claude-Jean (2003) 'Media Accountability Systems (M*A*S)', paper delivered at the Hilary Term Seminar Series, Programme in Comparative Media Law and Policy (PCMLP), Centre for Socio-Legal Studies, *Enlightened Self Interest or Just PR? Self-Regulation in the Media and Communications Sectors*, 3 February, www. selfregulation.info/iapcoda/030203-bertrand.doc

35   Ritter, J A and Leibowitz, M (1974) 'Press Councils: The Answer to Our First Amendment Dilemma', *Duke Law Journal* 5, 845.

36   This graph was drawn by the authors to illustrate the idea of a 'pyramid' of accountability as expressed by Neil Nemeth (2000) 'How a Typical American Newspaper Handles Complaints', in: David Pritchard (ed.) *Holding the Media Accountable: Citizens, Ethics, and the Law*, Bloomington, IN: Indiana University Press, p. 43.

37   LaMay, Craig L (Rapporteur) (2001) *Journalism and Emerging Democracy: Lessons from Societies in Transition, A Report of the Aspen Institute International Roundtable on Journalism*, Washington, DC: The Aspen Institute, at p. 25.

38   See: Beales, I (2005) *The Editors' Codebook: The Handbook to the Editors' Code of Practice*, The Press Standards Board of Finance. This work provides interpretative help for applying (in-house, at a newspaper) the UK PCC's code of practice by linking the articles of the code of practice with examples drawn from the body of adjudications of the UK PCC.

39   'Regional Newspapers: The Cinderella of Print', *The Economist*, 21 May 2005, p. 34. The article addresses the apparent negative impact of the fact that younger people use the Internet for news on the sale of big national newspapers, while regional newspapers are flourishing.

40   German Press Council: www.presserat.de/index.shtml

41   See: www.jmk.su.se/global03/project/ethics/sweden/swe2e.htm, The Swedish Press Editorial Advertising Committee. The rules against editorial advertising are the third and last part of the Swedish code of ethics for press, radio and television. It resembles the second part, professional rules, in terms of integrity. But here it's about credibility not for the single journalist, but for the entire media. Material that is published on editorial pages should not have any commercial influence and the news organisation should not accept any gifts or free trips, according to the rules. These issues are monitored by the Swedish Press Editorial Advertising Committee. Six members and three substitutes are appointed by The Publisher's Club, The Swedish Union of Journalists and The Swedish Newspaper Publishers' Association. The committee meets about five times a year and every meeting ends up in a report compiling the cases. The report is sent to the Swedish Press Cooperation Council, consisting of the mentioned press organisations. It is also distributed to *Journalisten*, the union newspaper, and *Pressens Tidning*, the magazine of the Swedish Newspaper Publishers' Association, where it can be published.

42   The UK PCC will take complaints about the online versions of newspaper and magazines provided that the publication subscribes to the Code of Practice and the material is some-thing that is covered by the terms of the Code. However, readers should note that the Commission is not equipped to deal with complaints about all the services – such as inter-active chat rooms – that a newspaper or magazine website may offer. See: www.pcc.org. uk/complaint/faq.asp

43   For a definition of 'content host' see Collins, M (2001) *The Law of Defamation and the Internet*, Oxford University Press, at p. 157: 'the operators of computer systems on which Internet content, such as web pages and bulletin board postings, is stored'.

44   *Loutchansky* v. *Times Newspapers, Ltd* (2001) *EWCA Civ.* 1805, (2002) QB 783.

45   *Dow Jones & Co., Inc.* v. *Gutnick* (2002) *HCA* 56, 10 December 2002, and *Berezovsky* v. *Michaels* (2000) *EMLR* 643 (H.L. 2000).

46   Schulz, D A and Wimmer, K (August 2005) 'Jurisdiction over Internet Publishers', *MLRC*, Issue 3.

47   *Dow Jones & Co., Inc.* v. *Jameel* (2005) *EWCA Civ.* 75 (3 Feb. 2005).

48   Jempson, M, 'Untangling the World Wide Web – When Errors Hit the Information Superhighway', paper prepared for the ONO – Organisation of News Ombudsmen – Annual Conference, London, 22–25 May 2005. The author, who is the Director of The

MediaWise Trust, refers to a case in which the web amplified and reproduced an erroneous story resulting in harm to the person who originally was wrongly accused of a crime. The story in question appeared in the UK *Sunday Mirror* on 25 January 2004 accusing a Bosnian refugee living in Montenegro of involvement in child trafficking. In April 2005 the newspaper admitted its error in court and paid damages. However, the (erroneous) story had been disseminated extensively. It is extremely difficult to track down online references and let those websites know that the original story was wrong.

49   See the Cluetrain Manifesto (at Cluetrain.org).

50   Jarvis, Jeff (27 March 2006) 'Blogs must beware the siren call of the celebrity', *The Guardian*: http://media.guardian.co.uk/mediaguardian/story/0,1740131,00.html

51   See: Mattin, David (15 August 2005) 'We are changing the nature of news', *The Guardian*: http://media.guardian.co.uk/mediaguardian/story/0,1549057,00.html. Traditional media also venture into the blogosphere: 'Traditionally it's been a percolation from the top down. We want to see news that comes from the people, upwards. *I don't see citizen journalism replacing traditional news, but instead we'll have a reciprocal flow* [emphasis added]. Our method is a way of providing news that is much more responsive to attitudes and concerns out there in the world. Even the way we lay it out is indicative of that difference: we don't have an editor at a desk deciding that one story gets lots of space, and another hardly any.'

52   www.jdlasica.com/articles/OJR-ethics.html

53   Membership of the UK PCC: www.pcc.org.uk/about/comm_members.htm

54   Cookson, R (2004) 'Watching the Watchdog', in Jempson, M and Cookson, R (eds) *Satisfaction Guaranteed? Press Complaints Systems Under Scrutiny*, Bristol: Mediawise, at p. 51.

55   Shannon, R (2001) *A Press Free and Responsible: Self-Regulation and the Press Complaints Commission 1991–2001*, London: John Murray, at p. 336.

56   See: www.jsn.fi/english/council.html#members

57   The Dutch Press Council: www.rvdj.nl/summ.html

58   Aznar, H (1999), op. cit., at p. 214.

59   Humphreys, P (1996), op. cit., p. 61.

60   Directive 2003/6/EC of the European Parliament and of the Council of 28 January 2003 on insider dealing and market manipulation (market abuse). Art. 22. www.europarl.eu. int/comparl/econ/lamfalussy_process/market_abuse_directive/market_abuse.pdf

61   See the joint consultation document produced by the UK's Treasury and Financial Services Authority: *UK Implementation of the EU Market Abuse Directive (Directive 2003/6/EC)*, June 2004, at p. 16. www.fsa.gov.uk/pubs/other/eu_mad.pdf. See also text of speech by Tim Toulmin, Director of the PCC, to the European Newspaper Publishers' Association on 29/04/2005, www.pcc.org.uk/press/detail.asp?id=156

62   Fact Sheet: Market Abuse, European Publishers Council. www.epceurope.org/factsheets/marketabuse.shtml

63   In the UK courts have addressed privacy cases on which there were adjudications taken by the self-regulatory body UK PCC. *Anna Ford* v. *Press Complaints Commission* (2001) *EWHC* Admin 683; *Campbell* v. *MGN Ltd* (2002) *HRLR* 28; and *R.* v. *Press Complaints Commission*, ex p. Stewart-Brady (1997) *EMLR* 185, Court of Appeal, Civil Division (LEXIS). See also: Pinker, R (2002) 'Press Freedom and Press Regulation – Current Trends in their European Context', *Communications Law* 7(4), 102–7, at pp. 103–4.

64   In *James Rupert Russell Mawdsley* v. *Guardian Newspapers Ltd* (2002) *WL* 31523276 (QBD), (2002) *EWHC* 1780, Morland J recognises at para. 34 the role of the Readers' Editor of the newspaper: '. . . Mr Mayes [*the newspaper's ombudsman*] carried out his role in relation to Mr Mawdsley's complaint honourably, independently and competently.' See also the article by Clare Dyer in *The Guardian*, 25 July 2002, www.guardian.co.uk/uk_news/story/0,3604,762719,00.html. In the case *Campbell-James* v. *Guardian Media Group Plc* (2005) *EWHC* 893 (QB), (2005) *All ER* (D) 161, the offer of amends was accepted but the apology was deemed late by the court, and hence the reduction on the award was less.

5 Mechanisms for self-regulation in the broadcasting sector in the European Union

For historical reasons, broadcasting is a heavily state-regulated sector, particularly in Europe in which there is also, on the one hand, self-regulation or self-monitoring by means of internal bodies at public service broadcasters (PSBs), as a way of implementing independence by keeping distance from the government of the day, and on the other, self-regulating islands in the commercial sector. Increased complexity in terms of more services brought about first by cable and satellite, and then digital technologies, has forced changes in the regulatory environment; the authorities felt the need to delegate more and more tasks of supervision to lower levels.[1] Therefore, we are witnessing a shift to self-regulation within a general context of a complex, co-regulatory environment. Self-regulation could be resorted to instead of government regulation to avoid constitutional free-speech issues when regulating more stringently than the requirements of statutory regulators. For example, by performing pre-publication control as carried out for the protection of minors by the FSF[2] in Germany and similar bodies in other countries. The trend is towards continued delegation. The regulatory environment thus created is one that permits the tasks of supervision of content to be discharged by increasingly autonomous mechanisms. The authorities retain supervision at a higher level (broad guidelines, judicial review, etc.).

Technological advances keep constantly challenging regulatory models. The phenomenon of the citizen journalist who is able to bypass the editorial control of content challenges the traditional model of broadcast media with an emerging amateur zone – technology allows anyone with access to Internet and low-cost equipment (e.g. a mobile phone with the ability to record audio and video) the capacity to reach many, as it became patently obvious in 2005:

> [T]he 7 July London bombings and the hurricanes in the US forced home the fact that citizens had a much larger role in the production of news than ever before. These collages of eyewitness accounts showed the immediate aftermath of the events long before any press camera could.[3]

Moreover, the growth of citizen journalism introduces the question of how the existing model for broadcasting will change. A post-broadcasting world may be one in which technology encourages a division between professional and amateur zones. As it is increasingly the case in the print media world, access to the 'one to many' media will become more widespread: 'You don't own the press, which is now divided into pro and amateur zones. You don't control production on the new platform, which isn't one-way. There's a new balance of power between you and us. "You" being big media.'[4] The regulatory regime will need, therefore, further adaptation.

Introduction: areas open for self-regulation in the broadcasting sector

In analysing broadcasting codes of conduct, the purpose was to review areas in which recent changes in the regulatory framework of broadcasting allow for further self-regulation in an area which has traditionally been highly regulated.[5] We review available mechanisms for regulation of the 'professional' broadcast media in both the PSB sector and in commercial broadcasting. In all the countries of the European Union there are special authorities responsible for licensing and supervising broadcasting. Most of the 15 countries surveyed have a long tradition of PSB, and the tendency across the countries of the European Union is to have separate regulators for commercial and PSB.

In the case of France and Italy, however, the (statutory) regulator for commercial channels has some limited competences over public service broadcasting. The regulatory bodies responsible for general supervision and licensing may be separate or combined in one regulator. These bodies enjoy a degree of autonomy from the government regarding the formulation and enforcement of programme standards.

Public service broadcasting is financed by taxation in most EU member states, and provided by a PSB – normally a statutory corporation. We use the term PSB here to refer to the corporation responsible for such programming. Where we refer to terrestrial free-to-air (FTA) broadcasters who receive no public financing, but whose licences nevertheless contain public service obligations, we do use the term 'PSB'. The European Commission has conducted extensive investigations into the legal definition of a PSB under the competition rules of the Treaty of Rome, as redefined in part by Protocol 32 to the Treaty of Amsterdam 1997.[6]

Sometimes regulators are assigned the enforcement of anti-trust rules in the interest of media pluralism (e.g. in the United Kingdom the former ITC[7] was required to ensure fair and effective competition in the provision of private broadcasting services, but the Director-General of Fair Trading and the Monopolies and Mergers Commission determined whether networking arrangements meet the requirements of competition law). The focus of this study is, however, on content regulation.

A general principle observed in all countries surveyed is that if a regulated commercial broadcasting sector is to be independent from the state the regulatory authority(ies) must be autonomous from government. Similarly, PSBs are also organised in ways to be independent from the government of the day. Hoffman-Riem[8] points out that legal forms offer little indication of the influence exerted in fact by the authorities. The independence of broadcasters could be entrenched in law, as it is the case in some of the German states. Or, in the case of the United Kingdom, even though independence may not be written in the law as such, the political culture points in the direction that government does not exercise powers that it may enjoy. Governments exercise important supervisory functions over regulators by, for example, selecting the main personnel and making financial decisions in some cases. But the experience in the countries studied in this report is that the individual regulatory body's independence rests in fact with rules concerning the composition and appointment of its members.

Self-regulation in the public service sector

Independence of the PSBs in most European countries is safeguarded by allowing PSBs in the member states to monitor themselves. PSBs are created by statute and are public law entities whose self-regulation aims at creating space between the broadcaster and the government. The monitoring takes place via internal bodies that control the PSB. In addition, independence may be fostered by the funding arrangements in place, such as the BBC's licence fees charged to UK viewers.

The composition of the bodies in charge of controlling the PSBs varies across the member states of the European Union. In some countries those bodies include representatives of social groups. Consider a few examples in which we see the different approaches of different societies to the general idea stated above.

Austria: The Austrian Broadcasting Company (ORF) self-regulates via four controlling bodies: the Board of Trustees, the General Overseer, the Committee of Viewers and Listeners and the Board of Inspection. In performing their duties the members of these boards are not subject to directives or orders from the government. The appointments, however, are made by the government following rules to ensure representation of different sectors. The 35 members of the Board of Trustees are appointed by the federal government in proportion to the political parties' fractions in the National Council and taking into consideration the candidates proposed by the parties. Nine members are appointed by the states that make up Austria, and a further nine are appointed by the federal government. Of the remaining 11, six are appointed by the Committee of Viewers and Listeners, and five are appointed by the Central Workers' Council. There is a requirement that other than the trustees representing political parties none of the other members should be a member or in employment at a political party.

The controlling function performed by the Board of Trustees is performed by approval of programme guidelines, production guidelines, etc., which the Director General prepares. The Director General, in turn, is appointed by the Board of Trustees, and is not bound to orders from the government. The role of the Director General is to manage the broadcaster and represent it.

To represent the interests of the audience, the Committee of Viewers and Listeners of 35 members has appointees chosen by the following organisations: the Federal Chamber of Commerce, the Conference of Presidents of the Agricultural Chambers of Austria, the Austrian Workers Congress, the Austrian Trade Unions Congress, the professional chambers of self-employed people, the Roman Catholic and the Protestant churches, etc. This Committee makes recommendations on programming and approves the level of licence fees paid by Austrian viewers and listeners.

Denmark: The Danish Broadcasting Law establishes that Danmarks Radio is managed by a board of 11 members which, although they are appointed by the government, have full decision-making powers over the broadcaster. The board formulates the general guidelines for activities of the broadcaster; it appoints the General Director as well as senior management. The Director General has responsibility for programming.

The PSB in Denmark operates in the regulatory environment created by the amended Broadcasting Law[9] which entered into force on 1 January 2003. This law gives a right to provide programme services as follows:

1   by the law itself in the case of the PSBs, which are two, one is Danmarks Radio and the other is TV2;[10]

2   by a system of licensing commercial services supervised by the Radio and Television Board (a regulator set up by the Minister of Culture);

3   by commercial services registered with the Radio and Television Board[11] (cable-network distribution of programmes does not require a licence or even registration with the Radio and Television Board).[12]

Germany: In the German system, federalism requires that the states of the federation have all responsibility for culture and media and there is no centralised regulatory authority at a federal level.[13] The two PSBs (ARD and ZDF) have managing councils independent from government. The federalism as brought into the broadcasting system of Germany means, in the case of the control of ZDF, that a broadcasting council is set up in which all the federal states that make up Germany are represented on an equal footing. On the other hand, the individual broadcasters of the ARD network are supervised by separate broadcasting councils, each with a membership between 19 and 77. Members are appointed for a term of four to nine years. As in the case of Austria and Denmark, various civil society groups have representation, such as churches, journalistic and cultural organisations, universities and unions. Other members are elected by the state legislatures, but the number of the nominees of the political parties does not exceed one-third of all members. The broadcasting councils have controlling powers such as:

1   the approval of programming principles and monitoring compliance;
2   the nomination of top management;
3   financing.[14]

United Kingdom: The BBC is a public corporation set up by Royal Charter[15] which regulates aims, competences, duties, constitution, sources of income and use of that income. In order to self-regulate the BBC relies on a variety of instruments and codes, such as the Royal Charter and a Complementary Licence and Agreement[16] signed between the BBC and the Secretary of State for Culture, Media and Sport, which gives more detail on how the BBC is to fulfil its duties.[17] The current Agreement and Charter came into force in January 2007.[18] It sets out a new regulatory framework for BBC self-regulation, and specifies new general aims and purposes for BBC public services. In particular the traditional self-regulatory scheme for the BBC – under which most content-related issues were dealt with internally by the BBC Governors – has been replaced by a more complex arrangement: the BBC Trust replaced the Governors and operates with more independence from the BBC, and Ofcom and the Trust are responsible for reviewing new BBC services before they are launched. A key aim of the reforms was to ensure separation of management and regulatory functions, and thus more effective regulation of the BBC than was provided by self-regulation.

The BBC is controlled by a Board of Governors or 'Trust' with 12 members appointed by the government. Among those members there is a chairman, a vice chairman and the national governors for Scotland, Wales and Northern Ireland.

The Trust has two duties in regulation of the BBC: it defines corporate strategy and acts as trustees of the public interest. They approve targets of BBC services and monitor its performance, and are responsible for ensuring that the public funding received through the licence fee is spent correctly. They appoint the BBC's senior staff.

Self-regulation of the BBC takes place via the direct accountability to the public of the Trust. The Trust each year publishes a statement of the goals, standards and services which viewers and listeners may expect, and once a year the Trust reports on how well the BBC has kept its promises. The BBC is also under parliamentary scrutiny, as it is required to present every year an annual report and accounts, must obtain Parliament's approval for the licence fee, etc.[19] (Since the Hutton Inquiry in 2003–4 these governance arrangements have come under increasing scrutiny. The previous chairman has published a discussion paper on changes to the arrangements and an internal review was conducted alongside the review of the Charter and Agreement.)

The Welsh Fourth Channel Authority (S4C) is a corporation under public law, whose purpose and functions are laid out in the Broadcasting Acts 1990 and 1996. S4C is controlled by a Board appointed by the Secretary of State for Culture, Media and Sport, which is responsible for defining the strategy of S4C and ensuring that the legal requirements are met. S4C is accountable to the public via the Board, which is also subject to parliamentary scrutiny.

In Ireland, the PSB also self-regulates,[20] and applies a number of codes for this purpose.[21]

Self-regulation in the commercial sector

Across the EU countries commercial broadcasting is a relatively new phenomenon, as broadcasting, unlike print media (understood as newspapers, not books), started as a state monopoly (with the sole exception of Luxembourg where there was never public sector broadcasting, although there have always been public service obligations imposed on RTL, the broadcaster, which has always been a commercial organisation).

The current regulatory 'geography' reveals an atmosphere of 'mixed' public service and commercial systems in Europe in which broadcasters are subject to a variety of more or less demanding regimes.[22] Statutory regulatory bodies find it increasingly difficult to cope with the sheer volume of material that they are responsible for regulating. Where regulators have a responsibility for detailed monitoring and reporting on media content, the trend has been towards a 'lighter touch regulation', i.e. more of the regulatory responsibilities are taken on by the producers and users of content rather than law or regulatory bodies of statutory creation. On the other hand not only are the means of regulation under challenge, but the justifications of regulation are undermined, as many argue that in an 'ecology' of more media, it becomes increasingly less justifiable to have central regulatory supervision of content. In this context, self-regulatory codes of practice are becoming the preferred solution in certain areas, as we see in the survey of the 15 member countries of the European Union.

Self-regulatory bodies operating in the commercial sector

Germany: The Freiwillige Selbstkontrolle Fernsehen e.V., FSF (Voluntary Television Review Body) is an organisation whose main concern is the protection of minors in relation to the representation of violence and sex on television and its effects on the recipients. The FSF was founded in 1993 by the largest German commercial broadcasters, as a response to a public outcry about the depiction of violence and sex on television.[23] It started its activities in 1994. The activities of the FSF are mainly the examination of programmes for their content of violence and sex and to produce guidelines on the content of daytime talkshows,[24] as well as fostering media education[25] aimed at the protection of minors.

The FSF exists to ensure that there is child protection over and above the limits set out in ordinary law.[26] It performs this task by means of pre-publication review. Under German law, a statutory regulator could not operate along the lines of the FSF. A regional Landesmedienanstalten (LMA, a public agency entrusted with the task of licensing and supervising commercial broadcasting), for example, cannot control content before publication because of the constitutional protection of freedom of speech and the ban on censorship.[27] In the restricted area of its jurisdiction, the pre-publication review of the FSF represents a more stringent content control than otherwise permissible in the environment of statutory regulation of commercial broadcasting.

The FSF has approximately 100 examiners, and films are examined by boards of five to seven people. Films are submitted to the FSF by the broadcasters indicating how they propose to broadcast (time, cuts if any, etc.). Decisions by that first board can be re-examined by a second board in case of appeal (by broadcasters, LMAs, the board of trustees of the FSF or those who sell programme licences to a broadcaster member of the system).[28] The decisions are made available to the LMAs. Assessment procedures in use at FSF are monitored by a committee of independent experts. In 2003 the FSF was approved by the KJM (an interstate regulatory commission for the implementation of the 2003 Interstate Treaty on the Protection of Minors and Human Dignity in the Media) for a period of four years.[29]

The decisions of the FSF are compulsory and can take various shapes: establish a time after which broadcast can proceed, or order cuts or not to broadcast at all. In its first decade of operation the FSF examined 56,569 titles. In 2,168 cases the examining board did not agree with the channel's request: in 981 cases, cuts were required to be made; 906 titles were approved for broadcasting, but only at a later time than applied for; 114 films were approved on condition of a later broadcasting time and further cuts; 167 titles were not allowed to be broadcast.[30]

The FSF operates in the legal environment for commercial broadcasting in which the fundamental rights of freedom of information and freedom of broadcasting as interpreted by the German Constitutional Court underpin the system.[31] Private broadcasters are bound by certain minimum standards with regard to balance and the expression of pluralism of views. These are controlled, however, after publication. Each German state has created an LMA. Private broadcasters intending to broadcast nationally, or to a limited geographic area (state, region or local) must be licensed by the LMAs having jurisdiction over the area(s) for which the licence is sought. Licensing requirements are set out in the Interstate Treaty on Broadcasting and in the 15 state media statutes for private broadcasting passed by each individual state (as regards PSBs, there are also 15 statutes). The state treaty sets out requirements of protection of pluralism and a balance of views and limits the number of channels each private broadcaster can control. The treaty also limits the interest a company may hold in a private broadcaster of national reach.[32]

Canada: Established in 1926, the Canadian Association of Broadcasters (CAB) represents the vast majority of Canada's private television and radio stations, including pay and pay-per-view services. Its main objective is to create, maintain and improve voluntary codes of conduct. Codes are administered by the Canadian Broadcast Standard Council (CBSC), an independent body created by the CAB in 1991, which is also responsible for dealing with public complaints about radio and television content. In spite of the voluntary nature of these codes, the Canadian

Radio-Television and Telecommunications Commission (CRTC), a regulator in the electronic media sector, requires, in certain instances, their adherence as one of the conditions of the broadcasting licence. In order to address concerns highlighted by the public and CRTC, the CAB has developed the following codes: Code of Ethics, CAB Voluntary Code Regarding Violence in Television Programming, CAB Sex-Role Portrayal Code for Radio and Television Programming and The Broadcast Code for Advertising to Children.

The first version of the Violence Code was adopted by the CAB in 1987. Four years later, Ms. Lariviere, a 13-year-old from Quebec, convinced that violence in programming contributed to the brutal rape and death of her younger sister, began a crusade against violence on television. Her petition, signed by over 1.3 million people, instigated the CAB to rewrite the Code.

Italy: In 2002 public and private broadcasters agreed to a 'self-regulatory code of conduct on television and minors' to protect minors from harmful content. In January 2003 a Supervisory Committee was set up. This system works within the statutory control in place, and to ensure compliance, the Supervisory Committee can refer non-compliance cases to AGCOM, the statutory regulator.[33]

Finland: In order to fulfil the requirements of protection of minors set out in the regulatory regime for television, broadcasters have agreed on a framework for the classification of programmes regarding their suitability for children as regards the depiction of violence and sex on television.[34]

Sweden: The Våldsskildrings rådet (Council on Media Violence) supports and stimulates the industry's efforts regarding self-regulation.[35] As in the example mentioned above, this organisation operates within the regulated environment of commercial broadcasting. The Swedish Ministry of Culture is responsible for the technical aspects of broadcasting and the Radio and Television Authority is in charge of awarding licences.[36] As is the case of all of the countries surveyed, award of a licence leads to demands on programme content, impartiality and diversity, which are requirements placed on the PSB and the only commercial television broadcaster already active on analogue terrestrial television.[37]

Netherlands: NICAM – *Nederlands Instituut voor de Classificatie van de Audiovisuele Media* (Netherlands Institute for the Classification of Audio-visual Media)[38] – is discussed in other chapters. Commercial broadcasting was first introduced in the Netherlands in 1992; however, Dutch commercial broadcasters had been operating from Luxembourg long before that date.[39] There is one regulator, Commissariaat voor de Media,[40] which is a statutory regulator.

United Kingdom: Before 2004, self-regulation took the shape of two industry bodies which carried out clearance activities for advertising submissions before commercials are broadcast: the Broadcast Advertising Clearing Centre (BACC) for television and the Radio Advertising Clearing Centre (RACC), while complaints were heard by the statutory regulator.[41] Since the end of 2004, broadcast advertising content regulation has been transferred, by contract, to a system established under the umbrella of the Advertising Standards Authority (ASA), the so-called one-stop-shop system. Under the Deregulation and Contracting Out Act 1994 (DCOA) the UK Parliament approved these changes. Even after the functions have been contracted out, Ofcom will be ultimately accountable under the DCOA for anything done, or not done, by the ASA(B) or BCAP (Broadcast Committee of Advertising Practice) in respect of the contracted out functions.[42]

More generally, legal and regulatory definitions will be adapted to a landscape of *regulatory* convergence as *technical* convergence becomes more and more of a reality in

the United Kingdom (and throughout the European Union). Service-based definitions (audiovisual service, etc.) are to be expected instead of definitions that are
network and platform based (digital broadcasting, mobile telephony, etc.). This trend
is visible in the UK regulatory regime introduced by the Communications Act 2003,
which aims to implement the EU communications framework.[43]

Accession countries: Poland – The National Broadcasting Council and the broadcasters prepared a 'Catalogue of Rules Underlying the Rating of TV Programmes
Intended for Various Age Groups of Children and Adolescents' and the signatories
established a standing Commission to control implementation.[44] Due to the broadcasters' non-compliance, the National Broadcasting Council, in order to implement
the rule,[45] has issued a regulation containing detailed methods of age and content-
based rating systems.

Self-regulation of journalistic ethics in the commercial sector

We have seen in Chapter 4 that a few press councils extend their code of conduct
(which addresses issues of journalistic ethics) to television and radio journalism. The
Finnish Code (and the mechanism of the Council for Mass Media) as well as the
Catalan Media Council and its code of ethics can be resorted to in cases of breaches
of professional standards in the print or the broadcast media.

In December 2002 the council of ethics of the Association of Journalists was
replaced by a press council in the Dutch-speaking part of Belgium. As in the case of
its Finnish and the Catalan counterparts, this council can hear complaints on alleged
breaches of rules of ethics by journalists in the print and the broadcast media. On its
board, journalists, print media broadcasters and broadcasters are represented. Its
decisions are published but the council has no disciplinary powers.[46]

Although the code of ethics applied by the Swedish Press Council and the Press
Ombudsman covers journalistic ethics in other media, these two bodies do not deal
with possible breaches of the rules in radio or television. Those breaches will be dealt
with by the broadcasting regulator.

Areas in the commercial sector in which the (self-)regulatory burden is taken on by the producers and users of content

Self-regulatory codes of practice in which more of the regulatory burden is taken on
by the producers and users of content (rather than statute or regulatory bodies of statutory creation) are becoming the preferred solution. In the United Kingdom, the
Communications Act[47] contemplates broadcasters preparing statements of
programme policy and monitoring their own performance. Already in 2001 the
popularly known 'Contracts with Viewers'[48] or statements of programming commitment[49] were being published on behalf of broadcasters, when the UK government
envisaged in the White Paper 'A New Future for Communications' a move towards
greater self-regulation.

Advertising[50] is an area in which there is scope for self-regulation in the broadcast
media.[51] There are precedents in other European countries (e.g. Italy[52]), and in the
UK print media where the ASA[53] has been in operation for many years. As noted
above, the ASA has covered the regulation of broadcast advertising under a system of
co-regulatory partnership with Ofcom since November 2004.[54]

Conclusions

Broadcasting is a digital media sector in which technological progress brought increased levels of complexity to a relatively stable licensing scheme, and policy changes have been in part responding to those changes. The European monopolistic model in which broadcasting developed with radio in the early twentieth century, and which was maintained with the advent of television, was first challenged by the opening of commercial services. The trend is towards continued delegation with the rise of digital. The regulatory environment thus created is one that permits the tasks of supervision of content to be discharged by increasingly autonomous mechanisms. The authorities retain supervision at a higher level (broad guidelines, judicial review, etc.), while industry bodies are increasingly involved with the day-to-day task of implementing codes of conduct.

The findings point to a heavily regulated sector in which there is, on the one hand, self-regulation or self-monitoring by means of internal bodies at PSBs, as a way of implementing independence from the government of the day, and, on the other, a commercial sector supervised by statutory regulators that apply a variety of codes which are imposed on licensees directly through a licence condition on the use of the electromagnetic spectrum. Breach of these codes of conduct will result in direct and heavy sanctions such as fines, the removal of the licence to broadcast, the obligation to broadcast apologies, and in some cases provision of a right to reply.

A few examples of self-regulatory bodies were identified for the commercial sector, which were mainly concerned with protecting minors. However, although their role is expanding, it is at present concentrated on areas located in the periphery of regulation, as they are also covered by the codes attached to the licence conditions, or in areas in which the authorities delegate and decision making is made at a lower level (for example, broadcasters self-police their programming duties). Self-regulation could be used instead of government regulation to avoid constitutional free speech issues when regulating more stringently; for example, by performing pre-publication control as carried out for the protection of minors by the FSF in Germany and similar bodies in other countries.

Convergence, and the great number and variety of channels and services available, seem to be opening up the field for more reliance on self-regulation: the environment makes supervision more difficult for statutory regulators as it becomes increasingly onerous to supervise all those new additional channels and services. Areas such as advertising, where there are precedents in self-regulation in other media, may come to broadcasting in the near future.

While in the past the detailed objectives of regulation were set out in legislation (and/or the licensing agreements signed with commercial broadcasters), in the future it is likely that more countries will move to a system that gives more autonomy to the industry for developing detailed objectives, within broad guidelines defined in statutory form. Whilst broadcasting remains a distinct service, however, these self-regulatory codes act within an existing spectrum licensing scheme in all cases. They provide self-regulatory 'islands' within a complex co-regulatory framework, therefore, with backstop powers remaining in the hands of the regulator.

Broadcasting convergence case study: the Association for Television on Demand

With the gradual rise of broadband provision via digital subscriber lines (DSL), several new players entered the audiovisual market post 2000, offering combinations of broadband service provision with on-demand television content, telephony in some cases, and premium video content. HomeChoice for example in the United Kingdom has achieved steady market growth, and with major telcos such as British Telecom entering the market a significant part of the European audiovisual market will be taken by such on-demand services. This develops a market segment that is an example par excellence of the regulatory challenges thrown up by convergence: what content standards, if any, should be applied, and what regulatory framework is appropriate for a service with niche audience, potential for increased consumer control, and a subscription model?

Ofcom signalled a reluctance to apply broadcast codes to on-demand services. In discussions between the relevant government department (DCMS) and representatives of the on-demand industry, it was made clear to the industry that video on demand (VOD) would remain outside the scope of the new broadcasting regime on the understanding that VOD operates an effective self-regulatory regime. Since then UK VOD providers have established the Association for Television on Demand (ATVOD).

ATVOD is a self-regulatory body, established to regulate the provision of on-demand programming, which emerged in the United Kingdom during the passage of the UK Communications Bill in 2002. According to ATVOD it:

> arose through the twin appreciations that: on-demand broadband services were based on a one-to-one connection between the viewer and the service provider, in contrast to the relationship between a broadcaster and its viewers; and in consequence, the world of linear broadcast regulation was not best suited for emerging on-demand services. (Andrea Millwood Hargrave, personal correspondence 2005)

As is clear from the ATVOD code, reproduced below, the framework is narrowly conceived as a mechanism for ensuring that children are protected, through the provision of password protection and that transparent standards are maintained. The code also provides for increased consumer self-regulation through clear labelling. The code makes reference to existing Ofcom codes as establishing benchmarks which can be referred to when establishing labelling of potentially offensive content. The interest for the industry in establishing the scheme is clear: if it is effective, VOD will be free of detailed statutory requirements for content.

The Association for Television on Demand

Code of Practice

Adopted 9 June 2004

Glossary

'Appeals Procedure'	means the Procedure of the ATVOD Independent Appeals Commission set out in Appendix 1
'Children'	means those aged 15 or under
'Customers'	means Subscribers and Viewers

'Broadcasting Regulatory Codes'	means (a) the ITC Code of Advertising Standards and Practice and (b) the ITC Programme Code, each as modified, amended, supplemented, consolidated, extended or replaced from time to time whether by the ITC or by OFCOM
'ITC'	means the Independent Television Commission
'OFCOM'	means the Office of Communications
'On-demand Provider'	means the operator of an On-demand Service. For the purposes of this definition, the operation of an On-demand Service shall include but not be limited to the aggregation, storage and delivery of video and audio programming and other content by means of an On-demand Service but shall exclude the *solus* operation of a telecommunications network (of any nature whether by cable, wireless or otherwise) over which an On-demand Service is delivered to Subscribers
'On-demand Service'	means a service where video and audio programming, commercial transactions, information and other consumer benefits are provided over a telecommunications network (of any nature whether by cable, wireless or otherwise) for reception at different times to the premises of individual Subscribers in response to requests made by individual Customers
'Procedures of the ATVOD Appeals Commission'	means the procedures adopted by the ATVOD Appeals Commission from time to time
'Subscriber'	means an account holder with an On-demand Provider (or its agent) authorized under contract to receive that party's On-demand Service
'Viewer'	means a viewer of an On-demand Service at the premises of a Subscriber
'VOD'	means Video-on-demand
'ATVOD Independent Appeals Commission'	means a body whose members are independent of ATVOD appointed to provide an independent means of appeal against adjudications and sanctions determined by the ATVOD Board pursuant to the ATVOD Complaints Procedure
'Young People'	means those aged 16 or 17

The Code of Practice

1   Introduction

1.1   On-demand Providers are committed to delivering a broad range of high-quality consumer services across the United Kingdom.

2   ATVOD and the Code

Remit and Scope of the Code

2.1   This Video-On-Demand Code of Practice (***the Code***) shall govern the conduct of the members of the UK Association for Television on Demand (**ATVOD**) in relation to their provision of On-demand Services within the United Kingdom.

2.2   The members of ATVOD (**Members**) shall be the signatories to the Code from time to time and each Member shall ensure maintenance of the standards and adherence to the Core Principles (defined below) contained within this Code. Membership of ATVOD shall be open to On-demand Providers whose services are available for reception within the UK (**Full Members**) and, on an associate basis, operators of telecommunications networks over which On-demand Services are distributed and suppliers of programming for On-demand Services (**Associate Members**).

2.3   The application of this Code shall be uniform and obligatory to all Members without modification or exception. A Member may not, by contract or otherwise, evade the application of the Code.

The ATVOD Board

2.4   The Members shall establish and maintain a regulatory body (**the ATVOD Board**) to administer and enforce this Code. The ATVOD Board shall be entitled to establish an administrative capability (**the Secretariat**) to facilitate the ATVOD Board's activities and its compliance with its obligations under the Code.

2.5   All Members will be obliged to share the costs incurred by the ATVOD Board and Secretariat. The funding formula shall require unanimous agreement by the ATVOD Board.

2.6   The ATVOD Board shall have a maximum of eleven Members and shall comprise an independent chairman (**the Chairman**), and two individuals independent of the Members, unconnected with the provision of On-demand Services, and selected, as far as possible, to reflect a diversity of background and experience, one representative of each Full Member and, for every four Full Members, one representative collectively appointed by the Associate Members. The Chairman and two independent individuals shall work on a part-time basis and shall be appointed by ATVOD for an agreed period.

2.7   The ATVOD Board and Members shall procure that, by no later than the fifth anniversary of the coming into force of the Code, a majority of the ATVOD Board shall comprise individuals independent of the Members. Such individuals shall be unconnected with the provision of On-demand Services and selected, as far as possible, to reflect a diversity of background and experience. They shall work on a part-time basis and shall be appointed by ATVOD for an agreed period.

2.8   The ATVOD Board shall:

(a)   set and maintain standards and, as appropriate, Core Principles and ATVOD Practice Statements (defined below) for the content of On-demand Services, and keep those standards, Core Principles and ATVOD Practice Statements under review;

(b)   ensure adherence to the Code;

(c)   consult the Members and other stakeholders including but not limited to the Department for Culture, Media and Sport, (DCMS), before changing those standards, Core Principles or ATVOD Practice Statements specifically or the Code more generally;

(d)   investigate and adjudicate upon complaints relating to the content of

On-demand Services and recommend action designed to achieve compliance with the Code where the Code has been breached. Subject to the provisions of section 8.2, the administration of the Code shall be reactive only – the ATVOD Board will not monitor Members' activities for breaches of the Code;

(e) promote and publicise membership of ATVOD to potential new providers of On-demand Services and/or programmes within the United Kingdom and to notify DCMS from time to time of the identity of its members;

(f) promote and publicise to Customers and third parties the existence of ATVOD, the identity of its Members, the objectives of the Code and the complaints procedure set out herein; and

(g) generally promote and publicise its role and publish reports on its work at regular intervals, including but not limited to an annual report setting out its achievements, commenting on adherence to the Code over the preceding 12 months and summarising complaints received by Members and/or made subject to the ATVOD Complaints Procedure.

ATVOD Practice Statements, Broadcasting Regulatory Codes and Changes to the Code

2.9   The ATVOD Board may from time to time issue to every Member policy statements regarding matters relating to the regulation of On-demand Services in the UK. After due and proper consultation with all Members and other interested parties, the ATVOD Board may by simple majority adopt such policy statements as practice statements (***ATVOD Practice Statements***). ATVOD Practice Statements shall thereby be incorporated into the Code and be binding on Members. For the avoidance of doubt, ATVOD Practice Statements may not seek to amend the constitution of ATVOD, the Core Principles or the ATVOD Complaints Procedure.

2.10   Save to the extent addressed by ATVOD Practice Statements, ATVOD shall ensure that the provision by its Members of On-demand Services within the United Kingdom shall be provided in accordance with the Broadcasting Regulatory Codes prevailing from time to time. For the avoidance of doubt, in the event of a conflict between a ATVOD Practice Statement and the Broadcasting Regulatory Codes, the ATVOD Practice Statement shall take precedence.

2.11   Save as in accordance with section 2.9, the ATVOD Board may amend the Code, including without limitation, the constitution of ATVOD, the Core Principles and the ATVOD Complaints Procedure, from time to time following consultation with Members and other interested parties and on no less than two months' notice. In performing its duty to review the Code in general and the Core Principles in particular the ATVOD Board shall give consideration at regular intervals to (i) the relevance and application of the prevailing Broadcasting Regulatory Codes to On-demand Services and (ii) prevailing Customer expectations of such On-demand Services.

2.12   Any change to the Code made pursuant to section 2.11 shall be made by formal resolution at a meeting of the ATVOD Board. Such a resolution will require a two-thirds majority of all Members present and entitled to vote (which, for the avoidance of doubt, excludes abstentions). When considering the adoption of ATVOD Practice Statements or changes to the Code, each Member shall be entitled to one vote.

Adherence to the Code and General Law

2.13 Each Member agrees that it shall abide by the Code and any ATVOD Practice Statements issued pursuant to section 2.9.

2.14 For the avoidance of doubt, and save for any express provisions to the contrary, nothing in this Code shall be taken to suggest that this Code regulates and/or that the ATVOD Board will adjudicate on the legality or otherwise of material accessible on On-demand Services. Where a complaint concerns the legality of such material, the ATVOD Board will advise the complainant to contact the On-demand Provider of the relevant material directly.

2.15 On-demand Services must comply with the law: they must not contain anything which is in breach of the law, nor omit anything which the law requires. Members recognise that compliance with the Code does not necessarily guarantee that they are acting within the law.

3   Statement of Policy: The Core Principles

3.1 This Code is based on two core principles (**the Core Principles**):

(i) Members recognise their responsibility to assist Subscribers in their efforts to protect Children and Young People from unsuitable material;

(ii) Members recognise their responsibility to provide accurate, timely and reasonably prominent guidance in relation to their offerings of (a) content reasonably expected to cause significant offence or upset to some Customers and (b) commercial services.

3.2 Subject to the general provisions below and any Practice Statements issued by the ATVOD Board, each Member shall be responsible for determining the most appropriate means by which it shall satisfy the Core Principles.

4   Protecting Children and Young People

4.1 Members will each institute and make available a reasonable, robust and effective access control system to enable Subscribers, should they wish, to prevent Children and Young People from watching content that might reasonably be considered unsuitable. This may be through personal identification number (**PIN code**) protection, and/or a content watershed or any other effective access control system (or combination of systems) reasonably identified by a Member.

4.2 In identifying which material should be susceptible to access control, Members shall have regard to the Broadcasting Regulatory Codes and ATVOD Practice Statements prevailing from time to time.

4.3 It is noted that the provision of access control systems during family viewing periods places a significant degree of responsibility on Subscribers to self-regulate their household's viewing. Nevertheless, the Members recognise that their responsibility is to make such access control systems available to the Subscriber and to promote their use; it is not the responsibility of the Members to enforce utilisation of such systems within the household.

4.4 Members shall ensure all access control systems and other safeguards provided for the protection of Children and Young People are clearly and regularly explained to Customers in general and Subscribers in particular. To this end, Members will regularly and actively promote the use of the access control systems available on their On-demand Services to Subscribers and Viewers alike to encourage their usage and will ensure that at all times their operating support systems make available in response to Customer enquiries adequate information about the operation of their designated access control systems.

Ensuring Subscribers are at least 18 Years Old

4.5   Where age-based access control systems are utilised by a Member in discharging its obligations under the Code, that Member shall institute and apply reasonable measures to ensure that its Subscribers are a minimum of 18 years of age.

5   *The Provision of General Guidance to Customers*

Protecting Other Groups

5.1   Any material reasonably expected by a Member as likely to cause significant offence or upset to some Customers will be clearly identified to the Customer prior to its distribution to the home. In identifying which material will require prior identification, the Members shall have regard to the Broadcasting Regulatory Codes and ATVOD Practice Statements prevailing from time to time and shall provide Customers with sufficient information and guidance as to the nature of the material so as to enable the Customer to make an appropriate choice at all times on whether or not to request the provision of the material.

Served Material

5.2   Members regularly distribute material to homes without the active on-demand selection of the Customer (***Served Material***). This may, for example, be done to promote and enhance understanding of services available to Customers, to communicate pricing or programming changes, to promote content available on the On-demand Service or to raise awareness of access control systems. Where Served Material is distributed to homes during family viewing periods without adequate access controls, Members will ensure such Served Material conforms to an appropriate family viewing policy set by the Member by reference to the ATVOD Practice Statements and the Broadcasting Regulatory Codes prevailing from time to time.

Ensuring Service Transparency

5.3   Members will assist Customer understanding of each service environment accessed within an On-demand Service and the content or services contained therein to enable Customers to make appropriate choices at all times. Members recognise that labelling, information announcements and classification details can be helpful in enabling Customers to make such choices.

Advertising and Sponsorship

5.4   Advertising, sponsorship and other commercial activities will be undertaken with regard to the Broadcasting Regulatory Codes and ATVOD Practice Statements prevailing from time to time.

Commercial Services

5.5   Members will use their reasonable endeavours to ensure Customers are able to understand fully the nature of every commercial transaction in general, and the price of the good or service offered, the payment options available and any material conditions in particular, prior to completion of a transaction.

6   *Data Protection and Privacy*

6.1   Members shall comply with UK legislation relating to data protection.

6.2   When registering on the Data Protection Register, all Members must in their application state that the data may be used for regulatory purposes and that ATVOD is a potential user of that information.

7   *Complaints*

7.1   Where a Customer or third party (*a **Complainant***) makes a complaint concerning a service provided by a Member, or asserts that a Member has acted in breach of the Code, the following procedure shall apply.

(a)   Where the complaint is notified to ATVOD, the Secretariat will direct the Complainant to contact the relevant Member direct if he/she has not already done so.

(b)   Where the complaint is made to the Member, or where the complaint is forwarded to the Member by ATVOD, the Member shall:

   (i)   promptly write to the Complainant to acknowledge receipt and furnish the Complainant with a statement explaining the ATVOD Complaints Procedure; and

   (ii)   use its reasonable endeavours to resolve the complaint within 20 working days of receipt.

(c)   Where a Complainant informs ATVOD that his/her complaint has not been resolved to his/her satisfaction by the Member within the time-frame set out in section 7.1(b), the Secretariat will:

   (i)   ask that the Complainant set out the complaint in adequate detail in an email or letter or by telephone and identify the cause of his/her continued dissatisfaction; and

   (ii)   forward the complaint to the Member's specified contact within two working days of receipt.

The Member must respond to the Complainant directly within 10 working days of receipt of notification of the complaint from the Secretariat, copying the Secretariat into the response.

7.2   Where, within a reasonable period of time (but not less than 20 working days) following delivery of the Member's response in accordance with section 7.1(c), a complaint remains unresolved to the satisfaction of the ATVOD Board or the Complainant, the ATVOD Board shall be entitled (in the exercise of its absolute discretion) to initiate the ATVOD Standard Complaints Procedure set out below.

7.3   Each Member shall provide ATVOD with a single point of Contact for the Member authorised to deal with complaints under the Code.

8   ATVOD Complaints Procedure

8.1   Complaints made subject to the ATVOD Complaints Procedure shall be determined by the ATVOD Board. The ATVOD Board may delegate its powers under sections 7 and 8 of the Code to a sub-committee (**the Adjudication Committee**) comprising not less than three members of the ATVOD Board, one of whom must at all times be independent of the Members. Any member of the ATVOD Board who represents (a) the Member which is the subject of a complaint, or (b) the Complainant in a particular complaint (**an Interested Party**), shall be replaced on the Adjudication Committee by an alternative member of the ATVOD Board whilst the complaint in which he is interested is considered and determined. References in section 7.2 above and sections 8.2–8.10 below to the ATVOD Board shall be construed as references to the Adjudication Committee where such committee exists.

Emergency Procedure

8.2   Where it appears to the Chairman (or any appointed deputy) that a breach of the Code has or is likely to have taken place which is serious and requires urgent remedy, the Secretariat, at the request of the ATVOD Board, may initiate the emergency ATVOD Complaints Procedure (**the Emergency Procedure**). Where the Emergency Procedure is initiated:

(a) The Secretariat will immediately investigate the complaint and notify its findings to the Adjudication Committee. If no such committee exists on initiation of the Emergency Procedure, the Chairman shall promptly appoint an Adjudication Committee.

(b) If all three members of the Adjudication Committee agree that there appears to be a serious breach of the Code requiring urgent remedy, the Secretariat will use its reasonable endeavours to notify the Member of the apparent breach and require the Member to correct the apparent breach immediately.

(c) Once the apparent breach has been corrected, the Secretariat shall provide to the Member all necessary information concerning the complaint and require the Member to respond in writing to the Secretariat within three working days.

(d) All relevant information will, in the absence of special circumstances, be laid before the Adjudication Committee within ten working days from the date of notification referred to in paragraph (b) above, following which the Adjudication Committee will decide (acting as experts and not as arbitrators) solely whether or not there has been a breach of the Code. No Interested Party shall be present at any meeting of the Adjudication Committee, included in any correspondence during or in which the complaint is being discussed or decided upon or otherwise involved in the adjudication of the Complaint save for the purpose of providing evidence at the request of the Adjudication Committee. Each case shall be considered and decided on its own merits.

(e) The Adjudication Committee may extend the time limits set out in this sub-section if it considers that their strict application might cause injustice.

The Standard Procedure

8.3   Pursuant to section 7.2, and save where the Emergency Procedure has been instigated, the Secretariat, at the request of the ATVOD Board, will initiate the Standard ATVOD Complaints Procedure as follows:

(a)   The Secretariat will seek from the Complainant and/or the Member as the case may be:

(i)   the Complainant's original complaint and all responses from the Member concerning that complaint;

(ii)   any additional relevant information considered likely by the Member or the Complainant to assist the Secretariat's consideration of the complaint.

(b)   The Secretariat may apply a discretionary non-refundable charge (*the Administration Charge*) of £250 towards the administrative costs of handling the complaint. The Administration Charge shall be levied upon the Member.

(c)   The Secretariat shall be entitled but not obliged to make further investigations into the complaint by whatever means it considers appropriate.

(d)   The Secretariat shall compile a report (*a Complaint Report*) setting out (but only to the extent permitted under data protection legislation):

(i)   the name and address of the Complainant;

(ii)   the name and address of the Member or Members the subject of the complaint;

(iii)   the original complaint;

(iv)   the manner in which the Secretariat investigated the complaint, specifying any investigation carried out by the Secretariat and the result of its enquiries into the complaint and exhibiting copies of all material documents received;

(v)   all material information available to the Secretariat concerning the complaint; and

(vi)   the conclusions of the Secretariat arising out of the investigations carried out concerning the complaint.

(e)   The Secretariat will present the Complaint Report to the ATVOD Board as soon as practicable by meeting in person or in correspondence, following which the ATVOD Board will decide (acting as experts and not as arbitrators) solely whether or not there has been a breach of the Code. No Interested Party shall be present at any such meeting, included in any correspondence during or in which the complaint is being discussed or decided upon or otherwise involved in the adjudication of the Complaint. Each case shall be considered and decided on its own merits.

Notification of Decision and Deadline for Appeal

8.4   Promptly upon determination of the complaint under sub-section 8.2 or 8.3 above, the Secretariat will provide a copy of the ATVOD Board's decision (*the ATVOD Adjudication*), in writing, to the Complainant and the relevant Member together with a notification of the parties' rights of appeal pursuant to the Procedure of the ATVOD Independent Appeals Commission (*the Appeals Notification*).

8.5   Subject to the parties' right to appeal to the ATVOD Independent Appeals

Commission, the final decision on complaints made subject to the ATVOD Complaints Procedure shall rest with the ATVOD Board.

Refusal to Adjudicate / Referral to Third Party

8.6 The ATVOD Board may refuse to adjudicate on a complaint where the subject-matter of the complaint is the subject of legal proceedings or where the complaint concerns the legality of material carried on a Service or where the ATVOD Board considers, after reasonable deliberation, the complaint to be frivolous, vexatious or persistently made without reasonable grounds. Where the ATVOD Board refuses to adjudicate, it shall provide its reasoning to the Secretariat for notification to the Complainant.

8.7 Where a complaint appears to fall within the ambit of a particular regulatory body or self-regulatory authority other than ATVOD (for example, OFCOM, the ISPA, ICSTIS or the Advertising Standards Authority), the Secretariat or ATVOD Board may refer the complaint to that body but may, should the ATVOD Board so wish in the exercise of its absolute discretion, nevertheless proceed to adjudicate upon the complaint in accordance with the above procedure.

Sanctions

8.8 Where the ATVOD Board determines, pursuant to section 8.1(e) above, that a Member has breached the Code, the ATVOD Board may by simple majority vote, having taken all relevant circumstances into account:
(a) require the Member to remedy the breach promptly; and/or
(b) require an assurance from the Member relating to future behaviour, in terms dictated by the ATVOD Board; and/or
(c) require the Member to reimburse to the Complainant any Service charges which the Complainant may have paid to the Member in connection with the matter giving rise to the upheld complaint; and/or
(d) require the Member to reimburse to ATVOD any reasonable amount in respect of administration charges incurred by ATVOD in determining the complaint; and/or
(e) suspend the Member from ATVOD for such period as the ATVOD Board shall determine in the exercise of its absolute discretion without any reimbursement to the Member of any fees previously paid to ATVOD whether in whole or in part; and/or
(f) publicise (by whichever means the ATVOD Board determines) the final decision of the complaint including the identity of the Member in question, the nature of the breach and any sanctions applied.

8.9 The failure of a Member to comply with any sanction imposed upon it will itself amount to a breach of the Code.

8.10 Prior to its adjudication, the details of any complaint to which the ATVOD Complaints Procedure has been applied shall be kept confidential by ATVOD, the Complainant and the relevant Member.

9 *Appeals*[55]

9.1 A Member or Complainant party to a complaint subject to the ATVOD Complaints Procedure may appeal against the ATVOD Adjudication to the

ATVOD Independent Appeals Commission. Appeals will be held in accordance with the Appeals Procedure set out in Appendix 1.

9.2 The ATVOD Independent Appeals Commission will accept and address appeals on the following grounds only:

(a) the ATVOD Adjudication was based on an error of fact;

(b) the ATVOD Adjudication was arrived at by the ATVOD Board's incorrect exercise of its discretion.

9.3 A written appeal must be lodged with the Secretariat within one month of receipt by the appellant of the ATVOD Adjudication and the Appeals Notification (as defined in the Appeals Procedure). Appeals to the Independent Appeals Commission must be made in writing to: The ATVOD Secretariat, (Address to be confirmed). Appeals must be accompanied by the written ATVOD Adjudication and must set out the reasons why the applicant is dissatisfied with the response received from ATVOD.

Notes

1 See Marsden, C (1999) 'Pluralism in the Multi-Channel Market: Suggestions for Regulatory Scrutiny', Council of Europe Human Rights Commission, Mass Media Directorate, MM-S-PL [99] 12 Def 2.

2 Freiwillige Selbstkontrolle Fernsehen e.V. (Voluntary Television Review Body).

3 Twist, Jo (2005) 'The Year of the Digital Citizen', http://news.bbc.co.uk/1/hi/technology/4566712.stm

4 Tom Curley, CEO of the Associated Press (2006) 'When the Audience Can Also Broadcast', http://journalism.nyu.edu/pubzone/weblogs/pressthink, 27 June.

5 For the reasoning behind the justification for the special regulation of broadcasting, see, for example, Barendt, E (1995) *Broadcasting Law: A Comparative Study*, Oxford University Press, pp. 5–9. For views on the matter in the United States, see: Bollinger, Lee C (1976) 'Freedom of the Press and Public Access: Toward a Theory of Partial Regulation', *Michigan Law Review* 75, 1.

6 Larouche, P (1998) 'EC Competition Law and the Convergence of the Telecommunications and Broadcasting Sectors', *Telecommunications Policy* 22(3), 219–42. Also, Larouche, P (2001) 'Communications Convergence and Public Service Broadcasting', at: http://infolab.kub.nl/uvtweb/bin.php3?id=00011353&mime=application/pdf&file=/tilec/publications/larouche2.pdf (accessed 15.03.03).

7 Independent Television Commission.

8 Hoffmann-Riem, W (1996) *Regulating Media: The Licensing and Supervision of Broadcasting in Six Countries*, New York: The Guilford Press, p. 288.

9 There is a translation into English of the Danish Broadcasting Act (*Lov om radio-og TV-virksomhed*) which is available at: www.fs.dk/uk/acts/a_tvuk.htm

10 The PSBs are Danmarks Radio (DR) – Danish Broadcasting Corporation: www.dr.dk, and TV2: http://tv2.dk

11 Sandfeld Jakobsen, Soren (2003) 'New Radio and Television Broadcasting Act', *IRIS* 2003:7/10.

12 Distribution in this sense is understood as the case when national or foreign programmes are distributed via cable systems unchanged and simultaneously. Owners of these cable networks, however, are under a 'must-carry' obligation as regards radio and television programmes of the public service broadcasters. If there is, on the other hand, subtitling or delayed transmission then the service requires a licence. Other broadcasters can be licensed by the Satellite and Cable Board to broadcast to an area exceeding one local area, and companies, associations and local authorities can be licensed to broadcast in one local area. Licensing of broadcasting by cable is under the responsibility of the Minister of Culture. The website of the Kulturministeriet (Danish Ministry of Culture): www.kum.dk

13 Legal Basis: Art. 5 GG (German Constitution): www.iuscomp.org/gla (available via the German Law archive in English language), and Interstate Broadcasting Agreement: www.alm.de/bibliothek/download/RSTV_JMStV.pdf (German).

14 Hoffman-Riem, W (1996) op. cit., pp. 148–49.

15 The Royal Charter of the BBC: http://access.adobe.com/perl/convertPDF.pl?url= http://www.bbc.co.uk/info/policies/charter/pdf/charter.pdf

16 Licence and Agreement of the BBC.

17 The UK Communications Act 2003 establishes in part 3 'Television and Radio Services' that Ofcom can regulate certain BBC services to the extent that there is provision to do so in the BBC Charter and Agreement, or pursuant to provisions of the Communications Act 2003 or the Broadcasting Act 1996. See Communications Act 2003 at 198 'Functions of OFCOM in relation to the BBC', www.opsi.gov.uk/acts/acts2003/20030021.htm

18 See: www.bbccharterreview.org.uk

19 The criticism of PSB self-regulation and the system of governance of the BBC was renewed after the Hutton Inquiry in 2004.

20 The RTÉ Authority: www.rte.ie/about/organisation/corporate_structure.html#authority. See also Statements of Commitments 2003: www.rte.ie/about/organisation/statements. html

21 RTÉ Programme-Makers' Guidelines: www.rte.ie/about/organisation/ProgrammeMak ersGuidelines.pdf; and the Irish Code of Fair Trading Practice: www.rte.ie/about/organi-sation/fairtrading.html

22 Smith, R C (1997) *Broadcasting Law and Fundamental Rights*, Oxford: Clarendon Press.

23 Schneider, A (1995) 'Child Protection on German Television – The Voluntary Television Review Body (FSF)', *IRIS* 1995(3): 7/13.

24 Niehl, T (1998) 'Daytime Talkshows on TV – Voluntary Code', *IRIS* 1998(99): 13/25.

25 German FSF, English summary: www.fsf.de/summary.htm

26 Schneider, A (1995) op. cit.

27 Ibid.

28 Schneider, A (1995) 'New Regulations Governing the Right to Apply for Review by the Voluntary Television Review Body (FSF)', *IRIS* 1995(5): 9/13.

29 Strothman, P (2003) 'Approval for FSF', *IRIS* 2003(7): 8/13.

30 German FSF, English summary: www.fsf.de/summary.htm

31 For a brief review of the constitutional cases that shape German broadcasting law see: Barendt, E (1995) op. cit., pp. 21–25.

32 Kirchner, J (1995) 'The Search for New Markets: Multimedia and Digital Television under German Broadcasting and Copyright Law', *EIPR* 17(6), 269–76, at pp. 269–71.

33 Benassi, M (2003) 'New Self-Regulatory Code of Conduct on Television and Minors', *IRIS* 2003(4): 10/21.

34 Österlund-Karinkanta, M (2000) 'Only Films for Minors to be Censored as of 1 January 2001', *IRIS* 2000(8): 9/19.

35 www.sou.gov.se/valdsskildring/council.htm (English version).

36 Radio-och TV-verket (Swedish authority for radio and television, the state licensing and supervisory authority): www.rtvv.se (Swedish), or in English version: www.rtvv.se/english/index.htm

37 Rosén, J (1999) 'Digital Terrestrial Broadcasting', *IRIS* 1999(5): 15/18.

38 www.kijkwijzer.nl/engels/ekijkwijzer.html

39 www.netherlands-embassy.org/article.asp?articleref=AR00000429EN. Dutch-language commercial companies include RTL 4 and 5 (which broadcast in Dutch from Luxembourg), Veronica, SBS6, TV10 and the Music Factory. It should be mentioned that RTL was in operation from Luxembourg before the time Dutch law authorised the licensing of private broadcasters based in The Netherlands.

40 Commissariaat voor de Media: www.cvdm.nl/pages/home.asp?flash=5

41 Douglas, T (2003) 'Self-Regulation: The Way Ahead for Advertising?', *Marketing Week*, 17 Oct., p. 17. With regard to experiences in the field of advertising self-regulation used for pre-vetting in the United States, see, for example, Abernethy, Avery M and LeBlanc

Wicks, J (2001) 'Self-Regulation and Television Advertising: A Replication and Extension', *Journal of Advertising Research* May–June, p. 31, and Rotfeld, H J, Abernethy, A M and Parsons, P R (2001) 'Self-Regulation and Television Advertising', *Journal of Advertising* 19, p. 18.

42 www.OFCOM.org.uk/consult/condocs/reg_broad_ad/future_reg_broad/section5/#content

Three new bodies have responsibility for broadcast advertising:

- The Advertising Standard Authority (Broadcast) (ASA(B)) – responsible for the handling of complaints about broadcast advertising.
- The Broadcast Committee of Advertising Practice (BCAP) – responsible for setting, reviewing and revising standards codes for broadcast advertising. The Advertising Advisory Committee of BCAP gives BCAP independent advice on advertising policy and code-setting issues. This committee has an independent Chairman and consists of expert and lay citizen-consumer representatives.
- The Broadcast Advertising Standards Board of Finance (BASBOF) is the body responsible for funding.

43 The EU framework consists of: (1) Directive 2002/21/EC on a common regulatory framework for electronic communications networks and services (Framework Directive); (2) Directive 2002/20/EC on the authorisation of electronic communications networks and services (the Authorisation Directive); (3) Directive 2002/19/EC on access to, and interconnection of, electronic communications networks and services (the Access and Interconnection Directive); (4) Directive 2002/58/EC concerning the processing of personal data and the protection of privacy in the electronic communication sector; (5) Directive 2002/77/EC on competition in the markets for electronic communications networks and services.

44 Mastowska, K (1999) 'Television Self-Regulation', *IRIS* 1999(5): 13/16.

45 Article 18 para. 5 of the Broadcasting Act of 29 December 1992: requires programmes or other broadcasts containing scenes or contents which may have an adverse impact upon a healthy physical, mental or moral development of minors, to be transmitted only between 11 p.m. and 6 a.m.; available at: www.krrit.gov.pl/stronykrrit/angielska/index.htm

46 Voorhoof, D (2003) 'First Decision of Council for Journalism – No Infringement of Journalistic Ethics by Commercial Television', *IRIS* 2003(6): 7/11:

47 UK Communications Act 2003; the relevant section is available at: www.legislation.hmso.gov.uk/cgibin/htm_hl.pl?DB=hmsonew&STEMMER=en&WORDS=statement+progr am+commun+act+2003+&COLOUR=Red&STYLE=s&URL=http://www.hmso.gov.uk/acts/acts2003/30021 – i.htm#muscat_highlighter_first_match

48 Goldberg, D (2001) '"Contracts with Viewers" Published', *IRIS* 2001(5): 6/10.

49 Prosser, T (2001) 'ITC Moves Towards Partial Self-Regulation and Lighter Regulation of Content', *IRIS* 2001(3): 12/16.

50 Higham, N (2003) 'The Challenge of Media Regulation', 21 Jan. 2003, BBC News: http://news.bbc.co.uk/1/hi/entertainment/tv_and_radio/2679593.stm; Grimshaw, C (2003) 'OFCOM Moots ASA Broadcast Role', *Marketing UK*, 30 Oct., p. 4.

51 Douglas, T (2004) 'Code War Breaks Out as Ofcom Tries to Force Pace', *Marketing Week*, 29 Jan., p. 19.

52 The Italian Code of Advertising and Sales Promotion. See: Capello, M (1999) 'Comparative Advertising Allowed by the Self-Regulatory Advertising Code', *IRIS* 1999(6): 13/25, in which she discusses implementation of the European rules on misleading comparative advertising. (Those rules were incorporated in the codes used by the statutory regulators in the UK; for example, see: Goldberg, D (2001) 'Radio Authority Publishes Revised Advertising and Sponsorship Code', *IRIS* 2001(2): 9/20.)

53 UK advertising codes for broadcast and non-broadcast advertising: www.asa.org.uk/asa/codes

54 www.asa.org.uk/asa/about/New+ASA

55 Appendices to the code, including a detailed appeals procedure, have not been included.

6 Internet content and self-regulation

The development of Internet content self-regulation over the past decade has been a rapid and creative process. Coordinated with reference to key policy statements such as the European recommendation (98/560/EC),[1] Internet self-regulation has drawn on previous traditions and tools of regulation in related sectors such as telephony, press and broadcasting, but has developed wholly new and peculiar paradigms that have raised fundamental constitutional issues relating to freedom of expression, privacy and other rights, as well as problems of enforcement and jurisdiction. Whilst an overall family resemblance of regulatory approaches has emerged on a global level, with some key regional variations, there is little indication that this system of Internet content self-regulation is stabilising as a paradigm, and no indication that the key problem of jurisdiction in a global medium has found resolution. The rate of change in the sector remains too fast to permit stabilisation of a regulatory scheme. Broadband rollout is leading to convergence with broadcasting, games and other services and the rollout of the wireless Internet leads to wholly new forms of service and regulatory dilemma. There remain tensions with fundamental constitutional rights, and uncertainties about effectiveness of regulation and about the range of new harms that emerge in the process of innovation. The harms associated with Internet content and the rationale for regulation of the Internet have been described in previous chapters. Alongside the general concerns with positive and negative externalities and market failure, rationales for some form of intervention include specific issues such as protection of children from inappropriate content and contact; spam; spyware; invasion of privacy; and also various forms of illegal content. Those that have received most attention in this respect include child pornography, copyright infringement, hate speech, and security against malicious code.

In this chapter we outline the main structures and paradigms of self-regulation of Internet content that have emerged in response to those rationales, and introduce some of the main tensions and dilemmas that are emerging in the sector. In what follows we refer mainly to Western Europe and to the key regions of the more open societies in the Asia Pacific region such as Japan and Australia, and North America. We outline the general level of activity of self-regulation and then pose some difficult questions about the overall effectiveness of these forms of regulation.

Figure 6.1 outlines the range of codes of conduct and self-regulatory activities that are incorporated into the Internet content value chain. This model aims to be simple, rather than exhaustive. The examples in the upper row outline technical measures embedded in the software code, and in the row below codes of conduct as publicly available rules to which ISPs and others subscribe. Internet actors and users often

	Content provider ➡	ISP ➡	ISP-user ➡	Search ➡	Access ➡	User
Code	Self-labelling of content (RSACi, PICS, ICRA); Trustmarks	ISP filtering (e.g. BT CleanFeed/ Telnor)	Reputational systems	Search level filtering	Login/access restrictions/ reputation management	Browser-level filtering; age verification
Code of conduct	Content standards codes; Privacy codes; BBC editorial guidelines; Government website guidelines; E-commerce codes	ISP code of conduct (ISPA, Euroispa code of conduct) -privacy codes -hotlines NTD codes	Terms of service (e.g. Wanadoo terms of service)	Search engine code of conduct German FSM	Computer misuse codes	Awareness/ literacy

Figure 6.1 Self-regulation and codes in the Internet value chain.

face a choice between a technical solution (software code) and a code of conduct when faced with a regulatory problem: in Internet content, as in other media, technical controls can functionally replace codes of conduct,[2] or they can operate in conjunction with them. Just as the possibility of parental control devices for television sets led to calls for the end of the watershed and relaxation of taste codes for broadcasting, the argument was made that the availability of filters reduces the need for Internet content codes of conduct.[3]

Content standards codes

As content convergence proceeds rapidly in the Internet sector, codes of conduct established for newspapers, broadcasters, games and other content sectors are increasingly applied to the content provided online by code subjects. Press self-regulatory bodies such as press councils and ombudsmen have applied their codes to newspaper content viewed online,[4] and broadcast content codes have either been applied directly, or adapted for application to online content of broadcasters. In addition, Internet disintermediation places new players in content provision roles, including private and public bodies. Government departments have developed their own web publishing editorial guidelines to increase trust and ensure quality control,[5] and other content providers – e-commerce providers and health information providers, for example – have developed their own editorial guidelines to protect quality. Some of these are embedded in an attempt to develop a 'quality seal' such as a trustmark.[6] These are examined further below. Finally, pure Internet content providers, such as those involved in provision of news, are experimenting with development of ethics codes purely for the online space.

Where a self-regulatory code is applied by an individual company there is a clear interest in protecting the brand of that company, and the decision to apply standards codes to online content is likely to be relatively straightforward. The BBC or the *Washington Post* will attempt to maintain the ethical standards established in broadcasting and print to their online content. However, different delivery mechanisms have differing levels of invasiveness, pervasiveness, publicness and influence,[7] and wholly new services such as user-generated content are being developed. This leads to varying approaches to content regulation standards. Less stringent controls are in some cases seen to be justified where a service is addressed to a niche adult audience, or where consumer control and choice can be enhanced through labelling and access controls. The BBC's editorial code has been adapted for online content. In most respects it is identical to the broadcast code, and where it differs it applies similar standards to new services.

In some cases, content providers do apply different standards online and offline. Obliged by the Independent Television Commission in May 2000 to cut scenes from the broadcast version of Lars Von Trier's *The Idiots*, the UK broadcaster Channel Four streamed them on its website in protest at censorship. Where broadcasters provide news services online, impartiality and independence standards tend to be identical to the broadcast code, and where codes are changed this is generally in the intention of applying the same principles to new services. Some of the editorial guidelines of major providers do indicate that there are differences. The *New York Times* website, for example, whilst providing a popup warning about shocking or upsetting content, does publish more violent and shocking imagery in the news sections of its websites than in the printed copy.

There is some evidence that content codes are converging to establish some common guidelines for 'big media' online. The BBC, for example, has now published online editorial guidelines which supplement its previously existing broadcasting code. Whilst in many cases these rules for online content replicate the broadcasting standards, they do differ, incorporating specific procedures for interactive services, for example the security implications of online 'grooming' and new commercial guidelines for linking and sponsorship.

Cross-sectoral codes, which apply to more than one company (such as the standards of press councils, advertising self-regulation, or film classifiers) and are based on the interests of the sector as a whole, are less clear cut in a situation of convergence: the decision to apply codes to different sectors will generally involve a complex negotiation and is less likely to happen spontaneously. The case of The Netherlands, where a single rating body applies icons to content on various platforms, remains an isolated one in Europe.

The debate about standards in online journalism has spawned several attempts to create codes of conduct for online journalistic ethics.[8] CyberJournalist.net has created a model 'Bloggers' Code of Ethics', reproduced in Figure 6.2. The code drew directly on established journalists' codes as it is based on the Society of Professional Journalists Code of Ethics.[9] The guidelines are purely advisory and without formal sanction.

Internet service provider (ISP) codes

ISP codes are dealt with in more detail below and form the focus of this study. They are a key site of Internet content regulation as they institutionalise the voluntarily adopted standards. In the European context they represent the outcome of negotiations at various levels: at the national level a single ISP representative organisation has emerged, often after a period of competition between alternative organisations. In some cases this process has been led strongly by government initiative, through the formation of stakeholder groups led by government. In Italy, government officials even produced the first detailed draft of the code of conduct. At the European level, the European Commission and Council of Europe have been active in coordinating the development of federated ISP organisations such as EuroISPA. The objective has been to perform the necessary single market and coordinating role, for example supporting transnational cooperation between hotlines and law enforcement through organisations such as InHope, the Internet Hotline Providers Association. At the national level, political entrepreneurs such as child protection organisations, and

The Bloggers' Code of Ethics – The Online News Association
April 15, 2003

Integrity is the cornerstone of credibility. Bloggers who adopt this code of principles and these standards of practice not only practice ethical publishing, but convey to their readers that they can be trusted.

A BLOGGER'S CODE OF ETHICS

Be Honest and Fair

Bloggers should be honest and fair in gathering, reporting and interpreting information. Bloggers should:

- Never plagiarize.
- Identify and link to sources whenever feasible. The public is entitled to as much information as possible on sources' reliability.
- Make certain that Weblog entries, quotations, headlines, photos and all other content do not misrepresent. They should not oversimplify or highlight incidents out of context.
- Never distort the content of photos without disclosing what has been changed. Image enhancement is only acceptable for technical clarity. Label montages and photo illustrations.
- Never publish information they know is inaccurate – and if publishing questionable information, make it clear it's in doubt.
- Distinguish between advocacy, commentary and factual information. Even advocacy writing and commentary should not misrepresent fact or context.
- Distinguish factual information and commentary from advertising and shun hybrids that blur the lines between the two.

Minimize Harm

Ethical bloggers treat sources and subjects as human beings deserving of respect. Bloggers should:

- Show compassion for those who may be affected adversely by Weblog content. Use special sensitivity when dealing with children and inexperienced sources or subjects.
- Be sensitive when seeking or using interviews or photographs of those affected by tragedy or grief.
- Recognize that gathering and reporting information may cause harm or discomfort. Pursuit of information is not a license for arrogance.
- Recognize that private people have a greater right to control information about themselves than do public officials and others who seek power, influence or attention. Only an overriding public need can justify intrusion into anyone's privacy.
- Show good taste. Avoid pandering to lurid curiosity.
- Be cautious about identifying juvenile suspects, victims of sex crimes and criminal suspects before the formal filing of charges.

Be Accountable

Bloggers should:

- Admit mistakes and correct them promptly.
- Explain each Weblog's mission and invite dialogue with the public over its content and the bloggers' conduct.
- Disclose conflicts of interest, affiliations, activities and personal agendas.
- Deny favored treatment to advertisers and special interests and resist their pressure to influence content. When exceptions are made, disclose them fully to readers.
- Be wary of sources offering information for favors. When accepting such information, disclose the favors.
- Expose unethical practices of other bloggers.
- Abide by the same high standards to which they hold others.

Figure 6.2 Bloggers' Code of Ethics (The Online News Association).

ministers under pressure from public opinion, spur the formation of policy stakeholder groups, and rules are developed in order to deal with a variety of potential
harms, with the broader view of heading off the threat of legislation, within the
regime of limited ISP liability.

Whilst codes of conduct have formed the central plank in the development of self-
regulation at the ISP level, ISPs have been under increasing pressure to engage in
filtering of content, and are under obligation to retain data for the purposes of law
enforcement in most European countries.

Search/ISP level technical controls

Some ISPs are already involved in filtering. Where this is conducted in collaboration
with government interests it has become the topic of growing scrutiny. In the United
Kingdom, British Telecom (BT; the largest telco/ISP) has, after public pressure to
block child pornography, developed a service known as CleanFeed. This enables ISP
level blocking of certain illegal websites. A list of illegal child pornography websites is
maintained by the industry body, the Internet Watch Foundation (IWF, see below,
pp. 123–4), and provided to CleanFeed. Users of the ISP,[10] are unable to reach those
blacklisted sites. Similar models have been adopted in Norway and are being developed in several other countries.[11]

In recent years, new types of filtering have emerged, some of which have been
criticised by free-speech advocates. For example, search-level filtering appears to be
used in China and, under a voluntary scheme, in Germany. The German scheme is
interesting as all the German major search engines have agreed to filter out harmful
content for their German audience. Google, Lycos Europe, MSN Germany, AOL
Germany, Yahoo, T-Online and t-Info have founded a self-regulatory organisation
that will voluntarily block a list of URLs considered to be harmful to the young. The
list is provided by a governmental media classification organisation. The search
engines will continuously check the central blacklist of indexed URLs and prevent
German subscribers seeing any of the banned websites. There will be a mechanism to
address possible gaps in the filtering by search engines, but provisions have been
made for users to complain about wrongful blacklisting.[12] Clearly this development,
whilst voluntary, warrants close attention. The sites blocked are those deemed harmful, rather than illegal, and the sites are blocked by private companies. The combined
search engines represent almost all search engines, and therefore blocking is likely to
be effective. In the United Kingdom, the Internet Watch Foundation (ISP organisation) maintains a list of not merely harmful, but illegal sites. These sites are blocked by
BT servers. Such arrangements are not without their problems. According to the
Guardian newspaper (25 May 2005): 'Technically skilled users of BT's Internet service
can use the system to find out which sites are blocked. . . . This means they are able to
gain access to a secret blacklist provided by the watchdog Internet Watch
Foundation.' Interestingly, there has been less discussion of the other major potential
problem, namely over-blocking: co-regulation of this form has been struck down in
the United States. A Pennsylvania state law that required ISPs to block identified lists
of child porn sites was struck down as unconstitutional in September 2004. The
Center for Democracy and Technology found that blocking the list had the result of
blocking access to over 1.5 million other sites with shared addresses. Whether the BT
list has the same effect is not clear, and there is no UK law requiring BT to block. The
central dilemma of course is transparency: to make public the list of 'banned' sites
used in any technical blocking scheme would have the perverse effect of advertising

the sites, but a lack of transparency regarding what is blocked and on what basis will tend to undermine the legitimacy of the scheme. Clearly, what is required is external audit of blocking databases against clear agreed criteria.

Terms of service

These are known to consumers as the often unread small print they agree to, usually by a click on a box, when agreeing to use an ISP. Most of these are contractual in that they embody a legally enforceable promise whereby users agree to the terms and rules under which they use the service, but can also be the subject of self-regulatory-type oversight and monitoring as they are publicly available statements of policy. Terms are sometimes subject to complaint, and are of course regulated by general contract law that aims to prevent unfairness. In 2004, Wanadoo UK's terms of service were subject to a number of complaints to the UK communications regulator Ofcom. It was alleged that the terms of service were 'potentially unfair [. . .] as it allows Wanadoo to inappropriately exclude or limit the legal rights of the consumer'.[13] After negotiation with Ofcom, Wanadoo agreed to change their terms of service. As ISPs are often subject to the regulatory oversight of the communications sectoral regulator, the broad liability waivers contained in these terms of service will be difficult to maintain where regulators do take up complaints.

Computer misuse codes

According to the World Internet Project, 41.6 per cent of Internet use in Germany takes place at home, 20.5 per cent in schools and workplaces, and 2.5 per cent in other locations.[14] Other countries have broadly similar ratios. Each of these forms of access may be subject to some form of self-regulation via a contract, but the second category of access in particular is likely to be subject to terms set out in a computer misuse or 'acceptable use' code. The Oxford University Department of Physics code, for example, defines the following as 'misuse of computing facilities':

> attempting to gain unauthorised access to a facility; making offensive material available over the Web; generating, sending or receiving pornographic material; using someone else's username and/or password; disregarding the privacy of other people's files; giving your username or password to someone else, or being otherwise careless with them; generating messages which appear to originate with someone else, or otherwise attempting to impersonate someone else; sending messages which are abusive or a nuisance or otherwise distressing; displaying offensive material in a public place; introducing programs with malicious intent; trying to interfere with someone else's use of the facilities; disregard for 'computer etiquette'; sending chain email; being wasteful of resources; software piracy (including infringement of software licences or copyright provisions); using the facilities for commercial gain without explicit authorisation; physically damaging or otherwise interfering with facilities.

There is huge variation between access codes, as different organisations will strike contrasting balances, between organisational efficiency and employee privacy for example. Sanctions vary, but computer misuse can be and has frequently been used as a justification of dismissal from employment, or disciplinary procedures in educational institutions.

It is unlikely that such oversight will be balanced by the assertion of rights to privacy from employer snooping, apart from some cases involving personal e-mail. Early attempts to assert user privacy in workplace Internet use have been contested. In the United States, it is particularly difficult to assert privacy of workplace under the Electronic Communications Privacy Act 1986, particularly where the employer is also the ISP. By contrast, a 2001 ruling of the highest court in France restricted employer access to private e-mail, even where the company prohibits private use of its computer systems. Nikon France SA, who sacked an employee for private use of their computer facilities, was found to have violated the employee's privacy. The court held that Nikon improperly dismissed its employee for using his workplace computer during work hours to send personal e-mails. In Britain, employers can gain freer access to records of employees' online activities, but remain subject to the Human Rights Act and Data Protection Act protection.[15]

Search codes of conduct

Search-level filtering for content, like ISP filtering, has been the subject of controversy worldwide. The lack of transparency of search-engine algorithms, together with the growing commercialisation of search, has led to increasing focus on the extent to which search itself acts as a regulator of speech online. Much of the criticism of major players such as Google has focused on the lack of transparency: where the site ranking of a search result is commercially driven, argue the critics, this directly contravenes established media ethics, such as the clear division between editorial and advertising content. Sites such as Google-watch.org have developed new critiques of these important gatekeepers. Where search engines conspire with other organisations, particularly law enforcement or government interests, other public interest concerns emerge. In this context, there have been the first developments of codes of conduct for search engines. One such code was developed by the German industry association: Freiwillige Selbstkontrolle Multimedia-Dienstanbieter e.V., FSM (Voluntary Self-Control for Multimedia Service Providers). The FSM, which has received funding from both the German government and the European Commission, developed a 'multimedia code' in 1997, and added a sub-code for search providers in 2004 (see Appendix 1).[16] This code – which is subscribed to by many of the smaller ISPs and search providers but does not include that with the largest market share, Google.de – is mainly aimed at transparency: placing duties on search providers to inform users about search features and reasons that sites are excluded or included, and making clear when 'sponsoring of links' occurs. It also places an obligation to forward complaints to FSM where they concern illegal content, including child pornography, unconstitutional organisations such as neo-Nazis, and acts of violence against children and animals. Sanctions are weak for this largely experimental code: code subjects can be excluded from the voluntary association, but only after several warnings (FSM Code, section 6).

User level

The self in self-regulation is not always the industry: it can also refer to the individual user, 'empowered' to exercise self-regulatory behaviour either relating to her own use of the network, or relating to that of children.[17] At the level of the individual user, self-regulatory activity focuses on influencing, shaping and limiting the choices that are made by users through education, awareness and decentralised filtering.

'Don't regulate, educate' has been a mantra of those concerned about growing support for regulation of Internet content.[18] The Council of Europe published an Internet Literacy Handbook in 2003 after consulting widely. The UK Communications Act 2003 places on the regulator Ofcom a duty to promote media literacy, and most other countries have government-led media literacy initiatives that were founded with the express aim of dealing with the issues of Internet 'danger' for children. The Internet Action Plans (IAP) for the European Commission funded 13 separate projects developing filtering tools in 2004, along with literacy and public information projects encouraging their use. Support for self and co-regulation continued after the initial IAP when the European Commission launched in 2005 the Safer Internet *Plus* programme (2005–8). The initiative endeavours to fund activities that promote safer use of the Internet and new online technologies, by way of education and awareness programmes coupled with national hotlines enabling the public to report illegal content. The issue of filtering of Internet content has been more controversial, and has been widely discussed in the literature.[19] We will not attempt to summarise ten years of technical debate on filtering. Though not all Internet users are aware of them, all major Internet browsers now provide the user with security and content settings options that include the ability to set a password that will protect content settings, to enable parents to control children's Internet behaviour. The key issues of controversy have been the technological problems of over- and under-blocking, the relative merits of centralised and decentralised, black- vs. white-list filters, the skills deficit (particularly parents' skills) and the involvement of industry vs. government bodies in rating of content.

Browser-level filters are based on word-recognition software, image recognition (e.g. fleshtones) or on red-light (black)/green-light (white) lists (i.e. databases of 'approved' or 'non-approved' sites). They can also be based on decentralised self-rating schemes such as ICRA, which relies on web designers themselves to rate their own sites according to agreed criteria. Successive generations of initiatives, dating back to PICS and RSACi standards, have attempted to establish an industry standard for decentralised self-rating whereby meta-tags are applied to websites enabling browser level filters, set voluntarily by guardians, to exclude inappropriate sites. The effectiveness and fairness of such schemes has been subject to question, and ultimately depends on browser settings. If children's filters are set to access only labelled sites, then they can be effective, but many people would argue that the ratio of labelled to unlabelled sites on the Internet (perhaps less than 1:100) would lead to unacceptable restrictions on Internet use. Those using filters based on labels would be able to reach only a tiny fraction of the total available content, and the experience of linking through a variety of sites – at the heart of the experience of the Internet – would become impossible.

An obvious consequence of the growth of various forms of self-regulation applicable to internet content is that the same content is often subject to numerous codes of conduct and accountable to several self-regulatory bodies. Figure 6.3 shows some of the overlaps. Taking, for example, content that is provided by a newspaper online, it may be subject to one or several offline codes developed for newspaper content or journalism. More generally, it could be subject to the ISP code and a specific online code provided by the newspaper itself or another body. And it could be involved in a self-labelling scheme such as ICRA. It is at least theoretically possible that the same content creator will be working within all of these regulatory schemes and more. Whilst these forms of overlap and potential conflict are by no means unique to online services, they do raise questions about the level of regulatory burden and the extent to

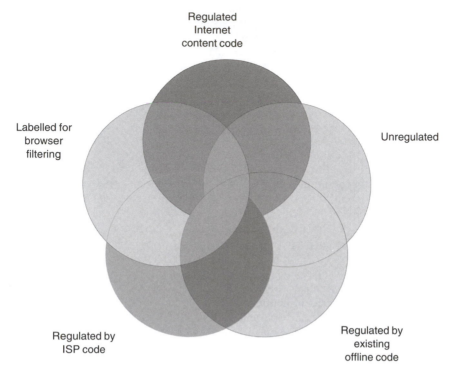

Figure 6.3 Internet content and self-regulation. Note: web content may fall under a number of regime types. Some Internet content is subject to multiple codes and labelling procedures. The web content of a newspaper for example may be subject to the pan industry guidelines of a journalistic ethics committee, to an ICP code of conduct and it may also label for ICRA. The ISP hosting the content may be the newspaper itself, or smaller companies may host externally and be subject to an external ISP code including take-down procedures.

which such a degree of overlap and potential conflict is undermining effectiveness of any single scheme.

Internet self-regulation of content: the early settlement

The first paradigm of Internet regulation was summarised by Marcel Machill *et al.* in 2001.[20] An adapted version of this scheme is shown in Figure 6.4. In this model the various forms of increased literacy and awareness, notice and take down, cooperation with law enforcement and other self-regulatory initiatives, create a virtuous circle. The key here is that the process is driven by complaints and monitoring by users themselves, and is self-perpetuating as long as it is supported by increasing levels of public awareness and media literacy.

This first settlement has become somewhat institutionalised on both sides of the Atlantic, and marked a compromise for a rapidly developing but fragmented ISP industry keen to avoid regulation, under pressure from rights holders and civil society to prevent illegality online. Governments competing with one another for investment

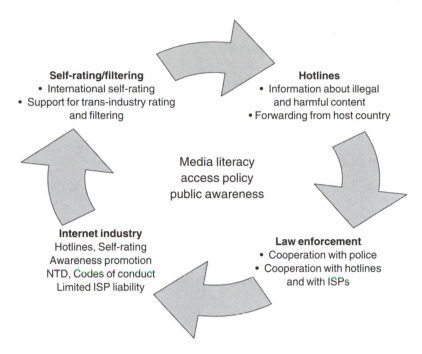

Figure 6.4 (Self-) regulation of Internet content: the early settlement (adapted from Machill *et al.* 2001).

in communications were cautious about placing burdens of regulation on a key strategic industry. This model of Internet content regulation, which is embedded in a co-regulatory framework outlined in the E-Commerce Directive in Europe and the Digital Millennium Copyright Act in the United States, attempted to assuage concern among parents, whilst addressing potential objections regarding both freedom of speech and regulatory burden. It also reflects the growing alarm of copyright holders that the Internet was bypassing traditional businesses based on publishing.

The framework is already being questioned. For one thing, governments are less worried about 'breaking' the economic dynamism of the Internet and are therefore less cautious about imposing regulatory burdens. Second, there are some signs that the first paradigm of Internet content self-regulation may be failing to deliver: significant indicators of continuing harm remain, both in terms of the level of trust in Internet transactions and in terms of the levels of exposure to harmful content as we saw in the first chapter of this book.

Notice and take down (NTD)[21]

Aside from a few fringe attempts (for example in Singapore and Australia) to apply broadcasting standards of taste and decency to Internet content, most countries accepted, some reluctantly, that it was not pragmatic to do so in this unruly, borderless medium. Consumers tended to rely more on brands as a guarantee of quality and safety, which helped facilitate the leverage of existing newspaper and broadcasting brands into online services. The focus of self-regulatory activity moved to *illegal* content; to obscenity, hate speech, defamation, copyright infringement and related areas. The question of the responsibility of the Internet service providers that carry such content to consumers was raised in numerous court cases and regulatory decisions during the early to mid 1990s. It was only with the publishing of the E-Commerce Directive[22] in 2000 that the European regime was clarified. Broadly, the current regime obliges those service providers to take down – or restrict access to – material posted on the Internet only when they have been told to take it down and they are satisfied it is illegal.

Notice and take down (NTD) is emerging as the key tool in Internet content regulation, and this method of regulation is being developed also to apply to mobile Internet services. The E-Commerce Directive underlies the NTD procedure as applied by ISPs in the United Kingdom. The framework is outlined in articles 14.3 and 21.2 and section 46. This reflects a liability regime that basically places an obligation on ISPs to remove illegal content only when the ISP 'obtains actual knowledge' of it. When ISPs have such knowledge, they must remove or disable access to the content. When the ISP receives notice, usually from a user or a hotline specifically set up for the purpose, of illegal content, then the ISP becomes responsible for taking it down if it is illegal. A similar NTD procedure has been instituted in the United States, under the Digital Millennium Copyright Act (DMCA). This obliges ISPs to take down material when they are notified of copyright infringement. The DMCA is more stringent regarding the procedure for NTD, outlining the need for specific staff needed to run the procedure and some rights for appeal.

This overall framework has been controversial both sides of the Atlantic, for various reasons: because it places a sensitive censorship role in private hands and because it is unclear whether ISPs have the resources or inclination to establish if content is in fact illegal. The dangers of NTD are numerous: some argue that it is under-effective, allowing illegal content to remain accessible, and others that, despite a specific duty to observe the principle of freedom of expression, it is administered sloppily, with legal content being removed without sufficient due process, rights of appeal or transparency.

The European E-Commerce Directive contains the following in paragraph 46:

> In order to benefit from a limitation of liability, the provider of an information society service, consisting of the storage of information, upon obtaining actual knowledge or awareness of illegal activities has to act expeditiously to remove or to disable access to the information concerned; the removal or disabling of access has to be undertaken in the observance of the principle of freedom of expression and of procedures established for this purpose at national level; this Directive does not affect Member States' possibility of establishing specific requirements which must be fulfilled expeditiously prior to the removal or disabling of information.

There are also problems of monitoring that are discussed by Ahlert, Frydman and others (Ahlert *et al.* 2003; Frydman and Rorive 2002). The US regime applies exclusively to copyright-infringing material, whilst the EC regime applies in general to illegal content, including copyright infringement. In Europe there has been some disquiet about a system that was devised to deal with categories of illegal and harmful content such as hate speech and child pornography being used primarily to police copyright infringement.

Hotlines and cooperation with law enforcement

The European Commission and national governments have given strong support to the development of a national network of hotlines for reporting of illegal Internet content. These hotlines are generally financed and managed through collective action of ISPs at the national level. Their objective is to deal quickly with the reporting, and where appropriate removal, of illegal content, and to collaborate with law enforcement on the national and the international level. These bodies, listed in Table 6.1, are emerging as a norm, and are increasingly being set up in the new member states of the European Union and also in central Europe. The European Commission provided a grant of 80,000 euros for the new Hungarian hotline *hotline. hu* in 2004, and 165,000 euros for the Polish hotline *hotline.org.pl*.

Hotlines are contacted by users who suspect they have found illegal content, and those hotlines then review the material, handing on to law enforcement/ISPs where necessary. The networks of hotlines, which receive public funding both through the European Commission and national bodies, are very developed in Europe.

Whilst this system appears to have worked well in the half-decade it has now been running, there does appear to be some danger of confusion about the exact breakdown of roles. Hotlines do make a judgement call about whether content is illegal, and ISPs may not, when they have the 'authority' of a hotline decision, invest sufficient time in the review procedure. Where responsibilities and procedures are not clearly laid out in the statutes of the hotline and code of the ISP, then there is clearly room for buck-passing between the two. Also, where it appears that ISPs are not engaging the resources necessary to make those judgement calls, it would seem obvious to suggest that ISP associations faced with notice to take down could engage the adjudication mechanisms at the national hotline rather than develop their own procedure. When the Directive is next reviewed, these procedures will come under

Table 6.1 National Internet hotlines

Country	Self-regulatory body	Year of commencement
Austria	STOPLINE	2000
Belgium	Childfocus Net Alert	2001
Bulgaria	SAFE-NET BG	2005
Cyprus	SaferNet	2004
Denmark	Red Barnet	2001
Finland	Northern Hotline – Nettivihje	2002
France	AFA Point de Contact	2002
Germany	IBSDE	2000
	Jugendschutz.net	2000
Greece	SAFELINE	2002
Hungary	InternetHotline.hu	2004
Iceland	Barnaheill Stopline	2001
Italy	Stop-It	2002
	Hot 114	2005
Lithuania	Hotline Lithuania	2005
Malta	Hotline Malta	2006
Netherlands	Meldpunt	2000
Poland	NIFC Hotline	2004
Spain	Protegeles	2000
UK	IWF	2000

scrutiny. Article 21.2 outlines the intention to review NTD and the attribution of liability under the Directive.

Publication of basic regulatory data on websites is a generally accepted standard for transparency of regulation, particularly regarding sensitive issues that impact on speech freedoms.[23] If data on Internet regulatory bodies' basic functions such as code revision, complaints received and adjudicated, outcomes and so forth are not available on the Internet we can say that they have failed to reach a basic standard of transparency. Our survey shows that there are many examples of good practice in this regard, but there are also areas of the European Internet self-regulatory regime that remain opaque and therefore it is difficult to gain an accurate picture of the overall level of self-regulatory activity. Table 6.2 outlines the annual levels of reports received by Internet self-regulatory hotlines (annual data for 2004 and 2005).

Most Internet self-regulatory hotlines are maintaining adequate levels of transparency when reporting on their activities and actions on their websites by means such as annual reports (see Table 6.2). Levels of awareness and the size of the market may play a key role in numbers of reports received. The high figures in the United Kingdom reflect higher levels of public awareness and the long-standing reputation of the IWF.

Clearly there may be perverse outcomes from the limited liability, mere conduit NTD model of Internet content regulation. In particular, this model encourages the ISP to be as ignorant as possible of the content transmitted, since knowledge implies responsibility. It may be a system that is designed more with ISP liability and less with the objective of preventing illegal or harmful activity in mind. This dilemma of 'hear no evil, see no evil, speak no evil' has operated as an uneasy compromise between desire to control illegal material and a concern for protection of freedom of speech rights. In the absence of any basic transparency of ISPs with regard to this issue it is impossible to evaluate the effectiveness of this procedure or its likely outcomes. The irony of the current situation is that its apparent defectiveness renders NTD tolerable: if it were more effective in removing content, and more transparent about removal and blocking, it is likely that there would be loud calls for reform.

Table 6.2 Reports received by national Internet hotlines in 2004 and 2005

	Reports received 2004	*Reports received 2005*
Austria	1,482	2,202
Belgium	2,172	–
Denmark	5,143	7,244
Finland	7,394[a]	–
Greece	58	294
Ireland	299	398
Italy	2,788	3,106
Netherlands	6,322	8,185
Poland	–	885[b]
UK	17,255	23,658

Source: Figures sourced from national Internet hotline websites.

Notes
a March 2004 to February 2005.
b January 2005 to September 2005.

Specific privacy codes

Alongside the general ISP codes that have been the subject of this study, a great many websites carry a privacy code, though this trend has been in decline in recent years. Several studies of privacy codes and compliance have been carried out, by the OECD, by the UK Information Commission, and others.[24] Privacy policies, like many others, generally incorporate a trustmark.

Trustmarks

Trustmarks, also known in the United Kingdom as kitemarks, have emerged as a key aspect of self-regulation of web content, through the application of a recognisable symbol (trustmark) to sites that have signed up to a common set of standards, usually codified into a written code of conduct. This form of self-regulation has been particularly evident in the case of those sites that require high levels of public trust in order to be successful, such as e-commerce and health information sites (Figure 6.5).

For this form of regulation to work, each stage of the process needs to be successful. There are numerous successful models of trustmarks in terms of the development of appropriate codes and pan-industry groups to monitor compliance, but the central and profound challenge for this model is effective monitoring of compliance with the code. Programme in Comparative Media Law and Policy (PCMLP) research showed that this is very rarely proactive, and generally complaints-driven (Wagemans 2003). Therefore in general, sites are very rarely removed from a trustmark scheme for non-compliance with a code (particularly where trustmark schemes are financially dependent on their members). Another key challenge lies with consumer awareness and brand recognition – which are obviously crucial if trustmarks are to impact consumer choices. Particularly where there is competition between trustmarks, the consumer is unlikely to recognise a purely Internet trustmark and the costs of investing in brand awareness through advertisement are likely to be prohibitively high. Therefore the efficacy of this regulatory tool, when it is entirely dependent on consumer awareness of trustmarks, must be questioned. If labels are machine-readable, and when media literacy and awareness schemes enlist the help of public education campaigns, schemes are more likely to be effective. If the latter course were to be seriously supported, it would be inappropriate that trustmarks were commercial enterprises. There is a strong argument for public funding here, and for a coordinating regulatory role to ensure that compliance is effectively monitored, and competition between trustmarks does not waste resources.

Conclusions

Figure 6.6 is a simplification, and it is also an ideal type: it does not match any national level procedure exactly, but takes elements from several, and includes optional extras. Some procedures enable the board themselves to initiate complaints (as in the United Kingdom and elsewhere), whilst others are genuinely user-driven. Not all have the same structures for cooperation with law enforcement or provision of blacklists to filtering providers. Under the Australian co-regulatory system the Australian Communications and Media Authority (formerly the Australian Broadcasting Authority and Australian Communications Authority) maintains a blacklist of sites that are inappropriate for children.[25] This blacklist is provided free of charge to those who maintain filters for browsers that enable 'child-friendly' surfing. The ISP

Quality Criteria for Health-Related Websites

Developed in widespread consultation with representatives of private and public eHealth websites and information providers, other industrial representatives, public officials, and representatives of government departments, international organisations, and non-governmental organisations.

These criteria should be applied in addition to relevant Community law

Transparency and honesty
- Transparency of provider of site – including name, physical address and electronic address of the person or organisation responsible for the site (see Articles 5 and 6, Directive 2000/31/EC on Electronic Commerce).
- Transparency of purpose and objective of the site.
- Target audience clearly defined (further detail on purpose, multiple audience could be defined at different levels).
- Transparency of all sources of funding for site (grants, sponsors, advertisers, non-profit, voluntary assistance).

Authority
- Clear statement of sources for all information provided and date of publication of source.
- Name and credentials of all human/institutional providers of information put up on the site, including dates at which credentials were received.

Privacy and data protection
- Privacy and data protection policy and system for the processing of personal data, including processing invisible to users, to be clearly defined in accordance with community Data Protection legislation (Directives 95/46/EC and 2002/58/EC).

Updating of information
- Clear and regular updating of the site, with date of up-date clearly displayed for each page and/or item as relevant. Regular checking of relevance of information.

Accountability
- Accountability – user feedback, and appropriate oversight responsibility (such as a named quality compliance officer for each site).
- Responsible partnering – all efforts should be made to ensure that partnering or linking to other websites is undertaken only with trustworthy individuals and organisations who themselves comply with relevant codes of good practice.
- Editorial policy – clear statement describing what procedure was used for selection of content.

Accessibility
- Accessibility – attention to guidelines on physical accessibility as well as general findability, searchability, readability, usability, etc.

Figure 6.5 Quality criteria for health-related websites.

blocking that BT CleanFeed and Telnor provide is also based on a blacklist that is built through consumer complaints, but again, this model has only been developed in certain countries.

As the orthodoxy for Internet self-regulation becomes institutionalised on a global level, many have claimed that it will lead to an inevitable 'chilling effect' on Internet speech (e.g. Hosein 2004). It is argued that repressive regimes will find it easy to maintain blacklists of 'inappropriate' content that includes dissident websites, and that

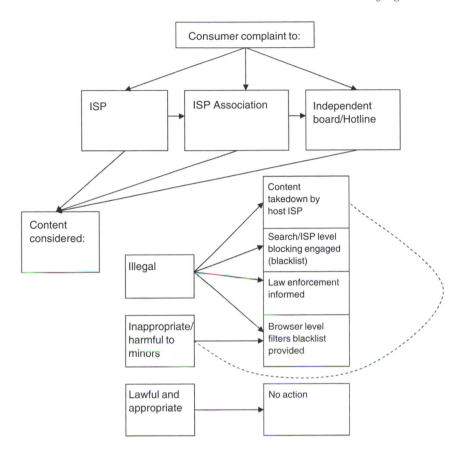

Figure 6.6 A self-regulatory content take-down procedure.

there is already an established tendency to do so, in China, Saudia Arabia, the Central Asian Republics and elsewhere.[26]

Some systems (such as Italy) oblige content providers to take down content that is not illegal, but is considered inappropriate or harmful (the dotted line of Figure 6.6). Others, such as the IWF in the United Kingdom, are reluctant to take down material that is, in a distinction adopted by the UK Home Office, 'unlawful but not illegal' (i.e. not subject to criminal sanction). This focuses the IWF hotline on the core mission of dealing with child pornography, rather than other forms of illegal content such as copyright infringement or defamation.

The extent to which this 'official' procedure for dealing with inappropriate or illegal content is the main self-regulatory activity remains unclear. As discussed below, many, perhaps most, complaints will go direct to the ISP, which incurs liability when it is informed of illegal content. Much of this is taken down immediately, without recourse to the supervisory board and the transparency/procedural standards that this would imply. The dotted line of Figure 6.6 represents a potentially problematic procedure that is discussed further below: the removal of legal content by an ISP through a notice and take-down procedure. In some cases, removal would follow review by a transparent and representative board of industry and civil society representatives. In others this does not take place, and content is removed through individual discretion and non-transparent procedures. Both raise fundamental concerns for freedom of expression which are explained further in Chapter 11.

APPENDIX 1

German FSM Code for Search Engine Providers. Translation by FSM

FSM Sub-Code for Search Engine Providers

(Code S)

Status: 21.12.2004
The aim of the Sub-Code for Search Engine Providers (Code S) is to improve consumer protection and to protect children and young people from inappropriate content when using search engines in Germany. Search engine providers generally operate as information finders and provide no content in their own right. They are, however, aware of their special role in finding information online. Code S thus expresses providers' awareness of its responsibilities and willingness to engage in voluntary self-monitoring. It applies exclusively to search engines in Germany and provides rules for searches conducted using them.

§ 1. Scope

1. Code S is binding for FSM members who are search engine providers or who have entered into a written agreement for the purpose of using search features of other search engine providers. Signatories to search features of other search engine providers shall within the scope of their capabilities strive to ensure that their provider complies with this Sub-Code. Code S constitutes a Sub-Code for specific member groups (search engines) within the meaning of Section 2 (2) of FSM's Articles of Association. A search engine is an online index of documents and images that are stored and published on computers connected to the Internet. The indexes are generated automatically using computer algorithms and are made publicly accessible to users worldwide.
2. Code S does not prejudice any best practice principles codified in law.
3. The code of conduct set out in Section 2 below is definitive. Save for the provisions it contains, Code S does not cover violations of other legal provisions, including those of advertising law, copyright law, data privacy law, consumer protection law, law on the freedom of expression or competition law.

§ 2. Code of Conduct

1. Signatories to Code S agree to inform users about their search engine features. They will also explain the circumstances under which websites are excluded from search results lists. The information must be made easily accessible to users.
2. Signatories to Code S agree to structure their search results pages as transparently as their resources allow. Search engine results which owe their positioning

on the results page to a commercial agreement with the search engine provider shall be marked accordingly. This can be done using terms such as 'advertisement', 'sponsor links', 'sponsored links' or 'sponsored websites'.

3. Within their capabilities, signatories to Code S strive to provide technical solutions that are suited to protecting children and young people from content that is harmful or dangerous. Consideration must, however, be given to the fact that no absolute guarantee can be given regarding the protection of children and young people from inappropriate content and that children should not use the Internet without parental supervision or that of a guardian.

4. The principle of the necessary minimum shall apply in the management of user data.

5. a) Signatories to Code S agree to involve the FSM Complaints Office as regards complaints that a link shown in the search results list violates the provisions of Section 2 (5) a of Code S. If following a preliminary investigation, it cannot be ruled out that one of the offences listed below has been committed, FSM will pass the complaint to the Federal Department for Media Harmful to Young Persons (BPjM). All other action is governed by the FSM Procedures for Search Engine Providers (VO-S). The list of offences includes:

   - Use of propaganda material and symbols of unconstitutional organisations as defined in Articles 86 and 86a of the German Criminal Code (StGB), and Article 4 (1) Nos. 1 and 2 of Germany's Interstate Treaty for the Protection of Human Dignity and the Protection of Minors in the Media (JMStV).
   - Incitement to hatred and violence against segments of the population (*Volksverhetzung*) and holocaust denial (*Auschwitzlüge*) as defined in Section 130 StGB and Section 4 (1) Nos. 3 and 4 JMStV.
   - Incitement to instigate or commit crimes (Section 130a StGB, Section 4 (1) No. 6 JMStV).
   - Depiction of acts of violence (Section 131 StGB, Section 4 (1) No. 5 JMStV) and of pornography featuring children, animals and violence (Section 148 (3) StGB, Section 4 (1) No. 10 JMStV).
   - Depiction of erotic poses featuring minors (Section 4 (1) No. 9 JMStV).
   - Glorification of war (Section 4 (1) No. 7 JMStV).
   - Violation of human rights (Section 4 (1) No. 8 JMStV).

   b) Where they have access to the URL and where the associated business expense can be reasonably expected, signatory providers also agree to remove or not to show any URL that has been indexed by the BPjM.

§ 3. Sanctions

If after applying the FSM Rules of Procedure for Search Engine Providers (VO-S) and the FSM Sub-Code for Search Engine Providers, the responsible FSM committee finds that a violation of Sub-Code S has occurred, it may implement sanctions under Section 6 VO-S.

§ 4. Final Provisions

Signatory members to Code S agree to review and revise both Code S and the list of sanctions every twelve months on the basis of practical experience.

Berlin
21 December 2004

Notes

1 Reproduced in Chapter 3 of this volume, Appendix 1.
2 The relationship between software code and law is well established (Lessig, L (1999) *Code and Other Laws of Cyberspace*, New York: Basic Books). The interplay between software-code-based regulation and self-regulation is less well explored, but for discussion see Price, M and Verhulst, S (2005) *Self Regulation and the Internet*, The Hague: Kluwer Law International.
3 See Price and Verhulst (2005), op. cit.
4 The German Press Council in 1996 adopted a decision extending its jurisdiction and code to complaints on online material; the UK PCC has adjudicated a growing number of complaints regarding online content, including content not also published on paper.
5 For example, New Zealand: www.e-government.govt.nz/web-guidelines. Government guidelines vary enormously. The major concern of the New Zealand guidelines is the issue of accessibility.
6 The Webtrader and TrustE trustmarks, and also the E-Health guidelines discussed below, are examples of content providers developing codes of conduct that are linked to publicly recognisable brands.
7 Tambini, D and Forgan, L (2000) 'Content', in Tambini, D (ed.) *Communications: Revolution and Reform*, London: IPPR.
8 See Chapter 4 on print media regulation.
9 www.spj.org/ethics_code.asp
10 See Ofcom (2005) *The Communications Market*, pp. 62–74.
11 These are discussed at length in: Clayton, Richard (2005) 'Failures in a Hybrid Content Blocking System', paper presented at a workshop on Privacy Enhancing Technologies. Dubrovnik, Croatia, 31 May.
12 Find the agreement at: www.fsm.de/?s=News&news_id=361&browse_page=2&s= News&news_id=358
13 Ofcom Complaint number CW/00779/08/04, www.ofcom.org.uk
14 www.worldinternetproject.net/2003 data (last accessed 08/05).
15 www.guardian.co.uk/bigbrother/privacy/yourlife/story/0,12384,785839,00.html; see also Porter, K M and Scheib, J (American Bar Association) (2002) 'Work Station or Purgatory? Steps toward a company policy on e-mail and using the Net', *Business Law Today* 11(6), 60 (Online).
16 www.fsm.de/?s=Subkodex+Suchmaschinenanbieter
17 Price, M and Verhulst, S (2005) *Self Regulation and the Internet*, The Hague: Kluwer Law International.
18 The phrase was coined by Professor Roger Silverstone of the LSE.
19 See Price and Verhulst (2005), op. cit.; Waltermann, J and Machill, M (2000) *Protecting Our Children on the Internet: Towards a New Culture of Responsibility*, Guetersloh: Bertelsmann Foundation. The EC commissioned a study, 'SIP-BENCH', to benchmark performance of filtering software in 2004.
20 Machill, M, Hart, T and Hauser, B K (2000) 'Structural Development of Internet Self-Regulation: Case Study of the Internet Content Rating Association (ICRA)', in Waltermann, J and Machill, M (2000), op. cit.
21 In this section we draw upon research conducted by Christopher Marsden, Christian Ahlert and Chester Yung: http://pcmlp.socleg.ox.ac.uk/text/liberty.pdf, and on the work of Frydman, B and Rorive, I, www.selfregulation.info/iapcoda/rxio-background-020923. htm
22 Directive 2000/31/EC of the European Parliament and of the Council of 8 June 2000 on certain legal aspects of information society services, in particular electronic commerce, in the Internal Market (Directive on electronic commerce).
23 Though standards of transparency are rarely formalised, they are mentioned when self-regulatory bodies are subject to audit. Following a consultation, UK regulator Ofcom included transparency in its criteria for transferring coregulatory bodies in 2004.

24 Global Report, Selfregulation.info 2003, p. 28: http://www.selfregulation.info/iapcoda/030329-selfreg-global-report.htm (last accessed June 2007).

25 Schedule 5 to the Broadcasting Services Act 1992 establishes the Online Content Co-regulatory Scheme. A review of this scheme was conducted in 2004: www.dcita.gov.au/–data/assets/pdf_file/10920/Online_Content_Review_Report.pdf

26 See the reports provided by the Berkman Center at Harvard University and by the consortium of researchers at: www.opennetinitiative.org

7 ISP codes of conduct

As the key actors within the provision of Internet services, and the link to the consumer, ISPs are crucial to the processes of rule-making, adjudication and complaints-handling for the Internet. While they maintain their own terms of service with their consumers, and many developed their own corporate codes of conduct, they are increasingly cooperating in Europe to develop pan industry national codes of conduct, and are under pressure from the EC to develop Europe-wide codes. This chapter contains an analysis of these codes. Our research focused on the ISP codes of conduct, monitoring the content, constitution, coverage, communication and compliance-related material in the code.

Case study: Italian ISP code, and the 'Internet and Minors' co-regulatory code

(i) Constitution

The Italian experience illustrates the interplay of EU, national government and industry institutions in Internet rule-making. According to the code drafters: 'following the resolution of the EU Telecommunications Council of 28 November 1997, the Post Office Board invited the operators of the Internet sector to undertake the work required to draw up a self-regulation code.' On a model also experienced in other countries, a working group was set up, composed of experts from the major ISPs and other interested parties, including AIIP (Italian Association of Internet Providers), ANEE (National Association of Electronic Publishing), Telecom Italia and Olivetti.

In May 1997, the draft code produced by the working group (see Appendix 1) was presented to the user and consumer associations in order to have their opinion on the document, establishing a loose framework for Italian ISPs. However, following further public debate, particularly about paedophilia websites, the government in 2002 judged that further action was necessary. It set up a working group on responsible Internet use, including an *ad hoc* group less dominated by ISPs with representatives of Save the Children and other civil society groups. This group produced a new draft code of conduct in May 2003, and a proposal for a government-appointed supervisory board. The code was greeted with protest from the ISP sector who objected that they were not consulted. They also argued strongly that the code, drafted by government officials, was not self-regulatory, but an attempt to assert government control over Internet content. After a difficult renegotiation of the code, which required three further meetings, the new working group, including the AIIP and two of the other key lobby groups, signed the code together with the Minister for Communications, and the board was established in February 2004.

(ii) Coverage

The new code is voluntary in the sense that the subjects of the code are those that freely download and sign it. Anybody can download, print and sign the forms of adhesion from the Ministry website. The current code includes clauses applying to signatories that are also content providers, obliging them to remove content on request of the Committee of Guarantee. It does not apply to those other sectors which also have Ministry-sponsored codes of conduct. The Internet code also establishes that members of the Committee of Guarantee will be appointed directly by the Ministry of Communications, though frequency of meetings were not specified.

(iii) Content

The Italian code is narrow 'at the moment' according to one of its drafters. Although it is detailed, many of the clauses are relatively weak. ISPs are encouraged but not obliged to use filters and age verification and to protect privacy by the code, and the code serves more to summarise and attract attention to existing law than to establish new more restrictive restrictions on content. The code is concerned only, given its title, with material considered harmful to minors, including violent and/or sexual content and offensive language. The code contains broad definitions of what might be considered harmful. Some board members have commented that definitions are disputed, but given a lack of transparency there is little means to ascertain how decisions are made on what content subject content providers may be induced to remove.

(iv) Communication

The communications strategy of the new co-regulatory institutions in Italy ostensibly is directed at linking with the government, regulator, ISPS, NGOs, consumers and law enforcement, but there does not appear to be a coordinated strategy for promoting the body, and no easily available record of numbers of complaints, adjudications, or council meetings.

(v) Compliance

At the time of writing there have been no disputes, and there is no publicly available record of the notice and take-down procedure in operation. Sanctions of the code are generally informal with public reports on violation of code, but include removal, after warnings, from the association.

European Internet service codes of conduct: what rules?

The content of ISP codes varies enormously from minimal, vague provisions to exhaustive and stringent provisions covering a wide variety of potential harms associated with Internet services. The issues least likely to be included in the code of conduct were issues of ICP coverage and provisions regarding hate speech online. This finding is very significant in that it shows that self-regulation, as it is set up by the 11 national ISP codes of conduct, has limited reach in dealing with some of the most pressing public concerns over Internet use – namely issues of sensitive and/or illegal content such as hate speech, incitement to violence and xenophobic speech. Understanding this observation, again, requires us to consider the fact that ISPs in many of the countries analysed have legislation prohibiting hate speech. Furthermore, the fact that each of the 11 country codes had a provision for illegal activity means that, in most of the countries not dealing explicitly with hate speech, this issue was covered under the provision of illegal activity.

Analysis

Figure 7.1 summarises the findings of the review by indicating each of the country's ISP codes' coverage of 11 issues: application to ICPs, provisions for review and amendment, regulation of information regarding business, provisions concerning illegal activity, provisions limiting access to material harmful to minors, provisions regarding hate speech, provisions regarding bulk e-mail, data protection and privacy provisions, complaint mechanism, provisions that regulate cooperation with law enforcement and third parties, and sanction mechanisms. The chart shows the penetration level of each issue in terms of the number of codes in which each issue was coded for.

Issue penetration and code completeness 5C analysis

(i) Introduction

The purpose of this study was to collect and analyse codes of conduct implemented by ISP Associations (ISPAs), evaluate the collected codes, and recommend acceptable minimum standards for ISP codes of conduct. The minimum standards for ISP codes of conduct are an important foundation for any successful self-regulation by the industry. In the European Union, especially, further development of ISPs presents special challenges for national associations, the industry, and the governments in harmonising existing codes of conduct or developing new EU-wide codes. The analysis and recommendations in this study present a basis for an approach to further cooperation of national ISPAs at the EU level.

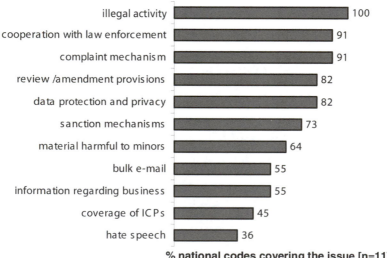

Figure 7.1 Main issues covered by ISP codes of conduct.

(ii) Background

Given that the process of constitution of ISP codes worked within general guidelines at both the national and the EU level, that each country adopted a different model of stakeholder involvement, and that the process was only loosely coordinated, we might expect that a broad range of rules emerged from the early development of Internet codes. What rules do ISP codes contain? Table 7.1 summarises the findings of the review by indicating each of the country's ISP codes' coverage of the 11 issues defined above.

As we saw in Chapter 1, national governments have traditionally avoided direct regulation of the Internet, and the new medium has been left to the industry to self-regulate. Recent interest of European institutions, most prominently the European Commission and the Council of Europe, has added the pan-European dimension to the issue of Internet self-regulation. As far back as 1997, the European Commission launched an Action Plan to investigate ways of making the Internet safer, and the Council Recommendation of 24 September 1998 made protection of minors and human dignity online an issue for the European Union. Most recently, the Council of Europe Convention on Cybercrime of 23 November 2001 set an important precedent in applying Europe-wide standards to the Internet.

Table 7.1 Issue penetration and code completeness

Y/N Issue	AT ISPA	BE ISPA	DE FSM	FR ISPA	IE ISPA	IT ISPA	NL ISPA	NO ISPA	UK ISPA	
A 5/4	Y		Y	Y	Y		Y			Designed to apply to both ISPs and ICPs?
B 7/2	Y	Y	Y		Y	Y		Y	Y	Formal provisions for review and amendment?
C 5/4		Y			Y	Y	Y		Y	Regulates information regarding business?
D 9/0	Y	Y	Y	Y	Y	Y	Y	Y	Y	Provisions concerning illegal activity?
E 5/4	Y		Y	Y	Y	Y				Provisions limiting access to material harmful to minors?
F[a] 3/6			Y		Y			Y		Provisions regarding hate speech?
G 4/5				Y	Y		Y	Y		Provisions regarding bulk e-mail?
H[b] 8/1	Y	Y		Y	Y	Y	Y	Y	Y	Data protection and privacy provisions?
I 9/0	Y	Y	Y	Y	Y	Y	Y	Y	Y	Complaint mechanism?
J 8/1	Y	Y	Y	Y	Y	Y	Y		Y	Provisions that regulate cooperation with law enforcement and third parties?
K 8/1	Y	Y	Y		Y	Y	Y	Y	Y	Sanction mechanisms?

Notes

a It is worth noting that all nine countries reviewed had coded for illegal content; this means that, in countries in which racist or xenophobic speech is illegal, it is incorporated in the code by reference.

b FSM code excludes issues covered by advertising, privacy, consumer and competition legislation.

(iii) Methodology

The codes of eight EU member states (Austria, Belgium, Germany, France, Ireland, Italy, the Netherlands and the United Kingdom), as well as the codes of Norway, Australia and Canada, were analysed. Of these, French, Italian, German, Austrian, Irish, Dutch and UK ISP associations are members of the EuroISPA.

The codes were translated from the original into English, and contacts were made with a number of ISPAs in order to verify the translations and seek clarification on sections of concern. The text of codes was analysed by applying general code of conduct methodology previously developed by PCMLP by Monroe Price.[1]

(iv) Main results

Of all the ISPA codes analysed, the Irish was the most stringent, or comprehensive. In this study, we use the word stringent or comprehensive to refer to codes that covered most of the areas of interest in self-regulation; i.e. answers to the questions in Table 7.1 were almost exclusively positive. The French and Canadian codes, by contrast, were the least stringent, covering fewer issues. In particular, the French ISPA code applied only to ISPs and not to ICPs, did not have an explicit review/amendment procedure, provided no guidance on information regarding business, provided no hate speech provisions, and had no formal sanctions mechanisms specified.

The observations must be viewed within the larger legal and media-regulatory framework. For example, although the French and a number of other national codes did not contain provisions for hate speech, they did refer to national legislation that makes hate speech in general illegal. This and other issues of legal and practical context are important in evaluating codes. Therefore codes that may be more stringent, or more comprehensive, do not necessarily result in a more regulated environment for ISPs in a country. This is an important distinction to maintain in viewing and analysing the results presented throughout this report. Figure 7.2 shows degrees of code comprehensiveness across the national cases of ISP codes of conduct.

Of all the issues examined (as outlined in the list of questions in Table 7.1), the main issue covered by each of the 11 ISP codes of conduct was illegal activity. All codes made explicit reference to a series of measures (from hotlines to fair practices to national legislation to cooperation with authorities) in condemning and/or otherwise strictly discouraging ISPs from engaging in conduct that was illegal mainly under national law. Cooperation with law enforcement and complaint mechanisms also ranked high on the list of issues included by national ISP codes. Figure 7.2 summarises the 11 issues analysed by their prevalence in 11 countries' ISPA codes of conduct.

The issues least likely to be included in the code of conduct were issues of ICP coverage and provisions regarding hate speech online. This finding is very significant in that it shows that self-regulation as it is set up by the 11 national ISP codes of conduct has limited reach in dealing with some of the most pressing public concerns over Internet use – namely issues of sensitive and/or illegal content such as hate speech, incitement to violence and xenophobic speech. Understanding this observation, again, requires us to consider the fact that ISPs in many of the countries analysed have legislation for prohibiting hate speech. Furthermore, the fact that each of the 11 country codes had a provision for illegal activity means that, in most of the countries not dealing explicitly with hate speech, this issue was covered under the

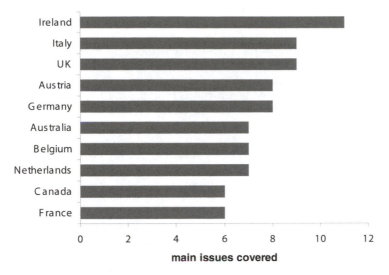

Figure 7.2 Code stringency by country.

provision of illegal activity. This is an important conclusion. Once again, this obser-vation is important when we consider the role of codes of conduct, and self-regulation in general, in regulating online content.

For Issue F (hate speech) note that all nine countries reviewed had coded for illegal content; this means that, in countries in which some form of racist or xenophobic speech is illegal, such as France, Germany and the United Kingdom, it is incorpo-rated in the code by reference, and national law applies.

For Issue H (data protection and privacy provisions) note that the German FSM code excludes issues covered by advertising, privacy, consumer and competition legislation.

As indicated above in the main summary of results (section iv), the summary of find-ings in Table 7.1 indicates a type of *issue penetration* in national ISP codes of conduct. All of the national ISP codes included provisions on illegal content (contained in all the codes in our survey), and this issue was closely followed by provisions for coopera-tion with law enforcement authorities or third parties (contained in 10 codes). In prin-ciple, this is an important link. It signifies that recognition of the existing national legal regime is a necessary foundation for a self-regulatory code of conduct. Furthermore, this (re)statement of already existing national legislation is coupled with provisions for cooperation with law enforcement authorities and third parties. In principle, again, this further legitimises and enforces the national standards on illegal online practice, and should also contribute to enforcement of the code. Yet only eight of the codes studied had clear sanction mechanisms specified.

The procedures for complaints, review and amendment were included in most of the national ISP codes (8 out of 11 for complaints; 10 out of 11 for review and amend-ment). This illustrates openness of the code both to industry and users (who can launch a complaint and therefore engage the self-regulatory system directly), and to the changing business and legal conditions. In the long term, this characteristic may prove valuable in both legitimacy and efficacy of codes.

Surprisingly, only slightly more than a half of the 11 codes of conduct analysed dealt with content issues such as protection of minors, bulk e-mail, and information regarding business. And less than half of the codes engaged directly issues of hate speech and responsibility of ICPs to the ISP self-regulatory framework. This low attention to content self-regulation that usually attracts highest public and media attention is important in understanding the structure and the role of ISP codes of conduct. Essentially, ISP codes of conduct avoided dealing with hate speech and other content self-regulation in countries where those issues were covered under the legal regulatory regimes, or where the government's concern for those issues overrode its willingness to leave the issue up to the industry self-regulation.

The following sections outline detailed ways in which the 11 ISP codes of conduct deal with the core issues of coverage, content, communication and compliance. First, under *communication* we present analysis of the common foundation for all codes, that is, provisions regarding illegal activity and co-operation with law enforcement and third parties. Then under the same rubric, we identify the answers to questions that lead us to analyse general openness of the code: complaints, reviews and amendments. In the next section, we turn to *content* concerns for e-business as well as individual users: data protection, privacy, bulk e-mail, and information regarding business. In the following section, protection of minors and hate speech are covered under the rubric of *content* and coverage of ISPs under the rubric of *coverage*. The final analysis section deals with the issue of sanctions under the general methodological rubric of *compliance*.

Illegal content and cooperation with law enforcement

Of the 11 ISP codes of conduct analysed, all 11 had provisions concerning illegal activity, and only the Norwegian ISP code did not have provisions regulating cooperation with the law enforcement and third parties. This convergence or overlap in the different codes of analysis is important as it helps us identify a common minimal foundation between the national codes.

Austria

In Austria, the ISPA code states that Internet content is subject to the applicable Austrian laws and that the members of the association, on discovery of publicly accessible, criminal content (termed 'illegal content'), will prevent access to the same using the technical and economic means at their disposal. Austrian ISPA members primarily learn about illegal content from the 'Internet Hotline', the ISPA contact point for illegal content, and from the competent authorities.[2] References to presumed illegal content from third parties are relayed to the Internet Hotline for processing.

The Internet Hotline is operated by the ISPA and serves to take reports of illegal Internet content (in particular child pornography and evidence of National Socialist reactivation), for the rapid examination of the reported contents, and, should this be recognised as illegal, relay these reports to every provider that can prevent access to this content and the competent national or international authorities. The Austrian Internet Hotline is incorporated into a network of international Internet report points to ensure efficient information relaying, even beyond the Austrian border.

The Austrian ISPA members ensure simple access for their customers to the Internet Hotline (e.g. via a link from their homepage to the Internet Hotline). Austrian ISPA members, on discovering illegal content and using any reasonable means available to them, immediately block access to the content or prove they have immediately occasioned the blocking of this content should the server concerned lie within the sphere of influence of the customer. In both instances, 'ISPA members, where technically and economically feasible, will secure the relevant evidence for the duration of one calendar month and, under no circumstances, deliberately delete such evidence.'[3] Paragraph 4 of the Austrian ISPA code also deals with cooperation with law enforcement authorities and third parties.

Belgium

In Belgium, the ISPA code's provisions concerning illegal activity and cooperation with law enforcement authorities are provided for by paragraphs 2, 3 and 4 of the code. It states that 'Members' services, products and promotional material are offered legally and with sincerity', and that 'Members are forbidden to accept or encourage anything of an illegal nature'. It instructs the members to 'ensure that their services and promotional materials do not lead to confusion because of non-compliance, ambiguity, overvaluation, modification or any other factor'.[4] Paragraph 3 of the code states that 'ISPs shall undertake in particular to fight against the presence of illegal or doubtful material on the Internet'. It encourages the members to 'pay particular attention to ensuring that the Internet is used legally'. The code states that ISPs do not have the ability to control everything that happens on the Internet; and that their task, therefore, consists merely of regulating the way in which their clients or third parties use or install Internet services. However, the ISPs are informed that they must assist the authorities without delay, in every way possible and according to the means and resources available to them. The Belgian ISPA code stipulates:

1. ISPs shall undertake to identify their clients.
2. ISPs shall add a 'good conduct' section to the general conditions. This section shall contain a reference to proper behaviour on the Internet. The reference to good conduct shall give the ISP an opportunity to take all useful measures (such as, for example, interrupting the service). ISPs shall also make available to their clients an e-mail address reserved for receiving complaints about illegal practices on the network.
3. The legal policy includes a Contact Point for receiving all complaints relating to activity that is illegal, runs counter to public morals (sexual activity, pornography, paedophilia, etc., without this list being comprehensive), contains elements of racism, xenophobia or ethnic cleansing, provokes or encourages criminal acts or associations of criminals, or contains games, lotteries, drugs or similar substances (for example, sites where the sale of substances banned in Belgium is promoted). This list is not comprehensive.
4. All activities that are criminal or run counter to the law or to public morals must be reported to the authorities.
5. The ISPA and ISP shall make a particular point of bringing to the attention of the public the existence of this contact point, most notably by displaying its web-site address on its sites and in its contractual conditions.
6. Communications between the contact point and the ISP shall be the subject of a separate note to be drawn up between the Parties.
7. Members shall comply with the requirements of the legal policy.[5]

On provisions for cooperation with law enforcement, paragraph 3 of the Belgian ISPA code states explicitly that ISPA members must assist the authorities without delay, in every way possible and according to the means and resources available to them. This paragraph of the Belgian ISPA code also states that all activities that are 'criminal or run counter to the law or to public morals must be reported to the authorities'.[6]

France

In France, the responsibilities of the French AFA (the French Internet Service Providers' Association) are classified between ISP responsibility concerning content produced and placed online by AFA users and content provided by third parties. Regarding content produced and placed online by AFA users on their personal pages, AFA members are not responsible for the content placed online by their users. But they check that the users comply with their general obligations. According to the AFA code, in practice, personal pages, which can at any time be modified by their authors, cannot reasonably be subject, as far as AFA members are concerned, to a systematic check of their content. AFA members have the possibility of detecting content that is 'manifestly illegal'. To date, three main means can be used: criticism from users, monitoring of pages most frequently consulted (and directly linked sites), and automatic detection of suspicious words (use of so-called crawler software). However, the effectiveness of software detection is reduced as soon as those responsible for the monitored sites have knowledge of the 'suspicious' words looked for by the access provider's computer program. The monitoring of pages most frequently consulted and the following up of criticism on the part of users make it possible to detect most manifestly illegal content, although not all.[7]

Regarding content produced and placed online by third parties, AFA distinguished between two important subgroups: newsgroups and direct messaging. In the case of newsgroups, the AFA states that 'Access Providers' have no means of preventing the setting up of discussion groups, which they do not initiate. That being the case, according to the AFA, the ISP can take no action until illegal discussion groups have appeared. AFA members can prevent the distribution of groups that do not comply with their General Conditions of User, or by means of a legal injunction. According to the code, in practice, AFA members suspend the distribution of the discussion groups: either by filtering the titles of newsgroups, or when the existence of such newsgroups is brought to their knowledge. Finally, filtered groups may, however, still be consulted through other access providers in France or abroad.[8] The case with direct messaging is similar: AFA members can take no action until after illegal discussion topics have appeared.[9] The issue of illegal content is also dealt with in Part III of the French AFA code, under 'Material Offensive to Adults'.

The AFA code of conduct states that, 'in conformity with the legal provisions in force, AFA members may, at the behest of police or judicial authorities, be required to reveal the identity of one of their Users'. This is the most important stipulation guiding AFA members on their cooperation with law enforcement authorities.[10]

Germany

The German code explicitly states that:

> Members shall take all actions, within the scope of legally determined responsibility and to the extent actually and legally possible and reasonable to ensure that content which is unlawful or impermissible, in particular pursuant to:

§130a of the StGB (Incitement to commit crimes);

§86 of the StGB (Dissemination of propaganda material of unconstitutional organizations);

§87 of the StGB (Treasonable conduct as an agent for sabotage purposes) is neither provided nor switched for use. (Part I, R.2, para. b, d, and e);

§184(3) of StGB (Dissemination of pornographic publications) is not provided nor switched for use (Part I, R.2, para. f).[11]

Regarding cooperation with third parties and law enforcement, in the Preamble, the Association states that it will cooperate with other voluntary self-monitoring bodies – also at the European and international level – in order to cover the global range of services, as well as the international nature of the networks and service providers. There is no other explicit statement on cooperation with third parties.

Ireland

The Irish code defines illegal content as that contrary to criminal law.[12] The responsibilities of members are defined as follows:

ISPAI acknowledges that it is the role of the State to make and to enforce the law. Members of ISPAI must observe their legal obligations to remove Illegal content when informed by organs of the State or as otherwise required by law. It should not, however, be the responsibility of a Member to determine the legality or suitability or to filter or otherwise restrict reception of or access to content material save where such action is taken following an identified breach (or anticipated breach) of the Code.[13]

Under section 4, the code states that members 'must use best endeavours to ensure that Services (excluding Third Party Content) and Promotional Material do not contain anything which is Illegal and is not of a kind likely to mislead by inaccuracy, ambiguity, exaggeration, omission or otherwise';[14] and that members 'must use best endeavours to ensure that Services (excluding Third Party Content) and Promotional Material are not used to promote or facilitate any practices which are contrary to Irish law'.[15]

The Irish code sets up the www.hotline.ie service to deal with illegal content, complaints, as well as cooperation with law enforcement and third parties. Section 7 of the Irish ISPAI code states:

ISPAI shall co-operate with www.hotline.ie in its efforts to remove Illegal material from Internet web-sites and newsgroups located in Ireland. Members are therefore required to adhere to www.hotline.ie procedures:

7.1 Members must register with www.hotline.ie.

7.2 Members must provide www.hotline.ie with a point of contact to receive notices from www.hotline.ie.

7.3 Members may from time to time receive notices from www.hotline.ie requesting the removal of specified potentially Illegal material from web-sites or newsgroups being hosted by Members. Provided it is technically practical to do so Members must comply with such notices within a reasonable time.

7.4   When requested by www.hotline.ie (where requested by a law enforcement authority) and where technically able to do so, Members must retain (subject to the provisions of the Data Protection Act, 1988) copies of removed material as may be required.

7.5   www.hotline.ie will actively seek to empower all end-users by providing information on ways end-users can protect themselves or their children from content which those end-users may consider harmful.

7.6   Following upon a Complaint made in relation to harmful Third Party Content, www.hotline.ie shall inform, where possible, the Complainant about the organisation hosting that content and will also forward the Complaint to the hosting company for them to take action according to their Acceptable Use Policy. Where the hosting company is a member of the ISPAI then that hosting company must follow the complaints procedure outlined in Section 11.2.

7.7   www.hotline.ie will not have any power to adjudicate on claims of infringement of copyright or advise or make any decision on matters of copyright law.[16]

Italy[17]

The Italian ISP code of conduct states: 'Any Internet party who becomes directly aware of the existence of subject-matter of an illicit nature which is accessible by the public, shall inform the legal authorities accordingly directly.' The obligation of the ISPs is further explicitly stated in regard to their cooperation with authorities and third parties: 'Access and hosting suppliers are obliged to make easily accessible online by all suitable means, including e-mail, information concerning the methods for reporting to the competent authorities any illegal or potentially harmful subject-matter of which they may become aware.'[18]

The Netherlands

The Dutch code deals with illegal content and cooperation with law enforcement authorities (third parties) under its section G.3: 'The provider and the subscriber keep themselves within the bounds of the Dutch law and regulations and observe Netiquette. The provider works in cooperation with the Report Centres recognised by the government and the NLIP for combating illegal content.'[19]

Norway

The Norwegian ISP code briefly regulates the ISPs' responsibility regarding illegal content: 'If the publisher's conduct on the Internet involves manifest and gross breaches of the law, the access provider and the host have the right to terminate the service.'[20] But the Norwegian ISP code does not provide a mechanism for cooperation with law enforcement or third parties.

United Kingdom

The UK ISP code states: 'Members shall use their reasonable endeavours to ensure the following: Services (excluding Third Party Content) and Promotional Material do not contain anything which is in breach of UK law, nor omit anything which UK law requires.' In two specific instances the code states that the members should not encourage anything which is any way unlawful,[21] and that the members are not used to promote or facilitate practices which are contrary to UK law.[22]

Regarding cooperation with law enforcement, the UK ISP code states that 'Members should provide to the police a 24 hour point of contact',[23] and that 'Members should cooperate with each other in investigating and deferring instances of Hacking'.[24]

Canada

In Canada, the national ISP association (CAIP) self-regulates concerns regarding illegal content by its Fair Practices Policy Statement. It states: 'Illegal Content and Conduct CAIP Members will not knowingly host illegal content or condone illegal conduct, and they will take action when notified about either.'[25] Further, the code stipulates: 'CAIP Members will advise customers with questions regarding the legality of specified content or conduct to obtain independent legal advice.'[26] In regard to cooperation with authorities, the policy of CAIP is that 'CAIP Members will cooperate where possible with government officials, international organizations and law enforcement authorities'.

Australia

Australia has developed a framework for Internet content self-regulation that contrasts with the European approach. The Broadcasting Authority, the ABA, was centrally involved in coordinating the Australian Internet industry to devise a code, and the Australian 'co-regulatory' scheme for Internet content is administered by the Australian Communications and Media Authority (ACMA) which replaced the ABA in 2005. The constitution of the scheme involved ministerial/legislative initiative. The Australian scheme is unique in its attempt to provide effective negative regulation based on broadcasting-type standards for 'offensive' or child-inappropriate content, as well as illegal content drawing on Schedule 5 of the Australian Broadcasting Services Act 1992.

The Australian code of 2005, which replaces the 2002 code, sets out contrasting responsibilities for content hosts and ISPs. Notice and take-down procedures for illegal content are set out, and the main aim of the codes is to set out the responsibilities of both hosts and ISPs for dealing with protection of children from inappropriate or harmful content. It also includes mobile content within the ISP code, rather than having a separate regime as is the case in Europe. The code refers to illegal content, restricted content (R18 Level) and prohibited content (X Certificate), drawing on the definitions based on the regulatory scheme for broadcasting. The code places broad 'reasonable measures' responsibilities on content hosts and ISPs to make consumers aware of filter products, to remove illegal content and block minors' access to both restricted and prohibited content. The ABA also maintains a list of approved filters that should be promoted by content hosts and ISPs.[27]

Openness of the code: complaints, reviews and amendments

Of the 11 codes analysed, only the Canadian one did not have explicit provisions for a complaint mechanism. When it comes to formal provisions for reviews and amendments to the code, only the French and the Dutch codes lacked these provisions.

In important ways, provisions specifying complaints mechanisms and formal review and amendment procedure together define openness of the code. The fact that the vast majority of ISP codes studied had these provisions indicates that, in addition to the codes' provisions for illegal content and cooperation with law enforcement, the openness of the code is the second minimal common foundation among the 11 national codes studied. In as much as self-regulation is a voluntary and participatory process, where members of the scheme recognise that it is in their own interest for various reasons, openness of the code – both through the complaint mechanism (on the side of members but also on the side of consumers) and through the review and amendment processes – may serve an important role to foster voluntary cooperation and broader participation of the industry members in the self-regulatory scheme.

Austria

The Austrian ISPA code deals with both the complaints mechanism and review/amendment provisions in paragraph 8 of the code. The code states that the ISPA members 'will adjust these Guidelines at regular intervals to changed actual or legal circumstances through new resolutions in accordance with the ISPA Association Statutes'.[28] Regarding complaints, the code instructs that:

> Objections due to any supposed non-observance of the Guidelines by ISPA members are to be reported in writing (by e-mail, fax or letter) to the ISPA. The ISPA Board, on receipt of such a written report, is to familiarise itself with the facts of the case through the obtaining of a written response (by e-mail, fax or letter) from the ISPA member concerned and is to judge the correctness and seriousness of the complaint. If the complaint is upheld, the ISPA Board, depending on the seriousness of the case and frequency of the non-observance of the Guidelines by the ISPA member concerned, may either issue a warning or terminate the membership of the member concerned under the terms of § 6 (4) of the 'ISPA Statutes' (Status 3.12.1998).[29]

Belgium

The Belgian ISPA code deals with the provisions for review and amendment in paragraph 5: 'ISPA may formulate remarks relating to the Internet in Belgium, and these remarks may be incorporated into the code of conduct. The code may be modified by decision of a 2/3 majority of the participants present at the Members' Meeting.'[30]

The mechanism for complaints is defined in paragraph 4 of the code:

> The procedure for dealing with complaints shall differ according to the origin of the complaint. In principle, there are three different procedures for dealing with complaints:
>
> a.   Complaint sent directly by a third party to an ISPA member: the member shall deal with the file until a satisfactory solution is found.
> b.   If the ISP does not provide a satisfactory solution, the third party shall refer his complaint to the ISPA committee.
> c.   The complaint may be referred directly to the ISPA committee.[31]

The code further states that complaints 'shall be dealt with according to the nature of the complaint', and that '[t]he committee shall determine the precise nature of the complaint'. The committee also reserves the right to hear the third party concerned beforehand, and 'will then inform the Member accordingly'. The first line of approach is informal, and if that fails, formal action is taken: 'If the Member refuses to comply with the committee's advices, or if he is found guilty of repeated non-compliance with the code, the committee may register the complaint officially against the Member and exclude him.'[32]

France

The French AFA code contains no formal provisions for the review and amendment procedure. On the topic of complaints, Part III states: 'If users are confronted on the network with contents which are illegal or which offend them, they can easily refer this to the access provider.'[33] The initial responsibility for responding to the complaint is up to the individual ISPs:

> An access provider which is a member of the AFA will quickly assess the complaint in view of the contract entered into with the User in question and will act on a case by case basis: [. . .] if the content placed on line or the attitude of the User in question is contrary to the General Conditions of Use, the access provider takes action requesting the User to change its attitude or the content in question.[34]

Germany

The German ISPA code states that members of the Association agree continually to review and revise the code. On the issue of complaint mechanism, this procedure is spelled out in detail in a separate complaint code, showing the Association's special concern for, and attention to, a formal complaint process as an important part of making the code of conduct legitimate and effective.[35]

Ireland

The Irish ISPAI code provides for review and amendment in section 3.5 of the code:

> The Code may be amended from time to time by 75 per cent majority vote of Full Members of ISPAI and each Member shall be given notice of any resolution to amend the Code in accordance with the Articles. Notwithstanding this process, the Code will be subject to review one year after its implementation following on consultations with the Internet Advisory Board.[36]

The Irish ISPA code deals with complaints in detail in section 11, entitled 'Complaints Procedure'. Section 11.2 provides different means for dealing with different forms of complaints:

> 11.2.1 where the Complaint is notified in person, resolution where possible, should be sought during the Complainant's personal attendance, or within five (5) Working Days where additional information is required;
> 11.2.2 where the Complaint is received by telephone, resolution where

>   possible, should be sought during the initial telephone call, or within
>   five (5) Working Days where additional information is required;
> 11.2.3   where the Complaint is received by e-mail, resolution where possible,
>   should be sought within five (5) Working Days via e-mail;
> 11.2.4   where the Complaint is received by letter, resolution where possible,
>   should be sought within ten (10) Working Days via post.[37]

In cases where a complainant notifies the ISPAI Secretariat of a complaint, the
Secretariat 'will direct the Complainant to contact the relevant Member directly if
the Complainant has not already done so'.[38] Where a complainant notifies the ISPAI
Secretariat of a complaint, 'the Secretariat will, if the Complaint relates to Third
Party Content, refer the Complainant to www.hotline.ie. Where the Complaint
concerns the legality of Third Party Content, the Secretariat will advise the
Complainant in the first instance, where possible, to contact the originator of the
material directly, in the second instance to contact the relevant ISP and in the third
instance to contact www.hotline.ie as provided for under Clause 7 hereof. Where the
ISP is a member of the ISPAI then the ISP will follow the complaints procedure in
Section 11.2.'[39]

In cases of anonymous complaints: 'Anonymous complaints are not accepted by
ISPAI but if deemed appropriate in the circumstances ISPAI may refer an anonymous complaint to the www.hotline.ie.'[40] Limits to accepting complaints are set in
section 11.6: 'ISPAI, at its sole discretion, will not accept Complaints which, in its
opinion, are vexatious, inexact, or wholly unjustified, trivial or of a minor nature and
the decision of ISPAI in the matter shall be final.'[41] Section 11.7 states what should be
done if a complainant is not satisfied with the decision of the Secretariat. In that case,
the Secretariat will 'attempt to resolve the Complaint informally by telephone at no
administrative charge to the Complainant within (5) Working Days';[42] and 'if the
Complaint cannot be resolved informally by telephone the Secretariat will inform the
Complainant that the Complainant may ask that the Complaint be dealt with
pursuant to the Complaints Procedure set out in Clause 11.8 hereunder'.[43]

The Irish ISPAI code further states the timing and the costs of dealing with
complaints:

> Where a Complainant asks for a Complaint to be dealt with pursuant to the
> Complaints Procedure the Secretariat will, normally within seven (7) Working
> Days of receiving a request in writing to deal with a Complaint pursuant to the
> Complaints Procedure, put in place the Complaints Procedure as set out
> herein.[44]

Italy

The Italian ISPA code entrusts review and amendment procedures to the Implementation Committee: 'The duties of the Implementation Committee are information,
prevention and regulation. The tasks entrusted to the Implementation Committee
are: the implementation and upgrading of this code through recommendations and
amendments.'[45]

The Italian code deals with complaints in its General Rule 13, under 'Proceedings'. Under 'Notification and investigation', it states:

> Notification of infringements must be made by Internet parties by means of an

application, sent by electronic mail (or by post or fax), containing a description of the infringement, and an indication of the URL of the site relating to the notified offence. Once the complaint has been received, the President of the Jury opens preliminary proceedings, sets a date for the decision and chooses within the Jury an investigating member charged with:

a)   notifying the parties concerned of the opening of the preliminary proceed-ings, the summons to a discussion, granting them a deadline of 3 days in which to file any conclusions and/or documents;

b)   examining the indicated application and preparing a report on the denounced matter in question, with the authority to consult the parties concerned.

On the expiry of this deadline the President convenes the Jury, which is obliged to take a decision regarding the proceedings, based on the investigator's report and the conclusions and/or documents filed by the parties concerned.[46]

Furthermore, the code mandates that:

The Jury is also given the right to extend the deadline for the decision if the proceedings are not sufficiently prepared or if it is necessary to acquire further elements for purposes of the decision, and informs the parties accordingly.[47]

The Netherlands

The Dutch ISPA code does not contain provisions for amendment and review. It provides a clear complaint procedure:

If a subscriber has complaints regarding the implementation of the agreement or the services of the provider, the subscriber may report these complaints (fully and clearly described) by e-mail within 3 working days to the helpdesk of the Provider (who is a member of the NLIP). In the case of no connection and/or no working e-mail, this may take place by telephone, fax or letter.[48]

The Dutch ISPA code also defines the actions of a special NLIP Disputes Committee, for dealing with the complaint:

If a subscriber is of the opinion that a complaint has not been dealt with correctly by the provider, he can bring it as dispute before the NLIP. The NLIP-Disputes Commission will then issue a judgement within 2 weeks. Before judgement of the dispute, the provider is also given a hearing. That judgement takes the form of weighty recommendation to the NLIP member concerned. Before a dispute is handled, a fee is payable. In 2002, this fee amounts to 35 Euros and is returnable to the complainant if he/she is found to be in the right. Possible disputes may be sent to the postal address of the NLIP or by e-mail.[49]

Norway

The Norwegian ISP code deals with review and amendment in its statement of purpose: 'A special council shall be established to develop and maintain standards that promote the above considerations.'[50] The Norwegian code deals with complaints in section 5 of the code, under 'The Council's Functions':

> The Council handles questions concerning breaches of these rules. The Council makes decisions in cases after an approach is made by any party who is bound by these rules. The same applies to complaints from other parties who are directly affected by the circumstances that gave rise to the complaint. The Council can take up cases on its own initiative. The Council can provide guidance to the public regarding other complaints arrangements as mentioned above in 3.3.[51]

United Kingdom

The preamble of the UK ISPA code states that from time to time the Council may issue policy statements regarding matters relating to regulation of the Internet in the United Kingdom. After due and proper consultations with the members, such policy statements may be adopted as practice statements by ISPA. Such practice statements shall be incorporated into the code and shall thereby be binding on the members.[52] The UK code also deals with the complaint mechanism explicitly, in Rule 8 and subsequently.

Canada

The Canadian CAIP code does not contain provisions for review and amendments, but it does reference review of member use policies mandated by the organisation. It states that 'Each CAIP Member's Authorized Use Policy will be a living document, enforced, reviewed and updated on a regular basis'.[53] The Canadian code also does not contain explicit reference to a formal complaint mechanism, but does contain a mandate for members. Fair Practices Policy Statement number 2.0 states that 'At a minimum, CAIP Members will provide customer service in the following areas: (i) sales, (ii) technical, (iii) billing and (iv) complaints'.[54] Regarding unsolicited bulk e-mail, the code states that 'Each CAIP Member's complaints procedure will deal with complaints about unsolicited commercial e-mail'.[55] On dispute resolution, the Canadian code mandates that 'CAIP Members will work to resolve any disputes with customers or members of the public in a manner that is fair, timely, effective and affordable'.[56]

E-business concerns: data protection, privacy, bulk e-mail, information regarding business

Issues of data protection, privacy provisions, bulk e-mail, and information regarding business play important roles in self-regulating business activity on the Internet. In this case, the pressure on the government to regulate this area of online activity is not motivated by the same forces that are concerned over, for example, content harmful to minors, hate speech, or even illegal content. Yet the overlap between the two sets of issues is significant, as data protection and privacy, as well as bulk e-mail, are related to distribution of content that may be deemed illegal or inappropriate by users or governments.

Data protection and privacy is the most important single issue of action for the 11 self-regulatory codes, in aggregate. Nine of the 11 national codes examined had data protection and privacy provisions, while the Canadian and German codes lacked the provisions. Bulk e-mail is related directly to data protection and privacy, but in this case a bare majority of codes contained separate provisions for bulk e-mail. Six national codes (French, Irish, Dutch, UK, Canadian and Australian) had provisions for bulk e-mail, while five national codes did not (Austrian, Belgian, German, Italian and Norwegian). The national codes were also split on the issue of information regarding business. The Austrian, German and Norwegian codes (which had no bulk e-mail provisions) were joined in the category of codes lacking provisions on information regarding business by France and Australia. Six national codes contained provisions concerning information regarding business (Belgian, Irish, Italian, Dutch, UK and Canadian).

Austria

Data protection and privacy. The Austrian ISPA code deals with data protection in four separate paragraphs of the code. Paragraph 3 states that: 'To provide Internet services, one pre-condition is the collection, storage and processing of data for operation and accounting. Thus, in the various areas of the Internet providers, data is stored and processed that, under the Austrian Telecommunications Law ("TKG"), are classified into "root data", "network data" and "content data".'[57] The Austrian ISPA members are instructed to 'respect the confidentiality of private data and correspondence and treat customer data and personal data confidentially'. The ISPA imposes the strict observance of telecommunications confidentiality on their members. The root data needed for customer identification, statements and similar is treated confidentially by the ISPA members and, for the provision of the Internet services, only processed for the duration of the legal relationship with the customer concerned. Parts of the root data may be passed on under the terms of the disclosure obligation contained in TKG § 96 ('Participant Index') or with the prior permission of the customer. Network or retrieved Internet data may be collected and stored to provide Internet services in various of the Internet provider's systems. The ISPA members in principle only store this data anonymously (i.e. without direct personal reference) and declare that they will not personally identify the subject of this data in the course of regular business. For accounting based on the service provided, ISPA members can also store person-related network data up until the expiry of the deadline for claiming or contesting payment for the relevant accounting period. Electronic post (e-mail) is – where there is no agreement with the customer to the contrary – automatically deleted by the ISPA member's server after delivery to the recipient or a certain period of time. To maintain Internet services, regular back-up copies of data must be made and kept, for example for restoration after systems failure. These copies are retained only for the necessary duration and safeguarded from unauthorised access.[58,59]

Paragraph 7 of the Austrian ISPA code deals with privacy of e-mail addresses in the case of online registration. It states:

> In the course of Online registration for various Internet services, among other things, e-mail addresses may be retrieved for inclusion in a database with the approval of the person registering. To prevent misuse of e-mail addresses, ISPA members inform the owners of the given e-mail addresses (e.g. via automatic re-mailer) of the inclusion of the e-mail addresses in a database. Rejection by the owner of the inclusion of the e-mail address in a database will be acted on by the respective ISPA member as soon as possible.[60]

Bulk e-mail and information regarding business. The Austrian ISPA code does not contain an explicit and formal mechanism for dealing with bulk e-mail or for dealing with information regarding business. Paragraph 2 of the Austrian code makes mention that financial feasibility is a measure of compliance.

Belgium

The Belgian ISPA code states that 'Personal data relating to clients may only be used by Members for legal purposes. Members must comply in every respect with the provisions of the law relating to the protection of privacy.'[61] Although the Belgian code does not deal directly and separately with information regarding business, it does deal with advertising practices and pricing information. It states that 'Members shall ensure that all advertisements placed by radio, TV, teletext, fax or other channels comply with the requirements of the law';[62] and that 'Members shall ensure in particular that the prices charged for their services are displayed clearly and unambiguously. Prices intended for the general public shall be inclusive of VAT. If options are available, this must be clearly indicated.'[63]

The Belgian code does not explicitly regulate bulk e-mail.

France

Data protection and privacy. The French AFA code provides explicit provisions for data protection and privacy, both in general and in regard to e-mail and user IDs. It states:

> AFA members make available the means of accessing the internet to their users and in carrying on this business, they consider that they have neither the rights nor the means of exercising control over the mass of information conveyed over their network web. They act as carrier (relayer) in the same way as a Post Office which knows the address and size of packages without knowing their content.[64]

Regarding e-mail privacy, the French code states:

> AFA members respect the confidentiality of private correspondence. Mail is usually erased from the servers on which they are saved before being delivered to the User's computer, as soon as they are received by the latter at a given time.[65]

The French code pays special attention to user identification of all possible means: 'All the items allowing Users to identify themselves and log onto the service are personal and confidential. All use of identification items falls under the responsibility of the User.'[66] The code explicitly limits and defines the ISP's ability to share information on users:

> AFA members are not allowed to communicate nominative information concerning their Users, outside cases authorized by law. In conformity with the legal provisions in force, AFA members may, at the behest of police or judicial authorities, be required to reveal the identity of one of their Users.[67]

Bulk e-mail and information regarding business. In the Principles section, AFA members are also concerned to limit the practice of sending out unsolicited electronic mail on a large scale ('spam'). To this end, they are putting in place computer tools designed to detect spam and reduce its transmission.[68] The French AFA code contains no separate provisions on information regarding business. But it does distinguish between different ISP customers in providing for AFA members' cooperation with law enforcement and third parties.[69]

Germany

The German ISP code does not contain separate provision for data protection and privacy. It deals with provisions on information regarding business only in its preamble, where it states that 'the Association will respect the basic right to economic freedom (provision of commercial services)'. Other than that, there are no specific provisions regarding business. The German code also contains no provisions regarding bulk e-mail.

Ireland

Data protection and privacy provisions. The Irish ISPAI code of conduct has a section on data protection and privacy, which states that 'Members shall comply with the Data Protection Act, 1988'[70] and that 'Members should have a "privacy statement" on their main website'.[71] Under the hotline Service provisions, the Irish ISPAI code states: 'When requested by www.hotline.ie (where requested by a law enforcement authority) and where technically able to do so, Members must retain (subject to the provisions of the Data Protection Act, 1988) copies of removed material as may be required.'[72]

Bulk e-mail. The Irish ISPAI code defines 'spam' as a 'means unsolicited material or information sent to an email address or newsgroup',[73] and it defines anti-spamming software as a 'means computer software used for filtering out Spam prior to it reaching e-mail addresses and/or newsgroups'.[74] Under the Best Practices section, the code states: 'Members will follow best industry practice in using Anti-Spamming Software.'[75]

Information regarding business. Under its general requirements, the Irish ISPAI code instructs members to 'use best endeavours to ensure that Services (excluding Third Party Content) and Promotional Material are not used to promote or facilitate any practices which are contrary to Irish law';[76] and to act fairly and reasonably in their dealings with Customers, other businesses and each other.'[77] The Irish ISPAI code has a special section on advertisements and promotions, including distribution of these over virtually all possible means of media communication (from Internet to radio):

8.1 Members must use best endeavours to ensure that Promotional Material transmitted by radio, television, tele-text, telephone, facsimile or any other form of communication shall observe the provisions of this Code and the Codes Of Standards, Practice And Prohibitions in Advertising, Sponsorship and other forms of Commercial Promotion Broadcasting Services published by The Independent Radio and Television Commission in the manner most reasonable and appropriate to the technology employed.

8.2 Members must use best endeavours to ensure that all Promotional Material complies with the provisions of the Code of Advertising Standards and the Code of Sales Promotion Practice which are supervised by the Advertising Standards Authority for Ireland.

8.3 Members must use best endeavours to ensure that Services and Promotional

Material comply with the Code of Practice applied by Regulator of Premium Telecommunications Services Limited (trading as RegTel) when access to them is made via a premium rate telephone call.

8.4 Members must, in addition to the provisions referred to at Clauses 8.1 to 8.3 above, use best endeavours to comply, where appropriate, with any other code of practice expressly regulating Promotional Material.

8.5 Members must ensure that charges for Services are clearly stated in any relevant Promotional Material. Members must clearly state the price of the goods or services including all taxes. Where additional charges (for example on-line charges) are payable, this should be stated.

8.6 Members must use best endeavours to ensure that textual pricing information relating to charges for Services is accurate, up to date, legible, prominent and presented in a fair and reasonable manner.

8.7 For commercial customers a contract will be deemed appropriate to satisfy the requirements of sections 8.5 and 8.6.

Italy

Data protection and privacy. The Italian ISPA code has extensive provisions for dealing with data protection and privacy. Its General Principle 4 states that 'All Internet parties must be identifiable', but 'Any Internet party, once identified, has the right to remain anonymous when using the Network in order to protect their own private sphere'.[78] The rule further states:

> The correct use of the Internet requires respect for fundamental rights and freedoms, and in particular of individual freedom, the right to access information, the freedom to meet together, protection of privacy, protection of personal data and confidentiality of correspondence.[79]

General Rule 5 of the Italian ISPA code deals with obligations relating to user identification:

> The parties must agree to the acquisition of their own personal data by whoever supplies them with access and/or hosting. The suppliers of the said services are obliged to register the data to make them available to the legal authorities under the terms of the law.[80]

The Italian ISPA code's Rule 7 deals with obligations concerning protection of fundamental freedoms and privacy. It states, in general:

> The suppliers of subject-matter shall inform their own clients of the technical limits of the protection of confidentiality of correspondence and private and personal data in the Network. Access suppliers shall provide their clients with indications as to the measures and products – which do not infringe the regulations in force – intended to ensure the confidentiality and integrity of their correspondence and data, in particular as regards encrypting tools and/or electronic signatures.[81]

Two specific sections of Rule 7 deal with secrecy of correspondence and private and personal data.[82]

Bulk e-mail. The Italian code has no separate provisions on bulk e-mail.

Information regarding business. Principle 4f of the Italian ISPA code states: 'Activities for commercial and/or professional purposes over the Internet are carried out based on the principles of correctness and transparency and are subject to the Italian and Community regulations regarding consumer protection, distance selling and advertising.'[83] Rule of Conduct 9 of the ISPA code addresses the ISP's responsibilities on information regarding business in more detail. For consultancy, the rule states:

> Services which offer information or consultancy quoting opinions must indicate clearly the identity, professional qualifications, and any post occupied by the expert or specialist. This indication must however be provided in compliance with professional ethics, which prohibit any form of publicity for certain categories of professionals. Each service must be supplied in terms and in a manner reflecting the seriousness of the discipline which is the subject of the consultancy, especially in the case of medical consultancy services.[84]

On information services, the rule states: 'Services offering information on data, facts or circumstances which are liable to undergo changes in the course of time must also contain an indication of the date and time to which the updating of the information supplied refers.'[85]

On prize-winning competitions, the rule states:

> Any service which institutes a prize-winning competition may only be activated after the relative authorisation order has been issued by the Ministry of Finance or, in the case of prize-winning operations limited to a single province, by the competent Finance Office, under the terms of the regulation issued by R.D.L. No. 1933 of 29.10.1938 and subs. mod, converted to law No. 384 of 27.11.1989, and by R.D. No. 1077 of 25.7.1940.[86]

On job opportunities, the rule states:

> A supplier of subject-matter, before implementing a service promoting job opportunities, must ensure that the supply of the service does not imply a violation of the order on the intermediation and/or intervention of workers. Services which offer professional training courses or other teaching courses are under the obligation not to make unreasonable promises or raise expectations of future employment or future remuneration by users.[87]

On advertising, the code states:

> The suppliers of subject-matter undertake to comply with the regulations laid down by the Advertising Self-disciplinary Code, both for advertising on behalf of the services offered, conveyed by means of those same services or through other means, and for advertising aimed at promoting other services or products, whereby the service only represents the vehicle of diffusion. The suppliers of subject-matter undertake to offer advertising space for communications of social importance on special conditions, based on the same rules provided for television advertising.[88]

The Netherlands

Data protection and privacy provisions. The Dutch ISPA code deals with privacy in its G.2 section:

> The provider gives no access to the subscriber's file to third parties. The provider gives notification to the subscriber in advance with regard to data which might under certain circumstances be disclosed to third parties. Within the provider's own organisation, this data is only accessible for operational purposes.[89]

Under confidentiality/security, the Dutch code states:

> The provider is responsible for security [. . .] with respect to the compilation of all data which might contain personal particulars, insofar as such compilations occur within the context of the execution of the agreement in the provider's system, as well as with respect to any associated records in the provider's administrative files. The confidentiality obligation applies for at least two years after the termination of the agreement, or so much longer as is required under the legal regulations.[90]

Bulk e-mail. The Dutch ISPA code provides compulsory recommended practices on spam, under the recommendations of the Security Committee:

> SPAM presents more and more problems, caused as much by the senders as by the recipients. The senders are becoming increasingly clever at concealing their identity. Every responsible provider should have brought mail relaying (the forwarding of mail from non-clients to non-clients) to a halt. The committee recommends the so-called football system: if it is suspected that a client is spreading SPAM, then a yellow card should suffice in the first instance (written/ verbal warning). If it is repeated, they are given a red card and the account is closed for an unspecified period of time. It is recommended that with line-rental clients who send SPAM, contact should first be taken up with the IT-manager at the site in question. If such actions are repeated, port 25 (the mail port) or even the whole connection can be closed down if necessary. The introduction of a 'clean-up fee' for clients who send SPAM is not seen as unreasonable.[91]

Information regarding business. The Dutch ISPA code deals with information regarding business within the mandatory section G.6, which is on Commercial Trading:

> The provider's services, products and promotional materials are offered in a lawful and sincere manner. Providers shall under no circumstances stimulate unlawful trading on the Internet. Providers will make every effort to ensure that their services and promotional materials are not misleading due to inaccuracies, exaggerations, modifications or in any other way. In conducting business with customers and other companies, the members will act in an appropriate, honest and reasonable manner at all times. Providers shall notify their customers regarding the existence of this Code and the complaints procedures. Providers must ensure that the prices for their services are clearly and unambiguously drawn up. In the case of individual connections these prices will be inclusive of VAT. If additional charges are made this fact must be clearly stated.[92]

There is also a separate, optional section, labelled 'QUALITY', which deals with the necessary measures the provider must take to be given a quality mark. The steps that must be taken are listed in paragraph 5 of the code.

Norway

The Norwegian ISP code deals with data protection and privacy in its section 4.3, under general obligations:

> The publisher is obliged to monitor material that is made available on his own website and to give due consideration to the interest of the general public and to the rights of others such as protection of reputation, protection of personal data, intellectual property rights, etc.[93]

The Norwegian ISP code does not contain provisions for dealing with bulk e-mail or information regarding business.

United Kingdom

Data protection and privacy provisions. The UK ISPA code contains specific provisions regarding data protection and privacy in Rule 4. It states:

1. Members shall comply with UK legislation relating to data protection.[94]
2. When registering with the Data Protection registry, all members must in their application state that the data may be used for regulatory purposes and that ISPA is a potential user of that information.[95]
3. Where services involve the collection of personal information, such as names and addresses, from individuals, members must make it clear to data subjects the purpose for which such information will be used. Members must also identify data user (if different from the member or data subject) and give the data subject opportunity to object to such usage.[96]

The UK ISPA code offers further privacy provisions in its Guidelines section: 'Members should advise customers regarding any software tools which they can use to protect their privacy.'[97]

Bulk e-mail. The Guidelines section of the UK ISPA code also provides provisions for dealing with bulk e-mail: 'Members should follow the best industry practice in using Spamming software, such that customers can elect to minimize the amount of spam sent to their e-mail account.'[98]

Information regarding business. The UK ISPA code contains provisions for honesty, fair-trading, customer contracts, and pricing. On honesty, the code states: 'Members shall use their reasonable endeavours to ensure Services (excluding Third Party Content) and Promotional Material are not of a kind that are likely to mislead by inaccuracy, ambiguity, exaggeration, omission or otherwise.'[99] On fair trading it states that: (1) 'In ... dealings with consumers, other businesses and each other, Members must act fairly and reasonably at all times';[100] and (2) 'Members must, upon request, bring to the attention of their Customers the existence of the Code and must notify them of the complaints procedure in the Code.'[101] On customer contacts, the UK ISPA code states that: (1) 'Members shall ensure that they bring their Terms and Conditions to the attention of all new customers before such customer registers for services';[102] and (2) 'Members must include in their contracts a provision requiring customers to comply with UK law in using any member services.'[103] On pricing information, the code states: (1) 'Members must ensure that charges for services are clearly stated in relevant promotional material';[104] and (2) 'Textual pricing information must be accurate, up to date, legible, prominent, and presented in such a way as does not require close examination.'[105]

Canada

Data protection and privacy provisions, and bulk e-mail. The Canadian CAIP code does not deal directly with privacy concerns or data protection. But privacy concerns are mentioned in commentary relating on avoiding bulk e-mail. Bulk e-mail is dealt within the Fair Practices Policy Statement number 5: 'CAIP Members will not knowingly allow their services to be used for the transmission of unsolicited bulk e-mail, especially unsolicited commercial bulk e-mail between parties that have had no previous commercial relationship.'[106] The code also contains a tip sheet for avoiding unsolicited bulk e-mail. This document is quite exhaustive and is included in the original version of the code.

Information regarding business. In its introductory statement, the CAIP code states: 'CAIP Members will communicate with customers in a clear, accurate and comprehensible fashion.'[107] The main section of the code dealing with information regarding business is the Fair Practices Document Policy Statement number 1, entitled 'Responsible Service'. It part two, it states:

> At a minimum, CAIP Members will provide customer service in the following areas: (i) sales, (ii) technical, (iii) billing and (iv) complaints.[108]

> CAIP Members will ensure that their representatives who deal with customers are trained in the area or areas for which they are responsible: sales, technical, billing and complaints. This responsibility exists even when all or part.of their customer support functions are outsourced.[109]

Further, the Canadian fair practice statement mandates that 'CAIP Members will provide a stable network for their customers';[110] 'When a CAIP Member chooses to specify a service level for one of its products, that service level must be supported with appropriate warranties in its contract';[111] 'CAIP Members will maintain appropriate levels of general liability insurance';[112] and 'When it becomes necessary to close down a point of presence (POP), CAIP Members will first notify their affected customers so as to give them a commercially reasonable amount of time to secure service from an alternate provider.'[113]

Australia

Data protection and privacy provisions. The Australian ISP code makes data protection and privacy one of its explicit objectives: 'to provide standards of confidentiality and privacy afforded to users of the Internet'.[114] Under principles, it states: 'In seeking to achieve its objectives this Code applies the following principles: [. . .] f. the privacy of users' details obtained by Code Subscribers in the course of business will be respected.'[115]

Bulk e-mail. The Australian code deals with bulk e-mail under ISPs' obligations in relation to Internet access generally. The code states:

ISPs will have procedures in place to deal with complaints from subscribers in respect of unsolicited email that promotes or advertises Internet sites or parts of Internet sites that enable, or purport to enable, end users to access information that is likely to cause offence to a reasonable adult. An ISP shall be deemed to have complied with this provision where they have provided complainants with, or directed them to, information describing methods by which receipt of unsolicited e-mail of this nature can be minimised.[116]

Bulk e-mail provisions are also in the Internet content host obligations in relation to hosting of content within Australia:

To the extent applicable, Internet Content Hosts will have procedures in place to deal with complaints from subscribers in respect of unsolicited email that promotes or advertises Internet sites or parts of Internet sites that enable, or purport to enable, end users to access information that is likely to cause offence to a reasonable adult. An Internet Content Host shall be deemed to have complied with this provision where it has provided complainants with, or directed them to, information describing methods by which receipt of unsolicited email of this nature can be minimised.[117]

Information regarding business. The Australian code does not deal separately with provisions regarding business.

Content concerns: coverage of ICPs, protection of minors, hate speech

When it comes to Internet content, the attention of the public and the media is usually centred around issues of pornography, incitement to violence, hate speech, and other content that may be deemed by some, or many, as inappropriate either for minors or for the public in general. Responsibilities for content regulation depend upon the definition of what constitutes an Internet provider. Most codes distinguish between ISPs and Internet content providers (ICPs). Nevertheless, prominent cases exist where an ISP would serve as an ICP, or where designers of the code wanted to include ICPs in general in the self-regulatory scheme. Because of this link between ICPs and ISPs, or the question whether ISPs should bear responsibility for content not provided for them, we analysed the 11 codes of conduct for whether they include ICPs in their regulatory scheme. Of the 11 codes, five included ICPs (Austrian, German, Irish, Italian and Norwegian) and six did not (Belgian, French, Dutch, UK, Canadian and Australian).

We also analysed the codes for provisions regarding protection of minors (restricting access to content that is or may be harmful to minors) and provisions regarding hate speech. We did not attempt to define either of these in a general form – as the definition ranges widely between the countries whose codes were studied – but instead relied on a particular description of both minors' protection and hate speech that was offered by the code we were analysing for existence of these provisions. Of the 11 codes studied, seven included provisions for protection of minors (Austrian, German, French, Irish, Italian, Canadian and Australian) and four did not (Belgian, Dutch, Norwegian and UK). Only four included provisions for hate speech (German, Irish, UK and Australian), while seven did not (Austrian, Belgian, French, Italian, Dutch, Norwegian and Canadian). It is important to note here, as was noted above in the introduction, that most of the countries (with exception of perhaps only Canada) that did not include hate speech in their code had strict national legislative regulatory mechanisms for preventing hate speech both online and offline.

Austria

Coverage of ICPs. The Austrian code differentiates responsibilities based on status of a member:

> To clarify the varying responsibilities of the ISPA members with regard to these Guidelines, various categories are allocated depending on the business concerned, whereby a member may also carry out various types of business and its conduct must comply with that of the business being carried out at the time:
>
> – Content Provider: any provider supplying their own contents on the Internet; they are fully responsible for these contents
> – Access Provider: any provider supplying access to the Internet for Internet users; they are in no way responsible for the transmitted contents
> – Host Provider: any provider providing storage space for outside Internet contents; they are in no way responsible for these contents and are not obliged to check through these contents; if they are notified of illegal contents, they act in accordance with § 4 of these Guidelines
> – Backbone Provider: any provider offering international Internet connections; they are in no way responsible for the transmitted contents.[118]

Protection of minors, hate speech. Because a variety of types of information is available over the Internet, the Austrian ISPA members 'regard it as their obligation, with regard to the possibilities and their influence, to enable access to the Internet for minors only with the verified permission of their legal guardians'.[119] Paragraph 6 of the Austrian code further states: 'ISPA is actively involved within the international organisation for the development of technical rating and filter systems. These can be recommended by ISPA members on readiness for use and depending on suitability.'[120] The Austrian ISPA code does not deal directly with hate speech because hate speech is defined under the Austrian criminal law. If a specific case of online hate speech is in fact illegal, then it is referenced by incorporation in paragraph 4, which deals with illegal content.

Belgium

The Belgian code applies only to ISPs, and not to ICPs. The Belgian code does not have any provisions dealing with protection of minors, and has no separate provisions for hate speech. In as much as hate speech is illegal, it is incorporated by reference in P.3 of the Belgian ISPA code of conduct.

France

The French AFA code does not cover ICPs. It also has no provisions regarding hate speech, which is regulated by law. On protection of minors, the code states:

> Subscriptions are refused to minors unless authorized by someone with parental

authority. AFA members offer their Users solutions allowing them to filter contents on their microcomputers (by PICS or Cyberpatrol for example), even before the corresponding contents are sent over the network.[121]

Germany

Coverage of ICPs, protection of minors. The German ISPA code does not extend to ICPs. It deals with protection of minors under Part I, Rule 3, outlining 'principles of conduct regarding the impairment of the well being of children/young persons':

1. Members shall take all actions, within the scope of legally determined responsibility and to the extent actually and legally possible and reasonable to ensure that content which is unlawful or impermissible, in particular pursuant to:[122]
   a) §8, Nos. 5 and 6 of the MdStV2;
   b) §184(1) of the StGB (Dissemination of pornographic publications) is not provided nor switched for use.[123]
2. Members shall take all actions, within the scope of legally determined responsibility and to the extent actually and legally possible and reasonable to ensure that content which may impair the physical, mental, or spiritual well-being of children or young persons is neither provided nor switched for use, unless:
   a) care is taken that children and young persons do not become aware of the services under normal circumstances, or
   b) users are offered technical arrangements which allow them to block the services according to their specific, individual needs.

Furthermore, the German AFM code instructs service providers to inform users of their options available in protecting minors' access and use to harmful material.[124]

Hate speech. The German AFM code deals with hate speech in Part I, Rule 2. It states:

Members shall take all actions, within the scope of legally determined responsibility and to the extent actually and legally possible and reasonable to ensure that content which is unlawful or impermissible, in particular pursuant to:[125]

a) §130 of the StGB1 (Incitement to hatred and violence against segments of the population (or minority groups) or publishing insults against them in such a manner as to endanger the peace or expose them to scorn or contempt) [. . .]
c) §131 of the StGB (Depiction of acts of violence, instigation to racial hatred) is neither provided nor switched for use.[126]

Ireland

Coverage of ICPs. The Irish ISPAI code applies to both ISPs and ICPs. In section 2.2 the code states:

ISPAI considers the provider of content (most commonly the user who posts a news article or a web page) as being responsible in the first instance not only for ensuring that the content is legal but also that the content is suitable for the intended audience.[127]

Under responsibilities of members, the Irish ISPAI code states:

> ISPAI acknowledges that it is the role of the State to make and to enforce the law. Members of ISPAI must observe their legal obligations to remove Illegal content when informed by organs of the State or as otherwise required by law. It should not, however, be the responsibility of a Member to determine the legality or suitability or to filter or otherwise restrict reception of or access to content material save where such action is taken following an identified breach (or antici- pated breach) of the Code:
>
> 2.3.1   Compliance with the Code does not guarantee that a Member is acting within the law. Any principles set out or established under this Code do not represent any legal grounds for liability.
>
> 2.3.2   This Code does not purport to cover any violations or alleged violations pertaining to 'competition law' or to 'copyright law'.
>
> 2.3.3   ISPAI supports its Members in any independent decision taken by the Member to proactively limit the accessibility of Illegal material via its Services, but strongly believes that no greater responsibility, standard of care or obligation should be placed on a Member who takes such action, than is placed upon those Members who do not take such proactive action.[128]

Protection of minors. The Irish ISPAI code does not provide direct and separate provi- sions for protection of minors, but does address the issue under suitability and hotline services. In section 2.2, the code states:

> ISPAI considers the provider of content (most commonly the user who posts a news article or a web page) as being responsible in the first instance not only for ensuring that the content is legal but also that the content is suitable for the intended audience.[129]

The section defines 'harmful' content as:

> content which includes any unlawful, libellous, abusive, offensive, vulgar or obscene material or any activities deliberately calculated to cause unreasonable offence to others, which whilst not necessarily Illegal, is none-the-less considered inappropriate and deliberately calculated to cause unreasonable anxiety, incon- venience or stress to others.[130]

Under the section defining its hotline service, the code states: 'www.hotline.ie will actively seek to empower all end-users by providing information on ways end-users can protect themselves or their children from content which those end-users may consider harmful'.[131]

Hate speech. Under the 'General Requirements', the Irish ISPAI code states: 'Members must use best endeavours to ensure that Services (excluding Third Party Content) and Promotional Material do not contain material inciting violence, cruelty, racial hatred or prejudice and discrimination of any kind.'[132]

Italy

Coverage of ICPs. The Italian ISPA code applies to both ISPs and ICPs because it keeps its membership open and voluntary. It states: 'Adherence to this Code is voluntary and open to all Internet parties operating in Italy or in the Italian language. The parties obliged to abide by this Code are all those who have signed it.'[133]

Protection of minors, hate speech. The Italian ISPA code has no provisions regarding hate speech. But it does have extensive provisions covering protection of minors. It defines 'Potentially offensive subject-matter or conduct' as that which 'concerns subject-matter or conduct which although it does not contravene the regulations in force, and is hence lawful, may prove offensive to some categories of users; the matter of protection of minors is particularly relevant'. Under Principle 4C, the Italian ISPA code states:

> The protection of minors imposes a refusal of any form of exploitation, particularly that of a sexual nature, and any communications and information which may exploit their credulity; respect for the feelings of minors also imposes special caution in the diffusion to the public of potentially harmful subject-matter.[134]

More specifically, the Italian ISPA code deals with protection of minors under its Rule of Conduct 6C:

> Any Internet party who becomes directly aware of the existence of subject-matter of an illicit nature which is accessible by the public, shall inform the legal authorities accordingly directly. Any Internet party who becomes directly aware of the existence of subject-matter accessible by the public which is contrary to the provisions of this Code, shall inform the self-disciplinary body. Access and hosting suppliers are obliged to make easily accessible on-line by all suitable means, including e-mail, information concerning the methods for reporting to the competent authorities any illegal or potentially harmful subject-matter of which they may become aware. The suppliers of subject-matter shall use tools capable of informing end-users of the presence of potentially offensive content, by means of appropriate signs, in order to prevent the involuntary viewing of such subject-matter. The suppliers of subject-matter undertake:
>
> 1. to make easily accessible on-line by all suitable means, including e-mail, information on the technical features, operating methods and tools for the use of filtering programs.
> 2. to carry out self-classification of their own subject-matter based on the classification system recognised as standard by the Code and to accept any variations in their own classifications which may be requested by the self-disciplinary entity.[135]

The Italian ISPA code entrusts the selection of the standard system of classification of subject-matter:

> to the Implementation Committee of the Code, taking into consideration the status of the technology, the diffusion of the systems on an international scale, and in particular, consistency with the choices made on the subject by the other member States of the European Union.[136]

The Netherlands

The Dutch ISPA code does not include ICPs. The code was drafted using the term 'provider', and from the context of the code that term can presumably be interpreted as an ISP that is not also an ICP. The Dutch ISPA code does not contain provisions for protection of minors, or explicit provisions for hate speech. However, to the extent that hate speech is illegal in the Netherlands, it is incorporated by reference into the code's provisions dealing with illegal content.

Norway

The Norwegian ISP code includes ICPs into its scope as long as they voluntarily join the code: 'These rules are applicable to any party who by agreement or other means has declared himself bound by them.'[137] The Norwegian ISP code does not include provisions for protection of minors, or for hate speech. However, to the extent that hate speech is illegal in Norway, it is incorporated by reference.

United Kingdom

The UK ISPA code applies only to ISPs, and does not include ICPs. The code does not deal with limiting access of minors to harmful content. But it deals briefly with hate speech by stating: 'Members shall use their reasonable endeavours to ensure the following: Services (excluding Third Party Content) and Promotional Material do not contain material inciting violence, cruelty or racial hatred.'[138]

Canada

Coverage of ICPs. The Canadian code does not apply to ICPs. In its introduction, the code states:

> Internet Service Providers have spoken repeatedly about self-regulation as a viable alternative to being regulated by the government. CAIP as a representative of Internet Service Providers has done so too. This Fair Practices Document is an effort to add substance to those words.[139]

Protection of minors. The Canadian code deals with protection of minors in its Policy Statement number 3: 'CAIP Members will make available information about the risks associated with Internet usage and about ways for customers to address these risks.'[140] The Canadian ISP association, CAIP, has also produced a 'Parent's Tip Sheet and Child's Pledge'. This document is quite exhaustive and is included in the original version of the code.

Hate speech. The Canadian code does not deal with hate speech separately; where illegal, it is included under reference to illegal content throughout the code of conduct.

Australia

Coverage of ICPs. The Australian code deals primarily with ISPs, but refers to ICPs' responsibility: 'In seeking to achieve its objectives this Code applies the following principles: [. . .] the responsibility for content made available on the Internet rests with the relevant Content Providers.'[141]

Hate speech, protection of minors. The Australian ISP code has no separate provisions for hate speech. To the extent that the racist or xenophobic speech is prohibited under the ABA, then it is incorporated by reference into the Code. But the code does include provisions for protecting minors, both under general obligations of ISPs and in regard to content host obligations in relation to hosting content within Australia. Under section 5.2, the code states:

> In respect of those of their subscribers who are Content Providers ISPs will: encourage them to use appropriate labelling systems, in respect of Content which is likely to be considered unsuitable for children according to the National Classification Code, though not Prohibited or Potential Prohibited content; and inform them of their legal responsibilities, as they may exist under the Act or complementary State or Territory legislation in relation to Content which they intend to provide to the public via the Internet from within Australia.[142]

Under section 5.3, the Australian code states:

> ISPs will take reasonable steps to provide users with information about: supervising and controlling children's access to Internet content; procedures which parents can implement to control children's access to Internet content, including the availability, use and appropriate application of Internet Content filtering software, labelling systems and filtered Internet carriage services.[143]

And under section 5.4, the code states:

> For the purposes of clauses 5.2 and 5.3 ISPs shall be deemed to have fulfilled these requirements where they direct users, by means of a link on their Home Page or otherwise, to resources made available for the purpose from time to time by the IIA, the ABA, NetAlert or other organisation approved by the IIA.[144]

Protection of minors is also dealt with under the section entitled 'Internet content host obligations in relation to hosting of content within Australia'. Here, Internet content hosts are instructed to:

> encourage Content Providers to use appropriate labelling systems, in respect of Content which is likely to be considered unsuitable for children according to the National Classification Code, though not Prohibited or Potential Prohibited content; and inform Content Providers of their legal responsibilities, as they may exist under the Act or complementary State or Territory legislation in relation to Content which they intend to provide to the public via the Internet from within Australia.[145]

In section 7.3, the hosts are instructed to:

> take reasonable steps to provide users with information about: supervising and controlling children's access to Internet content; procedures which users including parents and others responsible for children can implement to control access to Internet content, including the availability, use and appropriate application of Internet Content filtering software, labelling systems and filtered Internet carriage services.[146]

Finally, under section 7.4, the code states:

> For the purposes of this clause 7.3, Internet Content Hosts shall be deemed to have fulfilled their requirements where they direct users, by means of a link on their Home Page or otherwise, to resources made available for the purpose from time to time by the IIA, the ABA, NetAlert, or other organisation approved by the IIA.[147]

Sanctions

In principle, it is the sanctions part of any self-regulatory mechanism that is supposed to give it ultimate effectiveness. In other words, one of the ways to judge a code of conduct is to see how it is prepared to deal with instances where members who are subject to the code violate its rules, or forgo the code's recommendations. Nevertheless, the issue of sanctions, just like hate speech and most other provisions, needs to be viewed in a larger context. Of the 11 codes analysed, French, Canadian and Australian codes did not contain explicit sanction mechanisms. This absence of a sanction mechanism corresponds with a more regulatory approach to harmful content in national legislation (in France), a more advisory approach that consists of separate and detailed guidance sheets (in Canada), and a co-regulatory approach to implementing a code of conduct (in Australia).

Austria

The Austrian ISPA code of conduct does not contain explicit sanction mechanism provisions, but it does make reference to the 'ISPA Statute'. (Note that, regarding translation, statute in the Austrian context signifies internal governing rules, not statute in the classical, Anglo-American legal sense.) The Austrian ISPA code states:

> ... If the complaint is upheld, the ISPA Board, depending on the seriousness of the case and frequency of the non-observance of the Guidelines by the ISPA member concerned, may either issue a warning or terminate the membership of the member concerned under the terms of § 6 (4) of the 'ISPA Statutes' (Status 3.12.1998).[148]

Belgium

The Belgian ISPA code specifies a sanction procedure explicitly in paragraph 4 of the code:

> ... Initially, the committee shall approach the Member informally. If the Member refuses to comply with the committee's advices, or if he is found guilty of repeated non-compliance with the code, the committee may register the complaint officially against the Member and exclude him.[149]

France

There are no formal mechanisms whereby the French ISPA, AFA, can sanction members who do not abide by the code.

Germany

The German ISPA code deals with the sanction mechanism in some detail, in its Part II of the code. The code allows the German FSM association to:

a) Notify with demand to take remedial action, or expression of disapproval, or reprimand any member who breaches the Code. If FSM decides to sanction a member, the member voluntarily undertakes to comply with the sanction and ensure that the breach is not repeated.

b) Notifications with demands for remedial action and expression of disapproval shall remain unpublished but reprimands shall be made public in paraphrased form. Reprimands shall be published by the provider in the service concerned for a period of one month. If the service is terminated before the reprimand is given, the reprimand shall be published in a comparable place for the period of one month.

c) If a member, despite repeated demands, fails to take remedial action against a breach of the Code or fail repeatedly to comply with sanctions, the member may be excluded from membership in the FSM.[150]

Part III of the German FSM code, in its Rule 7, allows the FSM to sanction even non-members if:

1. The FSM receives a complaint regarding content that is offered, provided for use, or technically switched by non-members.

2. Any complaint about such services will also be decided on the basis of the provisions of this Code of conduct and handled in accordance with the grievance rules.

3. FSM shall inform the non-members of its decisions, and shall encourage the non-member to take remedial action, if appropriate. And non-member compliance with the sanction is voluntary.

4. Neither a decision to sanction nor any demand for remedial action against a non-member shall be published.[151]

Ireland

The Irish ISPAI code deals with sanctions within its section 12, together with complaints:

Where the Board decides, pursuant to a Complaints Hearing, that a Subject Member has breached the Code, the Board may, taking all relevant circumstances into account, impose any one or more of the sanctions set out herein:

12.1.1 The Board may require the Subject Member to remedy the breach of the Code within a reasonable time as agreed by the Board.

12.1.2 The Board may require a written assurance from the Subject Member, or any associated individual, relating to future behaviour, in terms required by the Board.

12.1.3 The Board may suspend the Subject Member from ISPAI without a reimbursement of membership fees in whole or in part.

12.1.4 The Board may convene an Extraordinary General Meeting of ISPAI for the purpose of considering an extraordinary resolution to expel the Subject Member from ISPAI, in accordance with Article 10 of the Articles.

12.1.5 The Board may, where the Subject Member is suspended or expelled pursuant to Clauses 12.1.3 or 12.1.4 above, publicise that fact.[152]

The limitations of the sanctions, in cases of doubt or third-party participation in the dispute, are laid out in section 12.2:

For the avoidance of doubt, where the Secretariat or Board refers a Complain to a third party pursuant to Clause 11.11 and that third party imposes a financial sanction on the Subject Member, the Board will not impose the financial sanction set out at 12.1.3 above.[153]

Italy

The Italian code deals with sanction mechanisms under its General Rule 13, entitled 'Proceedings'. This is the same rule that dealt with the issue of complaints. Under the title 'Decision and penalties', the rule states:

The Jury's decision is immediately communicated to the parties and must contain the measure which is subsequently to be adopted, with the respective grounds. In the event of a negative pronouncement, or if the decision establishes that the indicated offence is unfounded, the Jury closes the proceedings. In the event of a positive pronouncement, or if the decision establishes that the notified infringement persists, the Jury shall adopt the following measures:

1. communication of an intimation, containing a request to comply with the Jury's pronouncement within a 2-day deadline;
2. in the event of non-observance of the measure referred to in point 1, a formal admonition to be published on the site pertaining to the Internet self-regulation entity, with the request that the intimation referred to in point 1 be complied with.[154]

The Italian ISPA code further states, under the same rule:

The decisions and resulting measures are binding on all the parties adhering to this Code. The parties may appeal against the decision within 3 days to the Implementation Committee, which (a) if it deems the reasoning of the appellant to be well-founded, has the authority to modify or cancel the Jury's decision, in a justified act; (b) in the opposite case, the Implementation committee, in a justified act, confirms the decision taken by the Jury.[155]

The Netherlands

The Dutch ISPA code deals with sanctions through its dispute committee, ensuring 'that judgment takes the form of weighty recommendation to the NLIP member concerned'.[156] In administrating its quality mark part of the self-regulation scheme, the Dutch ISPA states:

If the ISP fails to bring performance back up to the required level within a reasonable period of time, then the following applies: In the first instance, strict instructions from the Disputes Committee or the Board; In the second instance, a temporary suspension imposed by the Board; In the third instance, suspension or cancellation of service, by the ALV on the recommendation of the Board.[157]

Norway

Under the Norwegian ISP code, the sanction mechanisms are under 'The Council's Authority': 'The Council's decisions are binding on any party who by agreement or declaration has undertaken to be bound by the present rules.'[158]

United Kingdom

Under the UK ISPA code, sanctions are governed by Rule 8.6 of the code.

Canada

The Canadian CAIP code contains no specific sanction mechanisms.

Australia

The Australian ISPA code contains no explicit sanction mechanisms. But there is an assumed incentive for ISPs to comply with the *de minimus* standards of the Australian co-regulatory model, the main incentive being the lack of formal legislation that may be imposed otherwise under the Australian Broadcasting Authority.

Summary and conclusions

In this section, first we summarise the findings of the analysis section, by repeating what was stated at the beginning of each section.

Of the 11 ISP codes of conduct analysed, all 11 had provisions concerning illegal activity, and only the Norwegian ISP code did not have provisions regulating cooperation with the law enforcement and third parties. This convergence or overlap in the different codes of analysis is important as it helps us identify a common minimal foundation between the national codes.

Of the 11 codes analysed, only the Canadian ISP code did not have explicit provisions for a complaint mechanism. When it comes to formal provisions for reviews and amendments to the code, only the French and the Dutch ISP codes lacked these provisions. Provisions specifying complaints mechanisms and a formal review and amendment procedure together define openness of the code. The fact that the vast majority of ISP codes studied had these provisions indicates that, in addition to the codes' provisions for illegal content and cooperation with law enforcement, the openness of the code is the second minimal common foundation among the 11 national codes studied. In as much as self-regulation is a voluntary and participatory process, where members of the scheme recognise that self-regulation is in their own interest for various reasons, openness of the code – both through the complaint mechanism (on the side of members but also on the side of consumers) and through the review and amendment processes – may serve an important role to foster voluntary cooperation and broader participation of the industry members in the self-regulatory scheme.

Issues of data protection, privacy provisions, bulk e-mail, and information regarding business play an important role in self-regulating business activity on the Internet. In this case, the pressure on the government to regulate this area of online activity is not motivated by the same forces that are concerned over, for example, content harmful to minors, hate speech, or even illegal content. Yet the overlap between the two sets of issues is significant, as data protection and privacy, as well as bulk e-mail, are related to distribution of content that may be deemed illegal or inappropriate by users or governments.

Data protection and privacy is the most important single issue of action for the 11 self-regulatory codes, in aggregate. Nine of the 11 national codes examined had data protection and privacy provisions, while the Canadian and German codes lacked the provisions. Bulk e-mail is related directly to data protection and privacy, but in this case a bare majority of codes contained separate provisions for bulk e-mail. Six national codes (French, Irish, Dutch, UK, Canadian and Australian) had provisions for bulk e-mail, while five national codes did not (Austrian, Belgian, German, Italian and Norwegian). The national codes were also split on the issue of information regarding business. The Austrian, German and Norwegian codes (which had no bulk e-mail provisions) were joined in the category of codes lacking provisions on information regarding business by France and Australia. Six national codes contained provisions concerning information regarding business (Belgian, Irish, Italian, Dutch, UK and Canadian).

When it comes to Internet content, the attention of the public and the media is usually centred around issues of pornography, incitement to violence, hate speech, and other content that may be deemed by some, or many, as inappropriate either for minors or for the public in general. The issue of content regulation is directly involved with a clear definition of what constitutes an Internet provider. Most codes distinguish between Internet service providers (ISPs) and Internet content providers (ICPs). Nevertheless, prominent cases exist where an ISP would serve as an ICP, or where designers of the code wanted to include ICPs in general into the self-regulatory scheme. Because of this link between ICPs and ISPs, or the question whether ISPs should bear responsibility for content not provided for them, we analysed the 11 codes of conduct for whether they include ICPs into their regulatory scheme. Of the 11 codes, five included ICPs (Austrian, German, Irish, Italian and Norwegian) and six did not (Belgian, French, Dutch, UK, Canadian and Australian).

We also analysed the codes for explicit provisions regarding protection of minors (restricting access to content that is or may be harmful to minors) and provisions regarding hate speech. We did not attempt to define either of these in a general form – as the definition ranges widely between the countries whose codes were studied – but instead relied on a particular description of both minors' protection and hate speech that was offered by the code we were analysing for existence of these provisions. Of the 11 codes studied, seven included provisions for protection of minors (Austrian, German, French, Irish, Italian, Canadian and Australian) and four did not (Belgian, Dutch, Norwegian and UK). Only four included provisions for hate speech (German, Irish, UK and Australian), while seven did not (Austrian, Belgian, French, Italian, Dutch, Norwegian and Canadian). It is important to note here, as was noted above in the introduction, that most of the countries (with the exception of perhaps only Canada) that did not include hate speech in their code had strict national legislative regulatory mechanisms for preventing hate speech both online and offline.

Table 7.2 summarises response sheet issues (otherwise called main issues in this report) not included in ISP codes of conduct, by country.

Table 7.2 Main issues not included in ISP codes of conduct, by country

Country	Areas **not** included in code	
Austria	8/11	
	C	Business regulation: not directly
	F	Hate speech: not directly, but prohibits content 'illegal' under Austrian law
	G	Bulk e-mail
Belgium	7/11	
	A	Only applies to ISPs
	E	Harmful to minors
	F	Hate speech: not directly, but prohibits content 'illegal' under Belgian law
	G	Bulk e-mail
France	6/11	
	A	Only applies to ISPs
	B	Review/amendment
	C	Business regulation
	F	Hate speech, not directly, but hate speech is illegal in France and thus is incorporated by reference in provisions regulating illegal content
	K	Sanctions
Germany	8/11	
	C	Business regulation
	G	Bulk e-mail
	H	Data protection and privacy
Ireland	11/11	
Italy	9/11	
	F	Hate speech, not directly, but if hate speech is illegal in Italy, then it is incorporated by reference in provisions regulating illegal content
	G	Bulk e-mail
Netherlands	7/11	
	A	Only ISPs ('providers')
	B	Review and amendment
	E	Harmful to minors
	F	Hate speech, not directly, but if hate speech is illegal in the Netherlands, then it is incorporated by reference in provisions regulating illegal content
Norway	6/11	
	C	Business regulation
	E	Harmful to minors
	F	Hate speech
	G	Bulk e-mail
	J	Cooperation with law enforcement or third parties
United Kingdom	9/11	
	A	Only ISPs
	E	Harmful to minors
Canada	6/11	
	A	Only ISPs
	F	Hate speech
	H	Data protection and privacy
	I	Complaint mechanism
	K	Sanctions
Australia	8/11	
	A	Only ISPs
	C	Business regulation
	K	Sanctions

Discussion

Emerging from the observations and analysis of the 11 codes is the finding that there are five building blocks of an ISPA code:

1   grounding the code in the existing legislation;
2   ensuring openness of the code both to members and end-users;
3   dealing with non-content users' issues such as data protection, privacy, bulk e-mail, and (to limited extent) information regarding business;
4   dealing with sensitive issues of protection of minors from harmful content and regulating hate speech;
5   enforcement and sanctions.

In grounding an ISP code of conduct in existing legislation it is not sufficient to identify ISPA members' responsibility to deal with illegal or criminal content. It is also necessary to specify a mechanism for cooperation with law enforcement authorities or third parties both in cases when self-regulation works (illegal content is identified and the ISP takes action) and when self-regulation fails (illegal content is identified but no action results).

In ensuring openness of the code, both to members and to end-users, it is necessary to provide provisions for a formal complaint mechanism. A formal yet uncomplicated complaint mechanism has an advantage of giving users confidence in the self-regulatory scheme. It is also likely to improve communication between ISPA members, users and the ISPA organisation. Furthermore, an open review and amendment procedure creates a participation incentive for ISPs, who can voluntarily join a code of conduct knowing that it can contribute to the evolution of the code's rules. With convergence of digital media, and evolving national and supra-national laws, it may be necessary to review and amend an ISP code in order to maintain its relevance and effectiveness.

Most of the codes quite explicitly spell out guidelines on data protection and privacy. This seems to be the minimum standard for a relevant ISP code of conduct. Yet further information on bulk e-mail and on information regarding business may be able to improve the relevance and effectiveness of the code in furthering these goals of protecting privacy and data. But these specific provisions may not be necessary, and in fact are not included in a number of well-drafted and functioning codes.

Content concerns, specifically protection of minors and hate speech, are the most publicised and perhaps the most sensitive and controversial issues in drafting and implementing an ISP code of conduct. Yet in countries where national legislation deals quite explicitly with hate speech and/or protection of minors, these content issues may not even fall into the sphere of self-regulation. ISPA codes of conduct that do not have a mandate to deal with hate speech or protection of minors should nevertheless specify explicitly how they provide for cooperation with law enforcement or third parties regarding this content. Depending on the scope of national legislation, it may not be necessary to make an assumption that issues of hate speech and protection of minors should be under the rubric of illegal content. Specifying the extent to which this sensitive content is regulated by law can help both end-users and ISPA members.

Finally, sanctions and enforcement may prove to be crucial for an ISP code of conduct once it is put into practice. But often implementation of codes depends less on the structure and comprehensiveness of a code than it does on will and organisation of the body responsible for self-regulation, as well as members of the industry and their relationship with the government. In all, there seems to be an emerging balance in the 11 codes of conduct studied – a balance between providing formal mechanisms of sanctions and avoiding complicated procedures that would prevent end-users and ISPA members from utilising the existing procedures. Ultimately, sanctions are a matter of application of the code, not merely of its structure.

Building on this analysis we can conclude that there is a plethora of issues that further complicates drafting and implementation of ISPA codes in practice. In principle, self-regulation should not create antitrust problems, and a code of conduct should not present foreign companies with barriers to market entry, both within and outside the European Union. An important issue is whether the culture of the industry is co-operative and whether its members are used to self-regulation, and here ISPs differ significantly from the broadcasters. In cases where industry is hesitant, clear incentives/motives have to exist and be emphasised in order to implement self-regulation. In addition, a 'best practice' code can be part of the self-regulatory mechanism. Multiplicity of codes, even on the national level such as in Australia, can make self-regulation less successful by introducing redundancy and confusion. So can failure to take into account current legal requirements (perhaps most notably and controversially hate and racist speech legislation in many EU states) or, in contrast, taking every single interest group's concern ('the Christmas tree phenomenon'). In general, ISP codes should aim to make users aware of the rights provided to them by the code, especially the rights of complaint. In addition, high media literacy can also empower end-users. ISPs are also faced with the fact that almost all other visual and audio media regulation mechanisms are bound to affect them more and more as convergence increases. To this extent, ISPs' codes of conduct need to consult other media codes of conduct as well as changing expectations of users in the different media industries.

Conclusions: Internet content and ISP codes

The first years of the Internet as a mass consumer phenomenon saw a cautious first settlement for content regulation. Whereas there was some agreement on the more extreme harms associated with the medium (e.g. child abuse) the desire to protect the economic dynamism of the sector led to a settlement involving limited liability with ISPs – considered mere conduits until informed of illegal content, and with little responsibility for harmful content. A self-regulatory approach to harmful content and procedures for dealing with harmful content were agreed in the E-commerce Directive and the Cybercrime Convention. This is further discussed in subsequent chapters.

This first settlement for Internet content in Europe is a convincing story. Whether it was in fact effective is another matter, and depends on whether success is measured in terms of preventing harms of one kind or another, or in terms of preventing state regulation. In terms of the latter it has been successful, but it would be difficult to sustain the argument that exposure to illegal or harmful content, or copyright infringement, has been effectively regulated.

The first Internet self-regulation paradigm, with ISP codes at the centre, is developing some international standards, but as we have seen these are not stable, and the processes of convergence are set to render standards even more unstable. Notice and take down, the central procedure for illegal content in the regime in Europe, has been widely questioned in the last few years, and a report of the OSCE High

Representative on Freedom of Expression from 2004 called for 'put back' rights to be incorporated into the regime.[159]

Sustainability problems continue with the maintenance of various Internet self-regulation solutions. The costs of maintaining generally accepted standards of due process when dealing with issues of fundamental rights are high. There is some evidence that ISPs do not have the incentives to prioritise the performance of these self-regulatory roles, particularly when the sector is more competitive. The European Commission asked European ISPs to come up with a pan-European code of conduct in June 2004. The fact that little progress was made on this surely estimates the limits of the co-regulatory approach.

Convergence is leading to multiple offline codes being applied to online content, and to an overlap of codes between content provider, ISP and statutory obligations. Codes for mobile operators have been developed. Issues of overlap and potential confusion between codes will continue to be pressing in the coming years.

There remains a good deal of public support for voluntary rating schemes such as ICRA and RSACi. These decentralised voluntary rating services do not, however, at present provide user security and child protection, because they have failed to persuade webmasters to invest the time necessary to self-rate. As a result too many sites are not rated, and children restricted to rated sites can access only a fraction of the web. Problems of jurisdiction remain, despite growing agreement that the country of origin principle should apply. There is often no agreement on jurisdiction that should apply. In the Guttnick case (libel of Australian businessman by US publication), for example, the High Court Judge ruled that the publication 'takes place where and when the contents are comprehended by the reader'.[160]

It is surprising that details of the notice and take-down scheme are not listed in more codes as it is essential that ISPs are more transparent in this regard. Clearly, analysis of codes can only take us so far. In particular, most codes have broad articles relating to illegal content and to cooperation with law enforcement. As they are situated in varying national contexts their behaviours will depend on the local law context, so where there are differences, the same code will be interpreted differently in different jurisdictions. Those fields where there are the most consequential differences in national law will be with regard to hate speech, defamation and obscenity. In regard to these fields jurisdictional issues are likely to complicate future pan-European cooperation in the field of Internet self-regulation.

In Chapter 11 we examine another broad issue area that is critical to the development of Internet self-regulation in a context of global norms on freedom of expression: the involvement of the state in self- and co-regulatory compact and the 'negative rights continuum'. Are there instances where state support for co-/self-regulation would be inappropriate?

APPENDIX 1

ITALIAN ISP CODE 1997

Contents

Introduction

Title I – Preliminary provisions and general principles

1. Definitions

2. Purpose of the Code

3. Field of application
   3a. Parties bound by the Code
   3b. Extension clause

4. General principles of the Internet Self-regulation Code
   4a. General principles of identification and the right to anonymity
   4b. General principles of responsibility
   4c. Principles of protection of human dignity, minors and public order
   4d. Fundamental freedoms and protection of privacy
   4e. Principles of protection of intellectual and industrial property rights
   4f. Principles of protection of consumers within the framework of electronic commerce
   4g. Principles for the application of the Internet Self-regulation Code

Title II – General rules of conduct

5. Obligations relating to user identification

6. Obligations relating to the protection of human dignity, minors and public order

7. Obligations relating to the protection of fundamental freedoms and privacy
   7a. Secrecy of correspondence
   7b. Private and personal data

8. Obligations relating to the protection of intellectual and industrial property rights

9. General obligations relating to special commercial and/or professional activities
   9a. Consultancy
   9b. Information services
   9c. Prize-winning competitions
   9d. Job opportunities
   9e. Advertising

Title III – Application of the Code

10. Preliminary statement

11. Implementation Committee
    Constitution and composition
    Duties and tasks
    Meetings

12. Self-protection Jury
    Constitution and composition
    Duration
    Chairman and Vice-Chairman
    Duties

13. Proceedings
    Notification and investigation
    Decisions and penalties

14. Illicit subject-matter and actions

Text of the Self-regulation Code

Introduction

The Internet is a **world wide web** whereby all the subject matter and services present can be accessed by any user wherever he may be, without geographic limitation. This characteristic of the Network is extremely positive, but it makes it difficult to regulate the subject-matter and services by means of a set of common rules, given the cultural, political and normative differences between the different countries.

The Internet is an interactive communication system which compared to traditional mass media, is based, and this is its most noteworthy feature, on the direct involvement of users in creating, as well as benefiting from the subject-matter and services.

The Internet is a **flexible tool** which makes it possible to communicate at multiple levels and in different ways: varying from 'publications' to public or private interaction, from purely textual features to multimedia communication, from message transmission to computer programs.

This flow of information and actions, which today already greatly supersedes any other form of traditional communication in terms of volume of communicative exchanges, may conceal illicit conduct according to some or all of the legal regulations, or subject-matter which is potentially offensive to some categories of users. It is therefore appropriate that measures be taken to limit any damaging effects which this subject-matter and conduct may cause.

For this reason, the operators in the sector feel the need to adopt a code of conduct which, in accordance with the specific characteristics of the Internet network:

*   take account of international experience and individual solutions in terms of self-regulation of the sector in other countries – with special reference to the member States of the European Union – in order to increase their effectiveness in a clearly international context;
*   is based on the right to freedom of expression and communication;
*   is studied in such a way as to evolve over time in accordance with the high rate of innovation which characterises the technologies linked to the Internet.

This code takes account, among other things, of the indications of the Council and the Commission of the European Union (Green Paper on the Protection of Minors and Human Dignity in Audiovisual and Information Services of 16 October 1996, Council Resolution of 17 February 1997).

Title I – Preliminary provisions and general principles

1. Definitions

For the purposes of this Code, the following definitions are used:

Internet (hereafter also called the Network): set of computer networks interconnected between themselves through telecommunication lines and communicating by using protocols of the TCP/IP family.

TCP/IP: protocol (communication language) used for transmitting data over the Internet.

Infrastructures: telecommunication lines and equipment necessary for the operation of the Network.

Access: connection to the Network, necessary for the purpose of using its resources.

Hosting: making available part of the resources of a server for purposes of distributing subject-matter or services through the Network.

Server: computer connected to the Network capable of apportioning services.

Subject-matter: any information made available to the public through the Network, made up, singly or separately, of text, sound, graphics, fixed or moving images, computer programs and any other element of communication.

Conduct: act or group of acts brought about through the Network or concerning the use of the Network.

Illicit subject matter or conduct: concerns subject-matter or conduct contrary to the regulations in force in Italy.

Potentially offensive subject-matter or conduct: concerns subject-matter or conduct which although it does not contravene the regulations in force, and is hence lawful, may prove offensive to some categories of users; the matter of protection of minors is particularly relevant.

Internet parties: all parties (physical or legal persons) who use the Internet.

User: anybody who accesses the Internet.

Suppliers of infrastructures: anybody who offers infrastructures over the Internet.

Access suppliers: anybody who offers access to the Internet.

'Hosting' suppliers: anybody who offers hosting on a server connected to the Internet.

Suppliers of subject-matter: anybody who emits subject-matter on the Internet.

World Wide Web: all the subject-matter present on the Internet and identified by a univocal address (URL).

Forums/discussion groups/newsgroups: discussion space of a thematic nature with deferred communication and made up of messages transmitted through the network on all the servers which host such a discussion space.

Chat/IRC (Internet Relay Chat): discussion space with communication in real time.

Electronic mail (e-mail): telematic system which enables documents of a private nature to be sent to one or more recipients determined by the sender.

Electronic commerce: activity of purchase and sale of goods and services carried out completely or partly through the Network.

Cryptography: method of codification of data which prevents their exploitation by unauthorised parties (who do not possess the key to decrypting the data); a useful technique, for example, for increasing the privacy of correspondence via e-mail.

Private communication: a communication is considered private when it is addressed exclusively to one or more recipients determined by the sender.

Public communication (subject-matter made available to the public):
the communication of subject-matter destined for recipients not determined
individually by a supplier of subject-matter.

Hypertext or link connection: function which makes it possible, by selecting
from within a given subject-matter a specific part of the text or a graphic
element, to go instantly to another subject-matter or server at any point of the
network.

The above definitions are subject to change by the bodies provided for by this Code
based on changes in the status of the technologies and the practice and use of the
Internet network.

2. *Purpose of the Code*

The purpose of the Internet Self-regulation Code (hereafter the Code) is to prevent
the illicit or potentially offensive use of the Network through the diffusion of an
appropriate culture of responsibility on the part of all parties active on the Network.

In particular, the aim of the Code is to:

- provide rules of conduct for all Network parties;
- provide users of the Network with informative and technical tools with which to
use services and subject-matter more knowledgeably;
- provide all Internet parties with an interlocutor to whom they can report any
cases of infringement of this Code.

The Code defines the rules by which the parties bound by this Code must abide.

3. *Field of application*

3A. PARTIES BOUND BY THE CODE

Adherence to this Code is voluntary and open to all Internet parties operating in Italy
or in the Italian language.

The parties obliged to abide by this Code are all those who have signed it.

3B. EXTENSION CLAUSE

Parties who are signatories to the code undertake to extend the binding nature of the
Code to third parties by including an appropriate clause in all contracts concluded
for the provision of Internet and hosting access.

4. *General principles of the Internet Self-regulation Code*

4A. GENERAL PRINCIPLES OF IDENTIFICATION AND RIGHT TO ANONYMITY

- All Internet parties must be identifiable.
- Any Internet party, once identified, has the right to remain anonymous when
using the Network in order to protect their own private sphere.

4B. GENERAL PRINCIPLES OF RESPONSIBILITY

- A supplier of subject-matter is responsible for the information he makes available
to the public.

- Any Internet party may carry out, simultaneously or separately, several different functions and perform various roles.

  For purposes of defining individual rights and responsibilities in the network, Internet parties should be distinguished on the basis of the functions and roles they perform at any time (and hence regardless of whether the role is performed continuously or occasionally, professionally or in private, for commercial purposes or otherwise).

- No other Internet party may be held responsible, unless their active participation is proven.

  By active participation is understood any direct participation in drawing up a specific subject-matter.

- The provision of technical services without knowledge of the subject-matter shall not presuppose the responsibility of whoever provided that service.

4C. PRINCIPLES OF PROTECTION OF HUMAN DIGNITY, MINORS AND PUBLIC ORDER

- Respect for human dignity entails the protection of human life and the refusal of any form of discrimination relating to origin, real or presumed ethnic, social, religious or sexual affinity, state of health or any form of handicap or because of professed ideas.

- The protection of minors imposes a refusal of any form of exploitation, particularly that of a sexual nature, and any communications and information which may exploit their credulity; respect for the feelings of minors also imposes special caution in the diffusion to the public of potentially harmful subject-matter.

- The use of the Internet Network imposes respect for the principles governing public order and social safety.

The Network must not be a vehicle of messages which encourage the committing of offences and in particular, incitement to the use of violence and any form of participation or collaboration in delinquent activities.

4D. FUNDAMENTAL FREEDOMS AND PROTECTION OF PRIVACY

- The correct use of the Internet requires respect for fundamental rights and freedoms, and in particular of individual freedom, the right to access information, the freedom to meet together, protection of privacy, protection of personal data and confidentiality of correspondence.

4E. PRINCIPLES OF PROTECTION OF INTELLECTUAL AND INDUSTRIAL PROPERTY RIGHTS

- All original intellectual creations, distinctive signs and inventions are protected as regards the author and his assignees, in accordance with Italian law, Community regulations and international treaties governing intellectual and industrial property.

4F. PRINCIPLES OF PROTECTION OF CONSUMERS WITHIN THE FRAMEWORK OF ELECTRONIC COMMERCE

- Activities for commercial and/or professional purposes over the Internet are carried out based on the principles of correctness and transparency and are subject to the Italian and Community regulations regarding consumer protection, distance selling and advertising.

4G. PRINCIPLES FOR THE APPLICATION OF THE INTERNET SELF-REGULATION CODE

- The Internet parties undertake to promote the use of the Code and to collaborate between themselves to find the best ways of applying it.
- They also undertake to accept and propose contractual texts which refer to the Internet Code.
- The signatory parties of the Code undertake to diffuse the decisions of the judging body and to ensure that the decisions of that body are complied with, by taking whatever measures may be necessary.
- The Internet parties undertake, in making subject-matter available to the public, to display prominently a statement concerning their adherence to the provisions of the Code.

This statement may, if feasible, take the form of an icon (as per the attached model).

This statement shall include a link to the text of the Code, as well as links to sites directly or indirectly involved in the self-regulation process (alert and complaints divisions).

Title II – General rules of conduct

5. Obligations relating to user identification

- The parties must agree to the acquisition of their own personal data by whoever supplies them with access and/or hosting. The suppliers of the said services are obliged to register the data to make them available to the legal authorities under the terms of the law.
- Once identified, a user may ask his access and hosting supplier for an identification other than his name (pseudonym) with which to operate over the Network (protected anonymity).

6. Obligations relating to the protection of human dignity, minors and public order

- Any Internet party who becomes directly aware of the existence of subject-matter of an illicit nature which is accessible by the public, shall inform the legal authorities accordingly directly.
- Any Internet party who becomes directly aware of the existence of subject-matter accessible by the public which is contrary to the provisions of this Code, shall inform the self-disciplinary body.
- Access and hosting suppliers are obliged to make easily accessible on-line by all suitable means, including e-mail, information concerning the methods for reporting to the competent authorities any illegal or potentially harmful subject-matter of which they may become aware.
- The suppliers of subject-matter shall use tools capable of informing end-users of the presence of potentially offensive content, by means of appropriate signs, in order to prevent the involuntary viewing of such subject-matter.
- The suppliers of subject-matter undertake:

1. to make easily accessible on-line by all suitable means, including e-mail, information on the technical features, operating methods and tools for the use of filtering programs.
2. to carry out self-classification of their own subject-matter based on the classification system recognised as standard by the Code and to accept any variations in their own classifications which may be requested by the self-disciplinary entity.

The selection of the standard system of classification of subject-matter is entrusted to the Implementation Committee of the Code, taking into consideration the status of the technology, the diffusion of the systems on an international scale, and in particular, consistency with the choices made on the subject by the other Member States of the European Union.

7. *Obligations relating to the protection of fundamental freedoms and privacy*

- The suppliers of subject-matter shall inform their own clients of the technical limits of the protection of confidentiality of correspondence and private and personal data in the Network.
- Access suppliers shall provide their clients with indications as to the measures and products – which do not infringe the regulations in force – intended to ensure the confidentiality and integrity of their correspondence and data, in particular as regards encrypting tools and/or electronic signatures.

7A. SECRECY OF CORRESPONDENCE

- The exchange of private correspondence over the Internet is based on the provisions of laws which govern the secrecy of correspondence.
- The general obligation of confidentiality is particularly strictly binding on parties who carry out commercial and/or professional activities over the Network.
- Companies which employ personnel with the power to access private correspondence for professional reasons undertake to respect confidentiality and to draw the attention of their collaborators to the criminal liability which could derive from any infringement of that confidentiality.

7B. PRIVATE AND PERSONAL DATA

- Information of a private and personal nature which is voluntarily transmitted by a subscriber or involuntarily during a connection between computers over the Network must be collected and used in compliance with the rights of the party to whom they refer, and more specifically, in compliance with the regulations in force concerning the processing of personal data.
- Suppliers of access by means of temporary links over the public telephone network are obliged to keep the date, times and PI number assigned by the connections made by each of their own users for a period of 24 months as from the connection. Suppliers of access by means of dedicated links are obliged to keep a record of the network addresses assigned to their own clients.

8. Obligations concerning the protection of intellectual and industrial property rights

- All original intellectual creations are protected as regards the author and his assignees, in accordance with the Italian law on copyright, Community regulations and international treaties.
- Databases are subject to protection on behalf of their authors and assignees, based on the law on copyright and the specific regulations governing rights to databases.
- A work may not be reproduced or made available to the public without the authorisation of the rights holder.
- Indications relating to the author of the work, the rights holder and the digital identification of the work may not be deleted or modified without the consent of the persons concerned.
- The automated transmission of the works for insertion in the network is not deemed to be a form of reproduction of the work.
- The citing of the work by means of hypertext links with other sites is lawful.

    Any form of citation involving reproduction of the work must be carried out in compliance with the specific regulations. The citation of a work which is subject to protection, in particular, must:
    - indicate the name of the author, the source and must not alter the elements which enable its digital identification;
    - be brief;
    - be incorporated in another work;
    - be justified by the nature of the work in which it is incorporated.
- The regulations governing trademarks are applicable to Internet parties.
- Internet parties shall abstain from substantial reproduction of the subject-matter of another site without authorisation, even if they are not subject to copyright protection. In particular, suppliers of subject-matter, prior to any use of works subject to protection, must ensure that they have obtained the relative rights and authorisation from the assignees.
- Hosting suppliers must include in contracts with clients a clause referring to this principle.
- When the maintenance of a given subject-matter on a site or a server ceases, due to the termination of contractual relations or on other grounds, the supplier of the service, in accordance with the contractual provisions, shall cease to keep the data supplied by his client.
- Before making any use over the Internet of a sign intended to distinguish a product or service or to indicate the address of a site, a supplier of subject-matter who intends to use that sign must ascertain that it is available.

9. General obligations relating to special commercial and/or professional activities

9A. CONSULTANCY

Services which offer information or consultancy quoting opinions must indicate clearly the identity, professional qualifications, and any post occupied by the expert or specialist. This indication must however be provided in compliance with professional ethics, which prohibit any form of publicity for certain categories of professionals.

Each service must be supplied in terms and in a manner reflecting the seriousness of the discipline which is the subject of the consultancy, especially in the case of medical consultancy services.

9B. INFORMATION SERVICES

Services offering information on data, facts or circumstances which are liable to undergo changes in the course of time must also contain an indication of the date and time to which the updating of the information supplied refers.

9C. PRIZE-WINNING COMPETITIONS

Any service which institutes a prize-winning competition may only be activated after the relative authorisation order has been issued by the Ministry of Finance or, in the case of prize-winning operations limited to a single province, by the competent Finance Office, under the terms of the regulation issued by R.D.L. No. 1933 of 29.10.1938 and subs. mod, converted to law No. 384 of 27.11.1989, and by R.D. No. 1077 of 25.7.1940.

9D. JOB OPPORTUNITIES

A supplier of subject-matter, before implementing a service promoting job opportunities, must ensure that the supply of the service does not imply a violation of the order on the intermediation and/or intervention of workers.

Services which offer professional training courses or other teaching courses are under the obligation not to make unreasonable promises or raise expectations of future employment or future remuneration by users.

9E. ADVERTISING

The suppliers of subject-matter undertake to comply with the regulations laid down by the Advertising Self-disciplinary Code, both for advertising on behalf of the services offered, conveyed by means of those same services or through other means, and for advertising aimed at promoting other services or products, whereby the service only represents the vehicle of diffusion.

The suppliers of subject-matter undertake to offer advertising space for communications of social importance on special conditions, based on the same rules provided for television advertising.

Title III – Application of the Code

10. Preliminary statement

Operators who are aware of the requirement to draw up rules of conduct for use of the Internet, thereby promoting this Code, represented by the Italian Association of Internet Providers, the National Association of Electronic Publishing, Olivetti and Telecom Italia, deem it appropriate to meet together voluntarily on an Implementation Committee for the purpose, as indicated below, of appointing the members of a Jury charged with upholding this Code.

The Implementation Committee may also promote the creation of a permanent associative structure aimed at diffusing and supporting this Code, endowed with statutes and appropriate administrative bodies. In such event, the following provisions will be of a temporary nature.

11. Implementation Committee

CONSTITUTION AND COMPOSITION

The promoters of this Code voluntarily constitute, under the terms of Articles 36 and following of the Code of Civil Law, a Committee for Implementation of the Code and hereby elect domicile at _____

The Implementation Committee is made up of three representatives for each promoter.

At its first session the Implementation Committee shall elect from among its members a Chairman and a Vice-Chairman and shall set up a common fund, under the terms of Article 37 of the Code of Civil Law, intended to finance the activities with which the committee and the Jury are charged.

DUTIES AND TASKS

The duties of the Implementation Committee are information, prevention and regulation. The tasks entrusted to the Implementation Committee are:

- the implementation and upgrading of this code through recommendations and amendments;
- the appointment of the members of the Self-protection Jury;
- the examination, in the second instance, of appeals against decisions taken by the Jury;
- a role of information and consultation for Internet users and parties;
- conciliation (through forms of mediation and arbitration) between Internet parties;
- the setting up and management of an Internet site with the function of diffusing the principles of the Code, information for all Internet parties on self-regulation, and support for the Jury's activity;
- the development of relations with the public authorities, independent authorities and category associations at national and international level;
- the development of relationships with similar organisations in other countries;
- study and research activities.

MEETINGS

The Chairman, by agreement with the Vice-Chairman, convenes meetings of the Implementation Committee and draws up the agenda. The Committee meets at an ordinary meeting twice a year and at an extraordinary meeting when requested by the Chairman or at least one third of the members. In such case the meeting must be held within 15 days of presentation of the request.

12. Self-protection Jury

CONSTITUTION AND COMPOSITION

The Self-protection Jury is set up by the Implementation Committee; it is composed of five members designated and appointed by the Implementation Committee and is domiciled at _____

DURATION

The members of the Self-protection Jury remain in office for one year, and its members may be re-appointed by the Implementation Committee.

CHAIRMAN AND VICE-CHAIRMAN

At the first session the Self-protection Jury elects a Chairman and a Vice-Chairman from among its members.

DUTIES

The duties of the Self-protection Jury are: upholding compliance with this Code, intervention in the event of being notified of an infringement by Internet parties, consumers or anyone involved in same, ascertaining and pronouncing itself on any infringements and the application of penalties *vis-à-vis* parties held responsible.

Furthermore, the Jury may also express preventive opinions on compliance with the Code of information to be made available to the public, the compatibility of specific subject-matter with rating principles, and self-certification criteria.

13. Proceedings

NOTIFICATION AND INVESTIGATION

Notification of infringements must be made by Internet parties by means of an application, sent by electronic mail (or by post or fax), containing a description of the infringement, and an indication of the URL of the site relating to the notified offence. Once the complaint has been received, the President of the Jury opens preliminary proceedings, sets a date for the decision and chooses within the Jury an investigating member charged with:

(a) notifying the parties concerned of the opening of the preliminary proceedings, the summons to a discussion, granting them a deadline of 3 days in which to file any conclusions and/or documents;
(b) examining the indicated application and preparing a report on the denounced matter in question, with the authority to consult the parties concerned.

On the expiry of this deadline the President convenes the Jury, which is obliged to take a decision regarding the proceedings, based on the investigator's report and the conclusions and/or documents filed by the parties concerned.

The Jury is also given the right to extend the deadline for the decision if the proceedings are not sufficiently prepared or if it is necessary to acquire further elements for purposes of the decision, and informs the parties accordingly.

DECISIONS AND PENALTIES

The Jury's decision is immediately communicated to the parties and must contain the measure which is subsequently to be adopted, with the respective grounds.

In the event of a negative pronouncement, or if the decision establishes that the indicated offence is unfounded, the Jury closes the proceedings.

Notes

1 Price, M and Verhulst, S (2005).
2 See § 4 of the Austrian ISPA code: 'Responsibility of ISPA members for Internet content'.
3 § 4 of the Austrian ISPA code: 'Responsibility of ISPA members for Internet content'.
4 § 2 of the Belgian ISPA code: 'General provisions of a commercial nature'.
5 § 3 of the Belgian ISPA code: 'Provisions concerning criminal activity and the claims procedure'.
6 § 3 of the Belgian ISPA code: 'Provisions concerning criminal activity and the claims procedure'.
7 Part II, R. 2 of the French AFA code.
8 Part II, R. 3.2 of the French AFA code.
9 Part II, R. 3.3 of the French AFA code.
10 Part I, R. 2.4 of the French AFA code.
11 Part I, R. 2 of the German FSM code.
12 Section 1.19 of the Irish ISPAI code.
13 Section 2.3 of the Irish ISPAI code: 'Responsibilities of members'.
14 Section 4.2 of the Irish ISPAI code: 'General requirements'.
15 Section 4.2 of the Irish ISPAI code: 'General requirements'.
16 Section 7 of the Irish ISPAI code: 'www.hotline.ieservice'.
17 Please note that references to the Italian code in this section refer to the 2002 ISPA code of Italy, not the co-regulatory code sponsored by the Ministry of Communications.
18 Rule of Conduct 6 of the Italian ISPA code: 'Obligations relating to the protection of human dignity, minors and public order'.
19 Section G.3 of the Dutch ISPA code: 'Laws and regulations'.
20 Section 4.9 of the Norwegian ISP code: 'Rights and obligations'.
21 R. 2.1.1 and R. 2.1.2 of the UK ISPA code.
22 R. 2.2.2 of the UK ISPA code.
23 R. 7.1.3 of the UK ISPA code.
24 R. 7.1.10 of the UK ISPA code; in addition, R. 5 of the UK ISPA code deals with cooperation with the Internet Watch Foundation (IWF).
25 CAIP Policy Statement No. 4: Illegal Content and Conduct.
26 CAIP Policy Statement No. 3.
27 This refers to a list of approved filtering services.
28 http://www.aba.gov.au/internet/codes/documents/IIA_Code.pdf
29 § 8 of the Austrian ISPA code: 'Declaration by the ISPA members re these Guidelines'.
30 P.5 of the Belgian ISPA code: 'Modification of the code'.
31 P.4 of the Belgian ISPA code: 'Internal procedure relating to members' non-compliance with the code'.
32 P.4 of the Belgian ISPA code: 'Internal procedure relating to members' non-compliance with the code'.
33 Part III of the French AFA code.
34 Part III of the French AFA code.
35 See the German AFM website at www.fsm.de for the complaints code.
36 Section 5.3 of the Irish ISPAI code: 'Scope of the code'.
37 Section 11.2 of the Irish ISPAI code: 'Complaints procedure'.
38 Section 11.3 of the Irish ISPAI code: 'Complaints procedure'.
39 Section 11.4 of the Irish ISPAI code: 'Complaints procedure'.
40 Section 11.5 of the Irish ISPAI code: 'Complaints procedure'.
41 Section 11.6 of the Irish ISPAI code: 'Complaints procedure'.
42 Section 11.7.1 of the Irish ISPAI code: 'Complaints procedure'.
43 Section 11.7.2 of the Irish ISPAI code: 'Complaints procedure'.
44 Section 11.8 of the Irish ISPAI code: 'Complaints procedure'.

> 11.8.1 The Secretariat will ask the Complainant to set out the Complaint in writing and to forward the written Complaint to the Secretariat together with a non-refund-

able payment of EUR 5.00 (IR£3.94) towards the administrative costs of handling the Complaint. The Secretariat is empowered to waive the said payment of EUR 5.00 (IR£3.94) at the sole discretion of the Secretariat.

11.8.2 The Secretariat, on receipt of the Complaint in writing, will forward the written Complaint to the Subject Member and will require the Subject Member to return to the Secretariat a written response to the Complaint within ten (10) Working Days of receipt of the Complaint. Failure by the Subject Member to return a written response to the Secretariat within ten (10) Working Days of receipt of the complaint will be considered a breach of the Code and shall result in the Complaint being referred to the Complaints Panel and the Secretariat will notify the subject Member accordingly.

11.8.3 In the event that the Complaint is not satisfactorily resolved within fourteen (14) Working Days after receipt of the Subject Member's written response required under 11.8.2 above the Secretariat may, at its discretion, refer the Complaint to the Complaints Panel which may then make further investigations into the Complaint in the manner deemed most appropriate and expeditious.

11.8.4 The Complaints Panel shall compile a 'Complaints Panel Report' setting out: (a) the name and address of the Complainant; (b) the name and address of the Member or Members the subject of the Complaint; (c) the original Complainant's wording as set out in the Complainant's Complaint; (d) the manner in which the Complaints Panel investigated the Complaint to include all details of such investigation and the result of all enquiries made by the Complaints Panel into the Complaint and exhibiting copies of all documents received by the Complaints Panel; (e) all information available to the Complaints Panel, concerning the Complainant, the Subject Member or Subject Members and the Complaint; (f) the conclusions of the Complaints Panel arising out of the Complaints Panel investigations carried out concerning the Complaint.

11.8.5 The Complaints Panel, on concluding its investigation into the Complaint and in the event the Complaint is not satisfactorily resolved, may issue a Complaints Panel Report for consideration by the next appropriate Board meeting. Any Subject Member or Complainant who is a member of the Board or any member of the Board who either represents the Subject Member or the Complainant, shall not be present at that portion of the Board meeting while such Complaint is being discussed and/or considered by the Board.

11.8.6 Where the Board determines, having considered the Complaints Panel Report, that a Subject Member is not in breach of the Code, the Board shall forthwith notify the Subject Member and the Complainant of its findings.

11.8.7 Where the Board determines, having considered the Complaints Panel Report, that a Subject Member may be in breach of the Code, the Board shall convene a Complaints Hearing to which it will invite the Subject Member to attend and/or be represented and the Board will, not later than twenty-one (21) Working Days before such Complaints Hearing, furnish the Subject Member with a copy of the Complaints Panel Report. The Board will be entitled, at its discretion, to invite the Complainant to attend and/or to be represented at the Complaints Hearing and in which case the Board will notify the Subject Member accordingly at least ten (10) Working Days before the Complaints Hearing.

11.8.8 The Board will, within twenty eight (28) days after the conclusion of the Complaints Hearing, issue a Complaints Decision in writing and the Secretariat will within seven (7) Working Days thereafter provide a copy of the Complaints Decision to the Complainant and to the Subject Member.

11.9 The Complainant and the Subject Member accept that the decision on any Complaint rests with the Board and the Board's decision shall be final and conclusive.

11.10 The Board may, at its discretion, refuse to adjudicate on a Complaint where the subject-matter of the Complaint is the subject of legal proceedings or where the Complaint concerns the legality of material carried on any Services or the Board may suspend its adjudication pending resolution of any concerned or disputed issue or any enquiry of whatsoever nature by the Courts.

11.11 Where a Complaint appears to the Board to fall within the remit of a particular regulatory body (e.g. www.hotline.ie or the Office of the Data Protection Commissioner or the Advertising Standards Authority for Ireland) the Secretariat or the Board may, on giving the Member ten (10) days notice, refer the Complaint to a named regulatory body or bodies and not adjudicate upon the Complaint or the Board may, where it deems necessary, confer with a relevant regulatory authority on giving the Member ten (10) days notice of the Board's intention to confer with the named relevant regulatory body or bodies.

45　P.11 of the Italian ISPA code.
46　General Rule 13 of the Italian ISPA code.
47　General Rule 13 of the Italian ISPA code.
48　'NLIP – Complaints Procedure' section of the Dutch ISPA code.
49　'NLIP – Disputes Committee' section of the Dutch ISPA code.
50　Section 1.3 of the Norwegian ISP code: 'Purpose'.
51　Sections 1.5–1.4 of the Norwegian ISP code.
52　Paragraph c, Preamble of the UK ISPA code.
53　Section 1.2 of the Canadian CAIP code: '1.0 Fair Practices Policy Statement – Responsible Service Policy Components'.
54　Fair Practices Policy Statement 2.0 of the Canadian CAIP code.
55　1.1, Policy Statement No. 5 of the Canadian CAIP code.
56　Policy Statement No. 6 of the Canadian CAIP code: 'Dispute resolution'.
57　§ 3 of the Austrian ISPA code: 'Confidential treatment of customer data by ISPA members'.
58　§ 3 of the Austrian ISPA code: 'Confidential treatment of customer data by ISPA members'.
59　TKG § 87 (3) states:

1. 'Root data' is all personal data required for the creation, the processing, alteration or termination of the legal relationship between the user and provider of telecommunications services or to prepare or issue a subscriber index; these are: (a) Family name and first name, (b) Academic level, (c) Address, (d) Subscriber number, (e) Credit worthiness.

2. 'Network data' is all personal data relating to the subscriber and user and which is required for the creation of a connection or the accounting for payment: (a) Active or passive subscriber numbers, (b) Subscriber address, (c) Type of terminal, (d) Charge code, (e) Total number of units to be charged for the accounting period, (f) Type, date, time and duration of connection, (g) Data quantity transferred, (h) Other payment information, such as advance payment, instalment payment, connection blocking or warnings.

3. 'Content data', the content of the information transmitted.

TKG § 96 (6) states:

The transfer of the data contained in a subscriber index to the regulatory body under the terms of § 26 and to a publisher of a multi-provider subscriber index as defined in para. 1 is permissible. Requests for this are to be granted by: (1) Providers having a market-dominating position, (2) Concession holders providing public voice transmission services if the request is made by another concession holder. To transfer the data, payment as pre-defined in the Business Terms and Conditions may be demanded, in the cases cited in paras. 1 and 2 to be oriented by the costs.

60 § 7 of the Austrian ISPA code: 'Dealing with E-Mail addresses in the case of Online registration'.
61 P.2 of the Belgian ISPA code: 'Data protection'.
62 P.2 of the Belgian ISPA code: 'Advertising'.
63 P.2 of the Belgian ISPA code: 'Information on prices'.
64 Part I, R. 2.1 of the French AFA code.
65 Part I, R. 2.2 of the French AFA code.
66 Part I, R. 2.3 of the French AFA code.
67 Part I, R. 2.4 of the French AFA code.
68 Part I, R. 1 of the French AFA code.
69 See part C.2.3 above.
70 Section 9.1 of the Irish ISPAI code: 'Data protection and privacy'.
71 Section 9.2 of the Irish ISPAI code: 'Data protection and privacy'.
72 Section 7.4 of the Irish ISPAI code: 'www.hotline.ie service'.
73 Section 1.29 of the Irish ISPAI code.
74 Section 1.2 of the Irish ISPAI code.
75 Section 6.3 of the Irish ISPAI code: 'Best practices'.
76 Section 4.2 of the Irish ISPAI code: 'General requirements'.
77 Section 4.4 of the Irish ISPAI code: 'General requirements'.
78 Section 4a of the Italian ISPA code: '4a. General principles of identification and right to anonymity' in the 'General Principle 4: General principles of the Internet Self-regulation Code'.
79 Section 4d of the Italian ISPA code: 'Fundamental freedoms and protection of privacy'.
80 Rule 5 of the Italian ISPA code: ' Obligations relating to user identification'.
81 Rule 7 of the Italian ISPA code: 'Obligations concerning protection of fundamental freedoms and privacy'.
82 Section 7a of the Italian ISPA code: 'Secrecy of correspondence' states:

> The exchange of private correspondence over the Internet is based on the provisions of laws which govern the secrecy of correspondence. The general obligation of confidentiality is particularly strictly binding on parties who carry out commercial and/or professional activities over the Network. Companies which employ personnel with the power to access private correspondence for professional reasons undertake to respect confidentiality and to draw the attention of their collaborators to the criminal liability which could derive from any infringement of that confidentiality.

Section 7b of the Italian ISPA code, 'Private and personal data', states:

> Information of a private and personal nature which is voluntarily transmitted by a subscriber or involuntarily during a connection between computers over the Network must be collected and used in compliance with the rights of the party to whom they refer, and more specifically, in compliance with the regulations in force concerning the processing of personal data. Suppliers of access by means of temporary links over the public telephone network are obliged to keep the date, times and PI number assigned by the connections made by each of their own users for a period of 24 months as from the connection. Suppliers of access by means of dedicated links are obliged to keep a record of the network addresses assigned to their own clients.

83 Principle 4f of the Italian ISPA code: 'Principles of consumer protection *vis-à-vis* electronic commerce'.
84 Section 9a of Rule 9 of the Italian ISPA code: '9a Consultancy' under 'Rule of Conduct 9: General obligations concerning special commercial and/or professional activities'.

85 Section 9b of Rule 9 of the Italian ISPA code: '9b Information services' under 'Rule of Conduct 9: General obligations concerning special commercial and/or professional activities'.

86 Section 9c of Rule 9 of the Italian ISPA code: '9c Prize-winning competitions' under 'Rule of Conduct 9: General obligations concerning special commercial and/or professional activities'.

87 Section 9d of Rule 9 of the Italian ISPA code: '9d Job opportunities' under 'Rule of Conduct 9: General obligations concerning special commercial and/or professional activities'.

88 Section 9e of Rule 9 of the Italian ISPA code: '9e Advertising' under 'Rule of Conduct 9: General obligations concerning special commercial and/or professional activities'.

89 Section G.2 of the Dutch ISPA code: 'Privacy'.

90 Section G.2 of the Dutch ISPA code: 'Confidentiality/security'.

91 Section 4 (Security), Recommended Practices of the Dutch ISPA code.

92 Section G.6 of the Dutch ISPA code: 'Commercial trading'.

93 Section 4.3 of the Norwegian ISP code: 'Rights and obligations'.

94 R. 4.1 of the UK ISPA code.

95 R. 4.2 of the UK ISPA code.

96 R. 4.3 of the UK ISPA code.

97 R. 7.1.5 of the UK ISPA code.

98 R. 7.1.6 of the UK ISPA code.

99 R. 2.3.1 of the UK ISPA code.

100 R. 2.4.1 of the UK ISPA code.

101 R. 2.4.2 of the UK ISPA code.

102 R. 2.5.1 of the UK ISPA code.

103 R. 2.5.2 of the UK ISPA code.

104 R. 3.2.1 of the UK ISPA code.

105 R. 3.2.2 of the UK ISPA code.

106 Fair Practices Policy Statement 5 of the Canadian CAIP code.

107 Section 2.0, Introductory Fair Practices Policy Statement of the Canadian CAIP code: 'Communications'.

108 Section 2.0, Fair Practices Policy Statement 1 of the Canadian CAIP code: 'Responsible Service'.

109 Section 2.3, Fair Practices Policy Statement 1 of the Canadian CAIP code: 'Responsible Service'.

110 Section 3.0, Fair Practices Policy Statement 1 of the Canadian CAIP code: 'Responsible Service'.

111 Section 3.1, Fair Practices Policy Statement 1 of the Canadian CAIP code: 'Responsible Service'.

112 Section 3.2, Fair Practices Policy Statement 1 of the Canadian CAIP code: 'Responsible Service'.

113 Section 3.3, Fair Practices Policy Statement 1 of the Canadian CAIP code: 'Responsible Service'.

114 Section 2.1, Objectives, of the Australian ISP code.

115 Section 3.1, Principles, of the Australian ISP code.

116 Section 5.7 of the Australian ISP code.

117 Section 7.8 of the Australian ISP code.

118 § 2 of the Austrian ISPA code: 'Fundamental responsibility of the ISPA members'.

119 § 6 of the Austrian ISPA code: 'Protection of young people – responsibility of ISPA members'.

120 § 6 of the Austrian ISPA code: 'Protection of young people – responsibility of ISPA members'.

121 R. 4, paragraph 1 of the French AFA code.

122 Part I, R. 3 of the German AFM code.

123 Part I, R. 3, subsection 1, paragraphs a and b of the German AFM code.

124 Part I, R. 3, subsection 2, paragraphs a and b of the German AFM code.
125 Part I, R. 2 of the German AFM code.
126 Part I, R. 2, subsections a and c of the German AFM code.
127 Section 2.2 of the Irish ISPAI code: 'Responsibilities of content providers' under 'Statement of policy'.
128 Section 2.3 of the Irish ISPAI code: 'Responsibilities of members' under 'Statement of policy'.
129 Section 1.2 of the Irish ISPAI code: 'Responsibilities of Content Providers'.
130 Section 1.20 of the Irish ISPAI code: 'Responsibilities of Content Providers'.
131 Section 7.5 of the Irish ISPAI code: 'www.hotline.ie service'.
132 Section 4.3 of the Irish ISPAI code: 'General requirements'.
133 Section P.3a of the Italian ISPA code: '3a. Parties bound by the Code'.
134 Principle 4C of the Italian ISPA code: 'Principles of protection of human dignity, minors and public order'.
135 Rule of Conduct 6C of the Italian ISPA code: 'Obligations relating to the protection of human dignity, minors and public order'.
136 Rule of Conduct 6C of the Italian ISPA code: 'Obligations relating to the protection of human dignity, minors and public order'.
137 Section 3.1 of the Norwegian ISP code: 'Scope'.
138 R. 2.2.1 of the UK ISPA code.
139 Introduction of the Canadian CAIP code.
140 Section 1.0, Policy Statement 3 of the Canadian CAIP code: 'Education'.
141 Section 3.1(e) of the Principles of the Australian ISP code.
142 Section 5.2 of the Australian ISP code.
143 Section 5.3 of the Australian ISP code.
144 Section 5.4 of the Australian ISP code.
145 Section 7.2 of the Australian ISP code.
146 Section 7.3 of the Australian ISP code.
147 Section 7.4 of the Australian ISP code.
148 § 8 of the Austrian ISPA code: 'Declaration by the ISPA members re these Guidelines'.
149 P.4 of the Belgian ISPA code: 'Internal procedure relating to members' non-compliance with the code'.
150 Part II, R. 6, paragraphs a–c of the German FSM code.
151 Part III, R. 7, paragraphs 1–4 of the German FSM code.
152 Section 12.1 of the Irish ISPAI code.
153 Section 12.2 of the Irish ISPAI code.
154 Section 7, General Rule 13 of the Italian ISPA code: 'Decisions and penalties' under 'Proceedings'.
155 Section 7, General Rule 13 of the Italian ISPA code: 'Decisions and penalties' under 'Proceedings'.
156 'NLIP-Disputes Committee' section of the Dutch ISPA code.
157 Section K.9 of the Dutch ISPA code: 'Enforcement'.
158 Section 6.1 of the Norwegian ISP code: 'The Council's authority'.
159 See Möller, Ch and Amouroux, A (2004) *The Media Freedom Internet Cookbook*, Vienna: OSCE.
160 *Gutnick* v. *Dow Jones* [22] HCA56.

8   Self-regulation of the electronic games industry

Introduction

The electronic games industry is not new – having existed offline for over thirty years – but is becoming a much more significant part of the media with games revenue exceeding film theatre revenue in many markets. Formerly a console-based, discrete activity, it is rapidly developing into a broadband-enabled online activity, with massive multiplayer gaming having originated in broadband pioneer South Korea. According to Price Waterhouse Coopers,[1] the global entertainment and media industries are expected to see accelerated growth of 7.3 per cent and will reach $1.8 trillion in annual sales by 2009. The global video game market is expected to be the fastest-growing component and increased from $25.4 billion in revenue in 2004 to almost $55 billion in 2009, growing at a 16.5 per cent compound annual rate. The introduction of the next-generation broadband-enabled consoles, as well as the continued growth of handheld and mobile gaming, will be key drivers of growth. The PC game market will continue to shrink with game sales projected to decline from $771 million in 2004 to $655 million in 2009 (see Figure 8.1).

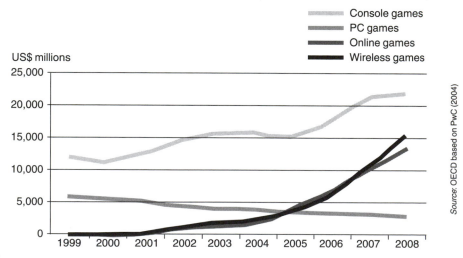

Figure 8.1 World computer games market to 2008. (From OECD (2005) 'Digital Broadband Content: The Online Computer and Video Game Industry', DSTI/ICCP/IE(2004) 13/FINAL, pp. 53–54, at: http://www.oecd.org/dataoecd/19/5/34884414.pdf.)

Europe may only be the third largest games market (after East Asia and North America) but it is the largest publisher of games, with about 40 per cent of games authored in the European Union. Additionally, Europe and East Asia have much higher levels of adoption of mobile games than North America. A corpus of legal scholarship concentrates on the virtual world's relationship with the law, with the 'State of Play' conference an annual event.[2] The effect of violent gaming on youth has been recently much debated in the media, and has led the American Psychological Association to pass a 2005 resolution which states in part:

> BE IT FURTHER RESOLVED that APA engage those responsible for developing violent video games and interactive media in addressing the issue that playing violent video games may increase aggressive thoughts and aggressive behaviors in children, youth, and young adults and that these effects may be greater than the well documented effects of exposure to violent television and movies.
> BE IT FURTHER RESOLVED that APA recommend to the entertainment industry that the depiction of the consequences of violent behavior be associated with negative social consequences.
> BE IT FURTHER RESOLVED that APA (a) advocate for the development and dissemination of a content based rating system that accurately reflects the content of video games and interactive media, and (b) encourage the distribution and use of the rating system by the industry, the public, parents, caregivers and educational organizations.[3]

There is a great deal of pressure on the industry, whether or not one accepts the APA's finding that video games can be more harmful to young people than television. Content rating is instituted in Australia under the co-regulatory schemes established by the National Classification Code of 1995, under the powers in the Broadcasting Service Act of 1992. In 2000, Section 5 of the Act became operational, extending the co-regulatory system to the Internet.[4] Further co-regulatory measures have recently been introduced in China and South Korea (with the stated objective of preventing games players' obsessive playing resulting in harm to self and others offline). As yet, less self-regulatory activity has focused in Europe on this issue of game 'addiction'. The focus has been on sex and violence.

European approaches to games rating

European concerns with computer games have reached the stage of pan-European action to regulate the content of games, in the new Recital 12 of the (2006) Recommendation on the Protection of Minors and Human Dignity as amended. This Recommendation covers new technological developments and complements Recommendation 98/560/EC. Its scope, on account of technological advances, includes audiovisual and online information services, such as newspapers, magazines and, particularly, video games, made available to the public via fixed or mobile electronic networks.[5]

The dominant model for self-regulation of the video game industry on the pan-European level is the Pan European Games Information (PEGI) rating system, implemented in the spring of 2003 by the Interactive Software Federation of Europe (ISFE).[6] The rating system is a result of a period of collaboration and negotiation between stakeholders from national self-regulatory organisations and the industry.

The project also received either advice or support from major video console manufacturers, experts in the field, and relevant stakeholders within the European Commission. As of September 2005, 16 European states were participating in the scheme. The most notable country not included was Germany (due to its new legislation on protection of minors that includes video games and the Internet within the larger national self-regulatory framework).[7]

PEGI was updated in August 2005 to take account of mobile and online gaming, extending its remit.[8] It has been referred to as a model example of pan-European regulation by Commissioner Reding in speeches in 2003 and 2005.[9] PEGI statistics for its first two years of operation show an implementation as in Table 8.1.

The PEGI age categories are 3, 7, 12, 16 and 18, and all the games also receive up to six content descriptors, warning that game's content includes discrimination, drugs, fear, bad language, sex, or violence (see Figure 8.2).

In 2003, we analysed the three national-level self-regulatory systems that served either as explicit models or as a starting point for designing and implementing the PEGI ratings. The three most prominent self-regulating bodies of the electronic game industry by 2003 included the Entertainment Software Rating Board (ESRB; a programme of the Interactive Digital Software Association in the United States), the Video Standards Council (VSC; a programme of the European Leisure Software Publishers Association in the United Kingdom), and the Kijkwijzer (a programme of the Netherlands Institute for the Classification of Audio-visual Media in the Netherlands).

Our comparative methodology was adapted to the case of the video game industry. In addition to the analysis of official procedures, structures and the relevant institutional histories of the three self-regulatory bodies, we also conducted interviews with experts involved in the work of each of the three bodies, held meetings and a workshop to discuss the problems of ratings and enforcement, and followed the dynamics

Table 8.1 PEGI statistics for April 2003 to March 2005

By age rating			By platform	
Years	*Games*	*%*	*Platform*	*Games*
3+	1,579	47.53	GameCube	218
7+	274	8.25	Game Boy Advance	279
12+	905	27.24	Playstation 2	733
16+	462	13.91	XBox	444
18+	102	3.07	PC	1,350
Total	3,322	100	Playstation 1	126
			Nokia mobile phone	50
			Macintosh	19
			Sony PSP	28
			Nintendo DS	28
			Gizmondo	8
			DVD Game	22
			Tapwave Zodiac	4
			Plug and Play	13
			Total	3,322

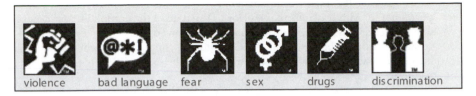

Figure 8.2 PEGI content descriptors.

that led to the evolution of the pan-European PEGI system from existing national ratings. We omit the 'SC' analysis and focus on the pan-European code.

Overall, our analysis found a set of important similarities between the three systems: they are all independent, non-profit organisations; they are founded by the industry and put a high priority on protecting industry interests; they have well-developed public outreach and publicity programmes designed to explain how their rating systems serve the public interest; they cooperate with the government either as required by law or as a sanction mechanism; they consider all parts of the producer–supplier–consumer chain and have developed programmes to address not only rating at production, but also distribution and marketing; they provide guidance on application of rating icons on packaging; they have an informal and internal procedure for evaluating their rating mechanisms and making changes to them; and they have a formal complaint and appeal procedure for settling disputes.

However, the three national self-regulatory systems also exhibited important differences in the areas of government cooperation and linkage; relationship with other industries' rating bodies, the mechanisms and the standards of the rating procedure; applicability of the codes and rules to the Internet; and independence of the complaints and appeals process.

Enforcement

Our analysis uncovered important distinctions in the ways the three national systems are equipped to deal with complaints, enforcement and cooperation with the government. Of the three, the US ESRB was most robust and well-developed in this area, although its structure and the process of dealing with complaints differed significantly from the European models. The ESRB procedure for appeals on a wide range of issues – from rating assignments to advertising to online privacy – is centred around the role of the general counsel. The ESRB General Counsel (or the ARC General Counsel in cases of complaints regarding advertising) reviews the substance of the written complaint and decides whether to initiate an investigation. Investigation and review are initiated only if very high standards are met.

For example, a complaint regarding a company's advertising practice will not be considered if the advertisement in question is:

1   'not national in character (i.e. is a commercial message and/or advertising or marketing material, that is not disseminated and/or targeted to consumers on a national level within the United States or to a substantial portion of the United States)',
2   'the subject of pending litigation or an order by a court',

3   'the subject of a federal government agency consent decree or order',
4   'permanently withdrawn from use prior to the date of the complaint and acceptable verification of such withdrawal has been received', or
5   'of such technical character that ARC could not conduct a meaningful analysis of the issues without sufficient merit to warrant the expenditure of the division's resources'.

In addition, the general counsel can refuse to investigate a claim if he/she finds it 'baseless, frivolous, or being presented for any improper purpose'. The final way out of considering a complaint is for ARC to appeal to its reserved 'right to refuse to open or continue to handle an investigation and review where a party has violated any of the procedures of ARC', the right whose purpose is 'to maintain a professional, credible, and unbiased atmosphere in which the ARC can effect a timely and lasting resolution to a case in the spirit of furthering voluntary self-regulation of advertising and the voluntary cooperation of the parties involved'.[10] Once the ESRB decides to launch an investigation or a complaint, it acts on behalf of the public interest or the complainant against the company that is subject of the complaint. Although complaints are generally remedied immediately, the ESRB has procedures in place to proceed to arbitration of any disputes. For persistently improper conduct, the ESRB may refer the offender to the appropriate governmental agency. The ESRB also has a detailed policy for handling complaints by game publishers, such as if a publisher would like to appeal the rating assigned to a game. These appeals are reviewed by an independent Appeals Board, which may award a less restrictive rating by two-thirds majority vote.

In contrast to the US ESRB model, a VSC complaints board is entrusted with addressing complaints regarding breaches of the VSC rules in the United Kingdom. The VSC's stated policy is to give more importance to correcting the breach than to imposing sanctions, although sanctions such as suspension of membership or referral to a third party can be imposed. After an assessment form has been submitted by a member, indicating the self-assigned rating, the VSC can object to the rating or decide that the game should be rated by the British Board of Film Classification (BBFC). In those cases, the VSC suggests a resolution to the company. If the company does not agree, the rating is assigned by the VSC Appeals Committee, which consists of the ELSPA General Secretary, a representative of the BBFC, a retailer, a member of the VSC Consultative Committee, and the VSC President. The committee is chaired by the President who can break a tie by casting a vote.

Our third model shows yet more variation in the way complaints are handled. NICAM's Independent Complaints Committee consists of four members with no ties with the industry. The types of complaint that apply to video games are general misclassification and failure to publicise Kijkwijzer ratings/pictogram meanings. In the film industry complaints include marketing, through previews, of films classified under older-age category than the feature. This could potentially apply to marketing of electronic games, but no specific provision for games exists at this point in time. A written complaint must be filed within six weeks of the violation, the committee decides on whether to hear the complaint within two weeks, and the decision is made within eight weeks of the hearing.[11] In addition, the NICAM Advisory Committee has set up the Coders Committee to deal with non-binding recommendations in case a producer has 'doubts about classification result such as arrived by the system'. More broadly, the Coders Committee can address other industry complaints regarding

NICAM regulations and the Kijkwijzer categories, and refer the complaints to the NICAM management.[12]

All three self-regulatory bodies had a method of cooperation with the government, including the law enforcement agencies in the area of enforcement. The ESRB voluntarily cooperates with the US Federal Trade Commission (FTC), as well as other government bodies. In cases where the ESRB itself concludes that there has been a violation of the agreements with the participants in any of its programmes, the ESRB can refer the case to the appropriate government agency. But conversely, participation in ESRB programmes like the ESRB Privacy Online Programme offers certain safe harbour provisions, protecting a company from actions of the FTC. A part of the rating process of the VSC is to refer games with realistic motion picture (or soundtrack) containing scenes of violence or sex not suitable for minors to the BBCF. After the referral, the VSC represents the interests of the industry before the BBCF, and has in the past argued against imposing stricter rating or censorship. The VSC cooperates with other governmental authorities in cases where it is obliged to do so by law, which is the case with BBCF referrals as well. This cooperation can be the result of a repeated breach of the VSC rules. NICAM is legally cooperating with the Media Authority, set up under the Dutch Media Act to ensure that no Dutch broadcasting licence holder broadcasts material that could cause serious damage to persons below the age of sixteen. According to the Media Act, this currently applies only to broadcasting and not to other media. NICAM's Complaints Committee was in part set up for the specific purpose of addressing the Media Authority's concerns.

Finally, when it comes to enforcing their decisions and employing sanctions, the three systems all rely on the voluntary character of self-regulation. The ESRB may take action in cases where the ESRB finds that a publisher may have obtained a rating improperly, or is improperly using the trademark rating icons of the ESRB. The possible forms of action that the ESRB General Counsel can take include, but are not limited to: mandatory relabelling of packaging, revocation of trademark licences, mandatory modification of advertisements, mandatory ESRB training, temporary suspension of rating services, recall of product, monetary fines of up to US$10,000, and the commencement of litigation or other legal action. In cases of violation of the ARC advertising code, the ESRB can also refer the file to the appropriate outside agency, release information regarding the referral to the press and to the media in which the advertising at issue has appeared, and may publish and report the advertiser's actions and ARC's referral. The ESRB Privacy Online policy provides for referral of companies to the FTC in cases where a company has signed up to participate in the programme but has failed to follow its principles and guidelines. VSC sanction mechanisms are reserved for repeated offenders, as the VSC's stated policy is first to seek industry's cooperation in improving practices to correct for the breaches of the rules. Once it decides to impose sanctions, the VSC can terminate membership in the organisation. The VSC can also use a referral to the government or the BBFC as a sanction mechanism. But in practice, VSC represents the interests of publishers in front of the BBFC. If the BBFC refuses to classify a game, it effectively acts to ban or delay its publication until an appeal.[15] NICAM can impose a warning or penalty as a result of a successful complaint before the NICAM Independent Complaints Committee. The fines are not specified for games, but for videos and film they are up to NLD 25,000 and for broadcasters up to NLD 50,000. The fines and warnings are public. The complainant or a party subject to the complaint can appeal the decision of the Complaints Committee. A separate, three-member NICAM Appeals Committee, with no ties to the industry, rules on the appeal within four weeks. But NICAM maintains a declaimer over complaints regarding actual content of the product.

Best practice: PEGI as a hybrid model system

From our analysis of the three systems, it becomes clear that the PEGI system resulted from the initiative of the UK ELSPA, and was importantly influenced by the British self-regulatory experience. However, the addition of content descriptors and more reliance on the manufacturers are only two of several important influences from the Dutch NICAM model. In that sense, the ISFE's PEGI rating system is a self-regulatory mechanism that incorporated the institutional and historical lessons of British self-regulation in the areas of films released on video, and later video games, with new and original thinking behind the Dutch experiment of cross-platform rating.

Because PEGI is the only pan-European system, it has the potential of serving as a best-practice model for other industries in search of a coordinated scheme of self-regulation across EU member state boundaries. The experience in this industry sector indicates that national self-regulatory agencies can serve as important advocates for implementing a pan-European system, but their initiative has to be accompanied by a consensus that there is indeed a need to implement a system that transcends national boundaries. In the case of video games, the pan-European system was also made possible by the fact that the UK ELSPA system was well developed and that the vast majority of the other member states either lacked any system of video games ratings or had only started to think about adopting their other media rating mechanisms to deal with this relatively new and expanding media industry. (See Chapter 9 for a discussion of the role of UK film ratings board in games rating.)

However, the exemption of one of the world's largest national markets for video games, Germany, from the PEGI system serves as an important reminder that even the most successful 'pan-European' self-regulatory models may not live up to all the member states' concerns or national legal requirements. Germany's laws on the protection of minors placed video and computer games within the overall media 'co-regulatory' framework, with a shared responsibility between a self-regulatory body on the federal level and länder governments on the local level. Such a national scheme, a priori, one can argue, precludes Germany from relying on an entirely voluntary pan-European system of video ratings.[14]

Trends, dilemmas, challenges

Video and computer games were among the most recent media to be subjected to public and government scrutiny over suitability of their content for children. Drawing on experiences of the video and film industries, the response of electronic game industries in both Europe and North America has been to introduce self-regulatory mechanisms of content rating according to age suitability. This is not to forget that some member states, such as Germany and until recently France, relied more heavily on the government to participate in determining what video game content should be available to minors.

The examination of the three self-regulatory mechanisms that predated the PEGI ratings showed considerable diversity of approaches to constitution, content, coverage, communication and compliance elements in their codes of conduct and practices. The United Kingdom has appeared as the most difficult case, as the Video

Recordings Act only has limited (but still significant) application to the electronic game industry. One way out of these complexities would have been to negotiate safe harbour provisions (as was the case with the ESRB and the FTC in the United States) or to amend legislation to introduce a government-endorsed self-regulatory body (as was the case with the Dutch Media Act and NICAM). The solution, however, was found neither in following a strictly American or a strictly Dutch approach, but instead adopting the ideas of the British-dominated ELSPA to a new pan-European system.

Another important decision that was to be made before PEGI was to come into force was whether to pursue video self-regulation within a national media self-regulatory scheme (i.e. Germany) or to separate the video games industry and address it through its own rating system (eventually the PEGI system). The experience of the Video Standards Council showed the difficulties of applying the same rating mechanism to videos and games as separate from films and music; with development and convergence of technology, the preferred approach is either the universal or the highly specialised. This problem is compounded by the challenge of interactive gaming, with development of consoles that allow playing against (or with) anonymous players, who can communicate during the game.

PEGI itself claims to be more co-regulatory than self-regulatory: 'One key feature of the PEGI system – probably the main driver of its success – is its unique combination of business and government input (on this ground, some would call it co-regulation rather than self-regulation).'[15]

Its composition, with an advisory board made up almost entirely of government representatives (14 out of 15 members), certainly supports that interpretation.[16] The ratings system has provided a model for the UK Independent Mobile Classification Body (IMCB)[17] – see Chapter 10. PEGI Secretary General Patrice Chazerand makes the point that the system works for three specific reasons:

- All the major industry players joined the system at its political inauguration in 2001–2, urged by the European Commission and Member States.
- It has been able to take advantage of the classification system expertise of NICAM and the appeals procedure expertise of VSC, in a telling example of pan-European systems using national expertise for comparative advantage.
- The continued success of the system has produced a virtuous circle of improved procedures (for instance, appeal) and pan-sectoral impacts (for instance, mobile and online markets).[18]

Research commissioned by PEGI in 2004, 15 months after launch, suggested that the pan-European system had resulted in greater player awareness of ratings than in Australia's system which had been developed in 2000:

> Compared with numbers taken in Australia, a territory with a smaller population and a common language, three years after the (Australian) OFLC launched its own age rating system, those coming out of the Nielsen survey look pretty encouraging: 59 per cent of respondents said that they were aware of a game rating system in Europe against 42 per cent in Australia. Among the players' community, the results are pretty close: 69 per cent for PEGI vs. 74 per cent in Australia.[19]

This highlights the communications and media literacy element of any code of conduct or ratings system. Without consumer awareness, and retailer education to actually enforce the ratings, the system is an empty vessel. The ISFE embarked on a media literacy course in 2005–6 to further publicise the ratings system. In the UK, for instance, a special 'games summit' was held on 5 December 2004, calling on retailers and parents to ensure that they did not allow children to play 18-rated games.[20] In some regimes, retailers have in addition legal obligations not to rent or sell 18-rated games to minors.

It appears that PEGI has proved the success of a co-regulatory system in a highly dynamic and rapidly converging industry. Using the examples taken from film classification and video classification, it has formed a pan-European system (except Germany) that has been acclaimed by the European Commission and adopted in part by the mobiles industry. Its effects are extending to online and mobile markets through the ratings system itself. Its success, however, may be more an exception than the rule, as the lack of institutional inheritance and prior art in regulation in this field permitted computer gaming to take a more self-regulatory approach than more established media. The similarities with mobile content self-regulation are striking, but the differences compared to many more established industries mean that the view of PEGI as a blueprint for all content regulation online is simplistic.

APPENDIX 1: PEGI Code of Conduct

CODE OF CONDUCT FOR THE EUROPEAN INTERACTIVE SOFTWARE INDUSTRY REGARDING AGE RATING LABELLING, PROMOTION AND ADVERTISING OF INTERACTIVE SOFTWARE PRODUCTS

Article 1: SCOPE

The present Code shall apply to all interactive software products including: videogames, computer games, education/reference works on CD Roms, distributed for retail sale by the members of the Interactive Software Federation of Europe (ISFE), or any other publisher or trade association which, without being members of this association, decide to comply with this Code.

This Code covers all products distributed electronically by whatever means, such as via the Internet, including on-line retailing of packaged products and on-line distribution, as far as these activities are initiated in the European Economic Area territories, and in Switzerland, within the control of the signatories to this Code.

The rules contained in this Code shall apply to the labelling of interactive software products, as well as to associated advertising and promotion by any means.

Article 2: PURPOSE

This Code reflects the interactive software industry's commitment and concern to provide information to the public on the content of interactive software products in a responsible manner. This industry's contribution complements existing national laws, regulations and enforcement mechanisms.

2.1 Firstly, this Code is intended to provide parents and educators with objective, intelligible and reliable information regarding the age category for which a given product is deemed suitable with specific reference to its content. The voluntary ratings implemented under the Code in no way relate to the difficulty of a game or the level of skill required to play it.

2.2 Secondly, this Code is intended to ensure that all advertising, marketing and promotion of interactive software products is conducted in a responsible manner.

2.3 Thirdly, this Code reflects the interactive software industry's commitment not to distribute market, advertise or promote interactive software products likely to offend human decency.

Article 3: INSTRUMENTS

In order to fulfil the objectives spelled out in Article 2, six principal instruments are available:

3.1. An **Advisory Board ('PAB')** including representatives from chief stakeholders (parents, consumers associations, child psychology experts, academics, media experts and the interactive software industry) (see Article 9 below). This body will see to the continuing adjustment of the Code to social, legal and technology developments.

3.2 A **Complaints Board** ('PCB') including, in the same manner as the Advisory Board, representatives from chief stakeholders, **(see Article 10 below)** and entrusted with the two following tasks:

- handle possible complaints about the consistency of advertising, marketing and promotional activities of any company participating to this Code with the age rating finally attributed or likely to be attributed under the PEGI system (see below)

- handle conflicts about the PEGI age ratings themselves including any publisher or consumer complaints about those ratings.

3.3. An **Enforcement Committee** ('PEC') in charge of implementing the recommendations of the Advisory Board and, more generally, of seeing to the enforcement of the rules and sanctions included in the present Code, including decisions of the Complaints Board (see Article 11 below).

3.4 An **Age Rating System** (*'PEGI': the Pan European Game Information System*), operated by ISFE with the assistance of an administrator, (the PEGI administrator') resulting in the granting of licenses to use a specific PEGI label ('the logo') which will indicate the age category most suitable for a product by reference to its content, as well as descriptors ('the descriptors') giving reasons for allocation of this age category. ISFE retains at all times the right to or rescind or recall any age rating or descriptor assigned to a product.

3.5 A Legal Committee, ('PLC') in charge of securing the ongoing coherence of the system with national legal frameworks and

3.6 A Criteria Committee, ('PCC') in charge of reviewing the Assessment Form ('Questionnaire') used for determining an age rating on a continuing basis.

Article 4: ISFE'S COMMITMENT TO THE CODE

The ISFE hereby commits to:

4.1 operate the PEGI System as efficiently as possible.

4.2 ensure comprehensive, thorough awareness and understanding of the Code and its purpose by all participants in the industry, including publishers and developers, wholesalers, retailers, trade media and advertising companies.

4.3 implement and maintain the appropriate structures to carry out the tasks of interpreting and updating this Code, making it public, settling disputes, and conducting studies and reports about the products concerned.

4.4 initiate any additional operations necessary to support the purposes of the Code.

Article 5: OBLIGATIONS OF ISFE MEMBERS

The members of ISFE shall:

5.1 abide by the Code as far as the labelling of products (see Article 7 below) and advertising and promotional activities (see Article 8 below) are concerned. It is understood that the obligation to label products according to the PEGI System, applies only as far as it does not lead to an infringement of future or existing national mandatory (governmental) rating and labelling systems applicable to interactive software.

5.2 abide by all decisions made by the PCB and PEC and provide all appropriate information to the PAB which oversees the implementation of this Code.

5.3 assist ISFE in delivering on its own commitments as stated in article 4.

Article 6: LEGAL AND REGULATORY ENVIRONMENT

The signatories to the Code shall ensure that the content, distribution by any means, promotion and advertising of the products covered by this Code comply at all times with existing and future laws and regulations at EU and Member States' level. It is therefore understood that the obligation to utilise the Code applies only as far as it does not lead to any infringement of existing or future national mandatory (governmental) rating and labelling systems applicable to interactive software and related websites.

Article 7: AGE RATING AND LABELLING

The main features of the PEGI System are described as follows. Their implementation shall be subject to guidelines to be enacted by the Enforcement Committee and to specific agreements to be entered into by the publishers and ISFE.

7.1 Prior to product release, the publishers shall, for each product and format and language version thereof complete an on-line Questionnaire, which assesses the content of the product using the following criteria: violence, sex, discrimination, drugs, fear and bad language.

7.2 The on-line Questionnaire shall automatically generate an age rating together with content descriptors indicating the reasons for classification of the Product in a specific age category.

7.3 The PEGI age rating groups shall be divided as follows: +3, +7, +12, +16, +18.

7.4 The PEGI administrator shall review the on-line Questionnaire according to the following rules:

7.4.1. Where the provisional rating is +3 or +7, the PEGI administrator shall approve the age rating by way of a licence to use the logo and descriptors, unless it has reasons to believe that the provisional age rating is misleading, in which case it shall review the product and reassess the rating assigned. Further, the administrator shall carry out regular random viewings on samples of +3 and +7 products.

7.4.2. Where the provisional rating is +12, +16 or +18, the PEGI administrator shall view the product in full prior to granting a licence to use the logo and descriptors.

7.4.3. In the event that the recommendation on the appropriate age rating is different from the one determined by the submitting publisher, an explanation for the variation shall be provided by the PEGI administrator. If the submitting publisher does not agree with the recommendation, it may appeal to the PCB, which will make the final decision as to the appropriate age rating recommendation.

7.4.4. In due course, the publisher will receive an authorisation to reproduce the logo and descriptors corresponding to the final recommendation on the product packaging, or equivalent place immediately visible to consumers where distribution is made via electronic means.

7.4.5. All product packaging associated with duly rated games intended for online play shall also include the 'PEGI Online' label as set out in Annex '1'

7.4.6 Publishers should also ensure that all websites under their control used to distribute games on-line shall only distribute games which fully comply with the PEGI system.

7.4.7 The logo and descriptors and, where appropriate, the 'PEGI Online' label shall appear on the outer packaging of the product in a size that permits the message to be perfectly legible and that is clearly visible to the consumer at the point of sale, in accordance with the templates determined by ISFE for each format.

7.4.8 The same principles are to apply to the making available to the public through other means but sale, such as rental or lending.

7.4.9 The publisher shall ensure that the logo and descriptors and 'PEGI Online' label are used in accordance with national legal requirements and that, in particular, they are not used in countries where the product is prohibited or subject to compulsory content classification.

Article 8: ADVERTISING AND PROMOTION

8.1/ Advertising materials shall, wherever practicable, show the age rating finally granted to the product concerned or, should the license be pending, show the final age rating expected, taking the higher age category as a reference in case of doubt.

8.2/ The design of print, broadcast and on-line advertising of these products shall comply with laws and regulations applicable to the age category concerned.

8.3/ More generally, the following principles will apply:

i. An advertisement shall accurately reflect the nature and content of the product it represents and the rating issued (i.e. an advertisement should not mislead consumers as to the product's true character).

ii. An advertisement shall not in any way exploit or a PEGI rating of a product as such a rating is intended as a recommendation only.

iii. All advertisements shall be created with a sense of responsibility towards the public.

iv. No advertisement shall contain any content that is likely to cause serious or widespread offence to the average consumer targeted.

v. Publishers shall not specifically target advertising for entertainment software products rated 16+ or 18+ to consumers for whom the product is not rated as appropriate.

vi. Publishers shall ensure that ancillary or separate products that are being sold or promoted in association with a core product contain content that is appropriate for the audience for which the core product is intended.

vii. Publishers shall not enter into promotion of interactive software products rated 16+ or 18+ with another company's brands, products, or events, if it is reasonable to believe that such company's products, brands or events will reach consumers for whom the interactive software product is not rated as appropriate.

viii. Publishers shall inform the public by means of a general statement of the existence of sponsorships and/or the existence of 'product placements' associated with any product. In this regard use of a trade mark or brand solely to provide authenticity to the game environment shall not be held to constitute either product placement or sponsorship provided that license holders do not receive payment in exchange for such use.

3

8.4 / The PEGI System shall be open to magazine publishers for the age rating of compact discs and/or DVDs attached to such magazines (cover discs) when they contain excerpts from interactive software products and/or audiovisual material related to such products provided that those products are published by companies which abide by this Code.

Article 9: ADVISORY BOARD ('PAB')

To ensure the continuing applicability of this Code taking into account potential social, legal and technological developments, an Advisory Board is established to interpret its provisions and to suggest appropriate implementation tools. The Board should be made of:

- parents/consumer organisations,
- child psychology experts,
- media experts,
- lawyers expert in European minor protection laws,
- academics,
- a representative from the Enforcement Committee,
- a representative from ISFE and the PEGI administrator.

Article 10 : COMPLAINTS BOARD ('PCB')

An independent Complaints Board is established with regard to this Code of Conduct with the following tasks in mind:

- handling possible complaints about the consistency of advertising, marketing and promotional activities of any company participating to this Code with the age rating finally attributed or likely to be attributed under the ISFE age rating system;
- handling possible rating conflicts between publishers and the administrator of the system, and process age rating complaints by consumers.

The PCB will draw on similar expertise to the PAB.

Article 11: ENFORCEMENT COMMITTEE ('PEC')

Compliance with this Code, the provision of advice to all companies deciding to subscribe to the Code as well as to its administrator, possible sanctions on companies infringing the Code, shall be entrusted to the PEC which shall be made up of carefully selected representatives of the industry, as nominated by the ISFE Board and elected by the General Assembly of ISFE.

Article 12 : INFRINGEMENT, CORRECTIVE ACTION, SANCTIONS AND ARBITRATION

12.1 The PEC and the PCB will jointly identify and document possible wrongful application and /or breaches of the Code. Reasonable, non-arbitrary discretion will be used in examining all relevant facts to make a determination of appropriate sanctions.

12.2 The PEC and PCB may suggest corrective action commensurate to the violation, to be implemented immediately. This corrective action may include:

- re-labelling of packaging,
- revocation and removal of logo, age rating and descriptors,
- recall of product inaccurately labelled
- modification of advertisements both on and offline

12.3 Failure to abide by the terms of this Code, including the failure to institute the corrective action referred to at **12.2**.above will expose offenders to the imposition of sanctions by the PEC including, but not limited to, the following:

- temporary suspension of product from the PEGI ratings system

- mandatory modification of any associated advertisements both on and off-line,

- permanent disqualification of product from the PEGI ratings system

- a fine of between €1000 and € 500,000 per violation depending on the gravity thereof and the failure to take appropriate remedial action.

4

12.4 Violations covered by these sanctions include

- presenting misleading or incomplete material to support the original application for a PEGI rating license,

- failure to submit changes, updates, or modifications that affect the ability of the publisher to comply with its obligations under the Code in a timely fashion,

- self-application or flawed display of logos, age ratings or descriptors the POL by the license holder,

- inappropriately targeted marketing, and, more generally,

- all steps or omissions that fail to show a sense of responsibility towards the general public. In this regard the deliberate failure by a publisher to disclose relevant content which is discovered after an age rating and content descriptors have been assigned shall be material grounds for consideration of high level sanctions by the PEC.

12.5 The PEC shall be able to take into account on the application of a publisher, or otherwise, any or all extenuating circumstances justifying moderation of any sanction to be applied.

12.6 Any PEC decision imposing a sanction on a publisher can be referred by that publisher, within thirty days of the date of the PEC decision, to final and binding arbitration by CEPANI, the Belgian Centre for Arbitration. Arbitration shall be the sole method available to challenge any decision of the PEC. Imposition of any sanction shall await the decision of CEPANI unless the PEC seeks interim measures from CEPANI pending that decision.

5

APPENDIX 2: Video violence[22]

American Psychological Association
Resolution on Violence in Video Games and Interactive Media

WHEREAS decades of social science research reveals the strong influence of televised violence on the aggressive behavior of children and youth (APA Task Force On Television and Society; 1992 Surgeon General's Scientific Advisory Committee on Television and Social Behavior, 1972); and

WHEREAS psychological research reveals that the electronic media play an important role in the development of attitude, emotion, social behavior and intellectual functioning of children and youth (APA Task Force On Television and Society, 1992; Funk, J. B., et al. 2002; Singer, D. G. & Singer, J. L. 2005; Singer, D. G. & Singer, J. L. 2001); and

WHEREAS there appears to be evidence that exposure to violent media increases feelings of hostility, thoughts about aggression, suspicions about the motives of others, and demonstrates violence as a method to deal with potential conflict situations (Anderson, C.A., 2000; Anderson, C.A., Carnagey, N. L., Flanagan, M., Benjamin, A. J., Eubanks, J., Valentine, J. C., 2004; Gentile, D. A., Lynch, P. J., Linder, J. R., & Walsh, D. A., 2004; Huesmann, L. R., Moise, J., Podolski, C. P., & Eron, L. D., 2003; Singer, D. & Singer, J., 2001); and

WHEREAS perpetrators go unpunished in 73% of all violent scenes, and therefore teach that violence is an effective means of resolving conflict. Only 16 % of all programs portrayed negative psychological or financial effects, yet such visual depictions of pain and suffering can actually inhibit aggressive behavior in viewers (National Television Violence Study, 1996); and

WHEREAS comprehensive analysis of violent interactive video game research suggests such exposure a.) increases aggressive behavior, b.) increases aggressive thoughts, c.) increases angry feelings, d.) decreases helpful behavior, and, e.) increases physiological arousal (Anderson, C.A., 2002b; Anderson, C.A., Carnagey, N. L., Flanagan, M., Benjamin, A. J., Eubanks, J., Valentine, J. C., 2004; Anderson, C.A., & Dill, K. E., 2000; Bushman, B.J., & Anderson, C.A., 2002; Gentile, D. A., Lynch, P. J., Linder, J. R., & Walsh, D. A., 2004); and

WHEREAS studies further suggest that sexualized violence in the media has been linked to increases in violence towards women, rape myth acceptance and anti-women attitudes. Research on interactive video games suggests that the most popular video games contain aggressive and violent content; depict women and girls, men and boys, and minorities in exaggerated stereotypical ways; and reward, glamorize and depict as humorous sexualized aggression against women, including assault, rape and murder (Dietz, T. L., 1998; Dill, K. E., & Dill, J. C., 2004; Dill, K. E., Gentile, D. A., Richter, W. A., & Dill, J.C., in press; Mulac, A., Jansma, L. L., & Linz, D. G., 2002; Walsh, D., Gentile, D. A., VanOverbeke, M., & Chasco, E., 2002); and

WHEREAS the characteristics of violence in interactive video games appear to have similar detrimental effects as viewing television violence; however based upon learning theory (Bandura, 1977; Berkowitz, 1993),_the practice, repetition, and rewards for acts of violence may be more conducive to increasing aggressive behavior among children and youth than passively watching violence on TV and in films (Carll, E. K., 1999a). With the development of more sophisticated interactive media, such as virtual reality, the implications for violent content are of further concern, due to the intensification of more realistic experiences, and may also be more conducive to increasing aggressive behavior than passively watching violence on TV and in films (Calvert, S. L., Jordan, A. B., Cocking, R. R. (Ed.) 2002; Carll, E. K., 2003; Turkle, S., 2002); and

WHEREAS studies further suggest that videogames influence the learning processes in many ways more than in passively observing TV: a.) requiring identification of the participant with a violent character while playing video games, b.) actively   participating increases learning, c.) rehearsing entire behavioral sequences rather than only a part of the sequence, facilitates learning, and d.) repetition increases learning (Anderson, C.A., 2002b; Anderson, C.A., Carnagey, N. L., Flanagan, M., Benjamin, A. J., Eubanks, J., Valentine, J. C., 2004; Anderson, C.A. & Dill, K. E., 2000); and

WHEREAS the data dealing with media literacy curricula demonstrate that when children are taught how to view television critically, there is a reduction of TV viewing in general, and a clearer understanding of the messages conveyed by the medium. Studies on media literacy demonstrate when children are taught how to view television critically, children can feel less frightened and sad after discussions about the medium, can learn to differentiate between fantasy and reality, and can identify less with aggressive characters on TV, and better understand commercial messages (Brown, 2001; Hobbs, R. & Frost, R., 2003; Hortin, J.A., 1982; Komaya, M., 2003; Rosenkoetter, L.J., Rosenkoetter, S.E., Ozretich, R.A., & Acock, A.C., 2004; Singer & Singer, 1998; Singer & Singer,1994)

THEREFORE BE IT RESOLVED that APA advocate for the reduction of all violence in videogames and interactive media marketed to children and youth.

BE IT FURTHER RESOLVED that APA publicize information about research relating to violence in video games and interactive media on children and youth in the Association's publications and communications to the public.

BE IT FURTHER RESOLVED that APA encourage academic, developmental, family, and media psychologists to teach media literacy that meets high standards of effectiveness to children, teachers, parents and caregivers to promote ability to critically evaluate interactive media and make more informed choices.

BE IT FURTHER RESOLVED that APA advocate for funding to support basic and applied research, including special attention to the role of social learning, sexism, negative depiction of minorities, and gender on the effects of violence in video games and interactive media on children, adolescents, and young adults.

BE IT FURTHER RESOLVED that APA engage those responsible for developing violent video games and interactive media in addressing the issue that playing violent video games may increase aggressive thoughts and aggressive behaviors in children, youth, and young adults and that these effects may be greater than the well documented effects of exposure to violent television and movies.

BE IT FURTHER RESOLVED that APA recommend to the entertainment industry that the depiction of the consequences of violent behavior be associated with negative social consequences.

BE IT FURTHER RESOLVED that APA (a) advocate for the development and dissemination of a content based rating system that accurately reflects the content of video games and interactive media, and (b) encourage the distribution and use of the rating system by the industry, the public, parents, caregivers and educational organizations.

REFERENCES

American Psychological Association. (1993). *Violence and Youth: Psychology's response: Vol 1: Summary Report of the American Psychological Association Commission on Violence and Youth.* Washington, DC: Author.
American Psychological Association, Advertising Council, & National Association for the Education of Young Children. (2002). Adults and Children Together [ACT] Against Violence Campaign.
American Psychological Association Task Force on Television and Society. (1992). *Report on televised violence.* Washington, DC: Author.
Anderson, C.A. (2000). *Violent video games increase aggression and violence.* U.S. Senate Commerce, Science, and Transportation Committee Hearing on "The Impact of Interactive Violence on Children." Tuesday, March 21, 2000. Hearing Chaired by Senator Sam Brownback, Kansas.
Anderson, C.A. (2002a). FAQs on violent video games and other media violence. *Small Screen, 179-180*, September & October issues.

Anderson, C.A., (2002b). Violent video games and aggressive thoughts, feelings, and behaviors. Chapter in S. L. Calvert, A. B. Jordan, & R. R. Cocking (Eds.). *Children in the digital age*, (pp. 101-119). Westport, CT: Praeger Publishers.

Anderson, C.A., & Bushman, B.J. (2002). The effects of media violence on society. *Science, 295*, 2377-2378.

Anderson, C.A., Carnagey, N. L., Flanagan, M., Benjamin, A. J., Eubanks, J., Valentine, J. C. (2004). Violent Video Games: Specific Effects of Violent Content on Aggressive Thoughts and Behavior. *Advances in Experimental Social Psychology, 36*, 199-249.

Anderson, C.A., & Dill, K. E. (2000). Video games and aggressive thoughts, feelings, and behavior in the laboratory and in life. *Journal of Personality and Social Psychology, 78*, 772-790.

Bandura, A. (1977). *Social learning theory.* Englewood Cliffs, NJ: Prentice Hall.

Berkowitz, L. (1993). Aggression: Its causes, consequences, and control. New York: McGraw-Hill.

Boland, M. (2001, December 17). Left in the dust: Oz distrib defies vidgame restriction. *Variety, 385*, p. 7.

Booth, L. (2001, November 26). Do you enjoy showering with men and picking on sissies? Join the military. *New Statesman*, p. 83.

Braun, C., & Giroux, J. (1989). Arcade video games: Proxemic, cognitive and content analyses. *Journal of Leisure Research, 21*, 92-105.

Brown, J.A. (2001).Media literacy and critical television viewing in education. In D.G. Singer & J.L. Singer (Eds.). *Handbook of children and the media*, (681-697) Thousand Oaks, CA: Sage Publications, Inc.

Buchman, D.D., & Funk, J.B. (1996). Video and computer games in the '90s: Children's time commitment & game preference. *Children Today*, 24(1), 12-15, 31.

Bushman, B.J., & Anderson, C.A. (2001). Media violence and the American public: Scientific facts versus media misinformation. *American Psychologist, 56*, 477-489.

Bushman, B.J., & Anderson, C.A. (2002). Violent video games and hostile expectations: A test of the general aggression model. *Personality and Social Psychology Bulletin, 28*, 1679-1686.

Bushman, B. J., & Cantor J. (2003). Media ratings for violence and sex: Implications for policymakers and parents. *American Psychologist, 58(2)*, 130-141.

Bushman, B. J., & Huesmann, L. R. (2001). Effects of televised violence on aggression. In D. Singer & J. Singer (Eds.). *Handbook of children and the media* (pp. 223-254). Thousand Oaks, CA: Sage Publications.

Calvert, S. L., Jordan, A. B., Cocking, R. R. (Eds.) (2002*). Children in the digital age: Influences of electronic media on development.* Westport, CT: Praeger

Carll, E. K. (1999a). *Effects of exposure to violence in interactive video games on children.* New York State Senate Hearings, Senate Majority Task Force on Youth Violence and the Entertainment Industry Hearing on "Video Game Violence: Fun and Games or Deadly Serious?" October 6, 1999 & November 23, 1999. Hearings chaired by Senator Michael A. L. Balboni.

Carll, E. K. (1999b). *Violence in our lives: Impact on workplace, home, and community.* Boston, MA: Allyn & Bacon.

Carll, E. K. (2003). *New media technologies and social change in the 21st century: Psychology's role.* Symposium, New media technologies, psychology, and social change, Carll, E. K., chair. American Psychological Association Annual Convention, Toronto, Canada.

Dietz, T. L. (1998). An examination of violence and gender role portrayals in video   games: Implications for gender socialization and aggressive behavior. *Sex Roles, 38*, 425-442.

Dill, K.E., & Dill, J.C. (2004). *Video game violence exposure correlated with rape myth acceptance and attitudes towards women.* Unpublished manuscript.

Dill, K. E., Gentile, D. A., Richter, W. A., & Dill, J. C. (in press). Violence, sex, race and age in popular video games: A content analysis. In E. Cole and J. Henderson Daniel (Eds.), *Featuring   females: Feminist analyses of the media.* Washington, DC: American Psychological Association.

Donnerstein, E., & Malamuth, N. (1997). Pornography: Its consequences on the observer. In Schlesinger, L. B. and Revitch, E. (Eds.) *Sexual dynamics of antisocial behavior.* Pp. 30-49.

Emes, C.E., Is Mr. Pac Man eating our children?. *Canadian Journal of Psychiatry*, May 1997; 42(4):409-14.

Eron, L.D., Huesmann, L.R., Lefkowitz, M.M., & Walder, L.O. (1972). Does T.V. violence cause aggression? *American Psychologist, 27,* 153-263.

Eron, L.E., Gentry, J.H., & Shlagel, P., (Eds.). (1994). *Reason to hope: A psychological perspective on violence and youth.* Washington: American Psychological Association.

Fisher, S. (1995). The amusement arcade as a social space for adolescents: An empirical study. *Journal of Adolescence, 18(1),* 71-86.

FTC, (2000). *Marketing violent entertainment to children: A review of self-regulation and industry practices in the motion picture, music recording, & electronic game industries.* Report of the Federal Trade Commission. Federal Trade Commission. Available online: www.ftc.gov/reports/violence/.

Funk, J.B., & Buchman, D.D. (1996). Playing violent video and computer games and adolescent self-concept. *Journal of Communication, 46(2),* 19-32.

Eron, L.E., Gentry, J.H., & Shlagel, P., (Eds.). (1994). Reason to hope: A psychological perspective on violence and youth. Washington: American Psychological Association.

Gentile, D. A., Lynch, P. J., Linder, J. R., & Walsh, D. A. (2004). The effects of violent video game habits on adolescent aggressive attitudes and behaviors. *Journal of Adolescence,* 27, 5-22.

Golde, J. A., Strassberg, D.S., Turner, C. M., & Lowe, K. (2000). Attitudinal effects of degrading themes and sexual explicitness in video materials, *Sexual Abuse, 12,* 223-231.

Herbert, B. (2002, November 28). The gift of mayhem. *The New York Times.* p. A35.

Hobbs, R. & Frost, R. (2003). Measuring the acquisition of media-literacy skills. Reading Research Quarterly, 38,(3), 330-355.

Hortin, J.A. (1982). Innovative approaches to using media in the classroom. Educational Technology, 22(5), 18-19.

Huesmann, L. R., Moise, J., Podolski, C. P. (1997). The effects of media violence on the development of antisocial behavior. In Stoff, D. M., Breiling, J., et al. (Eds.) Handbook of antisocial behavior, (pp. 181-193). John Wiley & Sons, Inc., New York, NY.

Huesmann, L. R., Moise, J., Podolski, C. P., & Eron, L. D. (2003). Longitudinal relations between children's exposure to TV violence and their aggressive and violent behavior in young adulthood: 1977-1992, *Developmental Psychology. 39(2),* 201-221.

Huntemann, N. (executive producer and director). (2000). *Game over: Gender, race and violence in video games.* [video]. (Available from the Media Education Foundation, 26 Center Street, Northampton, MA 01060)

Huston, A., Donnerstein, E., et al. (1992). *Big world, small screen.* Lincoln: University of Nebraska Press.

Jhally, S. (executive producer and director). (1994). *The killing screens: Media and the culture of violence.* [Video]. (Available from the Media Education Foundation, 26 Center Street, Northampton, MA 01060)

Kirsh, S.J. (1998). Seeing the world through "Mortal Kombat" colored glasses: Violent video games and hostile attribution bias. *Childhood, 5(2),* 177-184.

Komaya, M. (2003). Media literacy for Japanese third graders (No.132, ISSN 1346-8618, pp.45-60). Tokyo: National Institute for Educational Policy Research.

Lanis, K. & Covell, K. (1995). Images of women in advertisements: Effects on attitudes related to sexual aggression, *Sex Roles, 32,* 639-649.

Linz, D., & Donnerstein, E. (1989). The effects of counter-information on the acceptance of rape myths. In Zillman, D., & Bryant, J. (Eds.) *Pornography: Research advances and policy considerations.* Hillsdale, NJ: Erlbaum. Pp. 259-288.

Linz, D., Wilson, B. J., & Donnerstein, E. (1992). Sexual violence in the mass media: Legal solutions, warnings, and mitigation through education. *Journal of Social Issues, 48,* 145-171.

Knapp, D. (1996, October 16). Adolescent males blamed for violent gaming trend. Retrieved January 16, 2003 from http://www.cnn.com/TECH/9610/16/video.games/

Marriott, M. (2002, November 7). Game formula is adding sex to the mix. *The New York Times.* p. G1.

Mulac, A., Jansma, L. L., & Linz, D. G. (2002). Men's behavior toward women after viewing sexually-explicit films: Degradation makes a difference. *Communication Monographs, 69,* 311-328.

National Television Violence Study (1996). Mediascope: Studio City, CA.

Phillips, C.A., Rolls, S., Rouse, A., & Griffiths, M.D. (1995). Home video game playing in school children: A study of incidence and patterns of play. *Journal of Adolescence, 18(6),* 687-691.

Potter, W. J. (1999). *On media violence.* Thousand Oaks, CA: Sage Publications.

Reid, P., & Finchilescu, G. (1995). The disempowering effects of media violence against women on college women, *Psychology of Women Quarterly, 19*, 397-411.

Robinson, T.N., Wilde, M.L., Navracruz, L.C., Haydel, K.F., & Varady, A. (2001).   Effects of reducing children's television and video game use on aggressive behavior: A randomized controlled trial. *Archives of Pediatric Adolescent Medicine, 155*, 17-23.

Rosenkoetter, L.J., Rosenkoetter, S.E., Ozretich, R.A., & Acock, A.C. (2004). Mitigating the harmful effects of violent television. *Journal of Applied Developmental Psychology, 25*, 25-47.

Ryan, J., & Wentworth, W. M. (1999). *Media and Society*, Boston: Allyn and Bacon.

Singer, D.G. & Singer, J.L. (1994). *Creating critical viewers; a partnership between schools and television professionals.* New York: National Academy of Television Arts and Sciences, Denver, CO: Pacific Mountain Network.

Singer, D.G. & Singer, J.L. (1998). Developing critical viewing skills and media literacy in children. *The Annals of the American Academy of Political and Social Science, 557*, (164-179).

Singer, D.G. & Singer, J.L. (Eds.). (2001). *Handbook of children and the media.* Thousand Oaks, CA: Sage Publications

Singer, D.G & Singer, J.L. (2005). *Imagination and play in the electronic age.* Cambridge, MA: Harvard University Press.

St. Lawrence, J. S., & Joyner, D. J. (1991). The effects of sexually violent rock music on males' acceptance of violence against women, *Psychology of Women Quarterly, 15*, 49-63.

Strasburger, V. C., & Wilson, B. J. (2002). *Children, adolescents, and the media.* Thousand Oaks, CA: Sage.

Surgeon General (2001). Youth violence: A report of the Surgeon General. Rockville, MD: U.S. Department of Health and Human Services.

Surgeon General's Scientific Advisory Committee on Television and Social Behavior. (1972). Television and growing up: The impact of televised violence. Washington, DC: U.S. Government Printing Office.

Thompson, K.M., & Haninger, K. (2001). Violence in E-Rated Video Games. *Journal of the American Medical Association, 286*, 591-598.

Turkle, S. (2002). E-Futures and E-Personae. In Leach, N. (Ed.) *Designing for a digital world.* London: John Wiley & Sons.

Video game industry gets an "F." (2002, December 19). Retrieved January 16, 2003 from http://www.cbsnews.com/stories/2002/12/19/eveningnews/main533790.shtml

Walsh, D., Gentile, D. A., VanOverbeke, M., & Chasco, E. (2002, December). MediaWise video game report card. Retrieved January 15, 2003, from http://www.mediafamily.org/research/report_vgrc_2002-2.shtml

Notes

1   PricewaterhouseCoopers (2005) 'Global Entertainment and Media Outlook 2005–9', from www.pwcglobal.com/extweb/industry.nsf/docid/8CF0A9E084894A5A85256CE8006 E19ED?opendocument&vendor=none#IAAS

2   See: www.nyls.edu/pages/2713.asp

3   American Psychological Association (2005) *Resolution on Violence in Video Games and Interactive Media*, at: www.apa.org/releases/resolutiononvideoviolence.pdf. Released August 17 at: www.apa.org/releases/videoviolence05.html

4   See Wright, A (2005) 'Coregulation of Fixed and Mobile Internet Content', paper at conference, Safety and Security in a Networked World: Balancing Cyber-Rights and Responsibilities, Oxford, September, at: www.oii.ox.ac.uk/research/cybersafety/ ?view=papers

5   European Parliament (2005, 7 September) legislative resolution on the proposal for a recommendation of the European Parliament and of the Council on the protection of minors and human dignity and the right of reply in relation to the competitiveness of the European audiovisual and information services industry (COM(2004)0341 – C6– 0029/2004 – 2004/0117(COD)), at: www.europarl.eu.int/omk/sipade3?PUBREF=-// EP//TEXT+TA+P6-TA-2005-0330+0+DOC+XML+V0//EN&L=EN&LEVEL=0& NAV=S&LSTDOC=Y&LSTDOC=N

6   See Calvert, Justin (2002) 'New age rating system for games in Europe', *Gamespot*, 25 October, at: http://news.zdnet.co.uk/hardware/emergingtech/0,39020357,2124493,00. htm

7   The participating countries included Austria, Belgium, Denmark, Finland, France,

Greece, Ireland, Italy, Luxembourg, Netherlands, Norway, Portugal, Spain, Sweden, Switzerland and the United Kingdom.

8 See *PEGI Info Newsletter* No.7 at: www.pegi.info/pegi/download.do?id=12

9 See presentation by Secretary General Patrice Chazerand, Liverpool, 21 September 2005, at: www.fco.gov.uk/Files/kfile/AudiovisualConference_Draft_Programme.pdf

10 See 'Principles and Guidelines: Responsible Advertising Practices of the Interactive Entertainment Software Industry', Advertising Review Council of the ESRB, Second Edition as amended 31 Jan. 2001. New York: ESRB, 1 May 2001.

11 'Classification as Self-regulation', Kijkwijzer information packet, NICAM, Hilversum, Netherlands.

12 In 2003, the Coders Committee consisted of Mignon Huisman (KRO), Brenda Visser (RCV) and Harold Oomes (SBS group), who held their appointment for one year.

13 See the case of the 1997 game *Carmageddon* published by SCI, Take 2's *Postal* and BMG's *Grand Theft Auto* (as well as *Kingpin* and *Shadowman*). The cases are described by the VRC.

14 However, one could envisage a system where local governments could delegate the rating responsibility to a pan-European self-regulatory agency.

15 Chazerand (2005) Liverpool speech, op. cit., at: www.europa.eu.int/comm/avpolicy/revision-tvwf2005/docs/ip6-isfe.pdf. See also ISFE (2005) 'Position Paper on the Communication from the Commission "Challenges for the European Information Society Beyond 2005"', at: www.isfe-eu.org/index.php?PHPSESSID=804e6e3cfdc7506303904aa81afe850e&template[0]=matrice.html&template[1]=rubrique.html&oidit=T001:dfb8bc4a6dcf3052747cea0839f32f75

16 See ISFE (2005) 'Appendix to ISFE's Comments on Issue 6: Protection of Minors and Human Dignity', September, at: www.europa.eu.int/comm/avpolicy/revision-tvwf2005/docs/ip6-isfe-encl.pdf

17 See UK Independent Mobile Classification Body (2005) IMCB Guide and Classification Framework for UK Mobile Operator Commercial Content Services, p. 6, at: www.imcb.org.uk

18 *PEGI Newsletter* (www.pegi.info). See also Appendix 1 of this chapter.

19 See ISFE Press Release (2004) 'PEGI Celebrates Its First Two Years of Operations', 14 December, at: www.isfe-eu.org/index.php?PHPSESSID=ea3fccbb3951ccab88f9ca9a568e1772&template[0]=matrice.html&template[1]=rubrique.html&oidit=T001:96dec7f314175b346499b34f5ad64fda

20 See 'Video Games Warning' (2004), www.politics.co.uk/domestic-policy/video-games-warning-$7240904.htm

21 Courtesy of the ISFE as owner of the PEGI system.

22 Please also see www.apa.org

9 Self-regulation of the film industry

Introduction

In many ways, it is a mistake to apply the notion of self-regulation in a strict sense to the European film industry. In fact, the regulatory framework for the content of cinematographic art and entertainment – from the first black-and-white theatrical releases to television, video, on-demand movies, and DVDs – has deep roots in the classical models of statutory regulation. A large and diverse body of detailed statutory rules for protection of minors, and consumers in general, has been developed in every EU member state. However, even in the traditional area of classification for theatrical exhibition, national boards have started to move away from censorship and more towards advisory content ratings. The development of the EU audio-visual policy, the Commission's concern for the protection of minors, and the promotion of self-regulation have started to create a new legal and policy environment.[1] Technological changes have also led most classification boards to consider, at least, the role of the Internet, movies-on-demand, new advertising, and DVD/video distribution across EU member state boundaries.

Our analysis in this sector focused on examining the film classification systems in 17 European states, with attention to the beginnings of self-regulation that have started to appear in selected countries and parts of the film entertainment industry.[2] For this purpose, we have adopted our methodology to the film industry and analysed guidelines conceived broadly, ranging from a code of conduct in the cases of self-regulatory models to a set of guidelines and practices in the cases of more direct government regulation. Our analytical questions fall into areas of coverage, constitution, content, communication and compliance:

- *Coverage* refers to the scope of the classification system, focusing on the forms of film exhibition to which the classification applies, the extent different industry actors play in the process, the applicability of the rating across the production–distribution–consumption chain, applicability to the Internet, and its reach beyond national borders.
- *Constitution* refers to the organisation and character of the classification body, focusing on its governance and the body's relationships with the government, the industry, consumer groups, and other industries' rating bodies.
- *Content* refers to the system of screening and assigning age categories, comparing issues of content concern and the standards of different age categories of the EU member states.
- *Communication* refers to the mechanism by which the assignment of age ratings is

conveyed to consumers, in particular the rules governing its display in movie theatres and on DVD/video packages, public awareness, and ethics of advertising.

- *Compliance* refers to mechanisms for appeals, resolution of disputes, and sanctions at the classification body's disposal.[3]

Key indicators

Unlike in other industries (ISPs for example), film rating bodies keep detailed and generally easily accessible statistics on the number of films submitted for classification and ratings given. Especially when the rating bodies are part of a government ministry or other body, and further the work of such bodies subject to judicial review, detailed records of complaints and resulting actions are also kept and made available to the public. In comparison to industry-run bodies such as the Motion Picture Association of America (MPAA), ratings standards and justifications for rating decisions are also significantly more transparent across European cases.

For example, the database of films screened by the British Board of Film Classification (BBFC) shows changes over time in the number of movies screened and cut (Figure 9.1). The historical change seems to indicate, in the particular example of the United Kingdom, that (i) the number of movies screened has steadily declined after the Second World War, with a slight increase in the past decade, (ii) the number of movies cut by the BBFC has declined in recent years to a practically negligible level.[4] This trend is mirrored in other European countries, where rating boards have started to move away from the practice of cutting and outright censorship and toward a new role of providing advice to parents and other viewers. Other indicators, such as those kept by the MPAA in the United States, involve a comparison of commercial success of movies with different age ratings. Here, evidence indicates that a restricted age rating (such as R in the United States, or 18 and above in many European countries) significantly lowers the odds that a movie will make it to the top of the highest-grossing releases. Together, such indicators seem to suggest that there is a strong commercial incentive for releasing movies that are suitable for minors and are not to be cut by national film rating bodies.

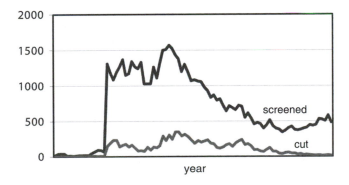

Figure 9.1 Films screened and cut by the BBFC, 1914–2003.

National models

Film classification for theatrical release is mandatory in ten countries in our sample, and voluntary in Austria, Denmark, Finland, Germany, Luxembourg and the Netherlands. The existing national systems sometimes exhibit high levels of complexity, and responsibility shared between different levels of government, stakeholders, the industry and the public. For example, in Austria, film classification and protection of minors are the subject of länder law, in each of the nine federal units, and it is länder governments that have jurisdiction over matters of film classification for screening in theatres.[5] The Austrian Board of Media Classification (ABMC) serves as a federal-level classification body with advisory powers only, but whose advice on classification is usually followed by the länder.[6] The regional aspect is also present in the United Kingdom, Germany, Spain and Belgium.

The classification of movies for distribution on video and DVD is not covered as thoroughly as theatrical release in four countries: Austria, Belgium, Luxembourg and Sweden. In Austria, there is no law for classification of videos and DVDs, and they bear the German FSK classification if imported from there.[7] In Belgium, videos and DVDs do not require mandatory rating, and are instead subject to the voluntary industry scheme set up by the Belgium Video Federation (BVF), but the imported videos and DVDs carry French and Dutch age category labels. In Sweden, although the classification of videos is voluntary, a rating protects the parties behind the video/DVD's distribution from possible prosecution under the Penal Code for pornography or violence.

Our analysis of guidelines and practices in film classification reveals a great level of attention to content, much more than in newer media sectors such as the Internet or electronic games. In discussing its rating practices, for example, the BBFC talks about 'difficult context issues, not only checking boxes'. Its screening committees address not only the content but also to whom it is addressed, including issues of appeal, context and effect of the content. The BBFC deals not only with film content but also videos (under the 1984 Video Recordings Act) and rates video games in certain specific circumstances. Whilst most video games are exempt from classification, those featuring realistic violence or sex do fall within the Act's scope. From 1994 the BBFC started to receive video games for formal classification. The first time the BBFC refused a certificate for a game was in 1997, when *Carmageddon* was refused on the grounds that it encouraged anti-social behaviour. This decision was later overturned on appeal on the condition that the game was fitted with a parental lock to prevent child access.

This high level of complexity and interpretation is not confined to the British example. A typical example of such complexity appears in rating violent content. Across Western Europe, different countries approach with different seriousness the representation of violence through comedy, satire, horror, science fiction, or documentary films.

In terms of diversity of content covered, all EU systems are formally at a similar standard. Violence and sex preoccupy a classification committee's concerns in most countries, while categories such as nudity, language, drug use and hate speech tend to be covered either in countries with stricter public morality standards (such as Britain and Ireland) or in countries with a special concern for limiting hate speech (France and Germany). In terms of defining age categories, important differences exist across the scale. Sweden's and Denmark's highest non-pornographic adult category is age 15. Age 16 is the default adult category in Austria, Belgium, Iceland

and the Netherlands. Age 17 is the highest category in Luxembourg, and all the other countries define adult audience by the 18 and over category.

Overall approaches to content differ from deciding what kind of content is suitable for public consumption to what kind of content children need protection from. Ireland and Portugal in particular outline in their guidelines the responsibility of the classification committees to take into account issues related to morality. While in Ireland this is done by the Censor's Office, in Portugal there is a voluntary Catholic community's content classification.

Hence, an analytic comparison of guidelines, practices and legal standards reveals a well-known empirical trend in classification standards across Europe. Sweden tends to tolerate a great deal more of nudity than countries such as the United Kingdom or Norway. Language, drug use, and discrimination preoccupy the attention of the popular classification systems of the BBFC and now the Dutch NICAM. France and Germany remain committed to screening movies for sensitive issues of hate speech, and have become increasingly concerned with protecting their underage viewers following highly publicised outbreaks of violence among teenagers.

Trends

An important changing aspect of content regulation is censorship, whether by complete banning of movies, or through mandatory cuts imposed by the rating board. There has been a steady trend towards relaxing censorship in several countries. Most recently the Finnish government worked for five years to abolish adult censorship. In Norway, the movement has been away from paternalistic protection and more towards the ratings playing an advisory role. In particular, the ratings regarding horror and science fiction are becoming less strict and a special value is placed on realism versus artistic or fantastic representation of questionable material. While censorship remains an option under the Norwegian law, the national classification board has committed itself to refraining from banning films and has allowed previously banned films to be distributed freely.

Adding to the complexity of the content rules is a continual revision procedure. Luxembourg is introducing a new law; Norway aims to put all media classification under one umbrella by 2005; Germany has introduced a novel co-regulatory framework; Italy has restructured its ministerial organisation of classification; NICAM is setting new standards in self-regulation; and French film classification officials are admitting a growing need to protect children and young people. Even the BBFC has recently altered its system. In August of 2002, it changed the age 12 classification to 12A, which allows those under 12 years of age to see a 12A movie if accompanied by an adult. This change is accompanied by a content descriptor, shifting the role of ratings away from censorship and towards parental advice and empowerment.

Good communication of the guidelines' standards, publicising of the age ratings, and comprehensive treatment of previews and advertising are emerging as a major strength of film classification systems across Europe. Specific guidelines on display of age categories and content descriptors (where applicable) are given by classification bodies. In cases where the classification system covers videos and DVDs, as discussed above, there exist formal rules on packaging and display. Public outreach and media education campaigns have also emerged as a crucial part of a successful classification system. This feature varies across different models of film classification. In cases where the classification system is a part of the government, such publicity campaigns are funded directly by the ministries responsible. However, even in cases of pure self-regulation such as NICAM, the government has worked with the industry to raise the profile of the newly introduced system and inform the parents about the meaning of the different age categories and content descriptors. In fact, the successful branding of NICAM's Kijkwijzer symbols and the public campaign behind them have been credited as crucial factors in determining the future not only of NICAM but also, possibly, of other self-regulatory schemes in media classification. The Dutch media campaign included television commercials, brochures for libraries, cinemas, video stores and children's healthcare organisations. As in most other countries, NICAM is relying on its website as an important means not only for communicating with parents and consumers but also with the public and the industry in general. The rating process itself is carried through distribution of an electronic questionnaire for the purposes of in-house self-rating.

Dilemmas and challenges

There is much room for speculation in discussing how the classification boards are adopting their roles to the new technologies, including the Internet and movies-on-demand. Here is where the reliance on self-regulation potentially holds the most promise, as demonstrated in the developing moves of the Dutch NICAM system. The Irish Ministry of Justice has also launched a special self-regulatory initiative under the Internet Advisory Board. Classification boards such as the Finnish one have incorporated movies-on-demand within the same framework they use for all films. And the BBFC was a subject of a difficult debate when it came to decisions on what its role should be in the rating of video games. Other strategies include dealing with the question of the Internet through regulation of advertising and of previews.

The movie industry involves exceptionally high stakes, financially, politically and culturally. Financially, the amount of money theatrical releases make is directly dependent on the rating given by a national rating body. Politically, rating bodies have to deal with complicated issues of public censorship and the pressure on them to liberalise their practices, which is growing across Europe. Culturally, cinema has been an established forum for national cultural production, with rating bodies being an integral part of a broader government framework for supporting national film production in several European countries (most notably perhaps France and Greece). It is difficult to contemplate a complete shift away from regulation towards more self-regulation even on the national level in many cases, not to mention the harmonisation of standards across EU member states and establishment of either pan-European rating bodies or pan-European age categories for theatrical releases.

At the same time, the fact is that English-language movies continue to dominate the European market for theatrical releases, and the vast majority of movies (including those that are commercially successful and seen by millions) come from the United States, where they have already undergone a self-regulatory rating procedure through the MPAA industry-run scheme. This well-recognised feature of globalisation is only compounded by increasing movement of goods across EU member state boundaries, including videos, DVDs, films on the Internet, and TV programming. These technological and economic developments are bound to continue to clash with the demands of governments to maintain control over the rating process in the majority of EU member states.

Notes

1 See European Commission, Green Paper on the protection of minors and human dignity, amended 30 June 1997 (original 1996); European Commission, 'Protection of Minors and Human Dignity in Audiovisual and Information Services, Consultations on the Green Working Paper', Commission Working Document SEC(97)1203, Brussels, 13 June 1997; European Commission, Council Recommendation 98/560/EC, 24 September 1998, Official Journal L 270 (7 Oct. 1998); European Commission, 'Communication from the Commission to the Council, the European Parliament, the Economic and Social Committee, and the Committee of the Regions on Certain Legal Aspects Relating to Cinematographic and Other Audiovisual Works', COM(201) 534 final, Brussels, 26 September 2001.

2 The units of analysis, therefore, were the guidelines for the process of classification. Our ultimate goal was to put the results of our analysis into a comparative perspective that unifies the analysis of self-regulation and codes of conduct across European Union member states and media sectors.

3 By adopting the methodology used in the analysis of self-regulation in other media we achieve two important goals: (1) we make our analysis comparable to the results of the other reports; (2) we analyse the film classification systems with special attention to variables relevant to self-regulation. Even in cases where content regulation conforms to the model of direct government regulation, we therefore expect to draw important comparative insight for furthering our knowledge of self-regulatory schemes, and more specifically self-regulatory codes of conduct.

4 See Chapter 11 in this book for a discussion of the case of Nigel Wingrove who took a case to the European Court of Human Rights when he was refused a certificate by the BBFC for his film *Visions of Ecstasy* which was deemed blasphemous.

5 Kinogesetze and Jugendschutzgesetze are the local laws dealing with public movie viewing and the protection of minors, respectively.

6 Established in 1948, the Board of Film Classification was the previous body tasked with this role, but it was changed into the ABMC in the summer of 2001.

7 In the federal unit of Salzburg, the law requires DVDs and videos to be labelled according to the German FSK classification system.

10 Mobile telephony-delivered Internet services and codes of conduct to protect minors from adult content

Mobile services (Table 10.1, Figure 10.1) have been used to serve web pages to European users since approximately 2000. The first generation of mobile Internet devices used Wireless Application Protocol (WAP) to deliver specially programmed, normally simplistic and graphic-poor pages over narrowband Global System for Mobile (GSM) networks. These 2G networks delivered data at about 65 per cent of the speed of the modems used for fixed-line computers circa 1994/5. The screen for GSM-only devices was typically monochrome and very small, and the pixilation (granularity) of the screen means that photographic images are cartoon-like. Text services (short messaging services, or SMS) on GSM devices have developed as 160-character text messages, rather than WAP-enabled chat or listserve.

The second generation of handsets, for General Packet Radio Services (GPRS), offers 64k colour screens, access at up to 26 kb/s to 2.5G networks, and larger screen size. Text is enhanced by images. The third generation – so-called smartphones and the data-card-connected personal digital assistants and laptop computers – are all enabled to receive web pages without recoding for WAP. These are therefore the first

Table 10.1 Explaining the evolving generations of standards and handsets for mobile Internet

	2 GSM	2.5 GPRS	3G	WiFi and Bluetooth	Smart phones
Download speed (kb/s)	9	26	64–384	c.5,000 (WiFi); 50,000 (WiFi5)[a]	Dependent on network
Typical phone					
Content types	SMS, WAP surfing and ringtones	Graphics, photos, games downloads and MP3	Video streaming and capture, broadband applications	All – including DVD quality video download	Public Internet

Note
a Depends on backhaul DSL speed.

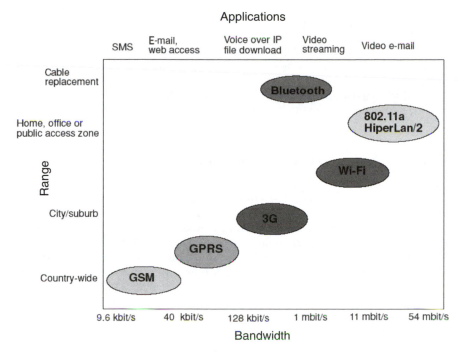

Figure 10.1 From GSM digital mobile handsets to advanced Internet access devices. (From Croxford and Marsden, C (2001) 'I Want My WiFi', White Paper, at: www. croxford.org/ivan/rethink/index.html.)

portable Internet devices. Accessing the WWW at GPRS speeds, increasing to 3G (perhaps 384 kb/s) and WiFi (up to several megabits), they can approximate the wired Internet use experience. With larger full-colour screens, they are fully specified Internet devices for image, sound and video.

From the consumer's point of view, the main differences between old- and new-generation mobiles are characterised by the different applications they facilitate, which can be summed up as follows:

- 2G allows SMS and WAP applications.
- 2.5G allows MMS, including low-resolution video, Java and BREW games.
- 3G allows rich media, streaming, full-motion high-resolution video.

This means that the concerns raised by the need to protect children from harmful material accessed via PCs might also be raised by mobile access to the Internet.

Such technological advances have, however, also led to the development of new business models for network operators, which focus largely on collecting revenue from online content. The models include:

- vertical integration: network operators offering their own content (e.g. Vodafone Live!);
- intermediation: network operators allowing third parties to provide content (payment authorised by the network operator);

- transit only: providing open access to the Internet (with payment, if any authorised by third parties such as Bango.net).

In the UK, mobile operator 3 was the first operator offering open access to the Internet for adult subscribers, whereas the other operators employed walled gardens. It is important to recognise the existence of these different models, as the possibilities for co- and self-regulation associated with the content delivery model will clearly vary according to the sources of content, and the contractual relationship with the content provider.

Legal and regulatory framework: mobile service

Mobile networks in Europe have very limited competition, with between three and six networks in major markets. The costs of terminating calls on mobile networks, previously unregulated, have recently been examined and regulated in the United Kingdom.[1] The first national commercial broadband network for mobile is that of Hutchison Whampoa's 3 service in the United Kingdom and Italy (as at 01/03/04). By end-2004, most EU member territories had metropolitan broadband wireless services – by 3G and WiFi 'hotspots' – which means that customers with handsets have a real Internet experience.

The European Commission has reported on member states' regulation of mobile content:

> Germany, France and Finland indicated that transmission via mobiles, in particular through UMTS [3G], is covered by regulation. Sweden considers that its legislation on illegal content is in principle applicable to mobile phone transmissions, but mentioned that this had not been tested in the courts. The Netherlands argued that the self-regulatory provisions had been drafted in a technologically neutral way, but were limited to 'hosted information'.[2]

In addition to these 'blanket' regulations of fixed content extended to mobiles, the United Kingdom and Norway responded by pointing to codes of conduct being developed to learn from fixed ISP self-regulation. The UK code is the central case study in this chapter.

Self-regulation in practice in mobile content

Mobile networks already have two examples of regulated self-regulation in place before codes of conduct are considered. These are:

- an ombudsman service for customer complaints over pricing and service;
- a premium rate regulator (for instance RegTel in Ireland or ICSTIS in the United Kingdom).

Both are shared with fixed-line telephony, and are mandated under European law.

Ombudsman scheme for consumer disputes

In the United Kingdom, Vodafone was instrumental in establishing OTelO, and T-Mobile and Orange in establishing the Communications and Internet Services

Adjudication Scheme (CISAS), an ombudsman for ISPs and phone companies. OTelO charges all members a fee; CISAS is free – an interesting example of regulatory competition.[3]

Premium service self-regulator

ICSTIS is a member of the International Audiotex Regulators Network (IARN), the European (and Australian) self-regulatory network for premium services. Operating since 1995, it held its 15th meeting in November 2002.[4] Member self-regulators have indicated that continuing support for IARN depends on resumed activity. IARN signals pan-European coordination in premium services, at a critical time when the mobile industry needs such a coordinatory network.

European broadcasters and fixed and mobile operators increasingly use premium services to fund interactive television 'reality' and quiz programmes, such as *Gross Bruder/Big Brother/Gran Hermano*. In the United Kingdom, mobile premium texting is doubling in value each year, and was worth £200million/€300million annually in 2003.[5] Total premium voice calls were worth €1billion in 2003, with mobiles about 10 per cent of that total. Directory enquiry calls were worth €400million. The entire UK premium rate industry – the largest in Europe – was worth €1.7billion.

Most complaints have tended to focus on adult, text message and dating services (Table 10.2). Interviewees have explained that many complaints and especially telephone enquiries relate to adult services, which are in fact spurious, based on family members discovering breaches of callers' anonymity. More recently, premium rate regulators' key new challenge has been dealing with downloaded autodiallers that are stored on users' PCs and trigger premium rate charges.

Table 10.2 ICSTIS 2002 Annual Report breakdown of complaint types and services

What are complaints about?			*What types of service cause complaints?*		
	2002	*2001*		*2002*	*2001*
Inadequate pricing	235	699	Adult entertainment	2,547	1,113
Misleading information	258	365	Fax	1,260	994
Failure to supply requested			Competitions	1,214	1,172
information	176	30	Text message	1,210	159
Inadequate contact details	156	224	Information	315	328
No prior permission	119	57	Ringtones and logos	271	375
Pricing prominence	113	184	Dating	268	113
Inappropriate promotion	92	88	Live conversation	146	104
Unreasonable delay	92	93	Consumer credit	142	443
Non-fulfilment of competition			Data capture	128	62
prizes	88	74			
Legality	69	110			

Note
ICSTIS (2003) Annual Activity Report 2002, at p. 7. Note that complaints increased by 60 per cent from 2001 to 11,552. http//www.icstis.org/icstis2002/pdf/ACTIVITY_2002.PDF

Other regulatory requirements on telephony content

- *Intercept, integrity and surveillance*: Networks must comply with network integrity and security measures to ensure surveillance is possible, that the European emergency number 112 is accessible.
- *Mobile handset theft*: Mobile networks also have systems to deactivate the SIM card of phones reported as stolen.
- *Number portability*: Further measures to monitor phone use include a Home Location Register (HLR) in each member state, to permit mobile numbers to be ported by subscribers from one network to a new subscription on a different network.
- *Spam blocking*: In several member states, unsolicited commercial messages (spam) are regulated by, for instance, the UK Telephone Preference Service (www. tpsonline.org.uk) and E-Mail Preference Service, again in common with fixed telephony. Mobile networks also undertake unilateral action.

Analysis of adult and illegal content regulation

In the position paper presented in November 2003, Ahlert *et al.* explain that:

> Major concerns for the self-regulatory framework include adult content (porn), interactive services, unsolicited messages, commercial transactions, location based dating, gambling, and peer-to-peer. The major necessary strategies for dealing with these concerns are content rating, filtering and blocking, notice-and-take-down procedures, public awareness, cooperation with the government.[6]

They identify the scale economies which make effective and sustainable regulation of the mobile Internet possible:

> The emerging market for 3G services in the European Union will be dominated by a few major mobile network operators, which in theory should make self-regulation a realistic and viable alternative to state regulation. Uncertainty of actual consumer uptake despite projected high popularity of 3G, media convergence, and the evolving EU regulatory framework all offer incentives for 3G mobile operators to invest in self-regulation.[7]

Note in the value chain shown in Figure 10.2 several innovations compared with the familiar fixed-line Internet value chain. First, for services in the mobile portal, there is a strong contractual sanction for mobile service providers (MSPs) failing to fulfil their self-regulatory duties, which in the fixed environment is true only for the largest portals, such as MSN, Yahoo! and AOL. Second, the pre-pay user has no regulatory sanction from the MSP, with no contract and no billing relationship, though the MSP could discover the identity and block service to the SIM card of users if unacceptable use is discovered. Third, the type of network control at the institution of work/research/education that the public access layer establishes is not relevant in the mobile environment except in the case of group contracts for mobiles given to employees.

Even before the start of the value chain there is a fourth critical difference: the MSP owns the network and can control the content flow onto networks in a manner

Mobile CP	Mobile SP	Mobile PrePay User	Public	Device control
Programme codes	Code of	Terms of	access	Filters,
Editorial and ethical	conduct	service	Not relevant –	awareness,
guidelines	Privacy	Not applicable	personal	zoning
Contract	policy		device	Effect unknown
with MSP				

Figure 10.2   Mobile CP programme codes.

unfamiliar to narrowband fixed ISPs. Therefore the lack of control over end-users is replaced by a control over the network. This is a critical change from end-to-end where control must be exercised close to or at the end-device, in that mobile networks can institute control in the network itself, are required to do so for law enforcement purposes, and choose so to do to stop spam overwhelming the network. That is not to suggest that as a policy choice such a radical departure from fixed Internet regulation is to be recommended, not least on free-speech grounds, but it does represent a different architecture of the ISP–network provider relationship.

The mobile industry has learned lessons from a decade of Internet regulation, and from earlier experience in Japan and South Korea, where 3G networks have operated since 2001/2. The early experience of spam, child prostitution and peer-to-peer breaches of copyright were noted prior to the drafting of the first European Code of Conduct, that of the United Kingdom.[8] It is predated by the broad content controls instituted across all electronic media distribution networks in Germany.[9] Note that smaller markets in the same language normally follow the larger: hence Austria and Switzerland follow Germany, and Ireland follows the United Kingdom.[10]

UK case study: constitution and coverage

The UK Code was drafted by a committee including all six UK network operators and virtual operators (3, Vodafone, Orange, T-Mobile, Virgin Mobile, O2). Informal consultation with content providers, infrastructure and handset suppliers and government at national and European Commission levels took place and with IAPCODE.[11] The Code itself was written in the 'regulatory vacuum' of 2003 as the new super-regulator Ofcom was being established, against a background of discreet coordinated lobbying by mobile networks, and pressure for self-regulation from Parliamentary debate during the passage of the Communications Bill 2002–3. There was therefore a combination of regulatory commitment (fostered by cooperation in 2002–3), resource freed by the handover period from existing regulators to Ofcom (second half 2003), and political pressure to establish a workable regime prior to the broad 3G launch in 2004. See Appendix 2 for the Code.

The six operators include all four of the largest pan-European operators.[12] A draft was presented for public consultation prior to the full publication of the Code in January 2004. Details of the Code's implementation (see below) were announced on 7 February 2004 with the launch of the Independent Mobile Classification Body (IMCB).[13] The Code itself is unremarkable, but its *ex ante* adoption, prior to many adult services being known to the general public, is exceptional and reflects high awareness in the sector both of potential harms and of the value of self-regulation. In part, this can be attributed to the market size and regulatory resources of the four giant companies behind the drafting.

Content

The main points of the Code are:

*   All commercial content unsuitable for under-18s will be classified as '18', and will only be made available to customers when the networks are satisfied that the customer is 18 or over.
*   The classification framework will be comparable to those applied to other media, and will be created by a body independent of the mobile operators.
*   Chat rooms available to under-18s will be moderated.
*   Parents and carers will be able to apply filters to network operators' Internet access service to restrict the content available via a particular phone.
*   Mobile operators will work to combat bulk and nuisance communications.

In addition, the Code observes the same 'notice and take-down' requirements with regard to illegal material as those applying to fixed-line ISPs. Thus Section 3 of the Code states:

> Mobile operators will work with law enforcement agencies to deal with the reporting of content that may break the criminal law. Where a mobile operator is hosting content, including web or messaging content, it will put in place notify and take-down provisions.

There are, however, several limitations on what the Code covers. The UK Code explains that:

> The Code covers new types of content, including visual content, online gambling, mobile gaming, chat rooms and Internet access. It does not cover traditional premium rate voice or premium rate SMS (texting) services, which will continue to be regulated under the ICSTIS Code of Practice.[14]

Nor does it cover wider Internet content not directly supplied by third parties to the mobile operator. Responsibilities here mirror those of fixed-line ISPs. However, the Mobile Entertainment Forum (MEF), a trans-Atlantic grouping of over 70 content providers, has issued its own Mobile Code of Conduct, dealing with premium content (Appendix 1). This may prove a precedent for a Code dealing with adult content.[15]

The Code also fails to cover issues which have already stimulated media concern such as the use of camera phones and Bluetooth technologies for content creation and distribution that does not require downloading from a website, or other forms of P2P file-sharing.

The extent of likely Internet filtering by mobile operators is somewhat unclear. Under Section 4, operators pledge to 'continue' to take action against spam – they already have prevented much content arriving on-net. To at least this extent, then, Internet content is to be filtered. Further, although the Code committed each operator to introducing an adult content filter, only Vodafone fulfilled its commitment, with the UK's other operators missing their agreed end of 2004 deadline.

The UK Code for Content does not have a central arbitrator for disputes: 'Each mobile operator may choose or need to use different organisational and technical solutions to enable it to meet aspects of the Code.' The content scheme is an opt-in self-classificatory scheme overseen by an independent classification body.[16] Content is classified as '18', adult content, or not – with optional interim ratings for younger children (in Section 7). Enforcement of the Code is formally dependent on individual operators and it is unclear how this will be recorded and publicised: 'Each mobile operator will enforce the terms of the Code through its agreements with commercial content providers.' However, in practice the IMCB is likely to set precedents for all operators: the IMCB has to end-2004 issued no rulings.

Communication

The six operators have consulted widely with stakeholders, and intend to display the Code on their websites, though navigation to the Code requires a specific search.[17] Encouragingly, the need to ensure brand awareness is not tarnished by adverse press and publicity is likely to make this a central element not only of a minor compliance budget (as with mobile phones and child exposure to radiation) but part of the massive marketing budget of the operators. The involvement of consumer groups in implementing redrafts and implementation of the Code is not known.

Compliance

Unlike the ombudsman schemes explained above, the UK Code for Content does not have a central arbitrator for disputes: 'Each mobile operator may choose or need to use different organisational and technical solutions to enable it to meet aspects of the Code.'[18] The content scheme is an opt-in self-classificatory scheme overseen by an independent classification body, the IMCB. Content is classified as '18', adult content, or not – with optional interim ratings for younger children (in Section 7). Enforcement of the Code is dependent on individual operators and it is unclear how this will be recorded and publicised: 'Each mobile operator will enforce the terms of the Code through its agreements with commercial content providers.'

This approach covers most of the potential areas of concern for parents, and demonstrates to government that the industry has taken its corporate responsibility seriously, but does still leave unanswered some important questions. Issues include how to build a relationship of cooperation between mobile operators and commercial content providers, particularly smaller non-MEF members, and raising awareness of the Code and the role of retailers. Also, the Code is heavily dependent on age verification procedures which are still far from foolproof and are open to fraud.

It is also worth noting that age verification procedures to be applied by the mobile industry are clearly only of use where a phone is being purchased or a new contract established; in so far as many children may just inherit or borrow phones from other family members or friends, it is vital that the Code and the child protection measures available are publicised as widely as similar measures for PC-accessed Internet. In other words some responsibility must lie with parents and carers, and not just government and industry.

It also still remains to be seen just how successful content rating systems will be. The UK body responsible for setting content rating guidelines, the IMCB, was only launched in February 2005 and, whilst it is initially up to the content production industry to label their services correctly, it will be mobile operators who are ultimately responsible for ensuring the appropriate rating of the content they carry. It remains to be seen how this relationship will develop but such a contractually required labelling system for 'commercial' content coming from third parties should work, because inappropriate content is to be filtered out at the 'gateway' between the network operator and the provider. Content on the open Internet will pose larger problems. Therefore, it is likely that the most effective approach will be to combine the utilisation of filtering software, content labels and URL block lists.[19]

Key indicators: what statistical evidence is there of usage of the Code?

ICSTIS, the UK premium regulator, and Vodafone commissioned research in 2003 to identify consumers' attitude to premium rate mobile services (Figure 10.3). It demonstrates overwhelming approval for child-access controls, and own-access controls.[20]

Since the UK Code was introduced in 2004, two other European countries introduced their own variant (Ireland and Italy), whilst dialogue is ongoing in at least one other state (France) as to the desirability and feasibility of such a code at end-2005. Australia has been holding a public consultation around proposals for changes to its rather more heavily regulatory framework for dealing with content delivered via mobile devices, whilst in the United States the Federal Communications Commission has seemingly asked for an industry-led mobile and wireless industry education campaign for parents, but also suggested that carriers review the adequacy of their existing code of conduct. Internationally, policy makers are sizing up to the opportunities and risks presented by the growth of 3G services and the increasing ubiquity of Internet-enabled mobile phones and other devices. In Japan, evidence of public concern leading to legislation to outlaw spam subject to opt-in, and to outlaw children's access to dating sites, has emerged.[21]

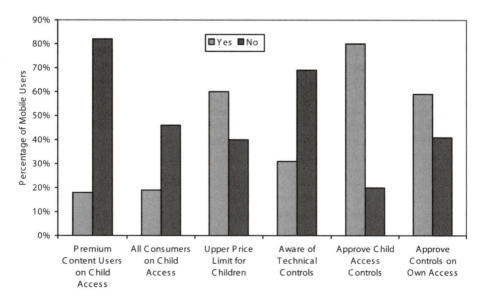

Figure 10.3 Consumer attitudes to mobile content, 2003 (ICSTIS/Vodafone).

Six differences between fixed and wireless Internet regulation

The Code itself is unremarkable, but its early adoption, prior to many adult services being known to the general public, is remarkable. In part, this can be attributed to the market size and regulatory resource of the four giant companies behind the drafting. However, there are also vital concerns that make the adoption of content controls by the mobile industry both different to narrowband ISPs and potentially a forewarning of broadband fixed ISPs' role: this Code is actually the first BSP Code.

There are several features of mobile phones which make such concerns either more and less pressing. For example, risks might be *decreased* in the sense that it is easier for network operators to adopt content controls, such as filters, as they are the only gatekeeper to the Internet for individual users of their services. In addition, network operators also have influence over which online services will be available to consumers as they currently have a degree of control over the user interface on their handset due to their role in providing the software and operating systems in conjunction with the handset manufacturers.[22] An *increased* risk is that children's use of mobile phones is much less open to supervision by parents and educators and might therefore pose a greater risk than PC-based access to the Internet.[23] These nuances can be summarised as follows:

1 *Ubiquity*: Given the increasing pervasiveness of colour screen technology in even standard mobile phone models, many secondary and even primary school students are likely to have phones with colour screens at the birth of the wireless Internet, whilst most children have only gained access to the Internet via PCs at a later stage in that technology's development.[24] This means the need for protective measures is pressing.

2 *Supervision*: Unlike PC-based access to the Internet, mobile use is more likely to be private and by its nature is mainly unsupervised. This may be tempered to some extent by the possibility of parental monitoring of itemised phone bills, although in the United Kingdom as elsewhere in Europe, large numbers of mobile users have pay-as-you-go accounts, with under-16s especially likely to have such accounts.

3 *Control*: With PCs, access to the Internet is provided and controlled by an ISP and users can choose which ISP they contract with after buying their PC. Such choice and competition amongst ISPs means that individuals could easily opt in or out of various filtering options by shopping around amongst ISPs. In the case of mobile-accessed Internet, however, a handset is usually bought as part of a contract with a particular operator. Even if it is practically possible to change network, this is not something which many customers would do on a regular basis. So long as this remains the case it is easier for network operators to adopt content controls, such as filters, as at any point in time they are the only gatekeeper to the Internet for individual users of their services. This feature, combined with the different models for content delivery described above means that mobile network operators can and do provide so-called 'walled gardens', which effectively limit Internet access to content approved by (and financially benefiting) the network operator.

4 *Filtering defaults*: It was widely expected that on mobile phones, filtering defaults when available would largely be opt-in, unlike opt-out Internet Explorer, AOL and Google, meaning that 2.5/3G mobile phone users would by default have

access to adult content. In the United Kingdom, this position has been reversed, in large part due to lobbying by child protection groups, meaning that those purchasing new mobile phones will now usually need to opt out of filtering applications, which will only be possible after age verification.

5   *Convergence of capture and distribution in one device*: Most devices now offer digital image capture capabilities and also enable distribution of these images – picture messaging is an example of this. This means that in principle, the distribution of inappropriate pictures, or even pornography is only 'one click away' from digital image capturing; but in a way that cannot be controlled by filters at the network level. This is a potential loophole in the widely acclaimed filtering strategies currently used by network operators, although it remains to be seen whether this will be a significant concern in practice.

6   *Peer-to-peer file-sharing*: Given that 3G bandwidth is still much slower than standard broadband connections, P2P file-sharing of photos, movies or music is still unlikely as it is time consuming and costly. However, as operators are now starting to offer seamless roaming packages whereby mobile phones can be used at home with standard wireless broadband connections and on the move with wireless hotspots, P2P may further drive usage of mobile-accessed Internet by children.

Technically, the mobile Internet can be much more restrictive than fixed Internet use. 3G services may not allow wider access to the Internet, limiting access to a 'walled garden' of online services. This may restrict uptake but does effectively eliminate networked P2P problems of illegal file-sharing via the Internet (though not by MMS, such as the picture messaging used in an infamous Irish schoolgirl pornography case of 2003/4[25]) even though this is perhaps an over-reaction to existing and emerging problems.

Similarly, filters may prove overly effective. Filtering technologies in use are much more effective in mobile phones – if the measurement for effectiveness is that some adult sites are simply fully blocked – than in the traditional fixed line environment. However, early anecdotal evidence also suggests that sometimes over-blocking occurs and perfectly legitimate services such as Hotmail or other Internet sites are not reachable. At the same time it remains to be seen how easy it is to get around the filters, as this will be one of the most crucial points in evaluating self- and co-regulatory approaches to mobile content.

Another difference, in terms of policy concerns, is history: the 3G debate profits from many lessons learned over a decade of Internet availability. Therefore broadcast video on 3G, whether time-delayed or live-streamed, presents fewer problems than the early video-over-broadband debates circa 1995 because of principles which were laid down then: don't regulate directly but expect networks to observe watersheds and adult content rules wherever possible. Revisions to the EU 'Television Without Frontiers' debate are being discussed just as video over mobile networks appears, but mobile platforms are currently excluded from direct regulation.

Most European countries trialled new distribution technologies in 2005–6 which deliver video content to next-generation mobile phones enabled with digital TV receivers. Full services will be launched only when analogue terrestrial television ceases to broadcast, and pose new challenges for self- and co-regulation. The video content delivery system differs from 3G services in that it is a broadcast, able to be transmitted to many users at once. For self-regulation purposes, the service currently falls under the UK Code of Practice for new forms of content on mobiles; however, issues specific to the distribution platform may require amendments to the Code with specific regard to the delivery of broadcast television on mobile platforms. There will also be duplication of codes, as content will be subject also to national regulatory authority standards and the revised Audio Visual Media Services Directive, assuming that the content is identical to that delivered on digital terrestrial television. The issue will generally revolve around whether the rationale used to regulate broadcast television to fixed devices is applicable also to its mobile reception.

Free speech only within a walled proprietary garden?

Technically, mobile Internet on-net can exclude off-net and really 'wall in' mobile Internet users. That would eliminate P2P including pornographic images by banishing mobile users from the wider Internet, which appears an over-reaction to existing and emerging problems, creating restrictions on speech freedoms. It is the approach which was initially taken by all UK operators, which in September 2005 (T-Mobile, 3) finally permitted 3G broadband mobile users to access the open Internet.

Legitimate adult content will be a major driver for wireless Internet profits: adult content filtering (Vodafone's Content Control bar, bango.net's filters) will be opt-in, not opt-out. Legitimate networks and content owners need to protect 'on-net' brand and limit liability from the porn and P2P piracy that 'off-net' users and cowboy site operators will create. Commercial adult content on the Internet is driven by the free referral site model: free porn in small doses leads to paid porn on 'official' sites.

Illegal and harmful content can be entirely user-generated and distributed. Legitimate 3G content owners make no money from off-net P2P adult content: because the receiver pays (unlike in fixed telephony and ISP access) and networks do profit per bit, mobile operators are perceived by consumers to have a higher duty of care. This is not to suggest that peer-to-peer should be regulated by networks on behalf of governments driven by moral outrage at well-publicised child porn cases. Evidence from Japan suggests that the mobile Internet has played a part in paedophilia and child prostitution and worse. Given the personalisation of Internet technology amongst children that is to be expected, but a balanced response is required.

Protecting children from profitable adult content in walled gardens is the first, and very least, that networks can do. They have learnt from the fixed Internet in taking such action early. But more will have to be done, especially with communication: educating consumers and introducing effective filters early where they are required. The opt-in filtering of mobile networks will help (though bango.net report that 1 per cent of its 5 million credit-card users opted to avoid adult content). Networks still have the dilemma of acting on the distribution of P2P illegal and harmful content, and the distribution of pirated and adult content. Networks have engaged in the debate early to make sure that regulatory action is reasoned, not tabloid-generated.

Conclusions

There may still be significant hurdles for workable codes of conduct to overcome: it remains to be seen whether there is any preferable alternative. Certainly it is hard to imagine the mobile or content industries welcoming a more directly regulatory solution. Self- or co-regulation is also likely to be the most appropriate response in the context of rapid technological advance; it will almost inevitably be easier for industry groups to assess the implications of such change and to revise their codes of practice accordingly. Self-regulation would have the benefit of being a more moderate response to the problem, but co-regulation would provide more transparency, accountability and room for public and governmental engagement. At the governmental level, EU Commissioner Viviane Reding has again made clear her commitment to co-regulation in the mobile communications market,[26] although this is not necessarily supported at the level of all European states: Spain, for example, has so far shown little appetite for controlling children's access via mobile phones to inappropriate material on the Internet. The latter point is important to note. There will inevitably be disagreement between states as to the extent of the risk posed to under-18s by mobile phones and Internet access. What is deemed to be inappropriate or even harmful in one country may be regarded as completely unproblematic in other European states. To this extent, the co-regulatory approach is an appropriate one, allowing public and governmental input to ensure a degree of variation between the codes applied in different countries.[27]

To be workable, codes must first and foremost be the result of genuine dialogue between government and industry with room for meaningful (rather than merely trivial) periods of consultation with non-governmental groups such as child protection or civil rights groups and the general public. Second, the establishment of such codes must be clearly understood both by those who are limited by its principles and those who seek its protection. Finally, it is essential that such codes be backed up by the creation of clear lines of accountability and monitoring. Given the importance of the rights and privileges that are protected and limited by these principles, it is essential that these are treated with respect.

APPENDIX 1: UK Mobile Code[28]

MMA CODE FOR RESPONSIBLE MOBILE MARKETING
A code of conduct and guidelines to best practice

December 2003

Mobile Marketing Association
www.mmaglobal.co.uk

Preface

The mobile is a more personal communication channel than any other, which can benefit consumers and businesses in many new ways. As it is more personal, however, particular care is needed not to abuse the power of the medium and to put control of the channel firmly in the hands of the user.

Since the Mobile Marketing Association was formed in 2000, it has been a committed advocate of permission-based marketing, the principle of which is that mobile users are able, and know how to, opt in and out at will of marketer communications.

The MMA is pleased to acknowledge that the new Privacy & Electronic Communications legislation being implemented across Europe will put regulatory force behind this principle.

For marketers mobile is a highly attractive new channel offering the ability to deliver far more valued and effective communications. However, a vast array of legislation and codes cover use of the medium and there are many new considerations of which to take account in developing its use. The goal of this Code therefore has been to provide:

1. The first comprehensive code of conduct and best practice guidelines for the industry, based on members' practical experience and the requirements of current legislation
2. A central reference source to the laws and regulations affecting mobile marketing
3. A step-by-step guide to planning and implementing mobile marketing activity

The MMA recognises that mobile is a fast evolving medium that will bring many new challenges as the market transitions from text to picture-based messaging to multimedia and location based services. The MMA Code is therefore a living document that will be refined and extended over time.

It is the MMA's intention to be the benchmark of best practice in the industry at each stage, so that membership of the MMA is a sign of adherence to the highest standards. Companies interested in joining the MMA should contact membership@mmaglobal.co.uk.

Contents

Appendix

1.   The British Code of Advertising, Sales Promotion and Direct Marketing (the "CAP Code")
2.   The Direct Marketing Association Code of Practice (the "DMA Code")
3.   The Direct Marketing Association Draft Code of Practice for SMS Marketing (the "SMS Code")
4.   The Data Protection Act 1998 (the "1998 Act")
5.   The Electronic Commerce (EC Directive) Regulations 2002 (the "E-Commerce Regulations")
6.   The Privacy and Electronic Communications (EC Directive) Regulations 2003
      (the "Electronic Communications Regulations")
7.   The ICSTIS Code of Practice (the "ICSTIS Code")
8.   The Consumer Protection (Distance Selling) Regulations 2000
      (the "Distance Selling Regulations")

A. Introduction

1. What is the MMA?

The Mobile Marketing Association ("MMA") is an independent body which has been set up to:

- act as the mobile marketing industry body, actively supporting and encouraging the development of responsible mobile marketing in the UK;

- develop a code of conduct for mobile marketing which will provide a means of self-regulation and establish accepted best practice policies and procedures;

- act as an independent industry voice to the general public, commercial entities and the government and governmental or other public bodies;

- respond to government consultations on areas of interest to its members and, where appropriate, to lobby the government in relation to these areas; and

- liase and co-ordinate as appropriate with other relevant industry regulators and bodies such as the ASA, DMA, MDA, MEF and ICSTIS.

Membership is open to any commercial entity that is engaged or otherwise involved in mobile marketing. MMA members include mobile marketing agencies, mobile ASPs and service providers, network operators, mobile marketing software providers, mobile data aggregators and vendors, traditional media and marketing agencies, consumer goods and services providers, media providers and industry lawyers and advisors.

2. What is mobile marketing?

Mobile marketing is any form of marketing, advertising or sales promotion activity aimed at consumers and conducted over a mobile channel.

Methods of communication for this type of marketing include voice files, SMS, MMS, WAP messaging, Java, SyncML and video and audio messaging.

3. What is the purpose of the MMA Code?

The MMA Code for Responsible Mobile Marketing (the "MMA Code") sets out practical mandatory standards and best practice guidelines in relation to the provision and operation of mobile marketing services based on the MMA's interpretation of the current relevant UK legislation applicable to this area and MMA members' experience of the medium. The MMA Code may be updated from time to time as new UK legislation comes into force and as practical knowledge of the ways in which the medium can be used develops.

While the MMA Code aims to highlight and provide guidance in those areas which the MMA views as key to ensuring legally compliant mobile marketing, the MMA Code is not intended to be a substitute for specific legal advice and compliance with the MMA Code does not guarantee legal compliance. Members should take their own legal advice where appropriate.

Please also note that the legal and regulatory position in relation to mobile marketing in other countries may be very different to that in the UK.

4. Who does the MMA Code apply to?

All members of the MMA in the UK must comply with the mandatory standards set out in the MMA Code (as updated from time to time) as a condition of membership. The MMA also strongly encourages its members to comply with the best practice guidelines set out in the MMA Code (as updated from time to time). All standards set out in the MMA Code are mandatory standards unless expressly referred to as being best practice, in which case they are included as best practice guidelines only.

Where possible Members should also encourage any non-MMA members with whom they are working in the mobile marketing field to adopt the MMA Code as best practice.

5. What happens if I do not comply with the MMA Code?
If the MMA:

- receives a complaint in relation to the mobile marketing activities of any MMA member(s); or

- otherwise becomes aware of any possible non-compliance with the MMA Code by any MMA member(s);

then the MMA board of directors will investigate this to establish if the MMA member(s) concerned has/have breached the MMA Code.

The relevant MMA member or members must give the MMA board of directors all reasonable assistance and co-operation in relation to such investigation.

If the MMA board of directors decides that there has been a breach of the MMA Code, then it will issue a written warning to the relevant MMA member(s). This warning may include:

- a request to withdraw or make amendments to the campaign or promotion complained of; and/or

- a set of recommendations for such actions to be taken by the relevant MMA member(s) to ensure future compliance.

If the relevant MMA member(s) do not rectify their non-compliance with the MMA Code or comply with any requests or recommendations set out in the warning within such time as may be specified by the MMA board of directors or, if they do not specify a time, within a reasonable time, then the MMA board of directors may:

notify the relevant MMA member(s) that their MMA membership has been suspended or terminated (and in this event no membership fees will be refunded); and/or

issue a notice on the MMA web site, in the MMA newsletter or by such other means as the MMA board of directors may see fit (including, where appropriate, by means of a press release) setting out details of the relevant MMA member(s) non-compliance with the MMA Code and any action taken by the MMA board in relation to this non-compliance (including any suspension or termination of the relevant MMA member(s) membership).

Where appropriate the MMA board of directors may also decide at any time to refer any complaint or other non-compliance matter to any other interested regulatory body such as the Office of the Information Commissioner, ICSTIS or the Advertising Standards Authority.

B. MMA Code

1. What does the MMA Code cover?

The main body of the MMA Code is set out as a series of frequently asked questions covering the following areas:

- general guidelines;

- first/key things to think about when setting up a mobile marketing promotion;

- special wording/information to be included in promotional material or mobile marketing communications;

- mobile marketing to children;

- games, competitions, prize promotions and prize draws;

- ongoing considerations when running a campaign;

- special requirements for mobile marketing relating to particular types of products or services;

- special requirements when using premium rate numbers;

- special requirements when using location based mobile marketing;

- special requirements if actually selling products or services to consumers via a mobile marketing mechanism; and

- complaints.

The Appendix to the MMA Code sets out some brief details of the key UK legislation and codes of practice to bear in mind when carrying out mobile marketing, including details of where to obtain further information on each of these. This is not a full list of all UK legislation or codes of practice which could potentially be applicable when carrying on mobile marketing, only those which the MMA believes to be particularly key in this area. It is intended to provide MMA members with a useful starting point for ensuring compliance but not as a substitute for legal advice. MMA members should obtain their own legal advice where appropriate.

There is a contents section at the front of the MMA Code to help you find your way around the main body of the MMA Code.

2. Are there any general guidelines that I need to think about when mobile marketing?

When carrying out mobile marketing you must take care not to abuse the personal nature and impact of this medium, which is what sets it apart from other marketing media.

All mobile marketing must be carried out in a manner that is:

- legal;
- decent;
- honest;
- truthful;
- permission-based;
- responsible;
- responsive; and
- respectful.

These are the general guidelines on which the rest of the MMA Code is based.

In addition, all mobile marketing must be carried out in accordance with all applicable UK legislation and codes of practice, in particular the key legislation and codes of practice referred to in the Appendix.

3. What are the first/key things that I need to think about when setting up a mobile marketing campaign?

3.1 Decide on your target group

Before doing anything else you need to:

- decide what target group the campaign is aimed at; and

- ensure that the proposed content/form of the campaign is appropriate for that target group.

For example, you must ensure that all content:

- is clear;
- makes sense;
- is not misleading or deliberately baffling; and
- is not offensive, explicit or sexually inappropriate;

bearing in mind that what is offensive or inappropriate will vary depending on the target group and the context of the campaign.

3.2 Some types of marketing where you need to be particularly careful

Given the personal nature of the mobile marketing medium you must take particular care to ensure that all content is appropriate to the relevant target group and in the context of the campaign. A significant percentage of all complaints received in relation to mobile marketing campaigns relate to what is perceived by the complainant as inappropriate content.

The following are particularly prone to potential complaints:

- marketing containing references to religion, political beliefs, race, gender, sexual preferences or orientation;

- marketing encouraging the recipient to ring a premium rate line (for example, to claim a prize or to reply to an urgent message) (please also see B9 below);

- marketing aimed at children (please also see B3.3 and B5 below);

- marketing relating to alcohol (please also see B3.3 and B8.2 below);

- marketing relating to gambling services or products (please also see B3.3 and B8.3 below);

- marketing relating to adult products (please also see B3.3 and B8.1 below);

- marketing suggesting that the target or someone they know may be ill, has been involved in an accident or has died or is about to die (for example, a spoof invite to a hospital appointment or to write someone's obituary);

- marketing suggesting that the target or someone they know may be being stalked or victimised in some way or is being threatened with violence (for example, use of a silent heavy breathing phone call);

- marketing suggesting that the target or someone they know is being contacted by the government or the military (for example, a spoof call up for military action or jury service);

- marketing suggesting that the target or someone they know is or has been involved in any criminal activity (for example, a spoof invite to come joyriding);

- marketing suggesting that the target of someone they know is or has been involved in a particular form of sexual activity or is of a particular sexual orientation (for example, a spoof message from an ex-girl/boyfriend).

3.3 Only market to an appropriate target group

You must take all reasonable steps to ensure that if you are involved in any of the above types of marketing that such marketing is only sent to an appropriate target group. In particular, you must:

- not send any marketing relating to alcohol, tobacco, gambling services or products, cosmetic surgery or adult products to under 18s;

- not send any marketing relating to medicines or diet products (such as artificial weight loss aids) to under 18s (this does not include non-commercial public health related marketing campaigns, such as tips on healthy eating or information relating to sexual health, which may be sent to under 18s subject to the restrictions set out in B5 below on marketing to children);

- only send marketing relating to adult products or material to recipients who are 18 or over and who have specifically consented to receive such adult marketing.

Please note that the mobile marketing of each of above types of products or services to recipients who are 18 or over while allowed in principle is subject to a number of specific requirements elsewhere in the MMA Code (see B5 and B8 below) and also in the majority of cases to specific UK legislative and/or regulatory requirements (for example, the marketing of tobacco is banned and the marketing of rolling papers and filters is subject to strict rules administered by the ASA).

Where marketing is not to be sent to a particular age group, then, subject to the exception set out below in relation to people who have responded to age-restricted promotions, such marketing must not be sent unless age verification can be confirmed. If the mobile number alone is the only form of targeting then no such age-restricted marketing may be sent.

If someone has made contact with you in order to participate in a promotion which is restricted to a particular age group and which has been promoted:

- in such a way that the fact that participation in that promotion is age-restricted has been clearly brought to that person's attention (for example by clearly highlighting this fact on the relevant promotional packs); and

- by way of a medium which is appropriate to the relevant age group (for example by way of advertisements placed in publications appropriate to that age group);

then you are entitled to assume that that person is within the relevant age group and to continue to treat them as falling within the relevant age group for the purposes of sending them further age-restricted marketing (assuming that they have opted in to receive further marketing – see B3.6 – B3.8 below) without taking any further steps to confirm their age.

Sponsorship of text alerts by adult brands, such as alcoholic drinks, will not be treated as marketing for the purpose of the above provided that such sponsorship is carried out in a manner which is not intrusive to those under 18s who may be signed up to receive such text alerts (for example, a simple tag at the end of the message "sponsored/powered by [insert name]") and that such text alerts are not solely or primarily targeted at under 18s.

3.4 Take care in relation to when and how often you are sending mobile marketing communications

When sending mobile marketing communications, you must be responsible in relation to the:

- timing (i.e. when the mobile marketing communication will be received);
- volume; and
- frequency;

of such communications, taking into account in each case the relevant target group and the nature of the campaign.

For example, it is not acceptable to send mobile marketing communications aimed at children to be received at a time when they might reasonably be expected to be asleep.

It is best practice not to send mobile marketing communications to be received between 10pm and 7am on week days or between 10pm and 9am on weekends or bank or public holidays, unless there is some special reason to do this (for example the specific nature of the campaign or the service being provided).

3.5 Where did you obtain the details of your target group and how can you use these?

In addition to the above, you also need to think carefully about where you obtained the details of your target group from and whether you are in fact lawfully able to send mobile marketing to these people.

In dealing with personal details, which can include mobile telephone numbers (even if you do not hold any other personal details about the user of the relevant mobile phone) as well as names, addresses and e-mail addresses (again whether held alone or in combination with any other personal details), you must make sure that you comply with the Data Protection Act 1998, and in particular the 8 data protection principles laid down in that act. See the Appendix for further details. This is in addition to any requirements set out in this MMA Code.

Please also see B7.2 below.

3.6 Using Opt in and Soft Opt in

The MMA believes strongly in permission-based marketing. Except in the limited circumstances set out below, you must only send mobile marketing to people who have agreed in advance to your doing this (i.e. on an "opt in" basis).

There is one exception to this. This is that you can send mobile marketing to people whose details you have obtained in the course of the sale of a product or service to that person or in the course of negotiations for the sale of a product or service (even if this does not actually result in a sale) provided that you:

> gave them the opportunity to opt out of receiving mobile marketing at the time you collected their details (this must have been free of charge except for the costs of transmission of the opt out);
>
> give them the opportunity to opt out of receiving further mobile marketing from you each time you send them a further mobile marketing message (again this must be free of charge except for the costs of transmission of the opt out); and
>
> only market to them in relation to your own products and services which are similar to the products and services that you originally sold to them or over which you were originally negotiating with them.

This "soft opt in" basis must only be used as set out above. Where details have been collected other than in the course of a sale or negotiations for a sale, this soft opt in cannot be relied on. For example, where details are collected as a result of promotional activities by charities and membership organisations which do not involve any form of sale, the soft opt in cannot be relied on and an express opt in must be obtained before any mobile marketing communications can be sent.

For the purposes of the MMA Code a "sale" will include any form of commercial transaction so that, for example, the payment of 24p to register a vote or to enter a competition will constitute a sale for the purposes of the above. This is based on the MMA's interpretation of the provisions of the Electronic Communications Regulations (see Appendix for further details) but is not a guarantee of compliance with these. A narrower view may be taken by the Information Commissioner in relation to interpretation and enforcement of the Electronic Communications Regulations in relation to this issue than is taken by the MMA.

It is best practice, wherever possible, to upgrade a soft opt in to a full opt in rather than relying on the soft opt in as a long term strategy. It is best practice to obtain this upgrade as soon as reasonably possible following the obtaining of the soft opt in.

It is best practice only to use any details obtained on a soft opt in basis for the purpose of contacting the relevant person to ask them to opt in to receive further mobile marketing communications from you and to delete that person's details if you have not received an opt in response from them within 48 hours of having requested this.

3.7 Asking someone to opt in

Where asking someone to opt in to receive mobile marketing communications from you, you must be very clear about exactly what this opt in covers.

For example, are you going to:

a only send them mobile marketing communications relating to your own products and services;

b send them mobile marketing communications relating to both your own and third parties' products and services;

c make their details available to other companies in the same group as you so they can send them mobile marketing communications in relation to their products and services;

d make their details available to unrelated third parties so they can send them mobile marketing communications in relation to their products and services.

It is particularly important that if you are planning to make their details available to third parties (whether related to you or not) you make this very clear up front.

Where appropriate you may want to split your opt in mechanism so that there are separate opt ins to mirror the different types of scenario set out in (a) to (d) above.

This has the advantage that where, for example, someone is happy to receive marketing from you in relation to your own products and services (scenario (a) above) but not any other type of marketing, they can opt in specifically to just receive this type of marketing. If the opt in is not split, this person will probably not give an opt in at all, as this will open them up to receiving types of marketing which they do not want to receive (scenarios (b) to (d) above) in which case you will lose the ability to market to them at all. (Also see B4.2 below).

You must also make sure that your marketing database is set up in such a way that you can clearly see who has given what level of opt in. For example, you must be able to clearly see who has opted in to receive mobile marketing from you and who has opted in for their details to be sent to third parties.

3.8 Using the opt in once you have got it

If someone has opted in to receive mobile marketing communications you must only send them communications which fall within the scope of that opt in. In particular, you must not make their details available to third parties to send them mobile marketing unless you made clear you were going to do this when you collected their details and they agreed to this as part of their opt in.

If you have collected someone's details for a purpose other than to send them mobile marketing and then decide that you want to use these details for mobile marketing then you must ask that person to opt in to this before you do so.

If you want to use someone's details for anything significantly different from what you originally told them you were going to do with their details, then you must ask that person to agree to this before you do so. For example, making details available to a third party for them to send mobile marketing to the individual where you had previously not told them you might do this.

3.9 Making sure the recipient knows who is contacting them and how they can opt out of further contact

You must not send any mobile marketing communications unless you have already provided the recipient with a valid address to which they can send an opt out request or you do so in the communication itself.

In addition, you must not send any mobile marketing communications where the identity of the person on whose behalf the communication has been sent has been disguised or concealed.

Please also see B4 below.

3.10 Some types of campaign where you need to be particularly careful re: legal compliance
Where you are intending to run a mobile marketing campaign involving any of the following:

- children;
- anyone outside the UK / EU;
- a competition or prize draw;
- gaming or betting;
- any regulated industry, for example financial services;
- online sales or sales via a mobile device;
- anything potentially offensive;
- anything particularly unusual;
- then you need to be particularly careful to ensure that your campaign is legally compliant.

4. Do I need to include any special wording or information in any mobile marketing communications or on any promotional material for any mobile marketing campaigns?

4.1 Wording/information to include in all mobile marketing communications

NB All the points below assume that you have already obtained opt in (or soft opt in) consent from the recipient of the mobile marketing communication to send them that mobile marketing communication (see B3.6 above).

You must make sure that **all** mobile marketing communications sent by you:

- are clearly identifiable as mobile marketing communications;

- clearly identify:
  - the person on whose behalf the communication is being sent; and
  - if this is a different person, the person to whom the recipient gave the permission to send them mobile marketing communications on which you are relying to send them this communication (the "permission holder");

- include clear identification of any promotional offers you are advertising together with an unambiguous explanation of any qualifying conditions regarding such offers;

- include clear identification of any promotional competition or game; and

- if you are using the mobile marketing communication to collect personal details in order to carry out further mobile marketing to the recipient and the recipient has not already given a clear opt in for you to do this, include suitable opt in wording.

In addition to the requirements above for wording/information to be **included** in the mobile marketing communication itself, you must also include **a means of accessing**:

- the basic information referred to in B4.3 below;

- any conditions for qualifying for participation in any promotional competition or game (which conditions must be clear and unambiguous);

- any other applicable terms and conditions; and

- if you are using the campaign to collect personal details, your privacy statement.

This means of access can be a web site address. If you are providing a web site address then it is best practice to also provide a phone number as well in case the recipient does not have easily available web access. You must not use phone numbers or other methods of access which exceed the national standard rate for this purpose. It is best practice where providing a phone number for this to be a free phone number where possible.

4.2 Opt in and opt out mechanisms

If you are using the campaign to collect personal details, you must provide a suitable mechanism for opting in or out of receiving further mobile marketing communications at the point at which these details are collected (see B3.6, B3.7 and B4.1 above). This mechanism must be clearly brought to the recipient's attention. In particular, when collecting personal details via a mobile phone the necessary opt in wording must not simply be included in a privacy statement accessible through a web site as this is not bringing it clearly to the recipient's attention.

In addition, each time you send a mobile marketing communication you must provide a clear response mechanism through which recipients can unsubscribe from further such mobile marketing communications. It is best practice to provide a response mechanism through which the recipient can unsubscribe simply by replying "STOP" or "STOP" plus a service identifier (such as one or more words or a number) to any mobile marketing communication. If you are not providing a "STOP" response mechanism, then you must provide a clear, memorable and easy to use alternative opt out route. For example a web site address or telephone number.

It is best practice to unsubscribe a recipient from a service where it is their clear intention to unsubscribe even if they have not used the correct unsubscribe mechanism. For example, where instead of replying "STOP" the recipient has replied "unsubscribe" or some other word or words to the same effect as "STOP".

If a recipient sends a response from which it is not clear whether or not they intend to unsubscribe or, if there is more than one service involved, which service(s) they intend to unsubscribe from, then it is best practice to contact that recipient once (but no more than once) in order to clarify their intentions.

If you are providing a web site address then it is best practice to also provide a phone number as well in case the recipient does not have easily available web access. You must not use phone numbers or other methods of access which exceed the national standard rate for this purpose. It is best practice where providing a phone number for this to be a free phone number where possible.

When putting in place your opt out mechanism you may want to bear in mind whether or not you wish to differentiate between different types of opt out. For example, where the recipient wants to opt out of receiving third party mobile marketing communications but is still happy to receive mobile marketing communications in relation to your own products or services.

4.3 Basic information which you must bring to the recipient's attention

Even if there are no terms and conditions as such in relation to the campaign you must still make sure that you have brought the following basic details to the recipient's attention in such a way that they have had an opportunity to easily access and read them (please see B4.1 for further guidance as to how to provide this opportunity):

- the name of the person on whose behalf the mobile marketing communication is being sent;

- that person's geographic address;

- that person's contact details (including an e-mail address);

- if that person is a registered company, their registered company number;

- reference to any codes of conduct that person is subject to and how these can be accessed electronically.

4.4 Some additional basic information requirements applicable in specific circumstances

Please note that there are specific requirements under the E-Commerce Regulations (please see Appendix) in relation to additional information to be provided;

- by people who are members of a regulated profession, such as lawyers, doctors or accountants;

- by people who are registered on a trade or similar register which is available to the public;

- where a mobile marketing communication is being sent as part of a service which is subject to a regulatory authorisation scheme; or

- where a mobile marketing communication is being sent as part of a service which is subject to VAT.

If these requirements are applicable to you then you must comply with them as well as with the above MMA Code requirements.

4.5 Use of hard copy promotional material

Where a campaign is being publicised by hard copy promotional material, such as a card given out in certain shops, then the basic information set out in B4.3 can be included on this card, together with suitable opt in wording (see B4.2) and a means of obtaining access to the full terms and conditions and privacy statement, for example a web site address, or phone number. This means of access must be straightforward and easy to use.

If you are providing a web site address then it is best practice to also provide a phone number as well in case the recipient does not have easily available web access. You must not use phone numbers or other methods of access which exceed the national standard rate for this purpose. It is best practice where providing a phone number for this to be a free phone number where possible.

If you are using a mechanism such as a card given out in shops/on the streets, then it is useful to give a code (this can be a code word or a number) which needs to be texted back to you in order to enter the promotion. This allows you to see that each person entering the promotion has seen the card and therefore the information held on the card.

Please note that this does not affect the requirements set out in B4.1 to include (as opposed to just making accessible) certain wording/information in all mobile communications.

4.6 Terms and conditions and privacy statement

At the start of any promotion, you must make sure that any applicable terms and conditions are brought to the recipient's attention in such a way that they have had an opportunity to easily access and read these.

In addition, if you are using the campaign to collect any personal details then you also need to make sure that a suitable privacy statement is brought to the recipient's attention in such a way that they have had an opportunity to easily access and read this.

Your privacy statement must contain at least the following details:

- who you are;
- what you collect and use personal information for;
- whether you will disclose this information to anyone else;
- that anyone whose information is being held by you is free to opt out of receiving further mobile marketing communications at any time;
- an explanation as to how to opt out of receiving further mobile marketing communications from you;
- who to contact to ask questions, check the information held is accurate or change this information;
- whether any personal information will be transferred outside the European Economic Area and if so why and what for.

Where you are also collecting details through a web site linked to the mobile marketing, the privacy policy must also make clear whether you are using any cookies on that site and, if so, what for and how these can be disabled.

The means of access to the terms and conditions and privacy statement must be straightforward and easy to use. For example, access through a web site address included in the mobile marketing communication and on any relevant hard copy promotional material as stated above.

If you are providing a web site address then it is best practice to also provide a phone number as well in case the recipient does not have easily available web access. You must not use phone numbers or other methods of access which exceed the national standard rate for this purpose. It is best practice where providing a phone number for this to be a free phone number where possible.

4.7 The approach to take to all information/wording to be provided

All terms and conditions, privacy statements, opt in/opt out wording and promotional material must be:

- clear;
- concise;
- easy to understand (bearing in mind the age of the target group); and
- customer friendly.

4.8 Some types of marketing where there will be additional requirements in relation to information to be provided

If you are sending mobile marketing to children then there are a number of additional things to bear in mind. See B5 below.

If you are including games, competitions, prize promotions or prize draws in your campaign then there are a number of additional things to bear in mind. See B6 below.

If you are sending mobile marketing in relation to any specially regulated products or services, for example financial services (including insurance), tobacco, alcohol or gambling, then you must make sure that you comply with any specific legal or regulatory requirements in relation to the marketing of such products or services and should take legal advice where appropriate.

If any sales are being entered into by consumers as part of a mobile marketing campaign so that there is no face to face contact between the consumer and the seller before the sale takes place then there is specific UK legislation that may apply to this (see Appendix) and you should take legal advice where appropriate.

5. What about children?

All mobile marketing to children must be carried out in a responsible and sensitive manner and the manner and content of such marketing must be appropriate to the target age group.

In particular, all mobile marketing must be carried out in accordance with the following guidelines:

Age	What you are/are not allowed to do
Under 12	*Collection of details* You must not collect any personal details from or send any marketing (however soft) to children under 12 years of age unless the child's parent or guardian has given their explicit and verifiable consent to this. Subject to the conditions below, if the child's parent or guardian has given such consent you may collect such limited details from the child as you need to send them further limited mobile or online communications (i.e. their name, their age, their mobile number and, if applicable, their e-mail address). You may only do this if you have first made clear to the child's parent/guardian (in clear user friendly language) why you are collecting the child's details and what you are going to use them for in such a way that it is clear that the child's parent/guardian understands what is involved and has agreed to this. *Use of details by you* You may use these limited details for relationship marketing purposes provided that: • such marketing is appropriate to the age of the child; and • such use falls within the type of use that you have told the child's parent/guardian that you are going to use the child's details for.

Making details available to third parties

You must not make the child's details available to any third party unless you have explained to the child's parent/guardian that you are proposing to do this and why and have obtained their explicit and verifiable consent to this.

12-13

Collection of details

Subject to the conditions below, you may collect such limited details from the child as you need to send them further limited mobile or online communications (i.e. their name, their age, their mobile number and, if applicable, their e-mail address).

You may only do this if you have first made clear to the child (in clear child friendly language) why you are collecting these details and what you are going to use them for in such a way that it is clear that the child understands what is involved and has agreed to this.

Use of details by you

You may use these limited details for relationship marketing purposes provided that:

- such marketing is appropriate to the age of the child; and

- such use falls within the type of use that you have told the child that you are going to use their details for.

Making details available to third parties

You must not make the child's details available to any third party unless you have explained to the child's parent/guardian that you are proposing to do this and why and have obtained their explicit and verifiable consent to this.

14-16

Collection of details

Subject to the conditions below, you may collect such limited details from the child as you need to send them further limited mobile or online communications (i.e. their name, their age, their mobile number and, if applicable, their e-mail address).

You may only do this if you have first made clear to the child (in clear child friendly language) why you are collecting these details and what you are going to use them for in such a way that it is clear that the child understands what is involved and has agreed to this.

Use of details by you

You may use these limited details for relationship marketing purposes provided that:

- such marketing is appropriate to the age of the child; and

- such use falls within the type of use that you have told the child that you are going to use their details for.

In addition, you may use these limited details to promote specific products or services provided that:

- such products or services are:

   appropriate to the age of the child;
   are the type of products or services which are regularly consumed by children of that age; and
   are within the average budget of children of that age;

- the manner and content of such promotion is appropriate to the age of the child; and

- such use falls within the type of use that you have told the child that you are going to use their details for.

Making details available to third parties

You must not make the child's details available to any third party unless:

- you have explained to the child's parent/guardian that you are proposing to do this and why and have obtained their explicit and verifiable consent to this; or

- you have explained to the child (in clear child friendly language) that you are proposing to do this and why in such a way that it is clear that the child understands what is involved and has agreed to this.

17   *Collection of details*

Subject to the conditions below, you may collect such personal details from the child as you need for the purpose of mobile marketing to them.

You may only do this if you have first made clear to the child (in clear child friendly language) why you are collecting these details and what you are going to use them for in such a way that it is clear that the child understands what is involved and has agreed to this.

Use of details by you

You may use these details for all reasonable marketing purposes provided that:

- such marketing is appropriate to the age of the child;

- any products or services being marketed or promoted to them are able to be legally consumed by children of that age and are otherwise suitable for consumption by them; and

- such use falls within the type of use that you have told the child that you are going to use their details for.

Making details available to third parties

You may make the child's details available to a third party provided you have explained to the child (in clear child friendly language) that you are proposing to do this and why and the child has agreed to this.

In addition to the above, you must comply with any specific requirements in relation to mobile marketing to children set out in any of the key legislation or codes of practice listed in the Appendix.

6. What if the campaign includes a game, competition, prize promotion or prize draw?

6.1 Information to include in the promotional material

Certain information must always be provided in the promotional material of any game, competition, prize promotion or prize draw. This is as follows:

- any significant terms and conditions and where these are located;

- any closing date of the game or competition;

- any age, geographical or other eligibility restrictions; and

- a description of the prizes and the number of prizes on offer in the case of games or competitions or any alternative prize that is available such as cash.

6.2 Information to include in the terms and conditions

In addition, the following must be included in the terms and conditions that relate to a game, competition, prize promotion or prize draw:

- any need to obtain permission to enter from an adult or employer;

- any requirements for proof of purchase;

- how and when winners will be notified of the results;

- any intention to involve winners in post event publicity;

- any conditions under which the entries may be disqualified; and

- any costs which an entrant might not expect to pay in connection with the collection, delivery or use of the prize or item.

6.3 Compliance with additional legal requirements

The laws that relate to lotteries and competitions are complex. In particular, there is a risk, if a campaign including an element that falls within the ambit of these laws is not structured in the right way, that you will be running an illegal lottery. If your campaign is going to include any game, competition, prize promotion or prize draw, then you must ensure that you comply with any additional legal requirements in relation to this area as well as the requirements set out in the MMA Code and should take legal advice where appropriate.

7.   Are there any ongoing considerations I need to think about?

7.1 Dealing with changes to the campaign

If you are running an ongoing mobile marketing campaign and you decide that you want to change any significant aspect of the way in which this is being run, for example the nature of a particular promotion forming part of the campaign, such as a competition or draw, then you must check to see if you need to revise your terms and conditions for this promotion.

Always include a term in your terms and conditions for any promotion that will allow you to change these if you need to.

7.2 Keeping your marketing database up to date

You must keep your marketing database accurate and up to date. If you have not had any contact with someone on your marketing database for 12 months (whether by mobile marketing communication, e-mail or any other direct form of contact) then you must delete that person from your database as you can no longer guarantee that that person's details will be accurate or that they will still want to receive mobile marketing communications from you.

It is best practice to contact everyone on your marketing database at least once every 3 to 6 months (whether by sending them a mobile marketing communication, an e-mail newsletter or any other direct form of contact) unless:

- they have opted out of receiving further mobile marketing or other marketing communications from you;

- they are signed up to a regular seasonal promotion or service which is sent less frequently; or

- there is some other special reason not to do this, for example it is inappropriate in the context of the specific nature of the relationship.

7.3 Opt out reminders

Where someone is signed up to a regular seasonal promotion or service, for example a service tied in to a particular sporting season, then it is best practice to contact that person:

- at the end of the season to remind them that you will contact them again at the start of the next season (unless they opt out in the meantime) and giving them the opportunity to opt out of this; and

- at the start of the next season (unless they have opted out in the meantime) to remind them that the promotion or service is about to restart and giving them the opportunity to opt out of this.

In addition to the MMA Code requirement to provide a clear opt out mechanism each time you send a mobile marketing communication (see B3 above) it is best practice to send each person on your database a mobile marketing communication every 6 months reminding them how they can unsubscribe from further mobile marketing communications.

Where appropriate you may also send this 6 months opt out reminder by another medium provided that a suitable opt out route is still provided. The opt out reminder does not have to be a separate contact just for that purpose and it may be linked to the best practice guidance set out above to contact everyone on your marketing database at least once every 3 to 6 months.

7.4 What to do if someone wants to opt out

If someone contacts you to unsubscribe from receiving further mobile marketing communications from you, then wherever possible you must take all reasonable steps to action this immediately so that they do not receive any further communications after the time of contacting you. If this is not possible, you must let them know when the opt out will be put into effect, warn them that some communications may still be received in the interim and take all reasonable steps to action the opt out as soon as possible and in any event within 28 days.

8.   Are there any special requirements in relation to marketing particular types of products or services?

There are a number of areas elsewhere in the MMA Code where special requirements are set out in relation to certain types of marketing. In addition to these you must also comply with the following requirements.

8.1 Adult

You must only send marketing relating to adult products or material to recipients who:

- are 18 or over; and

- have specifically consented to receive such adult marketing.

8.2 Alcohol

Mobile marketing relating to alcoholic drinks must not target under 18s.

Sponsorship of text alerts by alcohol brands is allowed provided that:

- the text alert service is not solely or primarily aimed at under 18s; and

- the sponsorship is done in such a way that it is not intrusive to under 18s who may be signed up to the text alert service. A simple tag line at the end of the message "sponsored by/powered by [insert name]" is acceptable. Anything more intrusive than that is not.

8.3 Betting and gaming

Mobile marketing in relation to betting and gambling must not:

- encourage addiction to gambling

- be misleading on the associated costs or chances or winning

It must also comply with all relevant regulatory requirements.

8.4 Employment/Business Opportunities

Mobile marketing in relation to employment/business opportunities must:

- not be offensive; and

- be clear who the person recruiting is and what the position is.

8.5 Financial services (including insurance)

Mobile marketing in relation to financial services must comply with all relevant regulatory requirements. For example, any FSA requirements or GISC requirements.

8.6 Health products and treatments/therapies

Mobile marketing in relation to health products and treatments/therapies must:

- not be misleading or offensive;

- make clear exactly what the product/treatment/therapy being promoted is or where to find further details about this; and

- be sensitively and clearly worded.

Particular care must be taken in relation to mobile marketing in relation to cosmetic surgery.

Sponsored text alerts are acceptable. For example, "Hayfever alerts sponsored by [insert name of Hayfever relief brand]".

8.7 Motoring

Mobile marketing in relation to marketing must not encourage drivers to interact while:

- driving; or

- in a petrol station.

8.8 Weight control

Mobile marketing in relation to weight control products must not:

- promote being underweight; or

- be offensive to overweight people.

Sponsorship of text alerts is acceptable. For example "diet tips sponsored by [insert name of slimming product]".

9. Are there any special requirements if I am using premium rate numbers?

Yes – if you are using premium rate numbers the ICSTIS Code of Practice will apply and you must comply with this in full. Please see the Appendix for further details.

10. Are there any special requirements if I am using location based mobile marketing?

The collection and use of location data relating to individuals is subject to specific legal requirements, in particular those set out in the Electronic Communications Regulations (see Appendix). If you are planning to collect or use such data in any way you must make sure that you comply with these requirements.

In addition, you must:

- only send location based mobile marketing (i.e. mobile marketing which is sent based on the location of the recipient at a given time) to people who have specifically agreed to receive this type of marketing; and

- each time you send a location based mobile marketing communication provide the recipient with a simple free of charge (other than the costs of transmission) means of opting out of receiving any further such location based mobile marketing communications at any time.

When asking people to opt in to receive location based mobile marketing you must make clear to them:

- that in order to send them such marketing it will be necessary to identify the location of their mobile device and so their personal location; and

- what you will be using these location details for.

Please note that if you are a network operator or provider there are some very specific requirements on you under the Electronic Communications Regulations in relation to the use of location data and provision of location based services and you must ensure that you comply with these in addition to the above MMA Code requirements.

11. Are there any special requirements if I am actually selling products or services to consumers via a mobile marketing mechanism?

If you sell goods or services to consumers:

- on the internet;
- on interactive digital television;
- by mail order, including catalogue shopping;
- by telephone;
- by fax; or
- by advertising on television or radio, in newspapers or magazines;

then the Distance Selling Regulations (see Appendix) may apply to your business and you must make sure that you comply with these.

12. What about complaints?

Complaint handling is part of brand management – a badly dealt with complaint can damage a brand far more than almost anything else.

You must make sure that all complaints are handled as quickly and efficiently as possible and that your complaint handling procedures are:

- clear;
- transparent;
- responsive; and
- customer friendly.

C. Contact the MMA

Please contact the MMA if you are interested in membership and/or our lobbying activities or you have any questions in relation to the MMA Code.

Our contact details are:

code@mmaglobal.co.uk

Our web site is at www.mmaglobal.co.uk/

Independent Mobile Classification Body

IMCB Guide and Classification Framework for UK Mobile Operator Commercial Content Services

First Edition
February 2005

Contents

Introduction General overview of IMCB

Background to IMCB and the Mobile Operator Code of Practice for New Content Services

On 19th January 2004 the UK Mobile Operators[1] (Vodafone, Orange, T-Mobile, 02, 3 and Virgin) announced a joint Code of Practice for the self-regulation of new forms of content on mobile phones. The six Mobile Operators have all signed up to the code designed to facilitate the responsible use of new mobile phone services whilst safeguarding children from unsuitable content on their mobile phones. Mobile technology advances mean that phones are being developed with enhanced features, such as colour screens, video and picture messaging allowing access to an increasing variety of services. Whilst many of the Commercial Content services which are delivered using this new technology will be suitable for all ages, some of the new services may, however, contain content which is only suitable for customers who are over 18 years of age. The Mobile Operators recognise that this may cause concern to parents whose children have mobile phones and have therefore worked together to develop the Code of Practice. This is intended to help protect children and give parents and carers the necessary information and tools to protect their children. A copy of the Code of Practice for New Content Services on mobile devices is available at www.imcb.org.uk.

With respect to Commercial Content, the Mobile Operators specifically committed to appointing an independent classification body to provide a Framework for classifying Commercial Content that is only suitable for customers 18 years and older. IMCB is the body chosen by the Mobile Operators to perform this role.

Terms of reference

IMCB is the Independent Mobile Classification Body responsible for setting a Classification Framework for certain new forms of mobile Commercial Content. IMCB Ltd is a not-for-profit company formed as a subsidiary of ICSTIS – the UK premium rate regulator – and Board members of IMCB have been drawn from the ICSTIS Committee. A multi-disciplinary team supports the Board. Premium Rate Services continue to be regulated by ICSTIS even where they are also Commercial Content services and need to be classified in accordance with this document.

As a body independent of the Mobile Operators, IMCB will:

- ❑ Provide and maintain the Classification Framework after consultation with the Mobile Operators and other stakeholders;

- ❑ Review and amend the Classification Framework after consulting the Mobile Operators and other stakeholders in light of changes in the law or changes in society's expectations. Evidence for this may come from consumer and public complaints, changes in standards by the Agreed Bodies or research;

- ❑ Publish information about the role and work of IMCB through an IMCB website and other appropriate means and, as part of this activity, IMCB will publish an annual report and summary of accounts;

- ❑ Deal with all complaints and disputes about the misclassification of Commercial Content in accordance with the complaints and dispute procedures set out in this document;

- ❑ Consult with the Mobile Operators over the appointment of new members to the IMCB Board.

---

[1] Any words used with capital letters denotes a defined term and is listed in the Appendix to this document

Remit

IMCB's remit is to determine a Classification Framework for Commercial Content against which Content Providers can self-classify their own content (whether provided directly or indirectly) as 18 where appropriate. Such content will be placed behind Access Controls so that, when combined with age verification arrangements, it is only available to those identified as 18 or over.

Commercial Content services which fall within IMCB's remit and the Classification Framework include:

- ❑ Still pictures
- ❑ Video and audiovisual material
- ❑ Mobile games, including java-based games

Services which fall outside IMCB's remit and the Classification Framework are:

- ❑ Text, audio and voice-only services, including where delivered as a Premium Rate Service and regulated by ICSTIS
- ❑ Gambling services (because they are age restricted by UK legislation)
- ❑ Moderated and unmoderated chat rooms (commercial unmoderated chat rooms will only be accessible by those 18 and over)
- ❑ Location-Based Services (which are the subject of a separate Mobile Operator code of practice available at www.imcb.org.uk)
- ❑ Content generated by subscribers, including web logs
- ❑ Content accessed via the internet or WAP where the Mobile Operator is providing connectivity only

Classification - Overview

The classification arrangements being put in place by IMCB will provide a common standard against which Content Providers can self-classify certain of their Commercial Content as 18. The Mobile Operators will be responsible for addressing instances of misclassification of Commercial Content through their own contractual arrangements with Content Providers.

The approach being adopted is that Commercial Content deemed suitable only for those 18 and over by Content Providers by reference to the Classification Framework set out in this document will be inaccessible to those under 18. Commercial Content that is not rated as 18 is Not Classified and will be unrestricted for the purposes of this document and IMCB provides no Classification Framework for unrestricted content.

This document has been created on the basis of research and consultations with a number of stakeholders. At a later stage IMCB intends to engage stakeholders in a review of this document and will consider further the requirements set out in it. The review will be undertaken in line with IMCB's remit described above.

The Internet

Content accessible through mobile devices available on the Internet falls outside of the remit of IMCB and these classification arrangements but the Mobile Operators have committed to offering filter solutions to parents and carers in order to help to protect their children. The Mobile Operators have also committed to providing advice to all customers on the nature of these new services and on ways in which they can help to protect themselves and their children. Some of the literature that provides this advice is available at IMCB's website – www.imcb.org.uk.

Funding

IMCB is funded by the Mobile Operators under a mutually agreed formula and in a way that does not fetter its independence. The funding for IMCB is wholly separate from that of ICSTIS. Summary accounts for IMCB will be published in IMCB's Annual Report.

Classification advice and general enquiries

IMCB provides a non-binding classification advice service for Content Providers who require advice on whether any particular content should be rated as 18 under the Classification Framework. Where there is doubt, however, IMCB would generally suggest caution. IMCB may charge for its advice in order to recover the costs associated with providing it.

Tel: 020 7357 8512
E-Mail: advice@imcb.org.uk

Contact details

IMCB
1st Floor, Clove Building
4 Maguire Street
London SE1 2NQ

Tel: 020 7357 8512
Fax: 020 7940 7456
E-mail: staff@imcb.org.uk

Media Enquiries: 020 7940 7474
E-mail: pressoffice@imcb.org.uk
Web: www.imcb.org.uk

Section One   Classification Framework - General

1.1 Classification Framework Structure
The Classification Framework has been drawn up taking account of the need to be consistent, as far as is possible, with standards for other media produced by the Agreed Bodies such as the British Board of Film Classification (BBFC) and Interactive Software Federation of Europe (IFSE)/ Pan-European Game Information (PEGI) for Mobile Games.

The Classification Framework has been designed to be flexible enough to accommodate the widest possible range of Commercial Content available in the market place, where this falls within the remit of IMCB. However, the Classification Framework cannot address itself to every specific piece of Commercial Content that might become available at any one time. The specific requirements and examples described in the numbered sub-sections of Section 2 are therefore not exhaustive but instead intended as an indication of the types of content that, under the Classification Framework, should be rated as 18. Content Providers should interpret these sub-sections in terms of the spirit of what is being sought. When self-classifying their content, Content Providers should also have regard to the context in which the particular material is included and use the Classification Framework as a guide to assist them.

1.2 Scope of the Classification Framework
The Classification Framework only applies to Commercial Content provided to UK customers of UK Mobile Operators. The Classification Framework applies regardless of whether the Content Provider is based within or outside the United Kingdom. It does not apply to locally provided services accessed whilst UK customers are "roaming" overseas; nor does it apply to overseas customers "roaming" in the UK.

1.3 Relationship to other bodies
If the provision of Commercial Content is by means of a Premium Rate Service it must also comply with the code of practice issued and enforced by ICSTIS.

If the Commercial Content is to be distributed over other platforms, such as video or through a games console, and requires classification by an Agreed Body, additional classification must also be obtained.

1.4 Legality
Content Providers have responsibility to ensure that the Commercial Content they are directly or indirectly providing is not unlawful or illegal.

1.5 Further information
As is made clear in the Classification – Overview, the arrangements put in place will mean that Commercial Content not classified as 18 is unrestricted for the purposes of this Framework. Some parents and carers may well consider that not all material which is unrestricted for the purposes of this Framework is suitable for everyone, and in particular younger children. However, nothing in the Code of Practice for New Content Services prevents Mobile Operators, and by extension Content Providers, from providing further information or advice about the age range for which the particular Commercial Content was designed.

We recognise that parents have the main responsibility for making sure that their children are properly educated about mobile phone technology. This responsibility is supported by the Mobile Operators through their commitment to provide advice to customers on the nature and use of new mobile devices and services. To this end, they support activities designed to improve the knowledge of consumers, including parents and carers, such as the "Be Aware" leaflet produced jointly by the Mobile Operators as a teacher's resource pack for school children.

6

Section Two   Specific Classification Framework requirements

In addition to the general guidance and provisions relating to legality contained in Section 1 the following requirements shall apply to all still pictures, video and audiovisual Commercial Content, including mobile games.

Where Commercial Content contains any content described in any of the sub-sections below it must be rated as 18 for the purposes of this Classification Framework. As a general guide it should be noted that if the content in question would be likely to be rated as 18 by an Agreed Body if it was relevant to that body, then it should be rated as 18 under this Classification Framework. In addition, the context and style in which the content is being presented, whether as a still picture or a video clip, should always be taken into account. Humorous content, such as violence or combat techniques in a children's cartoon, may therefore be acceptable.

2.1 Themes
No theme is specifically prohibited though these may be subject to other legal requirements. Content must not actively promote or encourage activities that are legally restricted for those under 18 such as drinking alcohol or gambling.

2.2 Language
Frequent and repetitive use of the strongest foul language.

2.3 Sex
Actual or realistic depictions of sexual activity, for example,

- ❑   Real or simulated sexual intercourse.

- ❑   Depiction of sexual activity involving devices such as sex toys.

- ❑   Sexual activity with visible pubic areas and/or genitals or including threats of sexual violence such as rape.

Note, however, that material which genuinely seeks to inform and educate such as in matters of sexuality, safe sex and health and where explicit images are the minimum necessary to illustrate and educate in a responsible manner may be permissible.

2.4 Nudity
Nudity where depicting pubic area and/or genitals (unless it is material which genuinely seeks to inform and educate such as in matters of sexuality, safe sex and health and where explicit images are kept to the minimum necessary to illustrate and educate in a responsible manner).

2.5 Violence
Graphic violence which in particular dwells on the infliction of pain, injuries or scenes of sexual violence. *In respect of mobile games in particular:*
Gross violence towards realistic humans or animals such as scenes of dismemberment, torture, massive blood and gore, sadism and other types of excessive violence.

Graphic, detailed and sustained violence towards realistic humans and animals or violence towards vulnerable or defenceless humans.

7

2.6 Drugs
Depictions which promote or encourage illegal drug taking or which provide instructive details as to illegal drug taking.

2.7 Horror
Any depiction of sustained or detailed inflictions of pain or injury including anything which involves sadism, cruelty or induces an unacceptable sense of fear or anxiety.

2.8 Imitable techniques
Dangerous combat techniques such as ear-claps, head-butts and blows to the neck or any emphasis on the use of easily accessible lethal weapons, for example knives.

Detailed descriptions of techniques that could be used in a criminal offence.

Section Three   Complaints and dispute procedures

Consumers

1.   If you are a consumer you can make a complaint if you believe that an item of Commercial Content should have been classified as 18.

2.   In order to complain you must first contact your Mobile Operator and explain the nature of your complaint. (Contact details can be found at www.imcb.org.uk or click here.)

3.   On receiving your complaint your Mobile Operator has 28 days to state whether it agrees that the Commercial Content you complained about should have been classified as 18.

4.   Your Mobile Operator will contact you directly to advise you as to its response to your complaint.

5.   If your Mobile Operator does not reply to you within 28 days from the date you made your complaint or does not agree that the classification was incorrect you can make a formal complaint to IMCB.

6.   To contact IMCB either go to the website at www.imcb.org.uk or write to them at:

IMCB
1st Floor, Clove Building
Maguire Street
London SE1 2NQ

Content Providers

7.   If a Mobile Operator decides that content you have provided should have been classified as 18 (whether or not there has been a complaint about it) and you disagree with this decision then you can, within 28 days of hearing of this decision, make a complaint to IMCB.

8.   Complaints must be made either through the IMCB website or in writing to the above address.

How IMCB deals with all valid complaints

9.   On receiving a complaint the matter is considered by an IMCB board member. The board member will ask for information from all relevant parties and any other information needed to determine the case and state the time in which this should be received, which will not be longer than 28 days.

10.   Once all relevant information has been received, a panel of the IMCB board ('the Panel') will consider the matter and make its decision ensuring that everybody involved has had an opportunity to respond to all the points raised.

11.   Any party can request an oral hearing. If any of the parties does make such a request the Panel will consider at its discretion whether an oral hearing should be held. Such a hearing will normally be held within 28 days of that decision under the control of the Chairman of the Panel and will be held in private unless the Panel decides otherwise.

12.   However the matter is dealt with by the Panel, it will provide its decision in writing to all the parties within 28 days, and its decision will be published on IMCB's website.

13.   The Panel does not have powers to make any order for costs of the proceedings.

Note: Full details can be obtained from IMCB.

Section Four Independent appeals arrangements for Content Providers and Mobile Operators

Classification Framework Appeals Body ("CFAB")

1. CFAB is a body of persons independent of IMCB appointed to hear appeals against decisions made by IMCB under the IMCB Complaints and Dispute Procedures. The Chairman is a qualified solicitor or barrister of not less than 10 years standing.

2. An appeal may be made on the following grounds:

    a. the disputed decision was based on an error of fact;

    b. the disputed decision was wrong in law or;

    c. IMCB exercised its discretion incorrectly in reaching its decision.

3. An appeal may be commenced by either a dissatisfied Content Provider or Mobile Operator lodging with the Clerk written notification of intention to appeal within 28 days of the decision of IMCB. Attached to the notification must be:

    a. the written determination of IMCB;

    b. details of the service in question; and

    c. notice of appeal setting out the grounds upon which the appeal is made and the facts and matters on which it is based.

Appeals Process

4. The Chairman may convene a conference of relevant parties in order to give appropriate directions for the preparation of the matter for consideration at the appeal.

5. If any of the parties requests an oral hearing then the Chairman will consider that request and may or may not decide to hold an oral hearing entirely at his discretion. If there is to be an oral hearing it would normally take place within 28 days of the decision that there should be such a hearing. If there is no oral hearing then CFAB will reach a decision on the matter on the basis of the papers before it once it is satisfied that it has all relevant information available and that any relevant parties have the opportunity to understand and respond to any relevant case made by another party.

6. There are particular provisions concerning the process leading to determination of the appeal in respect of witness statements, time limits and other relevant matters. There are also specific provisions relating to the conduct of any appeal hearing.

7. The CFAB does not have power to make any order as to costs of the appeal.

8. Within 28 days of an oral hearing, or otherwise as soon as is reasonably practicable, the written decision of CFAB will be provided to the parties and will be published on the IMCB website.

Note: Full details for CFAB appeals will be provided to all relevant parties on commencement of an appeal, or will be provided on request.

Appendix

Definitions used in the Classification Framework document

The following definitions apply in this document:

"Access Controls" are methods of preventing unrestricted access to content, including barring, PIN controlled access and subscription-only services

"Agreed Bodies" are the British Board of Film Classification (BBFC), Ofcom, Video Standards Council, Newspaper Publishers Association, Entertainment Leisure Software Publishers Association (ELSPA), Interactive Software Federation of Europe (IFSE)/Pan-European Game Information (PEGI)

"Chairman of CFAB" is the person being a qualified solicitor or barrister of not less than ten years' standing appointed to be Chairman of the Classification Framework Appeals Body

"Classification Framework" is contained within sections 1 and 2 of this a document, is produced by IMCB and sets out the criteria against which Content Providers need to classify their Commercial Content as 18

"Classification Framework Appeals Body" (CFAB) is a body of persons independent of IMCB appointed to hear appeals against decisions made by IMCB under the complaints and dispute procedures (section three)

"Code of Practice for New Content Services" is the code of practice first issued by the Mobile Operators in January 2004 setting out the Mobile Operator obligations to their customers with regard to new forms of content services

"Commercial Content" means content provided by Content Providers to their mobile customers. Mobile Operators act as the delivery and access provider and thus exercise an element of commercial control over the content delivered. Commercial Content includes pictures, video clips, Mobile Games, music, sounds and experiences such as gambling. It does not include content accessed via the Internet – where Mobile Operators are providing only connectivity

"Content Provider" means a Mobile Operator or a provider having a contractual relationship with a Mobile Operator, supplying Commercial Content to customers through a mobile device

"ICSTIS" is the Independent Committee for the Supervision of Standards of Telephone Information Services – the industry funded regulator for Premium Rate Services

"Mobile Operator" is a telecommunications network provider who has subscribed to the Code of Practice for New Content Services – at the release of this version they are 02, Orange, T-Mobile, Virgin Mobile, Vodafone and 3

"Not-Classified" is content for which no classification has been determined by IMCB.

"Premium Rate Service" is as defined in the code of practice issued from time to time by ICSTIS (currently 10th Edition)

12

18 is any content that is deemed suitable for persons only 18 years or older

"WAP" is wireless application protocol and is a carrier-independent, transaction-orientated protocol for wireless data networks

Notes

1 See www.ofcom.org.uk/static/archive/oftel/publications/mobile/ctm_2002/docs_ind ex. htm for a full list of documents submitted by Oftel, or the full Competition Commission report at: www.ofcom.org.uk/static/archive/oftel/publications/mobile/ctm_2003/ctm2. pdf. The Report is 15 chapters with 9 appendices and took a year to research and publish.

2 COM (2003) 776 Final, p.12, at: http://europa.eu.int/comm/avpolicy/legis/reports/com2003_776final_en.pdf

3 See www.arbitrators.org/cisas/ for ISP and mobile ombudsman; www.out-law.com/php/page.php?page_id=ispsandtelcosmust1069270107&area=news for news of CISAS' establishment and parentage; and www.otelo.org.uk/content.php?menuID=2&pageID=23 for details of the OTelO membership board. For legal measures, see Article 34 of the Universal Service Directive 2002/22/EC of 7 March 2002: http://europa.eu.int/information_society/topics/telecoms/regulatory/new_rf/documents/l_10820020424en 00510077.pdf

4 See www.iarn.org, last visited 3 March 2004, and interviews with national self-regulators, February–March 2004.

5 Source: IAPCODE estimate based on ICSTIS 2003 figures.

6 Ahlert, C, Alexander, M and Tambini, D (2003) 'European 3G Mobile Industry Self-Regulation: IAPCODE Background Paper for World Telemedia Conference', p. 2, at: www.selfregulation.info/iapcoda/031106-mobiles-revised-bckgrd.pdf

7 Ibid.

8 Mobile Network Operators (January 2005) 'UK Code of Practice for the Self-Regulation of New Forms of Content on Mobiles', available at: www.orange.co.uk

9 See Ahlert *et al.* (2003), op. cit. at p. 20 on the KJM interstate regulatory commission implementing the 2003 Interstate Treaty on the Protection of Minors and Human Dignity in the Media.

10 Interviewee from Austrian 3G network licensee, London, 30 January 2004.

11 Dialogue continued European networks, content providers, consumer groups and regulators met in London 29–30 January 2004 for the 'Delivering Adult Mobile Content Responsibly' conference which IAPCODE chaired for Total Telecom. Network operators were also present at the Safer Internet Action Plan's Safer Internet Day event on 6 February.

12 56 per cent of the 2000 European subscriber market was O2, Vodafone, T-Mobile and Orange – TIM and Telefonica Moviles, with less significant interest outside their domestic markets, are small in pan-European terms. See Ahlert *et al.* (2003), p. 4.

13 See the IMCB Classification Framework in Appendix 2.

14 UK Code, p. 2.

15 The Code was launched in the UK on 19 January 2005, and worldwide on 15 March 2005: see www.m-e-f.org/news032005.html

16 See www.imcb.org.uk

17 See for instance www.orange.co.uk/about/regulatory_affairs.html – the Code is the first download item in the middle of the page.

18 UK Code, p. 2.

19 Zittrain, J and Edelman, B (2004) 'Documentation of Internet Filtering Worldwide', in Hardy, C and Moller, C (eds) *Spreading the Word on the Internet: 16 Answers to 4 Questions*, Vienna: OSCE, pp. 137–48.

20 Beaufort International (2003) Premium SMS Services Research, p. 5, at: www.icstis.org. uk/icstis2002/pdf/SMS_RESEARCH_REPORT_MAY03.PDF

21 See ITU (2004) 'Shaping the Future Mobile Internet Society: The Case of Japan', Document SMIS/06, authored by Srivastava, L and Kodate, A, at: www.itu.int/osg/spu/ni/futuremobile/general/casestudies/JapancaseLS.pdf at p. 50: (2002, July) Law on regulation of transmission of specified electronic mail – spam law, and (2003, September) Law of regulating the act that attracts children using the Internet opposite-sex introduction sites – anti-paedophile law.

22 This is not the case with all newer devices, and indeed may change in the future if we see increasing convergence between palmtop PC and mobile phone functions. For example, some new PDAs and some smart phones run on Windows CE with voice communication as an additional feature incorporated into this Microsoft operating system.

23 Categories adapted and extended from Marsden (2004) 'Editorial . . . Illegal and Offnet: Is Peer to Peer the Next p Regulation Challenge?', at: www.selfregulation.info/iapcoda/0402xx-selfregulation-review.txt

24 Figures from the UK Department for Education and Skills show that in 2002 41 per cent of children between 5 and 18 owned a mobile phone, a figure which is likely to have increased still further since (DfES 2002). A recent consumer survey suggested that mobile phones are owned by over 5 million under-16s in the UK (mobileYouth, research report, 2005, London: Dhaliwal Brown Consulting, at http://www.statsmine.com/display_report.php/wireless_reports/mobileYouth_2005).

25 See: www.out-law.com/php/page.php?page_id=irishpoliceinvesti1074855914&area=news

26 Reding, V (2005) 'Mobile Communications: A Key Driver to Make Lisbon Succeed', delivered to the 3GSM World Congress, Cannes, 14 February.

27 See further Ahlert, C, Marsden, C and Nash, V (2005) *Protecting Minors from Exposure to Harmful Content on Mobile Phones*, for the European Internet Coregulation Network, at: http://network.foruminternet.org/article.php3?id_article=24

28 Please also see www.m-e-f.org

11 The privatisation of censorship?

Self-regulation and freedom of expression

1. Everyone has the right to freedom of expression. This right shall include freedom to hold opinions and to receive and impart information and ideas without interference by public authority and regardless of frontiers. This article shall not prevent States from requiring the licensing of broadcasting, television or cinema enterprises.
2. The exercise of these freedoms, since it carries with it duties and responsibilities, may be subject to such formalities, conditions, restrictions or penalties as are prescribed by law and are necessary in a democratic society, in the interests of national security, territorial integrity or public safety, for the prevention of disorder or crime, for the protection of health or morals, for the protection of the reputation or the rights of others, for preventing the disclosure of information received in confidence, or for maintaining the authority and impartiality of the judiciary.

European Convention on Human Rights, Article 10

Introduction: convergence, self-regulation and freedom of expression

Public policy debate concerning self-regulation of the media is deeply ambivalent. On the one hand, public opinion in democratic states tends to support self-regulation enthusiastically where the alternative is regulation by the state. On the other hand, if self-regulation is seen as effective, it can provoke uneasiness about 'privatised censorship' where responsibility for fundamental rights is handed over to private actors, many of which are centres of power in society.[1] The purpose of this chapter is to place the results of research on self-regulation across media industries in the wider context of freedom-of-expression concerns. The goal is to identify areas of conflict between the activities of self-regulatory bodies and freedom-of-expression rights, in order to understand the implications for freedom of expression of the restrictions on the content of speech that originate in the actions of those self-regulatory bodies.

We will consider how freedom of speech is understood in Europe, and address the areas of conflict or potential conflict between self-regulation and free speech. We will focus on whether imposing limits on freedom of expression via self-regulatory bodies is easier to justify than state regulation, and if so, with what conditions and to what extent limitations are tolerable in a system that takes rights seriously.[2]

Any form of content regulation in the media industry, whether through statute or code of conduct, may encroach on citizens' speech rights. Nonetheless, as is clear in Article 10 of the ECHR, free speech is not an absolute, and can be balanced against other rights, or the rights of others. In this chapter we therefore focus on the question of self-regulation and freedom of expression in terms of the legal situation.[3] We investigate the balancing of rights as carried out by self-regulatory regimes and mechanisms not in isolation, but as this interacts with the courts, the legislature and the executive. We argue that it is not possible to resolve the difficult question of speech rights and self-regulation at a high level of legal abstraction. We look instead at policy and socio-legal implications, for example through the analysis of the nature and extent of limitations imposed by self-regulatory bodies, and considering when and if these bodies are regarded as 'public authorities' sharing the power of the state. State, public and private organisations performing regulatory activities routinely balance the speech rights of citizens against other objectives; it is necessary to be aware of the detail of regulatory functions on a case-by-case basis. At a higher level of generality, we also need to revisit fundamental principles underpinning the justifications for free-speech protection. A framework for evaluating the impact of self-, co- and state regulatory functions[4] is outlined.

Limits imposed on freedom of expression by self-regulatory bodies

Before we consider the limits imposed on freedom of expression by self-regulatory bodies let us turn our attention to the various models for media content regulation contemplated in current frameworks of regulation in Europe. It is important at this stage to note that the array of limitations placed on content varies in different models of regulation. Partly because of the emergence of frameworks tailored for specific forms of speech and modes of delivery, there exist widely different legal systems, ranging from prior rating and classification (film and video, video games, ISPs, internal self-regulatory mechanisms at broadcasters, etc.) to post-publication self-regulation via complaints (journalistic ethics and press councils for print/online publications, such as the UK PCC and German Presserat; Ombudsman or readers' editor systems at newspapers and other systems of accountability). Controls on content are set up with various goals in mind, such as protecting the reputation of others,[5] protecting minors from harmful speech, the need to keep up standards of journalistic ethics or to protect consumers by making the media accountable. For the most part these different models of content regulation strike quite different balances between free-speech concerns and the degree of intervention deemed acceptable.

The following historical models of content regulation based on means of delivery can be distinguished in EU member states:

- The book model, not addressed in this study, gives all content rights to the communicator, and consequently regulatory intervention in content is deemed undesirable.
- The periodical print media model is strongly influenced by the concept of the free market of ideas, and so here content intervention is also deemed undesirable. Content regulation is based on ordinary law; above and beyond this, there is space for the ethical principles of the journalistic profession, which in turn help make the media accountable to its readership. The control on content via journalistic ethics is in some cases manifest as self-regulation, with or without a complaints commission charged with the task of implementing a code of conduct. The areas covered by the code concern voluntary regulation.[6]
- The European broadcast media model[7] involves the strongest content regulation

considered here. Controls are based on a broad notion of the public interest. The rationale is that frequencies used for broadcasting are scarce, therefore must be coordinated, and access not automatically granted to everyone. In addition to ordinary law there is close regulatory control of content based on statute and an array of codes connected to the award of a licence.

- The emerging Internet model of content regulation seems at first sight closer to the pure print model in EU countries, as it relies to a great extent on industry self-regulation by means of codes of conduct combined with technical controls. The model of content regulation for online news so far has been most similar to pure print media, but, as we have seen, games, mobile and other emerging variants present contrasting approaches.

New technological developments continually upset and erode these regulatory models and as a result may prompt new settlements, changing the boundaries between self-, co- and public regulation. On the one hand in the broadcasting sector, statutory regulatory bodies find it increasingly difficult to cope with the sheer volume of material that they are responsible for regulating. Technical progress makes available new services, for example on digital and interactive platforms.[8] The need to devolve at least part of the regulatory responsibility to the regulatee (or to pass part of the control to the consumer) is particularly felt for content, where the regulator had traditionally held responsibility for detailed monitoring and reporting. As we have seen, not only are the means of regulation under challenge, but the current justifications of regulation are undermined by technology, as many argue that, given increased volumes of media content, and higher levels of user control and choice, it becomes both less practical and less justifiable to have central regulatory oversight of content. In this context, self-regulatory codes of practice are becoming the preferred practical solution.

The acceptability of limits imposed on freedom of expression depends on the type of speech that is being conveyed. Not all content is treated in the same way. Commercial speech or 'commercial statements' in the wording of the ECHR, i.e. speech whose main objective is the proposal of a commercial transaction, is subject to a considerable degree of control.[9] The rationale is the potential of commercial speech for confusing or misleading the public. Political speech is subject to the lowest level of control. The rationale here is that the ability to criticise public officials in all matters of public interest must be wide-ranging in order to protect the health of democracy. As the European Court of Human Rights clearly expressed it in, for example, *De Haes and Gijsels* v. *Belgium*, even unpleasant or problematic information deserves to be protected:

> ... the Court reiterates that freedom of expression is applicable not only to 'information' or 'ideas' that are favourably received or regarded as inoffensive or as a matter of indifference but also to those that offend, shock or disturb the State or any section of the community. In addition, journalistic freedom also covers possible recourse to a degree of exaggeration, or even provocation.[10]

Artistic speech is in between those two extremes. Article 10 offers protection either in the case of prior control or ex post facto control. As regards the philosophical underpinnings of this right, both the justifications from democracy and self-fulfilment are deployed in the jurisprudence of the European Court of Human Rights, although the emphasis tends to be on the argument from democracy.[11] There is a gradation, and we see that reliance by the European Court upon the justification from democracy made the case law less tolerant of restrictions of political expression[12] while in cases in which freedom of expression is supported by concerns relating to self-fulfilment there is more scope for the member states to impose limits on freedom of expression (e.g. *Wingrove* v. *UK*).

Functions and models of self-regulation

For analytical purposes it is also important to distinguish different functions in the process of speech regulation. The legal traditions of liberal democracies (and hence the case law of the ECtHR) have not applied a blanket presumption in favour of freedom of expression: they have adjusted both for the type of content involved, and for the form of regulation. To take one example from English law, in *Venables* v. *News Group Newspapers Ltd and others*[13] we see the High Court prioritising the claimants' right to protection of their new identity over the freedom-of-expression rights of the defendant newspapers. The claimants had sought injunctions to protect their identities on their imminent release from detention – they were 10 years old when they had murdered a child. They had grown up and hence physically changed since their detention and a new identity could protect them from revenge. The injunction was granted: a restriction a priori, as the after-publication system offered by print media self-regulation would not be able to offer protection in the circumstances.

> The press code, as applied by the Press Complaints Commission, is not, in the exceptional situation of the claimants, sufficient protection. Criticism of, or indeed sanctions imposed upon, the offending newspaper after the information is published would, in the circumstances of the case, be too late. The information would be in the public domain and the damage would be done. The press code cannot adequately protect in advance.[14]

Concerns with freedom of speech can be radically different according to which control function is being undertaken, which kinds of speech, and the means of delivery for that speech. In Western Europe in some cases (rating content for taste and decency in broadcasting for instance) we see that a society is much more comfortable with state or governmental organisations undertaking regulatory functions than we would with others (monitoring news or political content in the press for example).

In Figure 11.1 the regulatory functions have been considerably simplified for analytical clarity. In practice many of the functions overlap. For each one, a variety of public, governmental, quasi-governmental and industry bodies are involved. Alongside the question of their role with regard to freedom of expression, and the balancing of public interest arguments for regulation or rights balancing freedom of expression, different traditions of freedom of expression place a differing emphasis on the relative importance of state, public or private curtailments of those rights.

With the basic philosophical justifications (outlined above) in mind, it is clear that concerns with freedom of expression differ across the various objects of regulation. There are, for example, some functions of regulation more appropriately carried out by a body independent of both government and the regulatee. Other functions are best left to the industry board or individual providers. In the latter case it may of course be necessary to define very well the standards and benchmarks of regulatory transparency and accountability before self-regulation can be defended.

Although over-arching categories fail to capture the complexity of regulatory tools and regimes, in order to make sense of regulatory schemes some approaches[15] have

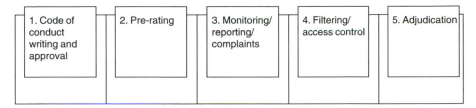

| 1. Code of conduct writing and approval | 2. Pre-rating | 3. Monitoring/ reporting/ complaints | 4. Filtering/ access control | 5. Adjudication |

Figure 11.1 Elements of self-regulation of content.

categorised them as either self-, co- or statutory regulation. Others[16] have taken a more functional approach, referring for example to self-monitoring. Categorisation facilitates the understanding of issues at a theoretical level; in practice, however, most individual media outlets operate in a complex ecology of all three main types of regulation. Regulatory schemes interact, for example when the ratings set by an industry-managed self-ratings board are applied within a legal framework governing broadcast licences or video retail and rental as is the norm in Europe. The press, on the other hand, is subject to civil (or criminal) penalty for defamation, libel, obscenity and hate speech, and at the same time is subject to self-regulatory codes that overlap with some of that general law. Models of co-regulation seem to allow governments not to abdicate from their ultimate goal of protection of the public from harmful content. (NB: co-regulation is generally termed 'regulated self-regulation' in German administrative law.[17])

This functional approach to self-regulation permits us to make explicit some policy concerns which are connected with the development of self-regulatory activity. Let us take the UK as a case study, and apply this functionalist view to regulatory activity, as we outline in Table 11.1. This table is a simplification, but it helps us spell out some of the freedom-of-expression concerns that arise with convergent content self-regulation, and it also helps us to transcend the polarised debates where those concerned with harms (e.g. child protection agencies) oppose those who defend free speech. We can see that the shift between self-, co- and state regulation is a complex one. Communications regulation more often than not involves elements of all three forms of regulation. Taking the example of Internet content regulation of illegal content: legislation determines the scope of what is forbidden. The role of the hotline, the Internet Watch Foundation (IWF), in dealing with illegal content, and the particular stress and focus taken by the IWF is determined by the IWF itself, and content is removed by ISPs themselves. Complaints come mainly from the public to a hybrid industry–public board which adjudicates. Some aspects of this chain, for example writing the criteria for determining what constitutes illegal material, and setting the operational priorities for the access control agency should arguably be kept away from government agencies. For legitimacy some role for parliament may be required. In others, we may be more relaxed, but – and this is the important point – only if sufficient safeguards of transparency and procedure are observed.

The European and the American experiences

As noted, the fundamental justifications for the protection of speech draw traditionally on three arguments – from truth, from democracy and from self-expression – which will have different relevance at different times.[18] For example, as a society we should be particularly concerned (and argue the point from democracy) if political

Table 11.1 Regulatory function and examples of institutions for the UK

| | Self-regulatory activity | | | State/formal regulation | |
| | Corporation/industry | Public/civil society | | State/governmental/quasi-governmental | |
Actor function	Internal corporate activity	Industry–civil society board	User	IRA	Government ministry/statute Ordinary law, plus:
Code writing	BBC Producer guidelines	PCC code committee	(Open consultation?)	Ofcom codes	Licence conditions
Pre-rating/content descriptors	PEGI	BBFC	ICRA	IWF blacklists	
Monitoring of content	Moderators/editors	Board of IWF, PCC,	User via ISP/hotlines	IRA	Government monitoring
Complaints	ISP staff	ICSTIS	User via ISP/hotlines		
Adjudications against code	Internal	IWF		Courts/IRA	Courts
Filter calibration, filter operation, access control	Notice and take down ISPs ISP/level filtering, BT/Telnor	Cinema/video stores	Internet browser, ICRA	Licensing	Licensing

speech regulation falls under governmental control as this would risk compromise of political pluralism. Governments wishing to remain in power have a very direct interest in closing down or controlling political debate and should not be given tools to do so. In the case of previewing and rating of content we would have a similar caution in relation to political speech but case law – as with the case of Wingrove (see below) – tends to illustrate the fact that prior restraint is of less concern where speech is artistic and not political.

The European tradition of free expression is enshrined in the national legal traditions of the countries surveyed in this study, as well as in the ECHR case law – in this chapter we take Strasbourg to illustrate the European tradition, as a reflection of a 'common European denominator' on the matter.[19] Unlike the First Amendment to the United States Constitution, which prioritises freedom of speech over other rights,[20] the system of the ECHR tends to be more comfortable with the idea of balancing the competing rights set out in the convention, giving free speech similar strength to other rights.[21]

The American tradition, however, appears less concerned with curtailment of speech rights by private organisations than the European one. This is illustrated by the Yahoo case, which concerned the possibility of French Internet users accessing websites selling Nazi memorabilia hosted in the United States. Under French law the display and sale of that type of merchandise is illegal. The key issue of difference between the legal reasoning of the courts in the United States and France lies in the conception of freedom of expression and the acceptability of limitations on free speech. In the United States, the answer to hate speech is to allow even more speech. The United States has repeatedly expressed free-speech reservations against outlawing hate speech, a concern which tends to be viewed in less absolute terms in Europe.[22] For example, the indictment in 1997 of Felix Somm, the head of the ISP CompuServe in Germany, for failure to prevent the dissemination of neo-Nazi material,[23] can be contrasted with the US Supreme Court's finding that it was unconstitutional to regulate expression on the Internet through the Communications Decency Act.[24]

In Europe, Article 10 sets out freedom of speech as a fundamental right subject to restrictions 'prescribed by law' and 'necessary in a democratic society'.[25] As a commentator put it, the question is often how far a member state can limit freedom of expression to protect third parties against damages.[26] In Strasbourg the question therefore is about managing the tensions arising out of the applicants' free-speech claims over the governments' exercise of powers that encumber those rights. In the adjudication of those tensions, the ECtHR indicates whether or not the burdens placed on free speech by the national authorities were within their 'margin of appreciation'. Our focus in this chapter is on limitations placed on free speech by self- (and to some extent co-) regulatory bodies. Pre-publication restrictions are viewed with suspicion, particularly in a First Amendment environment. In Europe, in contrast, there is still a measure of censorship, in varying degrees according to countries, regarding the a priori classification of films and video and, also, the quite detailed control of broadcast content.

Control over limitations placed by self-regulatory bodies: the interface between self-regulation and the state

Speech may be restricted prior to publication or penalties/redress imposed after. It is expedient, given new technology and globalisation, to regulate media industries through private or semi-private organisations funded (and in many cases entirely controlled) by industry. For some, this is positive for freedom of expression, as it moves content regulation away from the state or government. This view is particularly prevalent in US approaches to self-regulation where the First Amendment tradition focuses on a mistrust of state or government, and on expansive protection of free speech, particularly against viewpoint-based regulation.

An opposing view claims that this is a narrow, negative treatment of freedom of expression.[27] In this view, industry bodies increasingly regulate not only the voluntarily delegated content of their funding members, but the speech – as is the case with ISPs – of the broader population of users. Speech could be suppressed without the protections that the legal system grants when limitations originated with the authorities. Were the activities of industry bodies to take over these public functions, it is argued, such self-regulation would in fact constitute a direct threat to speech rights as it instates a so-called 'privatised censorship'. In these terms, the shift of regulatory authority to co-regulation and self-regulatory functions should be viewed with suspicion, as by means of self-regulation more onerous standards may be imposed in the shadow of the law.

Due to the increasing complexity brought about by technical progress across all mass media, coupled with the tendency towards devolving at least part of the content regulation to the regulatee or the consumer, equally, there appears to be a trend towards the deconstitutionalisation of freedom of speech. Are we in the presence of valid waivers to the fundamental right to free speech when parties enter into a voluntary self-regulatory regime? Are we leaving public law concerns behind and moving into the realm of contract? The apparent private erosion of rights granted by the (public) copyright law regime by means of the use of 'click here' adhesion contracts has been noticed some time ago.[28] Similarly, Lawrence Lessig warns about the use of (computer) code to regulate cyberspace as an 'invisible regulation' which is harder to resist than government regulation,[29] although he sees contract as less dangerous for rights than computer code because a court is the ultimate arbiter of rights set out in a contract.[30] Private law prioritises the discretion of the parties. The risk those authors are warning against is that the substantive choices that are being made in the shadow of the law appear to be the ones that are less protective of the values of freedom of speech or that favour too much the commercial interests of the industry.

If self-regulation means that the parties to a system privately establish the scope of their legal obligations instead of government imposing them, and a regime in which a code of conduct or a code of journalistic ethics imposes a voluntary set of restrictions on an industry and on stakeholders (e.g. consumers, readers, users, etc.), this does not necessarily lead to a situation in which fundamental rights are not taken seriously. If the result tends to be too often that parties suppress or limit speech – to an extent that the government may not,[31] or to an excessive degree – this may be an indication that not enough safeguards are in place and the discretion of the self-regulatory body in question may need to be reviewed and brought back to margins that are acceptable. Angela Campbell points out, for example, that in the United States self-regulation could be used instead of government regulation so as not to engage First Amendment protection (in her example, no constitutional issue arises if a station, a group of stations or an industry body chooses not to carry alcohol advertising).[32] If they were obliged by law or a statutory regulator not to carry a certain content First Amendment challenges would be more likely. Similarly, Internet filtering software voluntarily introduced by providers of content and others was viewed by First Amendment activists as a panacea that conciliates free-speech ideas with the protection of minors.[33]

The tendency we observed is that in Europe self-regulatory regimes all impose more onerous requirements than those of ordinary law. This can be seen across the media industries. Where consumers can choose between different companies' codes of conduct, these codes are less of a freedom-of-expression concern. A consumer may trade off some of the freedoms of choosing an ISP with a restrictive code for the increased security, for example. But where codes become sector-wide or cross-sectoral, there may be increased concerns. If all ISPs operate filter-level blocking based on a non-transparent blacklist provided by government (as the new Finnish code will require[34]) this is more likely to chill speech.

For this very reason it is likely that self-regulation – particularly if it continues to expand its scope, as we have seen in the trends highlighted by our research – will come under increasing scrutiny and challenge in Europe. If the concern is to make self-regulatory regimes more acceptable to all stakeholders and to the public, from the point of view of public interest, then it seems necessary to start viewing self-regulation in terms of specific safeguards and measures taken to limit liability of self-regulatory institutions themselves in the face of a challenge to their activities via ordinary law. A potential solution is to increase accountability to include procedural protection for rights (perhaps by means of court reviewability of decisions taken by self-regulatory bodies), or by strengthening the codes and/or the decision-making of those self-regulatory bodies. One possible way to achieve this would be to place them in the context of a co-regulatory regime where the privately agreed limitations may be audited by the authorities with the specific purpose that substantive free-speech rights are given due attention.

If we consider Meiklejohn's argument from democracy to protect free speech – the argument that the sovereign people have delegated a part, but not all, of their self-government to the state authorities – we can see that self-regulation of the media can be placed among that realm of rights to self-government which were not delegated to the state. The argument for self-regulation of the media as an alternative to legislation means using self-regulation mechanisms (codes, bodies able to apply a code, etc.) to provide a framework of limitations which in turn provides a system of accountability. Nonetheless, a self-regulatory regime can offer protection of freedom of expression of newspaper editors and proprietors, broadcasters, etc. against government regulation and also against those restrictions lobbied for by certain groups (protecting against low standards of journalism, intrusion into private life, etc.).

To make sense of self-regulatory mechanisms and their codes of conduct, and to include issues of accountability, we therefore suggest understanding those schemes as if they were contractual agreements – part of the discretion enjoyed by parties in the realm of private law. Parties enjoy freedom to agree to a mechanism and code. Admittedly, not all parties have equal bargaining power and the readership, audience or users agree to abide by a self-regulatory system by a 'click here' type of adhesion contract or by signing to in the small print of contracts with ISPs, for example. Hence the heightened need for transparency, consumer protection, stakeholder involvement and other ways of ensuring accountability and preventing abuse.

We recognise the existence of principled objections to intrusions on a fundamental right such as free speech, whether the intrusions result from state action or the action of private parties. The other side of the coin is that, like any right, free speech may, however, be subject to legitimate limitations. There is agreement among writers and practitioners at the level of fundamental principles that the freedom of expression of one person could harm another and therefore curbing certain forms of expression ensures fair play (that certain ideas do not dominate), which in turn furthers the goals of free speech.[35] There is agreement also at the more concrete level of the everyday functioning of the media that regulation is in order (for the reasons discussed in Chapter 2), and that the media are unlike any other regulatory object because, among other reasons, the media are systems of communication by which members of a society understand themselves and others. In a liberal democracy the mass media also fulfil the extremely important role of watchdog of the authorities. Limitations, of course, need to be imposed by an authority or a private party that enjoys legitimacy, and following transparent procedures. Limitations can be placed directly or indirectly, for example the informal influence from the authorities and threat of state action if nothing is done. Examples of the symbolic manoeuvring and dialogue between governments and media are numerous; state involvement in ISPs ranges from exhortation in ministerial speeches, to direct involvement in setting up task forces. In Italy, the 'voluntary' ISP code was drafted by the Ministry of Communications, for example.

The courts and self-regulation: interface between limits imposed via self-regulation and limits imposed by state authorities via regulation

Self-regulatory institutions have to judge the limits of free speech. As an English court said of the UK Press Complaints Commission:

the commission has to consider and balance in many cases the important but countervailing freedoms of privacy and of expression. The Commission then has to exercise a judgement on the particular facts as to when the right to privacy of a complainant ends and where the freedom of expression of the publisher against whom the complaint is made begins.[36]

A key question is to what extent self-regulatory bodies are likely to be challenged in court, in particular with regard to the standards set out in Article 10.[37] In the UK the courts have generally left a great deal of room for manoeuvre to self-regulatory organisations. Where reviewed, their curtailment of speech is rarely overturned. But there is very little case law (and none on ISPs or hotlines). In an analogous sector, the press, judges have repeatedly supported the view that although the PCC could be amenable to judicial review, its decisions should be left unchallenged under Article 10. In any case the PCC generally errs in favour of free expression in its adjudications and code.[38]

Turning from the PCC to the British Board of Film Classification (BBFC, the self-regulatory body of the UK film industry) allows us to consider a case in which Article 10 was invoked. The BBFC classifies films with the approval of central and local government, who retain the power to review decisions or refuse a local showing of a film classified by the board.[39] We should indicate that this case pre-dates the Human Rights Act 1998 (HRA) and the issue whether self-regulatory bodies can be considered 'public authorities' within the terms of the HRA.

Nigel Wingrove, a London-based film director, was refused a certificate by the BBFC for his film *Visions of Ecstasy*, deemed blasphemous (it addresses erotic fantasies of St. Teresa of Avila focused on the crucified Christ). Wingrove would have been liable to prosecution under the Video Recordings Act 1984 had the film been distributed. After his appeal was rejected by the Video Appeals Committee, Wingrove took his case to Strasbourg. Although the result may well be viewed as disappointing for free speech, the point we would like to highlight is procedural. The limitation placed on speech by the self-regulatory body here was subject to appeal to higher instances. We want to illustrate with this example a case in which self-regulatory bodies function within a system in which it is perfectly possible to challenge the balance of rights performed by those bodies. It is not a situation of privatised censorship without further recourse. It remains to be seen if other bodies exercising a semi-judicial function are open to similar challenge. ISP associations, hotlines and individual ISPs are currently protected by a limited liability regime, but they do exercise significant censorship functions.

There was an initial victory for Wingrove at the then Strasbourg Commission, which deemed the UK in breach of Article 10. The ECtHR, however, found for the UK government. The judgement stated that there had been no violation of Wingrove's freedom of artistic expression. The Court accepted the view that the UK government was entitled to consider the impugned measure necessary in a democratic society. In the sphere of morals or especially, religion, the margin of appreciation is quite wide.

In scholarly writings on the balance of rights reached by the BBFC, the ECtHR in *Wingrove* was seen as disappointing. Voorhoof[40] explains that the European Court did not rely on a survey of existing legislation in other European countries which could have perhaps countered the arguments of the UK government. Legislation on blasphemy exists only in few other European countries and those laws are rarely used. Strasbourg also missed the opportunity to explore the well-known inconsistency in the English law on blasphemy, which only extends to the Christian religion. Neither did the Court estimate the measure as disproportionate, even though it amounted to a total ban of the film. The European Court was persuaded that the values the BBFC and domestic law were trying to protect took priority over the concerns of freedom of expression. Prior restraint in this case was considered as necessary, because otherwise, in practice, the film would escape any form of control by the authorities.

We provide a second example. Self-regulatory bodies' exercise of their powers and the limitations they place on fundamental rights continued to be subject to Strasbourg review. In *Peck* v. *The United Kingdom*,[41] the applicant, Geoffrey Peck, had attempted suicide by cutting his wrists with a kitchen knife in Brentwood High Street in 1995. He had lost his job and his partner was terminally ill. His actions were caught on CCTV and an operator alerted the police. The police took Peck to a police station and he received medical help. The footage was broadcast and frames appeared in newspapers. Peck complained to the UK broadcast regulators BSC and ITC, and to the UK PCC. The broadcast regulators upheld Peck's complaints. The UK PCC, on the other hand, rejected it. Peck applied for judicial review of the press self-regulatory body, but this was rejected. He complained to Strasbourg. The European Court found that in the UK there was no adequate protection for privacy (Article 8 of the ECHR) as the self-regulatory and statutory regulators did not offer sufficient redress:

> The Court finds that the lack of legal power of the commissions to award damages to the applicant means that those bodies could not provide an effective remedy to him. It notes that the ITC's power to impose a fine on the relevant television company does not amount to an award of damages to the applicant. While the applicant was aware of the Council's disclosures prior to 'Yellow Advertiser' article of February 1996 and the BBC broadcasts, neither the BSC nor the PCC had the power to prevent such publications or broadcasts.[42]

We have seen that self-regulation operates in an area of freedom of choice associated with the sphere of the private. We have observed that via self-regulation limitations on speech rights can be introduced, and had those limitations been applied by law or a statutory regulator, challenges could be mounted on the basis of breach of fundamental rights. It seems, therefore, that self-regulatory mechanisms and codes could well be less protective of individual rights.

Are self-regulatory bodies public authorities?

The examples discussed above beg the question – are self-regulatory institutions bodies against which ECHR rights are enforceable? The question in the UK hinges upon whether or not the body in question can be considered a 'public authority' as expressed in the 1998 Human Rights Act, the statute that incorporated the ECHR into domestic law in the UK. In other signatory countries, there are different approaches to this question of how to define a public authority. Taking the UK again as a case study, we can ask how the dividing line between state and self-regulating bodies should be drawn. The reasoning of UK courts to declare the Advertising Standards Authority (ASA; the self-regulatory body for advertising) reviewable focuses on it being a body 'clearly exercising a public function which, if the ASA did not exist, would no doubt be exercised by a [statutory office]'.[43] We also supply some examples from other jurisdictions.

Editors control newspaper content, and television broadcasters likewise perform a gate-keeping function. But do ISPs, content ratings bodies or press councils have the right to interfere in this process? These questions are applicable in all the countries surveyed. We do object to regulators, states and governmental bodies getting involved in the filtering process behind publication if that results in free-expression rights being curtailed without transparency and due process. We object because interference in the marketplace of ideas by state authorities should be subject to the strongest inspection, as the marketplace enables democratic pluralism and debate about competing truth claims. Clearly, the extent to which a self-regulatory body – be it a press council, a video games or Internet content rating body – is viewed as a state or, in UK HRA terms, a 'public authority' is important to freedom of expression.

If one's view of freedom of expression defines it negatively, i.e. as the absence of state interference, then support for self-regulatory bodies will generally be viewed as conducive to speech freedom. At one level this is a technical question. EU member states all have a slightly different framework for assessing whether a body is to be considered a public authority and therefore whether Convention rights such as the right to free expression are enforceable against them. A parallel question arises with regard to which bodies are subject to the binding effects of EU directives. According to Craig and De Burca:

> a body which has been made responsible for providing a public service under the control of the State is *included* within the Community definition of a public body. Case law since then has not notably clarified the situation but has left it to the national courts to apply the loose criteria.[44]

How the question of applicability is resolved will have a fundamental impact on the nature of self-regulatory bodies, and their responsibilities to uphold freedom of expression. Taking the example of the UK, section 6 of the Human Rights Act makes it unlawful for a public authority to act incompatibly with Convention rights including Article 10. This applies to both pure public authorities such as statutory regulators, government departments and the police and also 'functional public authorities' which combine public and private functions. The upshot of this is that if industry self-regulatory bodies take on more public functions they will eventually trigger a greater responsibility to uphold freedom of expression and other convention rights. Should they fail to do so they could face judicial review under Article 10.

In the case *Selisto* v. *Finland* (2004) the ECtHR accepted that the exercise of the freedoms guaranteed by Article 10 carries with it 'duties and responsibilities' for a journalist as the statements made in an article may affect the reputation and rights of private persons. And these duties and responsibilities may be established by self-regulation and contained in a code of journalistic ethics. In the Court's own words:

> By reason of the 'duties and responsibilities' inherent in the exercise of freedom of expression, the safeguard afforded by Article 10 to journalists in relation to reporting on issues of general interest is subject to the proviso that they are acting in good faith in order to provide accurate and reliable information in accordance with the ethics of journalism.[45]

The converse theoretically also applies, with more worrying consequences. As regulatory functions are shifted from public authorities to private ones, the public may have fewer, if any, opportunities for redress on Convention rights such as Article 10. Put simply, the actions of self-regulatory bodies could fall outside the scope of ECHR

protection. However, member states of the Strasbourg system are under an obligation under Article 1 of the ECHR to ensure the effectiveness of the freedoms
contained in the Convention. If self-regulation is not effective the state cannot absolve
itself from responsibility by delegating to private bodies or individuals.[46] The key is
the adequate balance of the different interests:

> Restrictions on the information flow due to self-regulation may, however, qualify
> as legal restrictions under Art. 10 (2), hence rendering the state liable for not
> guaranteeing the fundamental right of journalists and the public's right to receive
> information and ideas on matters of crucial importance.[47]

There is no evidence that sufficient thought has been given to this issue by self-regulatory authorities or by those who fund them or in the broader policy framework. At
present, there is some dispute regarding criteria for deciding whether a body is to be
considered a public authority. In the UK, for example, the Parliamentary Committee
on Human Rights has recently expressed concern that the constitution and organisation of the authority, rather than the public nature of the function performed, determines whether a body is public or not. In such a context, the gradual transfer of
control over regulation of content to privately funded bodies would result in a lack of
remedy or reviewability of those decisions. Technically, the shift of emphasis might
lead to a decline in freedom-of-expression cases. So the simple example of reducing
risk of challenge by adopting self-regulation rather than statutory regulation – to use
the example cited by Angela Campbell (1999) – would be a solution that masks an
overall reduction in protection against the actions of regulators. In this view a shift to
self-regulation could lead to an overall diminishment of protection and redress, rather
than an improved climate of free expression.

The government and self-regulation

It is a cliché to say that self-regulatory institutions often find themselves in a relationship of threat and response with governments. Many self-regulatory codes are written
with the express aim of heading off potential statutory regulation and in many cases
governments go as far as drafting model self-regulatory codes to stimulate 'spon-
taneous' action by industry. This was the case in Italy, where the Department of
Communications took the initiative in convening a stakeholder group from the
Internet industry and drafting a code of conduct that would be 'voluntarily' applied
by ISPs. Leaving aside the strategic problems with this approach (in terms of legitimacy and sustainability of codes) it also raises the interesting case of when self-regulatory institutions cease to be self-regulatory because they are effectively
government-sanctioned bodies. Whilst the Italian code as originally drafted was not
implemented by the stakeholders, it would have been an interesting case were it
implemented. Not only was the code essentially imposed on the industry by government, but the code itself essentially consisted not in a set of agreed voluntary standards, but a summary of existing statutory standards, i.e. a guide to compliance with
existing law. It seems unlikely that such a code – were it enforced – would be viewed
as a pure form of self-regulation. In fact, it was largely rejected by the Italian ISP
industry in its original form. Frydman and Rorive[48] argue for the Internet industry
itself to self-regulate according to international standards. Under the European E-
Commerce Directive, ISPs, to avoid potential liability, must take down illegal content
that they are hosting, if notified of its presence. The liability of ISPs for third-party

content is an example of indirect public ordering. Since the ISP is not the originator of the speech the freedom-of-expression protections are not engaged by imposing liability on them rather than directly on the speaker. The difficulty with this approach (as we have seen above) is that ISPs might be too willing to avoid liability and hence be too quick at taking down material, thereby curtailing speech. The fact that the interaction will be in the realm of private law (limited as to whether the take down violated the contract between the user posting material and the ISP rather than as regards the broader constitutional implications of limiting free speech) might result in chilling effects on free speech.[49,50]

The ECHR requires limitations on speech to be 'prescribed by law' as well as 'necessary in democratic society'. Whilst this aspect of the role of communications self-regulation is yet to be tested in court, there is clearly a scope for discussion in many cases as to whether certain aspects of the self- and co-regulatory regime constitute rules that are 'prescribed by law'. At one end of a continuum, purely voluntary ethics codes of single companies are clearly not law, but at the other, codes that are encouraged through a legislative framework but administered by an industry association may be considered for these purposes to be law.

Important procedural considerations to ensure accountability: transparency, openness, due process, stakeholder participation

Free-speech considerations, as set out in Article 10, constitute a yardstick of first principles in the field of media regulation. Although it is arguable to what extent the 'horizontal effect' of the ECHR applies (i.e. its application between private parties, or between a private party and a self-regulatory body),[51] it is clear that self-regulatory bodies of the media must act in a way that is compatible with the provisions of the ECHR. Their activities – and codes and methods of implementation – are to be measured, ultimately, against the free-speech standards contemplated in the ECHR.

For the ECtHR there must be 'expression' and a 'restriction'. The triple test[52] applied by the ECtHR in the field of free speech is as follows:

- Is the restriction 'prescribed by law' (Art. 10 (2) ECHR)? Law means written or unwritten law. (The common law member states of the Council of Europe would have been discriminated against, as explained in the Sunday Times Case (No. 1),[53] if an institution such as contempt of court would have been declared not to satisfy the conditions of accessibility and foreseeability of an interference 'prescribed by law' for the sole reason that it was not set down in statutory form.[54])
- Is there a legitimate aim in the restriction placed on freedom of expression? There is a list of enumerated reasons in the case law of ECtHR, for example the restrictions based on the protection of public morals placed on pornography.[55]
- Is the restriction proportional to the aim sought by the authorities? Is the limit necessary in a democratic society? Free-speech concerns are balanced with opposing interests.

On the other hand, to prevent unlimited discretion on the part of self-regulatory bodies, it is of great relevance that good practices are adopted in their decision-making and other activities. Good practices make the action of those bodies less likely to hamper freedom of speech beyond the threshold of an interference deemed 'necessary in a democratic society'. Let us now focus on the guidelines for good (self-) regulatory practice discussed in more detail in chapters concerned with sectoral analysis:

- *External involvement in the design and operation of the self-regulatory scheme:* Two examples will illustrate this point of good practice. In the case of the video games industry the now dominant model for self-regulation on a pan-European level is the Pan European Games Information (PEGI) rating system, which was the result of a period of collaboration and negotiation between stakeholders from national self-regulatory organisations and the industry, and the project also received either advice or support from major video console manufacturers, experts in the field, and relevant stakeholders within the European Commission. Another example of ratings is the Platform for Internet Content Selection (PICS) which has the same shortcomings as any ratings system.[56]
- *Strong stakeholder involvement:* The Catalan Information Council had strong stakeholder involvement from its inception. This grassroots initiative by the Union of Journalists of Catalonia included members of civil society in all stages of its creation and functioning. At launch, the voluntary and consensual character of the council and code was emphasised and formalised by the signature of a document of creation; the council was established for a limited but renewable period of time. The agreement involves the provision of support, cooperation and financial support to the Council, and a promise to accept its moral authority and its decisions. Stakeholder participation fosters 'ownership' of the self-regulatory mechanism, increases its legitimacy, compliance and effectiveness, and from the point of view of free-speech concerns shows the mechanism in an altogether better light, which may well prevent challenges. The limits imposed via decisions taken by a self-regulatory body may be more likely considered as being within an acceptable field of discretion which does not breach fundamental rights.
- *Independence from the industry:* The key to achieving this lies in the membership of the board and the sources of financial support. To avoid the creation of a 'corporative' body, members of the public must be included in the main board. In the case of the UK PCC there is a majority of lay members and a minority of senior editors from across the industry (one of the advantages claimed for self-regulation is expertise), and an independent chairman who is appointed by the industry, but not engaged or connected with the industry.
- *Representation of consumers:* Press councils, for example, are not simply mechanisms for industry self-monitoring, and a way of opening up the mechanism is by means of including members of the public in their boards. Although one of the advantages claimed for self-regulation is industry expertise, the inclusion of the public makes the bodies less 'corporative' and distinguishes press councils from the tribunals created at professional organisations. In the case of the UK PCC and other press councils there is a majority of lay members and a minority of industry representatives. The approaches of the press councils differ as to, for example, the background of the members. Legal knowledge is deemed of importance at some councils, for example the chair is filled by lawyers in the Netherlands or Sweden. In the case of the UK, the PCC has a chairman appointed by the industry, but who is not engaged or connected with the industry.
- *Well-publicised rules and/or complaints procedure:* An example of good practice to ensure good communication of standards is NICAM, in which the Dutch

government worked with industry to raise the profile of the newly introduced system and inform the parents about the meaning of the different age categories and content descriptors. Successful branding of NICAM's Kijkwijzer symbols and the public campaign behind it have been credited as crucial factors in determining the future not only of NICAM but also, possibly, of other self-regulatory schemes in media classification. Another example of good communication (and of stakeholder involvement, and incidentally showing that these guidelines are intertwined) can be found in the discussion on self-regulation in mobile communication. The UK Code was drafted by a committee.[57] Informal consultation with content providers, infrastructure and handset suppliers and government at national and European Commission levels took place. The UK operators present included all four of the largest pan-European operators. A draft was presented for public consultation prior to the full publication of the code in January 2004.

• *Updating the scheme:* An example is the UK PCC where the Code of Practice is under constant review.

• *Reporting and publication requirements placed on self-regulatory bodies:* A standard for transparency of regulation is the publication of basic regulatory data on websites. Our survey on ISPs shows that there are many examples of good practice in this regard, such as active Internet self-regulatory hotlines. In the case of the print media, we praised the completeness of information available on websites such as the UK PCC or the German Presserat. There are also areas of the self-regulatory regimes that remain opaque and therefore it is difficult to gain an accurate picture of the overall level of self-regulatory activity. The Luxembourg Press Council is an example of an information-poor website. Ample disclosure of information is a good practice to enhance consumer trust.

Conclusions: the privatisation of censorship?

We close this chapter by posing again the question with which we began – 'Does media self-regulation advance or impede freedom of expression?' The answer depends upon issues such as how the powers of the self-regulatory institutions are in fact used as well as the strength and nature of the limitations that are being imposed on speech. We also need to make a clear distinction between freedom of expression in narrow legal terms and in practice. A blanket condemnation of self-regulation for being contaminated by the seed of censorship is as mistaken as the view that welcomes self-regulation on the sole grounds that it means (or appears to mean) less governmental intervention.

We have identified the possibility of a clash between the freedom-of-expression rights such as they are laid out in Article 10 of the ECHR, and the limitations on speech imposed by self-regulatory bodies. We acknowledge the tension that there is between the expediency and advantages offered by an industry self-regulating versus the need to take the limits imposed by the contractual and voluntary self-regulatory bodies seriously whenever they engage speech rights. We have tried to move the debate to the legal arena, beyond arguments of the left that believes self-regulation privatises censorship and that of the right that self-regulation means less government.

Once we see that self-regulation and freedom of speech need not necessarily be in opposition, a more constructive policy debate on the components that make up a self- or a co-regulatory regime can take place. From our analysis it emerges that self-regulatory bodies have the technical expertise which seems particularly relevant in a field in which there is fast technological change. Efficiency reasons justify regulatory decisions being taken at lower levels and in a decentralised manner, with courts being able to examine the correctness of the decision-making process in cases of complaints, thus ensuring that the protection of the law has opportunities to become effective. Procedural considerations are of great relevance. Regulatory decisions are strengthened by transparency in decision making and stakeholder participation. Curbs on free speech are justifiable when, for example, the balance of rights as set out in Article 10 is accomplished by bodies not only following, but which are seen to be following, impartial and legitimate procedures. This answer may be, however, too narrowly technical.

There are therefore two ways to answer the general question we posed at the beginning of this chapter. In legal terms the response is that whether curbs placed on free speech by self-regulation are justifiable depends on a number of variables, for example, the categorisation of self-regulatory institutions, their functions, and the extent to which they can be deemed as public/state authorities or if private, the extent to which their margin of action falls within contract or public law and the extent to which they could be subject to review by a higher authority. Even though this approach is useful in that it illustrates the basic legal concern with state and public authorities as well as the need to place fundamental (or constitutional) safeguards on any limitation of free speech, the answer may be ultimately unsatisfactory. The law is not clear, as the degree of 'horizontal protection' offered by ECHR for example (i.e. protection of speech rights against private bodies by controlling the restrictions placed on freedom of expression) has yet to be defined.

This research highlighted key background justifications that would be brought into play by courts and other bodies called upon to adjudicate in this new, fast-changing sector. What is abundantly clear is the need for caution as regards the free-expression implications of the current embrace of self-regulation, in other words, the margin of the acceptable in terms of private regulation via contractual and volunteer devices. The second way to answer the question we posed at the beginning of this chapter is by adopting a pragmatic and procedural case-by-case approach to those functions in regulation which were deemed by policy makers as more appropriately undertaken by private bodies. We argue that expedience should not dominate policy choices, and if self-regulation is an advantageous procedure for decision-making and control, then it is its implementation – including how due process considerations are taken into account – that will determine whether freedom-of-expression concerns are sufficiently respected.

What constitutes expression worthy of protection has been a new battleground with the rise of the Internet. The promise of the Internet, particularly to bring freedom of expression to closed societies, has brought with it a sometimes healthy scepticism of Internet policy per se: 'the best Internet policy is no Internet policy' we were told in the first years of the net. Our approach to freedom of expression has overwhelmingly focused on protecting *negative rights*, i.e. *freedom from* control as censorship. Most discussion of media freedom on the Internet remains focused on a case-by-case negative rights discussion. This is not to deny the importance of this: in conflict prevention and democratic transitions the role of the Internet is crucial.

Freedom from[58] control, particularly state control, is absolutely necessary in protecting broader freedom on the Internet. The question we would like to pose is whether it is sufficient. We must keep protecting the net from censorship. But we must not neglect the positive conditions for media freedom, nor should we be distracted by the crusade against censorship to the extent that we view the creation of any rules, or any dispute resolution as 'the thin end of the wedge'. Is it possible to identify rules that are steps on the slippery slope from those that are not? As Hosein put it discussing the Communications Decency Act:

> It is a case of the ever-articulated 'slippery slope' argument: if you begin with one form of content regulation, even with the most noble intents the rest will naturally follow. Other forms of regulation will arise either intentionally, using the 'verification' technologies to verify someone's geographic location to prevent access to non-indecent information, or less directly through the chilling of online speech for fear of surveillance or eventual censoring.[59]

Hosein takes some rather large steps in that paragraph. Whilst we can say that there is a danger of, as he calls it, 'chipping away at the marketplace for ideas', we need to be more specific about which forms of intervention and rule-setting are steps onto this slippery slope, and which are not. In order to assess the value or the threat posed by new developments such as co-regulatory search-level Internet filtering of the kind being deployed in the UK, Norway and Finland and elsewhere, we have to reach beyond the shrill opposition between rules and freedom posed in much of the debate. We need to acknowledge that rules can also open up spaces, and grow the space for debate. We also need to look beyond the law and return to the philosophical justifications of media freedom more generally: the arguments from truth, democracy and self-expression. Some rules genuinely do place us on a slippery slope to censorship, but others certainly do not.

Freedom to is also crucial. Free communication on the Internet will itself depend on maintenance of an open Internet. Real media freedom requires access and capabilities, content that can be easily shared, and public fora used by wide and overlapping communities of interest. There are various forms of rule-making taking place on the Internet, some private and some state led, some led by users themselves. It is the interplay between these public and private, voluntary and obligatory rules that will determine the future scope of freedom on the Internet.

Notes

1   See for example Hardy, Ch and Möller, Ch (2003) 'Putting Freedom Back on the Agenda: Why Regulation must be Opposed at All Costs', in Starr, S (ed.) *Spreading the Word on the Internet*, Vienna: OSCE.
2   A system in which 'the majority cannot travel as fast or as far as it would like if it recognizes the rights of individuals to do what, in the majority's terms, is the wrong thing to do'. (Dworkin, R (2000) *Taking Rights Seriously*, London: Duckworth, 9th impression, p. 204.)
3   Main legal instruments in the field of freedom of expression: *Universal instruments*: Universal Declaration of Human Rights 1948 (Article 19); ICCPR – International Covenant on Civil and Political Rights (Articles 19 and 20); *Regional instruments*: African Union: African [Banjul] Charter on Human and Peoples' Rights (Article 9); the Americas: OAS – Organization of American States, American Declaration of the Rights and Duties of Man and the American Convention on Human Rights (Pact of San Jose, promulgated 1969); and Europe: ECHR (Article 10); and an example of a *national instrument*: 1st Amendment to the US Constitution.
4   Gordon, W (2005) 'Copyright, Norms and the Problem of Private Censorship', in Griffiths, J and Suthersanen, U (eds) *Copyright and Free Speech: Comparative and International Analyses*, Oxford: OUP, pp. 71–72.
5   Collins, M (2001) *The Law of Defamation and the Internet*, Oxford: OUP, p. 344.
6   Barendt, E M (1995) *Broadcasting Law: A Comparative Study*, Oxford: Clarendon, p. 404.

7 Some view this control as excessive: Smith, P (1993) 'Censorship by Stealth', *Ent. L. R.* 4(3), 63–66.

8 In 2001, following extensive consultation, the former UK television regulator the ITC published its Guidance to Broadcasters on Interactive Television Services, on regulation of interactive advertising. The problem of sheer volume and an uncertainty about how many 'click throughs' in advertising can be regulated were identified as key challenges for the future.

9 The expression 'commercial speech' has American origins, but the ECtHR case law on the topic is developing: some ECtHR cases in which the restriction on expression was upheld in Strasbourg: *Markt Intern* v. *Germany* – 1989; *Jacubowski* v. *Germany* – 1994; *Casado Coca* v. *Spain* – 1994; *Lindner* v. *Germany* – 1999; and cases in which the restriction was deemed in breach of Art. 10: *Verein Gegen Tiefabriken* v. *Switzerland* – 2001; *Stambuk* v. *Germany* – 2002.

10 *De Haes and Gijsels* v. *Belgium*, Judgement by the European Court of Human Rights, 24/02/1997.

11 Griffiths, J (1999) 'The Human Rights Act 1998, Section 12 – Press Freedom over Privacy', *Ent. L. R.* 10(2), 36–41, at p. 40.

12 There is abundant case law supporting this position. To name one recent example: in 2005, in *Turhan* v. *Turkey*, the applicant was the author of a book entitled *Extraordinary War, Terror and Counter-terrorism* and under national law had been ordered to pay damages to a Secretary of State, since certain passages of his book were held to have been defamatory. The ECtHR found this to be a violation of Art. 10 ECHR as in a democratic society there is ample freedom to be critical of the authorities.

13 9 *BHRC* 587.

14 9 *BHRC* 587, paragraph 96.

15 See: Schulz, W and Held, T (2004) *Regulated Self-Regulation as a Form of Modern Government: An Analysis of Case Studies from Media and Telecommunications Law*, Eastleigh: University of Luton Press.

16 Palzer, C (2002) 'Co-Regulation of the Media in Europe: European Provisions for the Establishment of Co-Regulation Frameworks', *IRIS* 2002(6), www.obs.coe.int/oea_publ/iris/iris_plus/iplus6_2002.pdf.en

17 See: McGonagle, T (2002) 'Co-Regulation of the Media in Europe: The Potential for Practice of an Intangible Idea', *IRIS* 2002(10), www.obs.coe.int/oea_publ/iris/iris_plus/iplus10_2002.pdf.en

18 See for a full discussion: Barendt, E (1985) *Freedom of Speech*, Oxford University Press; Craufurd-Smith, R (1997) *Broadcasting Law and Fundamental Rights*, Clarendon Press; Schauer, F (1982) *Free Speech: A Philosophical Inquiry*, University of Cambridge Press; Sunstein, C R (1993) *Democracy and the Problem of Free Speech*, The Free Press.

19 Ganshof van der Meersch, W J (1980) 'Reliance in the Case-Law of the European Court of Human Rights, on the Domestic Law of the States', *Human Rights Law Journal* 1(13), 19. See also Leonardi, D A (1996) 'The Strasbourg System of Human Rights Protection: "Europeanisation" of the Law Through the Confluence of the Western Legal Traditions', *European Review of Public Law* 8, 1139–96. An alleged breach of the ECHR may be gauged against a set of common principles coming from the general body of the laws of the member states taken as a whole and, incidentally, by which the ECHR itself was inspired.

20 Schauer, F (2004) 'Media Law, Media Content and American Exceptionalism' (Iris Special: 'Political Debate and the Role of the Media: The Fragility of Free Speech'), *European Audiovisual Observatory*, 12/2004, pp. 61–70, at p. 67.

21 See: Craig, J D R (1998) 'Privacy and Free Speech in Germany and Canada: Lessons for an English Privacy Tort', *EHRLR* 2, 162–80, at p. 165.

22 Rosenfeld, M (2003) 'Hate Speech in Comparative Perspective: A Comparative Analysis', *Cardozo Law Review* 24, 1523.

23 Rappaport, K L (1998) 'In the Wake of Reno *v.* ACLU: The Constitutional Struggle in Western Constitutional Democracies with Internet Censorship and Freedom of Speech Online', *Am. U. Int'l L. Rev.* 13, 765, at p. 791.

24 Cabe, T, student note (2002) 'Regulation of Speech on the Internet: Fourth Time's The

Charm?', *Media L. & Pol'y* 11, 50, at p. 55. See on the European Union and the United States approaches to Internet regulation: Caral, J M E A (2004) 'Lessons from ICANN: Is Self-Regulation of the Internet Fundamentally Flawed?', *International Journal of Law and Information Technology* 12, 1, at p. 7.

25 See also: Black, J (1996) 'Constitutionalising Self-Regulation', *MLR* 59, 24, pp. 24–55.

26 Mahoney, P (1997) 'Universality versus Subsidiarity in the Strasbourg Case Law on Free Speech: Explaining some Recent Judgments', *EHRLR* 4, 364–79, at p. 368.

27 By 'negative' we mean the notion of negative rights (Berlin, I, 1969, 'Two Concepts of Liberty', in Berlin, I (2002) *Four Essays on Liberty*, Oxford: Oxford University Press) and freedom of expression as a negative right which is defined against state interference rather than as a positive right which can be claimed in itself.

28 McManis, Ch R (1999) 'The Privatization (or "Shrink Wrapping") of American Copyright Law', *Cal. L. Rev.* 87, 173–90.

29 Lessig, L (1999) *Code and Other Laws of Cyberspace*, New York: Basic Books, at p. 99. See also, by the same author, (2004) *Free Culture: How Big Media Uses Technology and the Law to Lock Down Culture and Control Creativity*, Penguin Press. Available free for non-commercial use under a Creative Commons licence on: http://cyberlaw-temp.stanford.edu/freeculture.pdf

30 Lessig, L (1999), op. cit., at p. 136.

31 See the discussion on the conflict between contract law and free speech rights as regards contracts of silence *vis-à-vis* the First Amendment in the United States, Garfield, A E (1997–98) 'Promises of Silence: Contract Law and Freedom of Speech', *Cornell L. Rev.* 83, 261, at pp. 343–60.

32 Campbell, A J (1999) 'Self-Regulation and the Media', *Federal Communications Law Journal* 51, 711, at p. 717.

33 Weinberg, J (1996–97) 'Rating the Net', *Hastings Communications & Ent. L. J.* 19, 453, at p. 454. The software may of course filter too much or too little; see for example: Birnhack, M D and Rowbottom, J H (2004) 'Symposium: Do Children Have the Same First Amendment Rights as Adults? Shielding Children: The European Way', *Chi.-Kent. L. Rev.* 79, 175, at p. 213.

34 'Finnish ISPs Must Voluntarily Block Access', *Home EDRI-gram*, Number 3.18, 8 September 2005, at: www.edri.org/edrigram/number3.18/censorshipFinland

35 Kerr, R L (2002) 'Impartial Spectator in the Marketplace of Ideas: The Principles of Adam Smith as an Ethical Basis for Regulation of Corporate Speech', *Journalism and Mass Communications Quarterly* 79(2), 394–415, at p. 407.

36 Silber, J, Judgement *R (on the application of Ford)* v. *The Press Complaints Commission* [2001] *EWHC Admin* 683, CO/1143/2001, 31 July 2001.

37 Pinker, R (2002) 'Press Freedom and Press Regulation – Current Trends in their European Context', in *Communications Law* 7(4), 102–7, at p. 104, and Pinker, R (1999) 'Human Rights and Self-regulation of the Press', in *Communications Law* 4(2), 51–54, at p. 53.

38 Silber, J expressed in the judgement that 'the Commission correctly in my view accepts for the purposes of the present permission application, that it is arguable whether it is a Public Authority for the purposes of s 6 of the Human Rights Act 1998 and is amenable to judicial review', in: *R (on the application of Ford)* v. *The Press Complaints Commission* [2001] *EWHC Admin* 683, CO/1143/2001, 31 July 2001.

39 Bradley, A W and Ewing, K D (2003) *Constitutional and Administrative Law*, 13th edn, Harlow: Pearson Longman, p. 523.

40 Voorhoof, D, 'European Court of Human Rights: Banning of Blasphemous Video Not in Breach of Freedom of (Artistic) Expression', *IRIS* 1997: 1/8.

41 Case of *Peck* v. *The United Kingdom*, application 44647/98, 28 January 2003.

42 Case of *Peck* v. *The United Kingdom*, paragraph 109.

43 *R* v. *ASA*, ex p. The Insurance Service [1990] 2 *Admin. L. R.* 77, per Glidewell LJ.

44 Craig, P and De Burca, G (2003) *EU Law Text, Cases and Materials*, Oxford University Press, p. 211.

45 http://cmiskp.echr.coe.int/tkp197/view.asp?item=1&portal=hbkm&action=html&high light=selisto%20%7C%20finland&sessionid=3810400&skin=hudoc-en, at paragraph 54.

46 Thorgeirsdottir, H (2004) 'Self-Censorship Among Journalists: A (Moral) Wrong or a Violation of ECHR Law', *EHRLR* 4, 383–99, at pp. 397 and 398.

47 Thorgeirsdottir, H, op. cit., at pp. 398 and 399.

48 Frydman, B and Rorive, I (2002) *Racism, Xenophobia and Incitement Online: European Law and Policy*, www.selfregulation.info/iapcoda/rxio-background-020923.htm

49 Birnhack, M D and Rowbottom, J H (2004) 'Symposium: Do Children Have the Same First Amendment Rights as Adults? Shielding Children: The European Way', *Chi.-Kent L. Rev.* 79, 175, at pp. 205–7.

50 Similarly, as regards how the conflict between the private law of contract and the funda-mental human rights set out in ECHR may work out in English law, see: McKendrick, E (2000) *Contract Law*, 4th edn, Basingstoke: Palgrave, pp. 13–16.

51 Ahlert, C, Marsden, C and Yung, C (2004) 'How "Liberty" Disappeared in Cyberspace: The Mystery Shopper Tests Internet Content Self-Regulation' (as summarised in Tambini, D (2004) 'How ISPs Could Curb Our Freedom', *The Guardian*, 17 May).

52 Voorhoof, D (1998) 'Guaranteeing the Freedom and Independence of the Media', in *Media and Democracy*, Strasbourg: Council of Europe Publishing, p. 35.

53 (1979–80) *EHRR* 2, 245, paragraph 47. Relevant for the study of this case are: Teff, H and Munro, C R (1976) *Thalidomide: The Legal Aftermath*, Chichester: Saxon House, and Duffy, P J (1980) 'The Sunday Times Case: Freedom of Expression, Contempt of Court and the European Convention on Human Rights', *HR Rev.* 5, 17–53.

54 Cremona, J J (1990) 'The Interpretation of the Word "Law" in the Jurisprudence of the European Court of Human Rights', *Selected Papers 1946–1989*, 188, lists various cases where the word 'law' occurs.

55 Birnhack, M D and Rowbottom, J H, op. cit., at p. 193.

56 Birnhack, M D and Rowbottom, J H, op. cit., at pp. 213–14. The PICS system is a rating system that content providers and third parties can use to rate materials: in theory it allows user control of material suitable for children in a way that is flexible and not imposed by a centralised source, but as with any filtering software it might become dominated by the big businesses that have the ability to self-regulate and if it does not fulfil expectations might lead to further calls for statutory regulation (or censorship).

57 The committee included the UK six network operators and virtual operators (3, Vodafone, Orange, T-Mobile, Virgin Mobile, O2) and the consultant Hamish McLeod, who acted as spokesman for the group.

58 The distinction between positive and negative rights will be familiar to many. It is attrib-uted to Isaiah Berlin. In his 1958 lecture 'Two Concepts of Liberty' he distinguished between freedom from outside interference and freedom to which entailed the liberation of the human. Berlin, I (1969), op. cit.

59 Hosein, I (Gus) (2004) 'Open Society and the Internet: Future Prospects and Aspirations', in Möller, Ch and Amouroux, A (eds) *The Media Freedom Internet Cookbook*, Vienna: OSCE, p. 250, www.osce.org/publications/rfm/2004/12/12239_89_en.pdf

12 Conclusion

Current challenges in media self-regulation

This book has offered an overview, a collection of key resources, and a review of the key challenges for media self-regulation. In this final chapter, we attempt to distil the key points for practitioners who may be reflecting on their own self-regulatory strategy in the light of recent developments and also for recommendations for public policy. The first decade of the commercial World Wide Web was one in which there was broad-based public policy support for self-regulation in general, and particularly in communications. What emerges from reflection on that decade and upon the vogue for more complex co-regulatory structures increasingly determines the framework for freedom of communication on the Internet, and therefore for freedom of communication generally.

Harm, the public interest, speech freedoms and institution building

In communications, as in other business sectors, there are clear incentives for service providers to develop a code of conduct and a self-regulatory framework. Even those who argue that private organisations' first responsibility is to their shareholders would agree that trust in products can be improved, and markets thereby expanded by creating clear criteria of quality and ethics and maintaining them. Most now accept that some form of collective self-restraint across a sector – particularly a new sector – may be both necessary and cost-effective.

This general tendency of providers to self-regulate has been well illustrated by this study of self-regulation in the converging digital media sectors. The framework of Internet self-regulation – through codes of conduct and national hotlines – is well established in Europe, and self-regulation has developed with support from state and civil society. There are now many 'model codes' already developed by public authorities for deployment by the private sector, and an array of bodies, both private and public, ready to advise on self-regulation.[1] At every point in the delivery chain basic self-regulatory functions have been developed: services for rating and filtering of content are being deployed by users, by providers and by private bodies; service providers accept liability for content and procedures for restricting access under certain conditions; filters, trust marks and access controls impact on the user–content relationship.

Codes of conduct have been developed to specify and also to publicise the evolving regime under which users conduct their communications. Some codes are specific to individual companies and others apply across entire sectors or even several distinct markets. Some are restricted to one national market and others cross boundaries. As we have seen, procedures are often imperfect and sometimes lack the basic standards of due process and transparency. On some occasions codes are developed as part of a genuine attempt to take corporate responsibility for harm and increase trust, and in others they are a fig leaf, adopted with the specific and limited goal of seeing off a threat of legislation. And whilst there is a growing awareness that effective self-regulation requires significant resources, actors are actively seeking allegiances that will enable further international and intersectoral cooperation in this field, thereby reducing costs.

With the development of self-regulation in the communications sectors that are currently converging on the Internet come significant strategic challenges. On the one hand, basic rights concerns are raised. Whilst in a constitutional and legal sense freedom of speech may be protected by a preference for self-regulation over-regulation by public authority – simply because the state plays a lesser role in speech restriction – the users attempting to access ideas and express themselves may be indifferent to the source of controls. A walled garden administered through cooperation by parents, teachers and service providers may feel just as restrictive to a student or a child as one administered by a public regulatory agency. Self-regulation may involve fewer obligations and pressures for transparency and fairness in the processes of speech regulation. In countries with a higher level of constitutional protection against state control of speech we find that there remain other concerns for freedom of expression: a film made unavailable because it was rated by an industry body, and as a result a major retailer has refused to stock it, may be just as difficult to access as one listed by a culture ministry.[2] Whilst the self-regulatory solution may appear to be a dynamic and responsive solution, inherently conducive to free expression, it may in fact offer fewer safeguards for freedom of expression if it is less transparent and operates with lower procedural standards.

On the other hand, new challenges are thrown up by the process of technological convergence itself. Internet content is the paradigm case of convergent self-regulation. Codes of conduct that were first applied only to parallel sectors such as broadcasting and the press are being applied to online content, and codes that were applied to Internet content are now overlapping with codes applied to other sectors such as games and mobile Internet access. But as we have seen from the review of converging content sectors, the converging media markets each in fact have a complex co-regulatory system involving a combination of licensing, public regulation by an independent regulatory agency (IRA), self-regulatory board and the ultimate possibility of legislation should self-regulation fail. In some cases, for example video on demand or premium content on the Internet, new self-regulatory bodies are developing. These tend to be adapting to the changing ecology of self-regulation by establishing niche roles in an entrepreneurial manner. Clearly, the extent to which such bodies can flexibly adapt to convergence, without maintaining false boundaries between industry sectors, will be crucial for their medium-term sustainability. Should self-regulatory organisations constitute new barriers to market entry, to convergence between sectors, or to cross-border trade, they will begin to have a negative impact on economic performance and consumer welfare.

Global standards and international variation

What is effective Internet self-regulation? There is no agreed answer to that question. If the benchmark of effectiveness is that users are unable to receive content that is either illegal in their jurisdictions or that they consider inappropriate to receive, then much remains to be done. Even taking the case of the most extreme pornography featuring children, experts agree that the amount of material available via the Internet continues to grow, and it is easier rather than more difficult to find. The use of the Internet as a distribution mechanism for the most distressing evidence of illegal terrorist acts, and of incitement to those acts clearly illustrates the difficulty of censoring the Internet. The central problem is not only the end-to-end nature of the Internet – the fact that it is possible to upload anonymously and in remote countries, and to mirror sites – but the problem of jurisdiction, the diversity of applicable standards and of law applying to Internet content, and the varying inclination of various authorities to implement standards.

One interesting development is the emergence of international content standards. We saw this first with child pornography itself, which until the advent of the Internet was not illegal per se in some countries. Whilst standards and definitions do differ, there is now a near total global agreement on illegality of child pornography, and an international network of hotlines that is growing to deal with the problem, as discussed in Chapter 7. In other areas such as extreme pornography and hate speech, standards are much more varied across the globe and international cooperation is more difficult. Regulators and law enforcement have to rely more on criminal prosecutions of users who download material, and policy makers fall back on the creation of new categories of content that it is illegal to download.[3]

Media self-regulation in new democracies in Eastern Europe and the CIS

With the development of international practices in the area of Internet content come several dilemmas: to what extent can practices developed in a few advanced democracies be applied effectively in isolation from other countries, many of which have different political cultures? And if there is a need to make self-regulation more effective, what concerns might we have about sharpening the tools of Internet co-regulation when they may be applied elsewhere – in countries that remain despotic and bent on controlling the subversive potential of the Internet?

The performance of self-regulation in the media sector of the new democracies is patchy. Taking the former Soviet Union, and the new EU accession states as examples, we see nonetheless that self-regulation is picking up momentum across the region.[4] Many local initiatives in self-regulation have the support of overseas funding organisations such as the UK government's Department for International Development (DFID), the European Union, the United States Agency for International Development (USAID), the Open Society Institute and several others.[5] Local organisations throughout Eastern Europe and the Commonwealth of Independent States (CIS) are starting self-regulatory initiatives. For example, the Russian Union of Journalists now opens membership of its ethics tribunal to civil society, which would bring the current Grand Jury system in line with modern Western European press councils.[6] The struggle between the governmental authorities wanting to impose regulation on the media and the media offering self-regulation as an alternative, running through the history of press councils in Western Europe, also plays out in the East. An example was the attempts in 2002 by the Russian Federal Legislature to introduce anti-terrorist amendments to the Russian Law on Mass Media in order to regulate coverage of events such as the siege and later rescue operation of hostages held by Chechen rebels in a Moscow theatre. The media asked President Putin to use his veto, which he did. The (Moscow) media persuaded the authorities to rely on self-regulation to 'put their house in order' and thus avert the threat of legislation.

Beyond the field of journalistic ethics, there are self-regulatory bodies in other sectors, notably the long-established practice in advertising. Although the codes set up by the industry may be weakened by the lack of implementation mechanisms, the advertising self-regulatory bodies generally provide expertise for administrative inquiries concerning complaints regarding the content of advertising or the bodies are consulted by the authorities when contemplating reform of legislation.[7] Self-regulatory mechanisms are seen by the industry as a regulatory approach that addresses a perceived need, but at the same time offers protection for editorial freedom by maintaining arms-length distance from the authorities and/or the powerful. To the public, self-regulation brings alternative dispute resolution mechanisms faster than the courts.

Self-regulation in the new EU member states

In new EU member states, self-regulation does not have a long-standing tradition. One of the fields where it is rapidly gaining greater importance is in advertising. At the time of joining the European Union, four (Hungary, the Czech and Slovak Republics and Slovenia) out of ten countries had already established self-regulation organisations (SROs) and were members of the pan-European trade body EASA (European Advertising Standards Alliance). Another five (Poland, Lithuania, Cyprus, Latvia and Estonia) planned to establish self- and co-regulatory systems by the end of 2005.

Another good example of media self-regulation in new member states is in the press, where the era of freedom of expression started in the late 1980s and early 1990s. In most of these countries, laws on publishing and broadcasting were passed in the early 1990s. Around the same time codes of ethics for journalists were adopted (Slovakia – 1990; Malta and Poland – 1991; Latvia – 1992; Slovenia – 1993; Hungary – 1994; Lithuania – 1996; Cyprus – 1997; Estonia – 1998; Czech Republic – 2000).[8]

With regard to the Internet, self-regulation is in its early stages in the new member states. Only three new member states (Hungary, Estonia and Slovenia) have self-regulation for ISPs at end-2004 and of these, only Hungary has established a code of conduct. Four other states (Cyprus, Hungary, Lithuania and Poland) have created hotlines for reporting illegal and/or harmful content.

In general, self-regulation is regarded as something new. Although media self-regulation and professional ethics are familiar concepts within most of the new member states, there appears to be difficulty, on the part of those applying regulations, in interpreting which are statutory and which are self-regulated.[9] This can be attributed to the political climate within these states prior to the dissolution of the Soviet Union, and the socio-economic structures that were, and no longer are, the norm. The rapid adjustment to Western standards is an evolutionary process which will take time. Implementation of self-regulatory ideas may differ, often sharply, from the Western European models from which inspiration was drawn, but the institutional idea of self-regulation has been introduced and clearly seems to be gaining momentum.

The effective use of self-regulation, like democratic citizenship, requires a delicate balance of self-interest and enlightened self-interest that may not be present in the newest democracies. The development of successful self-regulatory bodies in former dictatorships such as Spain show that this is, however, a temporary condition that can be resolved given conducive civic and economic conditions.

On the other hand, there is a growing body of evidence, mostly provided by the pioneering work of the OpenNetInitiative and Harvard University's Berkman Center, and the work of Edelman and Zittrain,[10] that non-democratic countries are developing effective tools of Internet filtering, blocking and censorship. Many have argued that the tools of self-regulation, because they constitute an apparatus, and even some software tools for finding, listing, removing and blocking content provide legitimacy to the actions of authoritarian regimes. This is a very difficult problem to resolve. In advanced democracies we need to self-regulate in order to promote positive freedom: to ensure that we can use this new medium as a means to promote democracy, self-expression and the search for truth without fear or harm. Self-regulation, including software solutions, can be technologies of freedom in that sense. In authoritarian countries, on the other hand, we see the same or similar technologies being used in the service of state censorship, and rightly our concern there is with negative freedom: freedom from the state. The question is whether we can concern ourselves with both.

An independent, self-regulating Internet: myth and reality

Clearly, the ideal of a pristine Internet, free from regulation, is a myth, and not a particularly helpful one. Internet communication, like all communication is a social practice that comes with responsibilities, ethics, norms, disputes and harms. Whether the necessary rules are formal or informal, and whether they should be agreed with the specific involvement of state institutions or formal democratic accountability are pragmatic questions to be resolved through public debate case by case. As the Internet embeds itself further in everyday life, so too will concerns about content and its consequences, and we contend that in Europe, and even in the United States, the illusion that the Internet can constitute a 'free' sphere separate from social life will fade. The debate about the Internet content layer – which is part of social life and regulated as such – must as far as possible be separated from debates about Internet infrastructure. The principle of end-to-end can be retained whilst ensuring that users themselves are empowered to use and trust the medium.

In discussions of media freedom and the Internet, we have been rightly concerned with the problem of censorship. But discussions of regulation need also take on the positive question of what form of policy intervention may be acceptable – even required – if the medium of the Internet is to be more fully free. In our approach to the Internet we need to have a sense that norms, rules and codes are necessary in all human communication. In 2003–4, several major companies, including Microsoft, have removed discussion group services from their servers and no longer offer them. Providing discussion groups led to an increased possibility that their servers hosted illegal content, and moderated discussion proved too expensive to provide. So it was the inability to develop affordable rules and codes that resulted in the closing of some public fora for debate.

The Internet requires us not only to consider freedom of speech but in some ways it requires us to return to first philosophical principles with the notion of free speech. At one level the question is an age-old one about the value of universal human rights principles in a widely diverse world where some have access to a cornucopia of information services and others remain excluded. But rules, whether formal or informal, are required for communication, and these will emerge. In discussions of Internet regulation we want to move the debate on from a sterile opposition between rules and freedom. There is no freedom without rules; the challenge is to ensure that rules are democratically set at the necessary minimum, procedurally fair, accountable and in the public interest. In freedom of expression more generally, the three-part test that applies is that restrictions must be:

1   provided in law;
2   for the purposes of safeguarding a legitimate private or public interest;
3   necessary to secure this interest.[11]

Only if we acknowledge this do the real challenges for Internet governance come into view. 'No rules is good rules' is an easy position to take. But the task is more difficult and pressing. We need to identify bad rules, and think harder about how rules are agreed and upheld.

Shaping self- and co-regulation: key issues

Those developing self-regulatory strategies will have to take into account this broader concern with free expression, and it is their activities that will shape the future of rule-making on the Internet more than governments. However, they do so in a context that is not of their own choosing. In the current environment they will have to take the following into account:

*   *Competition*: Developing codes of conduct, like standards setting more generally, can be a part of a repertoire of anti-competitive practices.[12] Whilst it may be desirable from a public policy perspective to exclude 'rogue' providers, doing so may result in a reduction of competition, against the consumer interest. This issue has been the subject of a great deal of attention from regulators, particularly where independent regulators are considering whether to encourage, and how to audit, self-regulatory activities.[13] At one level the problem is unavoidable. Adam Smith noted that wherever competing companies come together in the same room they will seek to collude.[14] And if codes of conduct and enforcement do improve standards they are almost certain to raise barriers of entry, so safeguards must be put in place to ensure that this is not subject to abuse.
*   *Convergence*: Any attempt to develop a code of conduct in media sectors should have a convergence strategy. Sooner or later the following issues will emerge: (a) content that does not fall within definitions of the sector; (b) content that falls within definitions of several sectors. This could result in expensive disputes or regulatory arbitrage, or disputes between regulators. Proactive strategists in self-regulation may aim to achieve efficiency gains by cooperating across sectors (as has NICAM in the Netherlands) or across countries (as has PEGI). Those that attempt to remain specialised in a sector may find themselves isolated and unable to compete in the market for self-regulation.
*   *Audit, co-regulation and public engagement*: Globally, the pressure is for improved standards in self-regulation, and external audit of self-regulation. This may be formal, as in the Ofcom (2004) criteria for considering transfer of powers to self-regulatory bodies, or the UK DCMS Select Committee's report into Privacy and Related Matters of 2003, or informal through public analysis and debate. Co-regulation as an audit of self-regulatory bodies introduces some backstop guarantees of quality and due process whilst retaining the freedom of operation

of the regulator. Whether this co-regulatory development is to be considered an attack on free speech cannot be resolved in the abstract.

Challenges for sustaining the global Internet

Isaiah Berlin made a rather pessimistic note in closing his essay 'Two Concepts of Liberty',[15] implying that contained in the orientation to positive liberty was a seed of repression, as a concern with 'freedom to' was often at the core of authoritarian movements. We have been using his concept of liberty in a more restricted and pragmatic sense, not as a tool in the critique of moral philosophy, but perhaps we need to take this seriously. Some would say[16] that *any* attempt to regulate the Internet, or any policy that would even shape it into a safer place should be resisted. We would say that this argument is potentially damaging for instilling media freedoms in the positive sense.

The 'Declaration of Independence of Cyberspace' cited at the beginning of this book was premature and unrealistic. Freedom of expression on the Internet is not about the absence of rules, or even of law. It is about ensuring that the procedures of rule-making are fair, transparent and democratic. This has been a challenge in any media sector, but the more so in a global medium, which is why international organisations and international debate are so important.

There are tendencies in the development of self-regulatory institutions that give rise for concern, and should be monitored. These include:

* Tendencies to 'mission creep', whereby self-regulatory bodies expand the range of their activities and the categories of content that are regulated, either through empire building or through pressure from government and civil society. For instance, the Internet Watch Foundation (IWF) in the United Kingdom was set up specifically as an agency dealing with child pornography. The body now also takes responsibility to take down other forms of illegal content such as racist and copyright-infringing material, and the UK government is also consulting on adding new categories of illegal pornography which the IWF could be used to take down. Clearly the presence of an institution invites all sorts of 'Christmas Tree' dangers whereby more and more categories of content are 'hung from' the existing list of illegal content the IWF should remove, 'because it is there'.
* Self-regulation in advanced democracies that enjoy protection of freedom of speech could provide an inappropriate model for countries that do not. Russia and China both made announcements of self-regulatory schemes for the Internet in recent years. In China's case the 2002 code, coordinated by the Internet Society of China and signed by many of the key ISPs included the following article:

Article 9   We Internet information service providers pledge to abide by the state regulations on Internet information service management conscientiously and shall fulfil the following disciplinary obligations in respect of Internet information service:

1.   Refraining from producing, posting or disseminating pernicious information that may jeopardize state security and disrupt social stability, contravene laws and regulations and spread superstition and obscenity. Monitor

the information publicized by users on websites according to law and remove the harmful information promptly;

2.　Refraining from establishing links to the websites that contain harmful information so as to ensure that the content of the network information is lawful and healthy;

3.　Observing laws and regulations concerning intellectual property rights in the course of producing, posting and propagating information on the Internet;

4.　Encouraging people to use the Internet in an ethical way, to enhance the Internet ethical sense and reject the spread of harmful information on the Internet;

5.　If the Internet service provider discovers information which is inconsistent with the law on its website, it will remove it.[17]

This code of conduct, which would appear to constitute specific obligations on service providers to restrict religious and political speech, and promptly remove content that 'disrupts social stability', would give some cause for concern in a country where many had hoped the Internet could provide a healthy alternative to state media. The code clearly in some respects resembles the codes of conduct that have been developed in European countries, justifies those that argue that the rise of codes and soft takedown obligations constitute a step onto a serious slippery slope towards restriction of expression.

To conclude the book, we state the conclusions that we draw from our research for the sustainable development of self-regulation,[18] to guarantee consumer rights, freedom of expression and an Internet free of censorship by either government or private actor. Regulability – which Lessig famously argued was a fact[19] – must in our view be used to the advantage of all Internet users, to ensure the continued development of the medium into a ubiquitous and positive pluralistic medium. We make *eighteen* recommendations on media self-regulation, which specifically can help the effective development of media codes of conduct, of which twelve apply to the 'new media': co-regulation of Internet content, online computer games and mobile.

Our key finding is that technological progress brings about change and self-regulation can respond more rapidly and efficiently than state regulation. There is no universally acceptable recipe for successful self-regulation, as regimes must be adjusted to the needs of each sector and other circumstances (technological change, changes in policy to respond to changes in technology, a country's legal system, case law of European courts, and so on).

To illustrate, broadcasting is an area in which technological progress brought complexity and the increase of self-regulation responds in part to policy changes prompted by those technological changes. The European monopolistic broadcasting model which developed with radio, maintained for television, was first challenged by commercial terrestrial services. Further pluralism brought about first by cable and satellite, and then digital technologies including the Internet, forced changes in the regulatory environment, and public authorities increasingly delegated the power to regulate to market actors. The trend is towards continued delegation (with regulatory authority audit of the resources, procedures, transparency, stakeholder participation and market effect of the self-regulatory scheme adopted).

Key recommendation: resourcing self-regulation

Adequate resourcing is the key to successful self-regulation. Policy on self-regulation must take into account a broader view of the sustainability, effectiveness and impact on free speech of self-regulatory codes and institutions. We recommend applying an auditing procedure for establishing self-regulatory institutions and codes. Given the centrality of speech freedoms in constitutions, we hold that this regulatory audit burden is a minimal price to pay for effective self-regulation in the public interest.

Convergence, the single market and future trends in self-regulation

Significant economies of scale are likely to be realised through functional integration of certain key aspects of the content regulation value chain horizontally across sectors and across EU member states. Computer games rating has illustrated the potential for developing a common pan-European ratings structure. Germany and the Netherlands operate a cross-media rating and labelling scheme. In a situation of increasing cross-border trade within the European Union, this trend is set to continue. An important use of the Internet is to access news. Journalistic ethics online, often an extension of systems developed for the print media over decades, has the potential for a pan-European structure. Online news services, online versions of newspapers, and news aggregators, as well as self-regulatory mechanisms to which they may belong, could soon acquire relevance beyond national borders. The readership may start seeking access to self-regulatory bodies and complaint mechanisms located outside national jurisdictions.

Although the *legislative* role of the European institutions is currently limited (with no European constitutional settlement following the failure at ratification in summer 2005), several recommendations have been made as cited below. And it is likely that, in a single-market context, there will be a significant self-interest on the part of industry in self-regulation. More research and development, benchmarking and technical assistance in disseminating best practice between member states is clearly essential to assist industry bodies in the exploitation of economies of scale and scope in self-regulation across the various converging media sectors in the single market (SS.4.10–15), and to ensure greater effectiveness of self-regulation.

The general trend is towards an expansion of scope of co-regulation, often at the expense of statutory regulation. IRAs such as Ofcom in the United Kingdom are exploring the possibility of 'sunsetting' particular regulations in the event that co-regulatory alternatives can be found.

Recommendation 1

Clear procedures for auditing self-regulatory schemes should be devised and implemented, according to transparent criteria. We explain the criteria and process in Recommendations 12–15.

Funding and sustainability of media self-regulatory regimes

Where there is a clear industry interest in self-regulation to improve market penetration, or to head off threats of statutory regulation, there are adequate market incentives for resources to be allocated to self-regulatory activities. However, the calculation of enlightened self-interest required is vulnerable to changing personnel and market structures such that self-regulatory institutions, where they do not have access to levy funding, will not enjoy the funding necessary to meet standard requirements of transparency, accountability and due process.

Recommendation 2

Where funding is provided to encourage self-regulation, funding should be directed to those self-regulatory institutions that are able to fulfil public interest criteria, including freedom-of-expression tests, and therefore likely to develop into self-sustaining codes and institutions.

A wide variety of models of self-regulatory tools exist. Some of these are based on adequate standards of transparency, inclusion, due process, resources and so forth, and some clearly are not. As a result there is some concern with the development of codes that insufficient standards apply to both law enforcement/child protection and protection of freedom-of-expression rights. If these mechanisms are improperly structured we can expect public harm to result in the medium term.

Recommendation 3

The European Commission, Council of Europe, and OSCE should develop and publish clear benchmarks for acceptable levels of transparency, accountability and due process and appeal, particularly with regard to communications regulation that may impact upon freedom of expression.

Recommendation 4

Self-regulatory institutions should follow the guidelines for transparency and access to information that are followed by public and government bodies according to international best practice. At the very least, self-regulators should provide summaries of complaints by clause of code of conduct, numbers of adjudications and findings of adjudications on their website. Failure to conform to these baseline standards of transparency should be viewed as a failure of self-regulation.

Self-regulation and freedom of expression

Self-regulation has an ambivalent and tense relationship with fundamental rights to freedom of expression. At one level this depends on definitions. In some cases, and particularly in the United States, case law tends to favour a view of freedom of expression as a negative right: it exists where there is an absence of state interference with communication. In other traditions, freedom of expression is equally endangered by private bodies such as corporations. In the former case, self-regulation is likely to be viewed favourably in terms of its impact on freedom of expression as by definition expression is not endangered by non-state entities. However, this does not mean that positive rights to free speech are protected by self-regulatory institutions. On the contrary, because self-regulatory institutions are not public bodies, they may be less accountable. Self-regulation could be used instead of government regulation to avoid constitutional free-speech issues when regulating more stringently: for example, broadcasting pre-publication control as carried out by the FSF in Germany and similar bodies in other countries.

Self-regulation offers a complaints procedure and alternative dispute resolution. However, here again there is a danger lurking, as there may be less protection for rights than with the protection offered by the law. For example, injunctions, fines and sanctions may be unavailable within a self-regulatory regime, or a decision of a self-regulatory body may not be reviewable by a court. Similarly, victims may not be able to access financial compensation if complaints are resolved by self-regulation rather than in court.

Multi-stakeholder participation in co-regulation

A key lesson is that it is essential to achieve a balance between the self-interest of the industry represented on the board of a self-regulatory body and the participation of lay members. This combination strengthens its legitimacy. This, in turn, may lead to a virtuous circle in which the enlightened self-interest of the industry can help the media to willingly fund the mechanism of code implementation, and abide by the decisions of a self-regulatory body.

Recommendation 5

Industry professionals should constitute a minority on boards of content self-regulatory bodies. Measures should be adopted to ensure that bodies that are 100 per cent funded by their industry are not captured by it. These measures could include: fixed tenure for board members, dismantling separate 'funding boards' (who may attempt to hold regulatory boards to ransom), and replacing them with a compulsory levy on industry participants, as currently applies to premium telephony in, for instance, the United Kingdom. This transparent and guaranteed funding then permits industry participants to play a much greater expert role in advising the regulator, with less conflict of interest.

Technical knowledge and media self-regulation

Despite recent progress, consumer groups often lack the technical and legal knowledge of the application of media self-regulation to a given media sector, for example the Internet, especially in new capabilities of mobile and broadband.

Recommendation 6

If co-regulation is to operate successfully, it is essential that IRAs or ministries, in cooperation with the European Commission, ensure that a continual programme of technical and regulatory education be provided to consumer groups for their effective participation and trust in co-regulatory fora.

Internet co-regulation

The following twelve recommendations are directed to those public and private institutions engaged in Internet regulation. The response to the extensive surveys conducted in the research for this book has been exceptionally meagre, demonstrating a lack of resources devoted to self-regulation within ISPs. In part, this may be because self-regulation in the sector is so recent compared to the other sectors studied. Following the cross-sectoral analyses, we recommend a significant role in inculcating a regulatory culture by the IRAs in each country. The several countries conforming to best practice may find the co-regulatory audit concept, in particular, a relatively low hurdle to cross. Nevertheless, we believe that co-regulation will encourage publicity for those best practice schemes, and therefore better public awareness of their work. For the other under-resourced market actors and their schemes, co-regulatory audit will act as a much-needed reality check on the resource required for effective self-regulation in sectors where freedom-of-speech concerns are so critical. We begin with four recommendations on strengthening the relationship between industry self-regulatory codes and user-based solutions: holistic thinking and media literacy, filtering, hotlines and trustmark accreditation.

Holistic thinking about all unsolicited content types

Inappropriate and harmful content is becoming a massive problem – unsolicited adult content is part of a larger content category including unsolicited commercial communication (spam) and unsolicited code (including malicious code – viruses and spyware). It threatens trust in the medium as a whole, including e-commerce and even e-mail. Legislation is dealing with some of these issues, such as spam.

Recommendation 7

Self-regulation arrangements should take account of these new initiatives and any changes to their role that may result. There is insufficient 'joined up' thinking at national and regional level about the interrelationship between different layers of the Internet: content, physical and software protocols. Adult content cannot be regulated in isolation from other types of content regulation, such as spam blocking, and their effect on other layers.

Filtering and hotlines

Where filtering rules and self-regulatory hotlines have been instituted, there has been a heroic assumption that users will install technical solutions and be aware of hotlines, and that the 100 billion web pages will be self-classified or policed effectively. This is becoming increasingly unlikely.

Recommendation 8

Technical enthusiasts or global user communities without real self-interest cannot achieve the coordination that is necessary. Future studies of filters and hotlines should continue to focus not only on the technical capabilities of filtering technology or police cooperation, but on the skills of users, parents, children and others and awareness and ease-of-use of these technologies.

Moreover, end-user software, for instance filters and search engines, raise significant problems for freedom of expression. For instance, popular search engines may have rules for search that prioritise content inappropriately for specific cultures: by language, content type or software format.

Recommendation 9

It is essential that studies of filters be instituted that examine the freedom-of-speech implications of commercial ranking of sites, pages, content types and languages. ISP or portal judgements of speech freedoms must be subjected to national law as well as international standards of freedom of speech (for example, standards set out in regional and international human rights agreements).

Trustmarks and accreditation

Accreditation for website content can work in the case of national e-commerce trust-marks because buyers and sellers have one common concern – security and reliability in the transaction. Content website accreditation has no such over-riding concern that can create network effects in accreditation. Also, trustmark schemes that offer accredited sites a visible marker have failed in most cases because of low levels of consumer awareness of trustmarks and the high costs of advertising trustmarks.

Recommendation 10

Support for trustmarks in the future should depend on demonstration of adequate consumer awareness of the kitemark or the possibility of a public sector awareness campaign.

Notice and take down: 'put back' in the revision of the E-Commerce Directive

The opacity of self-regulatory regimes is also a cause for concern in the notice and take-down regime for ISPs. Where an ISP substitutes its own judgement of harmful or potentially illegal content, with or without trained legal advice, it does so 'in the shadow of the law'. This privatisation of enforcement of freedom of expression is a continued cause for concern. Where there is even a suspicion that notice and take-down procedures are not being adhered to, legitimacy of self-regulation and the ISP industry suffers. Presently ISPs appear to be substituting their view of illegal, harmful (and copyright infringing) content without effective legal procedures for content producers to respond and appeal. This is a direct infringement of freedom of expression on the Internet, which is unchecked by current legislation.

Recommendation 11

We recommend that 'put back' be seriously considered as a policy option when the E-Commerce Directive is reviewed.

Co-regulation: resource audit role of IRAs

There is a lack of credibility in Internet co-regulatory fora generally. This is in part due to lack of technical and regulatory expertise, but also due to a lack of wider industry partnership. It is particularly difficult for regulatory staff in smaller and medium-sized media businesses to make the internal business case to dedicate scarce staff time to the development of self-regulatory solutions. ISPs often do not have the resources necessary to meet high standards of transparency, accountability and due process in self-regulation. Decisions to take part in self-regulatory schemes are often taken without sufficient knowledge of the longer-term cost implications.

Recommendation 12

Industry must take an active part in co-regulatory initiatives. Whereas large multinational corporations (such as Microsoft, AOL and ISP subsidiaries of national telcos) and voluntary actors (typically from research or educational backgrounds) are active participants, proactive measures need to be taken to fully engage with user groups and smaller for-profit content and access providers.

Recommendation 13

IRAs should convene a co-regulatory forum on a quarterly basis located at their offices, with minutes and participants published on the IRA website. This will introduce much-needed transparency into the co-regulatory process, to ensure all commercial operators take content co-regulation seriously. Effective co-regulatory schemes will find this no extra burden, but indeed a stimulus for new members and educational function for the consumer.

Recommendation 14

Accrediting co-regulatory codes of conduct and behaviour can only be carried out under the auspices of IRAs, who have the regulatory resource, stakeholder participation and competition law exclusion to effectively institute a voluntary kite-marking scheme. IRAs may choose to sub-contract the scheme's functioning to a third party.

Recommendation 15

IRA audit of self-regulatory activity, incorporating assessment of market structure and interests in self-regulation and an assessment of impact on fundamental rights, must take place within a dynamic and pragmatic framework which encourages rather than discourages self-regulatory activity where it is appropriate. We also recommend a 'national resource audit of ISP and content sectors' – to answer essential questions of effective and sustainable ISP self-regulation:

- Who is engaged in the notice and take-down regime?
- What is the dedicated legal resource in each ISP?
- Are the crucial code writing and adjudication functions sufficiently independent from industry?
- Who performs the freedom-of-expression function in each ISP?
- Does the self-regulatory industry scheme, as well as individual ISPs, have sufficient resource 'ringfenced' away from industry participant control, to operate efficiently, transparently and fairly?

Benchmarking and research for a forward-looking agenda

Accession states to the European Union have substantial need of technical assistance in formulating co-regulatory schemes. Such assistance is needed in legislative and technical areas as much as in co-regulation itself. In particular, stakeholder/consumer groups require assistance in playing an effective role in co-regulatory discussions.

Recommendation 16

The European Commission is urged to establish expert groups in these areas. It is therefore suggested that a technical advisory board (TAB) be established for co-regulatory schemes, best practice and policy research. The TAB can take composition from national experts (in the manner of the moribund DGInfoSoc Legal Advisory Board). It requires an active secretariat and a willingness to consult at short notice where issues of content regulation arise. Its members must be appropriately qualified.

The TAB would need to advise the European Commission on achieving a progressive, forward-looking agenda, actively engaging industry and stakeholder interests (including technical stakeholders) through partnerships with for instance the spam forum now established by the OECD.

Recommendation 17

Co-regulatory practice needs to take account of rapidly developing technologies and content types in (a) broadband and (b) mobile Internet networks.

The TAB would be required to engage with other advanced Internet stakeholders from East Asia and North America, and from sectors including software, content and hardware developers. Without these inputs, its work would be limited in scale and scope to a regional and narrow view of the Internet.

Recommendation 18

The TAB would be required to pursue an active engagement with stakeholders from across the many media and communication sectors, and from multinational stakeholders active in European markets, as well as representatives from European media industries and other national and regional stakeholders.

Conclusion: responsible Internet self-regulation

A self-regulated Internet is subject to pressures to fragment and privatise, and will make its own rules, which will impact on the real freedoms experienced by users. And the necessary soft rule-making in some countries can easily be tweaked in ways that restrict democratic debate in others. The question is not rules or no rules. It is whether the rules of the Internet are set in a way that is transparent, fair and accountable, and represents the public interest rather than the state or any private entity. That is why we need more debate and more research about co-regulation.

The challenge of Internet policy and regulation is the same as the challenge of communications policy and regulation more generally. It is to combine the strong approach to negative rights (fighting government censorship) with a recognition of the necessary role of rules and rule-making broadly in the development of communications freedom. Communication without rules is impossible. On the most mundane level we observe rules of etiquette and grammar, but we must also acknowledge that communication will only take place if participants view the activity as safe. If our experience of the Internet – or any other public forum – is an experience of being attacked, by fraudsters, phishers or pornographers, for example, we may not use it. A minority of technically confident users will. Unless security can be guaranteed, the ideal of the Internet as a space of free communication will remain a fiction, whether in Amsterdam or in Azerbaijan.

In order to gauge the value or the threat posed by new regulatory developments such as search-level filtering of the kind being experimented with in Germany, or ISP-level filtering in Norway and the United Kingdom, we have to rise above the at times shrill opposition between rules and freedom posed in much of the debate. We have argued that we must acknowledge that rules can also open up spaces for debate. The ecology of co-regulation will be a fertile one during the process of convergence because all the organisms involved have incentives to control the process of rule-making and establish competing rules. But that ecology will benefit from some cultivation and husbandry on the part of informed public policy makers, who will periodically review and audit self-regulation. We hope to have provided some pointers for those involved, and a plea for the centrality and the limitations of the value of freedom of expression in the debate. Policy makers will have to return not only to the constitutional principle of freedom of expression, but to the fundamental philosophical justifications of that freedom, which are the arguments from truth, from democracy and from self-expression. And pragmatism is called for: some rules genuinely place us on a slippery slope to censorship, others do not.

Notes

1 The Australian Competition and Consumer Commission issued guidance to self-regulatory bodies in 2002. The Institute for Business Ethics and other bodies have specialised in advising organisations on improving their self-regulatory activities.

2 See Ahlert, C, Marsden, C and Yung, C (2004) 'How "Liberty" Disappeared in Cyberspace: The Mystery Shopper Tests Internet Content Self-Regulation' (as summarised in Tambini, D (2004) 'How ISPs Could Curb Our Freedom', *The Guardian*, 17 May); OpenNetInitiative (2004) 'A Starting Point: Legal Implications of Internet Filtering', at www.opennetinitiative; Australian Broadcasting Authority (2004) 'Five Years On: Internet Content Regulation in Review', Update December/January, at 17–18.

3 In July 2005, following a murder by a user of extreme pornography, the UK Government Home Office began consulting on the creation of a new offence of downloading extreme, violent pornography.

4 See the International Press Council's (IPC) website at the University of Missouri: www.media-accountability.org. A number of former Eastern bloc countries are now piloting press councils and other self-regulatory ideas: www.presscouncils.org/html/frameset.php?page=news&PHPSESSID=cf2e343be3711d9b5ad6897263c9bb0a

5 See the website of the Moscow Media Law and Policy Institute at Moscow State University, with details and decisions of two regional press councils in Nizhny Novgorod and Rostov-on-Don, as well as the experience of developing in-house ombudsmen at newspapers in the Krasnodar region: www.medialaw.ru/selfreg/index.htm

6 Website of the Grand Jury of the Russian Union of Journalists: www.ruj.ru/b_jury/new.html. Members of the Union also use as precedent the experience of the Tribunal for Information Disputes created in the Yeltsin era in Russia although it was later closed. See: Krug, P (2002) 'Information Tribunal Made Permanent Under President's Supervision', in Price, M, Richter, A and Yu, P (eds) *Russian Media Law and Policy in the Yeltsin Decade*, The Hague: Kluwer Law International, p. 144.

7 Golovanov, D (2005) 'Regulation of Advertising in the Broadcasting Sector in Countries of the Former USSR', *IRIS Plus* 2005–04, p. 8, www.obs.coe.int/oea_publ/iris/iris_plus/iplus4_2005.pdf.en

8 Available at: www.presswise.org.uk

9 Buchanan, S and Hammerer, L (2005) *Freedom and Accountability, Safeguarding Free Expression Through Media Self-Regulation*, London: Article 19.

10 www.opennetinitiative.org

11 These restrictions on limitations are provided both in the UN Human Rights Committee

and in the European Convention on Human Rights. See the discussion in Mendel, T (2004) 'Restrictions on Freedom of Expression', in *IRIS Political Debate and the Role of the Media*, Strasbourg: Council of Europe.

12 Pitofsky, R (1998) Chairman, Federal Trade Commission. 'Self Regulation and Antitrust', paper presented to Washington DC Bar Association Symposium, Washington, DC, 18 February, www.ftc.gov/speeches/pitofsky/self4.htm

13 See the Report of the Joint Parliamentary Scrutiny Committee (The Puttnam Report), 2003.

14 Smith, A (1976) *An Inquiry into the Nature and Causes of the Wealth of Nations*, volume 1, Campbell, R H and Skinner, A S (general eds), Todd, W B (textual ed.), Oxford: Clarendon Press.

15 Berlin, I (1969) 'Two Concepts of Liberty', in Berlin, I, *Four Essays on Liberty*, London: Oxford University Press.

16 Hosein, I (Gus) (2004) 'Open Society and the Internet: Future Prospects and Aspirations', in Möller, Ch and Amouroux, A (eds) *The Media Freedom Internet Cookbook*, Vienna: OSCE, p. 250, www.osce.org/publications/rfm/2004/12/12239_89_en.pdf

17 www.isc.org.cn/20020417/ca102762.htm

18 See further Marsden, C (2004) 'Co- and Self-regulation in European Media and Internet Sectors', *Tolley's Communications Law* 9(5), 187–95; Marsden, C (2005) 'Co-Regulation in European Media and Internet Sectors', *Multimedia und Recht* 1, 3–7; Marsden, C (2004) 'Co- and Self-regulation in European Media and Internet Sectors: The Results of Oxford University's Study', in *The Media Freedom Internet Cookbook*, op. cit., pp. 76–100.

19 Lessig, L (1999) *Code and Other Laws of Cyberspace*, New York: Basic Books.

Bibliography

Abernethy, A M and LeBlanc Wicks, J (2001) 'Self-regulation and Television Advertising: A Replication and Extension', *Journal of Advertising Research* 41(3), 31–37

Aznar, H (1999a) *Comunicación Responsable: Deontología y autorregulación de los medios*, Barcelona: Editorial Ariel

—— (1999b) *Etica y Periodismo: Códigos, estatutos y otros documentos de autorregulación*, Barcelona: Paidós

Barendt, E (1995) *Broadcasting Law: A Comparative Study*, Oxford University Press

Barendt, E and Hitchens, L (2000) 'The Press and the Press Complaints Commission', in Barendt, E and Hitchens, L (eds) *Media Law: Cases and Materials*, Harlow: Pearson Education

BBC Licence and Agreement, http://access.adobe.com/perl/convertPDF.pl?url=http://www.bbc.co.uk/info/policies/charter/pdf/agreement.pdf

BBC Royal Charter, http://access.adobe.com/perl/convertPDF.pl?url=http://www.bbc.co.uk/info/policies/charter/pdf/charter.pdf

Beales, I (2005) *The Editors' Codebook: The Handbook to the Editors' Code of Practice*, London: The Press Standards Board of Finance

Benassi, M (2003) 'New Self-Regulatory Code of Conduct on Television and Minors', *IRIS* 4, 10/21

Bertrand, C-J (2002) *Arsenal of Democracy: Media Accountability Systems*, London: Hampton Press

Blinderman, E, Price, M and Verhulst, S (2000) *Codes of Conduct and Other Self-Regulatory Documents: Emerging Patterns of Norm Formulation and Enforcement on the Internet*, Guetersloh: Bertelsmann Foundation

Blumler, J (1986) *Television in the United States: Funding Sources and Programming Consequences*, London: HMSO/Home Office

Boddewyn, J J (1988) *Advertising Self-regulation and Outside Participation*, New York: Quorum Books

Bollinger, L C (1976) 'Freedom of the Press and Public Access: Toward a Theory of Partial Regulation', *Michigan Law Review* 75, 1–42

Bröhmer, J and Ukrow, J (1999) *Self-regulation of the Media in Europe: A Comparative Legal Study, Prepared at the Request of the Federal Government Commissioner for Cultural Affairs and the Media*, Saarbrücken: Institute of European Media Law

Burkert, H (2000) 'The Issue of Hotlines', in Waltermann, J and Machill, M (eds) *Protecting Our Children on the Internet*, Guetersloh: Bertelsmann Foundation

Campbell, A J (1999) 'Self-Regulation and the Media', *Federal Communications Law Journal* 51, 711

Capello, M (1999) 'Comparative Advertising Allowed by the Self-regulatory Advertising Code', *IRIS* 6, 13/25

Clements, B (1998) 'The Impact of Convergence on Regulatory Policy in Europe', *Journal of Telecommunications Policy* 22(3), 197–205

Collins, R and Murroni, C (1996) *New Media, New Policies*, London: Polity Press/IPPR

Collins, R and Purnell, J (1995) *Managing the Information Society*, London: IPPR

Collins, R, Garnham, N and Locksley, G (1987) *The Economics of Television*, London: Sage

Communications Act (2003) UK, www.legislation.hmso.gov.uk/cgi-bin/htm_hl.pl?DB= hmso-new&STEMMER=en&WORDS=statement+program+commun+act+2003+& COLOUR=Red&STYLE=s&URL=http://www.hmso.gov.uk/acts/acts2003/30021 – i.htm#muscat_highlighter_first_match

Communications Decency Act (1996) US, Title 47 USCA, 223(a) and (d)

Cowie, C and Marsden, C (1999) 'Convergence: Navigating Through Digital Pay-TV Bottlenecks', *Info* 1(1), 53–66

Craufurd-Smith, R (1996–97) 'Getting the Measure of Public Services: Community Competition Rules and Public Service Broadcasting', in Barendt, E M (ed.) *Yearbook of Media and Entertainment Law*, Oxford: Clarendon Press

—— (1997) *Broadcasting Law and Fundamental Rights*, Oxford: Clarendon Press

DCMS (1999) *Regulating Communications. The Way Ahead. Results of Consultation Paper*, London: Department of Culture, Media and Sport

Department of Journalism and Ethics at Stockholm University, www.jmk.su.se/global03/ project/ethics/sweden/swe2a.htm

Douglas, T (2003) 'Self-regulation: The Way Ahead for Advertising?', *Marketing Week* 17 Oct, 17

—— (2004) 'Code War Breaks Out as Ofcom Tries to Force Pace', *Marketing Week*, 29 Jan, 19

ESRB (2001) 'Principles and Guidelines: Responsible Advertising Practices of the Interactive Entertainment Software Industry', Advertising Review Council of the ESRB, Second Edition as amended 31 Jan, New York: ESRB

European Commission (1999) *Results of the Public Consultation on the Convergence Green Paper: Communication* [Com(1999)108]

Federation of Electronic Engineers (2000) *FEI Response to Oftel on 'Encouraging Self and Co-Regulation in Telecoms to Benefit Consumers'*, Document No. FEI 00/0313 of 18 September

Feintuck, M (1997) 'Regulating the Media Revolution: In Search of the Public Interest', *The Journal of Information, Law and Technology (JILT)* (3), http://elj.warwick.ac.uk/jilt/ commsreg/97_3fein/

—— (1998) *Media, the Public Interest and the Law*, Manchester University Press

'Freedom and Accountability: Safeguarding Free Expression Through Media Self-Regulation – Article 19' (2005), London: International Federation of Journalists

Frost, C (2000) *Codes of Conduct and Regulation: Media Ethics and Self-regulation*, Harlow: Longman

Gaines, S E and Kimber, C (2001) 'Redirecting Self-Regulation', *Journal of Environmental Law* 13, 157–85

Gibbons, T (1998a) 'Aspiring to Pluralism: The Constraints of Public Broadcasting Values on the De-regulation of British Media Ownership', *Cardozo Arts and Entertainment Law Journal* 16(2–3), 450–67

—— (1998b) 'De/Re-Regulating the System: The British Experience', in Steemers, J (ed.) *Changing Channels: The Prospects for Television in a Digital World*, London: John Libby Media

—— (1998c) *Regulating the Media*, 2nd edn, London: Sweet and Maxwell

Goldberg, D (2001a) '"Contracts with Viewers" Published', *IRIS* 5, 6/10

—— (2001b) 'Radio Authority Publishes Revised Advertising and Sponsorship Code', *IRIS* 2, 9/20

Goldberg, D, Prosser, T and Verhulst, S (1998a) *Regulating the Changing Media: A Comparative Study*, Oxford University Press

—— (1998b) *EC Media Law and Policy*, London: Longman

Graham, A and Davies, G (1997) *Broadcasting, Society and Policy in the Multimedia Age*, Eastleigh: University of Luton Press

Hills, J and Michalis, M (1997) 'Technological Convergence: Regulatory Competition. The British Case of Digital Television', *Journal of Policy Studies* 18(3/4), 219–37

Hoffman-Riem, W (1996) *Regulating Media: The Licensing and Supervision of Broadcasting in Six Countries*, New York: The Guilford Press

House of Commons, Culture, Media and Sports Committee (2003) *Privacy and Media Intrusion*, HC 458, London: HMSO

Humphreys, P J (1996) *Mass Media and Media Policy in Western Europe*, Manchester University Press

Independent Television Commission (1997) *ITC Code of Conduct on Electronic Programme Guides*, London: ITC

Jacobs, J A (1996) 'Comparing Regulatory Models – Self-Regulation vs. Government Regulation: The Contrast Between the Regulation of Motion Pictures and Broadcasting May Have Implications for Internet Regulation', *Journal of Technology Law & Policy* 1(1), 4

Jigenius, P-A (1997) 'Media Accountability in Sweden: The Swedish Press Ombudsman and Press Council', in Sonnenberg, U (ed.) *Organising Media Accountability*, Maastricht: European Journalism Centre, www.ejc.nl/hp/mas/jigenius.html (accessed 12.10.05)

Jimenez, R (1997) 'Media Accountability in Spain: The Spanish Press Ombudsman', in Sonnenberg, U (ed.) *Organising Media Accountability*, Maastricht: European Journalism Centre, www.ejc.nl/hp/mas/jimenez.html (accessed 12.10.05)

Kirchner, J (1995) 'The Search for New Markets: Multimedia and Digital Television under German Broadcasting and Copyright Law', *EIPR* 17(6), 269–76

Kirkman, D A (1996) *Whither the Australian Press Council? Its Formation, Function and Future*, Sydney: The Australian Press Council

Larouche, P (1998) 'EC Competition Law and the Convergence of the Telecommunications and Broadcasting Sectors', *Telecommunications Policy* 22(3), 219–42

—— (2001) 'Communications Convergence and Public Service Broadcasting', at: http://infolab.kub.nl/uvtweb/bin.php3?id=00011353&mime=application/pdf&file=/tilec/publications/larouche2.pdf (accessed 15.03.03)

Levy, D (1999) *Europe's Digital Revolution: Broadcasting Regulation, the EU and the Nation State*, London: Routledge

Marsden, C (1999) 'Pluralism in the Multi-Channel Market: Suggestions for Regulatory Scrutiny, Council of Europe Human Rights Commission', Mass Media Directorate, MM-S-PL [99] 12 Def 2

Mastowska, K (1999) 'Television Self-Regulation', *IRIS* 5, 13/16

McGonagle, M (2003) *Media Law* (2nd edn), Dublin: Thomson Round Hall

McGonagle, T (2002) 'Co-Regulation of the Media in Europe: The Potential for Practice of an Intangible Idea', *IRIS* 10, www.obs.coe.int/oea_publ/iris/iris_2002/iplus10_2002.pdf.en

MMLPI – Moscow Media Law and Policy Institute, at the Faculty of Journalism of Moscow State University, www.medialaw.ru/selfreg/index.htm

Mosdorf, S, Liikanen, E, Grainger, G, Dyson, E, Strossen, N, Meng, N C and Cole, J (2000) 'Comments on the Memorandum on Self-Regulation of Internet Content', in Waltermann, J and Machill, M (eds) *Protecting Our Children on the Internet*, Guetersloh: Bertelsmann Foundation

Munro, C (1997) 'Self-regulation in the Media', *Public Law* 6–17

Murray, A and Scott, C (2002) 'Controlling the New Media: Hybrid Responses to New Forms of Power', *Modern Law Review* 65(4), 491–516

Murroni, C and Irvine, N (1998) *Access Matters*, London: IPPR

Murroni, C, Collins, R and Coote, A (1996) *Converging Communications – Policies for the 21st Century*, London: IPPR

Murschetz, P (1998) 'State Support for the Daily Press in Europe: A Critical Appraisal. Austria, France, Norway and Sweden Compared', *European Journal of Communication* 13(3), 291–313

Napoli, P (1999) 'The Marketplace of Ideas Metaphor in Communications Regulation', *Journal of Communication* 49(4), 151–69

Nemeth, N (2003) *News Ombudsmen in America: Assessing an Experiment in Social Responsibility*, Westport, CT: Praeger

Niehl, T (1998) 'Daytime Talkshows on TV – Voluntary Code', *IRIS* 9, 13/25

Nixon, H (1998) 'Fun and Games are Serious Business', in Sefton-Green, J (ed.) *Digital Diversions*, London: UCL Press

Noam, E M (ed.) (1985) *Video Media Competition: Regulation, Economy, and Technology Change*, New York: Columbia University Press

Ofcom (2004) *Consultation Document 'Criteria for Transferring Functions to Co-regulatory Bodies'*, www.ofcom.org.uk/consultations/past/co-reg/?a=87101

O'Malley, T and Soley, C (2000) *Regulating the Press*, London: Pluto

Österlund-Karinkanta, M (2000) 'Only Films for Minors to be Censored as of 1 January 2001', *IRIS* 8, 9/19

Palzer, C (2002) 'Co-Regulation of the Media in Europe: European Provisions for the Establishment of Co-Regulation Frameworks', *IRIS* 6, www.obs.coe.int/oea_publ/iris/iris_plus/iplus6_2002.pdf.en

PCMLP (1999) *Parental Control of Television Broadcasting, a Report for the European Commission DG Culture*, Oxford: PCMLP

Pinker, R (2002) 'Press Freedom and Press Regulation – Current Trends in Their European Context', *Communications Law* 7(4), 102–7

Pitofsky, R (1998) Chairman, Federal Trade Commission. Self Regulation and Antitrust Paper presented to: Washington DC Bar Association Symposium, 18 February, Washington, DC, www.ftc.gov/speeches/pitofsky/self4.htm

Price, M (1995) *Television, the Public Sphere and National Identity*, Oxford University Press

Price, M and Verhulst, S (2000) 'In Search of the Self: Charting the Course of Self-Regulation on the Internet in a Global Environment', in Marsden, C (ed.) *Regulating the Global Information Society*, New York: Routledge

—— (2005) *Self Regulation and The Internet*, The Hague: Kluwer Law International

Price, M, Richter, A and Yu, P K (eds) (2002) *Russian Media Law and Policy in the Yeltsin Decade: Essays and Documents*, The Hague: Kluwer Law International

Prosser, T (1997) *Law and the Regulators*, Oxford: Clarendon Press

—— (2001) 'ITC Moves Towards Partial Self-Regulation and Lighter Regulation of Content', *IRIS* 3, 12/16

Raboy, M (1998) 'Public Broadcasting and the Global Framework of Media Democratization', *Gazette* 60(2), 167–80

Raboy, M *et al.* (1998) 'Global Media Policy – A Symposium on Issues and Strategies', *The Public* 5, 63–105

Radio-och TV-verket (Swedish authority for radio and television, the state licensing and supervisory authority): www.rtvv.se (Swedish), or English version: www.rtvv.se/english/index.htm

Review of Press Self-Regulation (Chairman Sir D Calcutt QC), Department of National Heritage, London: HMSO, Cm 2135, 1990

Rosén, R (1999) 'Digital Terrestrial Broadcasting', *IRIS* 5, 15/18

RTÉ Authority: www.rte.ie/about/organisation/corporate_structure.html#authority; also, Statements of Commitments 2003: www.rte.ie/about/organisation/statements.html

RTÉ Programme-Makers' Guidelines: www.rte.ie/about/organisation/ProgrammeMakers Guidelines.pdf

Sandfeld Jakobsen, S (2003) 'New Radio and Television Broadcasting Act', *IRIS* 2, 7/10

Schauer, F (2004) 'Media Law, Media Content and American Exceptionalism', in Closs, W and Nikoltchev, S (eds) *Political Debate and the Role of the Media: The Fragility of Free Speech* (IRIS Special), Strasbourg: European Audiovisual Observatory

Schily, O (2000) 'Worldwide Communication – A New Culture of Common Responsibility', in Waltermann, J and Machill, M (eds) *Protecting Our Children on the Internet*, Guetersloh: Bertelsmann Foundation

Schneider, A (1995a) 'Child Protection on German Television – The Voluntary Television Review Body (FSF)', *IRIS* 3, 7/13

—— (1995b) 'New Regulations Governing the Right to Apply for Review by the Voluntary Television Review Body (FSF)', *IRIS* 5, 9/13

Schulz, W and Held, T (2004) *Regulated Self-Regulation as a Form of Modern Government: An Analysis of Case Studies from Media and Telecommunications Law*, Eastleigh: University of Luton Press

Seymour-Ure, C (1996) 'Media Accountability: Markets, Self-Regulation and the Law', in Seymour-Ure, C (ed.) *The British Press and Broadcasting since 1945*, Oxford: Blackwell Publishers

Shannon, R (2001) *A Press Free and Responsible: Self-Regulation and the Press Complaints Commission 1991–2001*, London: John Murray

Strothman, P (2003) 'Approval for FSF', *IRIS* 7, 8/13

Sunstein, C (2000) 'Television and the Public Interest', *California Law Review* 88, 499

Swedish Press Editorial Advertising Committee, www.jmk.su.se/global03/project/ethics/sweden/swe2e.htm

Tambini, D (2000) *Communications: Revolution and Reform*. London: IPPR

Thorgeirsdottir, H (2004) 'Self-Censorship Among Journalists: A (Moral) Wrong or a Violation of ECHR Law', *EHRLR* 4, 383–99

Tillmanns, L, 'Media Accountability in Germany: The German Press Council', in Sonnenberg, U (ed.) *Organising Media Accountability*, Maastricht: European Journalism Centre, www.ejc.nl/hp/mas/tillmanns.html (accessed 12.10.05)

UK PCC – Press Complaints Commission: www.pcc.org.uk/2002/statistics_review.html

Voorhoof, D (1997) 'European Court of Human Rights: Banning of Blasphemous Video not in Breach of Freedom of (Artistic) Expression', *IRIS* 1, 6/8

—— (1998) 'Guaranteeing the Freedom and Independence of the Media', in Council of Europe (ed.) *Media and Democracy*, Strasbourg: Council of Europe Publishing

—— (2003) 'First Decision of Council for Journalism – No Infringement of Journalistic Ethics by Commercial Television', *IRIS* 6, 7/11

Waltermann, J and Machill, M (2000) 'Responsibility on the Internet – Self-Regulation and Youth Protection', in Waltermann, J and Machill, M (eds) *Protecting Our Children on the Internet*, Guetersloh: Bertelsmann Foundation

Worthy, J and Kariyawasam, R (1998) 'A Pan-European Telecommunications Regulator?', *Journal of Telecommunications Policy* 22(3), 1–7

Ypsilanti, D and Xavier, P (1998) 'Towards Next Generation Regulation', *Journal of Telecommunications Policy* 22(3), 643–59

Internet and telecoms regulation references

ACLU v. *Reno*, Supreme Court Case No. 96–511, 1997

Ahlert, C, Alexander, M and Tambini, D (2003) 'European 3G Mobile Industry Self-Regulation: IAPCODE Background Paper for World Telemedia Conference', www.selfregulation.info/iapcoda/031106-mobiles-revised-bckgrd.pdf

Arnback, J (2000) 'Regulation for Next Generation Technologies and Markets', *Journal of Telecommunications Policy* 24 (Online)

Balkin, J M, Noveck, B S and Roosevelt, K (2000) 'Filtering the Internet – A Best Practices Model', in Waltermann, J and Machill, M (eds) *Protecting Our Children on the Internet*, Guetersloh: Bertelsmann Foundation

Beaufort International (2003) 'Premium SMS Services Research', p. 5, at: www.icstis.org.uk/icstis2002/pdf/SMS_RESEARCH_REPORT_MAY03.PDF

Benkler, Y (1998) 'Communications Infrastructure Regulation and the Distribution of Control over Content', *Journal of Telecommunications Policy* 22(3), 183–96

Birnhack, M D and Rowbottom, J H (2004) 'Symposium: Do Children Have the Same First Amendment Rights as Adults? Shielding Children: The European Way', *Chi.-Kent Law Review* 79, 175–227

Blackman, C R (1998) 'Convergence Between Telecommunications and Other Media', *Journal of Telecommunications Policy* 22(3), 163–70

Bohlin, E, Brodin, K, Lundgren, A and Thorngren, B (eds) (2000) *Convergence in Telecommunications and Beyond*, Amsterdam: Elsevier

Burk, D L (1997) 'The Market for Digital Piracy', in Kahin, B and Nesson, C R (eds) *Borders in Cyberspace: Information Policy and the Global Information Infrastructure*, Cambridge, MA: Harvard University Press

Caral, J M E A (2004) 'Lessons from ICANN: Is Self-Regulation of the Internet Fundamentally Flawed?', *International Journal of Law and Information Technology* 12(1), 1–31

Cerf, V (1994) *Guidelines for Conduct on and Use of Internet Draft v0.1*, 14 Aug, at: www.isoc.org/internet/conduct/cerf-Aug-draft.shtml

Collins, M (2001) *The Law of Defamation and the Internet*, Oxford: OUP

Dutton, W H and Peltu, M (2005) 'The Emerging Internet Governance Mosaic: Connecting the Pieces', Oxford Internet Institute, University of Oxford, Forum Discussion Paper No. 5

Elkin-Koren, N (1995) 'Copyright Law and Social Dialogue on the Information Superhighway: The Case Against Copyright Liability of Bulletin Board Operators', *Cardozo Arts and Entertainment Law Journal* 13, 345, 399–410

European Commission (1999) Internet Action Plan: European Commission

Frydman, B and Rorive, I (2002) 'Regulating Internet Content Through Intermediaries in Europe and the USA', *Zeitschrift fur Rechtssoziologie* Bd.23/H1, July, 1–31

Grewlich, K W (1999) 'Cyberspace: Sector-Specific Regulation and Competition Rules in European Telecommunications', *Common Market Law Review* 36, 936–69

Hardy, T (1994) 'The Proper Legal Regime for "Cyberspace"', *University of Pittsburgh Law Review* 55, 993, 1042–46

Holznagel, B (2000) 'Responsibility for Harmful and Illegal Content as Well as Free Speech on the Internet in the United States of America and Germany', in Engel, C and Keller, H (eds) *Governance of Global Networks in Light of Differing Local Values*, Baden Baden: Nomos

Hosein, G (2004) 'Open Society and the Internet', in Moeller, C and Amouroux, A (eds) *The Media Freedom Internet Cookbook*, Vienna: OSCE, 242–264

Huidobro Moya, J M (2002) *Comunicaciones Móviles*, Madrid: Thomson Paraninfo

ICSTIS (2003) Annual Activity Report 2002: www.icstis.org/icstis2002/pdf/ACTIVITY_2002.PDF

Kahin, B and Keller, J H (eds) (1997) *Coordinating the Internet*, Cambridge, MA: MIT Press

Kahin, B and Nesson, C R (eds) (1997) *Borders in Cyberspace: Information Policy and the Global Information Infrastructure*, Cambridge, MA: MIT Press

Kesan, J P (2003) 'Private Internet Governance', *Loloya University Chicago Law Journal* 35, 87–137

Lemley, M (1999) 'Standardizing Government Standard Setting Policy for Electronic Commerce', *Berkeley Technology Law Journal* 14(2), 745–58

Lessig, L (1996) 'Reading the Constitution in Cyberspace', *Emory Law Journal* 45, 869

—— (1999a) 'The Limits in Open Code: Regulatory Standards and the Future of the Net', *Berkeley Technology Law Journal* 14(2), 759–70

—— (1999b) *Code and Other Laws of Cyberspace*, New York: Basic Books

Levi-Faur, D (2004) 'On the "Net Policy Impact" of the European Union Policy Process: The EU's Telecoms and Electricity Industries in Comparative Perspective', *Comparative Political Studies* 37(1), 3–29

Levy, B and Spiller, P (1994) 'The Institutional Foundations of Regulatory Commitment: A Comparative Analysis of Telecommunications Regulation', *Journal of Law, Economics and Organisation* 10(2), 201–46

Leyden, J (2004) 'Digital Certificate Regime Wins UK Gov Plaudits', *The Register*, 22 April, at: www.theregister.co.uk/2004/04/22/pki_self_regulation

Machill, M, Hart, T and Kaltenhäuser, B (2002) 'Structural Development of Internet Self-Regulation: A Case Study of the Internet Content Rating Association', *Info* 4(5), 39–55

Marsden, C (ed.) (2000) *Regulating the Global Information Society*, New York: Routledge

Marsden, C and Verhulst, S (eds) (1999) *Convergence in European Digital TV Regulation*, London: Blackstone

Mobile Network Operators (January 2004) *UK Code of Practice for the Self-Regulation of New Forms of Content on Mobiles*, available at: www.orange.co.uk/about/regulatory_affairs.html

Nissenbaum, H (2001) 'Securing Trust Online: Wisdom or Oxymoron?', *Boston University Law Review* 81(3), 635–64

Noam, E (1993) 'From the Network of Networks to the System of Systems: An End of History in Telecommunications Regulation?', *Regulation* 16(2) (Online)

Price, M and Verhulst, S (2000) 'The Concept of Self-Regulation and the Internet', in Waltermann, J and Machill, M (eds) *Protecting Our Children on the Internet*, Guetersloh: Bertelsmann Foundation

Reidenberg, J (2002) 'Yahoo and Democracy on the Internet', *Jurimetrics* 42, 261–80

Resnick, P and Miller, J (1996) 'PICS: Internet Access Controls Without Censorship', *Association for Computing Machinery* 39(10), 87–93, at: www.w3.org.PICS.iacwcv2.htm

Rights Watch White Paper (July 2003) 'A Way Forward for Notice and Takedown', www.rightswatch.com/White_Paper_20030704_v1_FINAL.pdf (last accessed May 2007)

Ritter, J A and Libowitz, M (1974) 'Press Councils: The Answer to Our First Amendment Dilemma', *Duke Law Journal* 5, 845–70

Schulz, A and Held, T (2001) *Regulated Self-Regulation as a Form of Modern Government*, Hamburg: Verlag Hans Bredow Institut

Shah, R C and Kesan, J P (2003a) 'Incorporating Societal Concerns into Communication Technologies', *IEEE Technology and Society Magazine*, 22(2), 28–33

—— (2003b) 'Manipulating the Governance Characteristics of Code', *Info* 5, 43–9

Shapiro, C and Varian, H R (1999) *Information Rules: A Strategic Guide to the Network Economy*, Harvard Business School Press

Srivastava, L and Kodate, A (2004) 'Shaping the Future Mobile Information Society: The Case of Japan', paper presented at the ITU/MIC Workshop on Shaping the Future Mobile Information Society, Seoul, 4–5 March, available at: www.itu.int/osg/spu/ni/futuremobile/general/casestudies/JapancaseLS1.pdf

Stiglitz, J E (1985) 'Information and Economic Analysis: A Perspective', *Economic Journal* 95(suppl), 21–41

Tambini, D (2001) *Communications: Revolution and Reform*, London: IPPR

Thierer, A and Wayne Crews Jr, C (2003) *Who Rules the Net*, New York: Cato Institute

Thorgeirsdottir, H (2003) *Journalism Worthy of the Name: A Human Rights Perspective on Freedom Within the Press*, Lund: Lund University

Tickle, K (1995) 'Comment: The Vicarious Liability of Electronic Bulletin Board Operators for the Copyright Infringement Occurring on Their Bulletin Boards', *Iowa Law Review* 80, 391, 416

Volkmer, I (1997) 'Universalism and Particularism: The Problem of Cultural Sovereignty and Global Information Flow', in Kahin, B and Nesson, C R (eds) *Borders in Cyberspace: Information Policy and the Global Information Infrastructure*, Cambridge, MA: Harvard University Press

Wassink, E (2004) 'Statistiken zum Jahr 2003', in *Deutscher Presserat 2004 Jahrbuch*, Constance: UVK

Working Group on Intellectual Property Rights, Information Infrastructure Task Force (1995) *Intellectual Property and the National Information Infrastructure*, 1–6, 114–24

General self-regulation and other references

Almond, G A and Verba, S (eds) (1989) *Civic Culture Revisited*, London: Sage Publications

Arato, A and Cohen, J-L (1992) *Civil Society and Political Theory*, Cambridge, MA: MIT Press

Ayres, I and Braithwaite, J (1992) *Responsive Regulation: Transcending the Deregulation Debate*, Oxford: OUP

Baldwin, R, Scott, C and Hood, C (1998) *A Reader on Regulation*, Oxford: OUP

Black, J (1996) 'Constitutionalising Self-Regulation', *The Modern Law Review*, 59, 24–55

Council of Europe (1998) Proceedings of the Information Seminar on Self-Regulation by the Media, Strasbourg, 7–9 October

Doyle, C (1997) 'Self Regulation and Statutory Regulation', *Business Strategy Review* 8(3), 35–42

Ellickson, R C (1998) 'Law and Economics Discovers Social Norms', *Journal of Legal Studies* Part II, XXVII, 537–52, fn 58

Froomkin, M A (1999) 'Of Governments and Governance', *Berkeley Technology Law Journal* 14(2), 617–33

Fukuyama, F (1992) *The End of History and the Last Man*, London: Penguin

Gordon, W J (2005) 'Copyright Norms and the Problem of Private Censorship', in Griffiths, J and Suthersanen, U (eds) *Copyright and Free Speech: Comparative and International Analyses*, Oxford: OUP, p. 67

Habermas, J (1974) 'The Public Sphere', *New German Critique* (3), 49–55

—— (1989) *The Structural Transformation of the Public Sphere*, Cambridge: Polity

Hall, P A and Soskice, D (eds) (2001) *Varieties of Capitalism: The Institutional Foundations of Comparative Advantage*, Oxford University Press

Huntington, S P (1996) *The Clash of Civilizations and the Remaking of World Order*, New York: Touchstone

Jayasuriya, K (1999) 'Globalization, Law and the Transformation of Sovereignty: The Emergence of Global Regulatory Governance', *Global Legal Studies Journal* 6, 425–55

Kaul, I, Grunberg, I and Stern, M (eds) (1999) *Global Public Goods: International Cooperation in the 21st Century*, New York: Oxford University Press

Keleman, D R and Sibbitt, E C (2004) 'The Globalization of American Law', *International Organization* 58, 103–34

Levi-Faur, D (2003) 'The Politics of Liberalization: Privatization and Regulation-for-Competition in Europe's and Latin America's Telecoms and Electricity Industries', *European Journal of Political Research*, 42(5), 705–40

MacCormick, N (1993) 'Beyond the Sovereign State', *The Modern Law Review* 56, 1–18

Maxwell, J W, Lyon, T P and Hackett, S C (2000) 'Self-Regulation and Social Welfare: The Political Economy of Corporate Environmentalism', *Journal of Law and Economics* 43(2), 583–617

McLean, I *et al.* (2003) *Identifying the Flow of Domestic and European Expenditure into the English Regions, Report Commissioned by the Office of the Deputy Prime Minister*, 5 September, www.nuff.ox.ac.uk/projects/odpm

Milgrom, P and Roberts, J (1992) *Economics, Organization and Management*, Englewood Cliffs, NJ: Prentice Hall

Moe, T M (1997) 'The Positive Theory of Public Bureaucracy', in Mueller, D C (ed.) *Perspectives on Public Choice: A Handbook*, Cambridge University Press

National Consumer Council (UK) (2000) 'Models of Self-Regulation: An Overview of Models in Business and the Professions', www.ncc.org.uk/regulation/selfregulation_position.pdf (last accessed May 2007)

—— (2003a) 'Better Business Practice: How to Make Self-Regulation Work for Consumers and Business', www.ncc.org.uk/pubs/pdf/self-regulation_gpg.pdf (last accessed May 2007)

—— (2003b) 'Three Steps to Credible Self-Regulation', www.ncc.org.uk/regulation/selfregulation_position.pdf (last accessed May 2007)

North, D C (1990) *Institutions, Institutional Change and Economic Performance*, Cambridge University Press

Ogus, A (1995) 'Rethinking Self-Regulation', *Oxford Journal of Legal Studies* 15, 97–108

Ohmae, K (1991) *The Borderless World: Power and Strategy in the Interlinked Economy*, New York: Harper Business

Oswell, D (1999) 'The Dark Side of Cyberspace: Internet Content Regulation and Child Protection', *Convergence* 5(4), 42–62

Owen, B (1999) *The Internet Challenge to Television*, Cambridge, MA: Harvard University Press

Paterson, J and Teubner, G (1998) 'Changing Maps: Empirical Legal Autopoiesis', *Social and Legal Studies* 8, 451–86

Picciotto, S and Scott, C (eds) (1996) *International Regulatory Competition and Coordination*, Oxford: OUP

Putnam, R D (2002) *Making Democracy Work: Civic Traditions in Modern Italy*, Princeton, NJ: Princeton University Press

Reidenberg, J (2004) 'States and Internet Enforcement', *University of Ottawa Law & Technology Journal* 1, 213–30

Richardson, M and Hadfield, G (1999) *The Second Wave of Law and Economics*, Sydney, NSW: Federation Press

Scott, C (2000) 'Accountability in the Regulatory State', *Journal of Law and Society* 27(1), 38–60

The Economist (2005) 'Survey of Corporate Social Responsibility', 22 January

Thomson, M, Grendstad, G and Selle, P (eds) (1999) *Cultural Theory as Political Science*, London: Routledge

Trompenaars, A and Hampden Turner, C (1993) *The Seven Cultures of Capitalism: Value Systems for Creating Wealth in the United States, Japan, Germany, France, Britain, Sweden, and the Netherlands*, New York: Doubleday

—— (1997) *Riding the Waves of Culture: Understanding Cultural Diversity in Business*, London: Brealey

Wagemans, T (2003) 'The role of selfregulation in creating trust in electronic business', unpublished seminar paper: http://selfregulation.info/iapcoda/030127-wagemans.doc (last accessed June 2007)

Webley, S and Le Jeune, M (2002) *Ethical Business – Corporate Use of Codes of Conduct*, London: Institute of Business Ethics

Williamson, O (1985) *The Economic Institutions of Capitalism: Firms, Markets, Relational Contracting*, New York: Free Press

Winn, N (1998) 'Who Gets What, When and How? The Contested Conceptual and Disciplinary Nature of Governance and Policy-Making in the European Union', *Politics* 18(2), 119–32

Index

Page numbers in **bold** indicate figures and tables.

DATE DUE